CW00819357

IN THE MIDST OF WARS

IN THE MIDST OF WARS

An American's Mission to Southeast Asia

EDWARD GEARY LANSDALE

With a Foreword by WILLIAM E. COLBY
and an Introduction by CECIL B. CURREY

FORDHAM UNIVERSITY PRESS
New York
1991

Copyright © 1972 by Edward Geary Lansdale
All rights reserved
First edition published by Harper & Row, Publishers
LC 91–70451
ISBN 0–8232–1314–5
Fordham University Press Edition 1991

Printed in the United States of America

CONTENTS

	Foreword	*vii*
	Introduction	*ix*
	Acknowledgments	*xxix*
	Preface	*xxxi*
	Acronyms	*xxxiii*
1.	*To Manila, 1950*	1
2.	*Learning About the Enemy*	17
3.	*With Magsaysay*	32
4.	*Politburo Capture*	60
5.	*Psychological Action*	69
6.	*1951 By-Election*	85
7.	*Philippines 1952–53 and Indochina 1953*	96
8.	*The 1953 Presidential Election*	115
9.	*Assignment: Vietnam*	126

10. *Last Half of 1954* 154

11. *Trinh minh The* 184

12. *Early 1955* 202

13. *1955 Pacification Campaigns* 228

14. *United Sects Front* 224

15. *Confrontation in Saigon* 260

16. *Battle for Saigon* 282

17. *Midyear 1955* 313

18. *Beginnings of the Republic* 324

19. *Last Days in Vietnam* 335

20. *A Course for America* 365

Postscript 377

Index 379

MAPS

Philippine Islands 3

South Vietnam, 1954–1956 132

Saigon-Cholon, 1954–1956 133

Illustrations follow page 148.

FOREWORD

This reprint of Edward Lansdale's account of his service in Southeast Asia is not only a contribution to history and a tribute to a fine American, it is a well-timed lesson for our nation as we see the end of the Cold War and must consider the policies, the programs, and the tactics we should adopt for the new era facing us.

Ed always put the individual citizen at the center of his efforts, and reached out to understand him and his surroundings, however far an Asian peasant might be geographically and culturally from the middle Americans with whom Ed grew up. When we followed his approach, as in the Philippines, we succeeded in finding good leaders and helped them in the fight against their, and our, enemies. When we pushed Ed (and them) aside and put our faith in overwhelming force, as in Vietnam, we ultimately failed.

This account of Ed's work covers his spectacular success in the Philippines, where he worked closely and effectively with President Ramon Magsaysay, and his difficulties in trying to repeat the success in the early days of South Vietnamese independence from the French (1954–1956). The far more tangled political problems of the new republic and its leader, President Ngo Dinh Diem, were perhaps more than Ed's simple and straightforward approach could handle, especially as his influence was diluted by a massive American presence, with its cacophony of advice and influence upon the embattled Vietnamese leader. But Ed's account is important and useful, even in its depiction of this turmoil, as an analysis of some of the problems which later engulfed the small nation and its great ally.

But the real message of this book is how Ed kept his compass firmly on freedom, for the new nations he helped during their birth pangs, and for the plain people whose fate was being determined by the forces rampaging over their heads. It is an important message for Americans to hear again in the full flush of victory over Cold War Communism, to keep freedom still as the chief goal—and tactic—as we face whatever new threats arise to the ordinary peoples of the Middle East, Asia, and the rest of the world.

—WILLIAM E. COLBY

INTRODUCTION

I first heard of Edward Geary Lansdale while researching and writing my pseudonymous *Self-Destruction: The Disintegration and Decay of the United States Army During the Vietnam Era* (W. W. Norton, 1981). He seemed such a mysterious figure, sometimes wearing an Air Force officer's uniform and regularly turning up in troubled areas of Southeast Asia. When he spoke, his recorded words—so far as I was able to uncover them— seemed filled with uncommon good sense. Yet the historical literature which mentioned him was sparse and no one seemed to know much about either him or his work, other than that he served as the role model for Alden Pyle in Graham Greene's *The Quiet American* (1955) and Barnum Hillandale in Eugene Burdick's and William Lederer's *The Ugly American* (1957). A few years later I determined to see if I could cast some light on this man and his ideas. So in 1984 I wrote a letter to the Office of the Joint Chiefs of Staff asking if he was still alive; if so, I asked for his address to be given to me.

Only a few days later, when I answered my telephone, I heard a gruff voice saying: "I understand you've been asking about me." It was Lansdale, who had been informed by Pentagon officials of my queries about him. We arranged for an initial meeting at his home in McLean, Virginia; its outcome would determine whether he would cooperate with me in crafting his biography. In the months and years that followed, we became friends. Plagued by ill-health, he still found energy to sit long hours talking with me. He wrote letters of introduction for me to friends and acquaintances in the Philippines and the United States. I shared in one of his birthday parties, he visited me in my Florida home and my wife and I took him on an excursion to Walt Disney's Epcot Center in Orlando, Florida, and I interviewed him on a regular basis at his home. Our relationship continued until, early on Monday, 23 February 1987, when I had completed only three rough draft chapters of his biography, he died peacefully during his sleep, aged 79. I attended his funeral at Arlington National Cemetery.

He had been an extraordinary man. Brought up in a family where his father was one of the pioneers of the automotive age, and schooled at U.C.L.A., Lansdale moved to San Francisco where he plunged into the world of advertising. His ideas and straightforward approach quickly brought him such clients as Levi Strauss, Wells Fargo, Union Trust, Nestlé, and Italian Swiss Colony Wines.

With the outbreak of the Second World War, Lansdale joined the army and served simultaneously with Army Intelligence and the Office of Strategic Services. War's end found him in the Philippines, a nation whose land and people he came to love. Before rotating home at the conclusion of the hostilities he transferred to the newly created Air Force, which he hoped would be receptive to innovative ideas. It assigned him as a teacher of strategic studies at a Colorado air base and then sent him to a military school for instructors in Alabama. Recalling his heady days as an OSS operative, he called upon friends in the Pentagon to rescue him. They responded. Within weeks of his return to Colorado he was recruited by a secret government action agency called the Office of Policy Coordination (which later fused with the CIA).

For years thereafter, while as a fiction of convenience he remained an Air Force officer until his retirement, he was on loan to other agencies, primarily the CIA. Neil Sheehan has recently written in his *Bright and Shining Lie* that Lansdale was the midwife at the birth of Vietnam. So also did he act as attending physician to the health of the Philippines. Reassigned there in 1950, he worked as an adviser to Ramón Magsaysay, helping that Filipino patriot put down the cancer of a rebellion then flaming throughout much of the land, headed by a Marxist insurgency known in the Tagalog language as the *Hukbo ng Bayan Laban Sa Hapon*, abbreviated as Hukbalahap or Huk. Lansdale devised tactics, implemented by Magsaysay, that ensured a truly popular election there for the first (and almost the last) time in history. He successfully advocated to Magsaysay policies that helped the government destroy the Huks as a threat to Filipino society. Upon his arrival there, Lansdale found the nation ill and tottering, drained by political leeches, bloodied by an internal insurgent conflict. He left it strong and whole, under the guidance of a magnificent leader. In those years, from 1950 to 1954, Lansdale formulated his views on how to contend successfully against insurgent movements.

His work there completed, CIA sent him to Vietnam in 1954 to attempt two things: to weaken the newly formed northern government of Ho Chi Minh through whatever means possible and to strengthen the government of the southern regions headed by Ngo Dinh Diem. While notably unsuccessful in his efforts in Hanoi, he quickly became Diem's confidant in Saigon. Asians have not had too much reason to trust westerners, yet in the Philippines Magsaysay had treated Lansdale like a brother. Now, within three weeks of meeting Ngo Dinh Diem, the diminutive premier asked Lansdale to move into Independence Palace with him. Wanting to blend with the background, Lansdale diplomatically refused and remained in his own quarters.

The trappings of power, so often important to other men, were not to his liking. Although never as close to Diem as he had been to Magsaysay, Lansdale provided him with advice which, had it been followed, might well have changed the course of modern Vietnamese history.

What had he done? Simple things. He urged Diem to travel out of Saigon into the countryside—to see and be seen—and to show more interest in his own people. He encouraged other Asians, especially Filipinos, to offer their help to Vietnam. He spirited plotters away to the fleshpots of Manila so as to interrupt their planned coups against Diem. He contacted the heads of rival groups and convinced them to support the Diem government. He helped organize a Vietnamese veterans organization and advised Diem on methods of establishing a working civil service bureaucracy. He made a quick trip back to Washington to drum up additional support for Diem's infant government. He urged Diem to assign the southern army to civic action work projects out among the rice paddies. He convinced him to implement a number of social, economic, and political reforms including building schools, repairing roads, teaching personal and public hygiene, and teaching rural inhabitants that there might be benefits in aligning themselves with the Saigon government. He tried, without result, to persuade Diem to allow opposition political parties to function freely. (By refusing, Diem made it inevitable that a renewed insurgency would once more rise up against him in the south.) He helped Diem begin a nation that almost succeeded in becoming a stable state. Diem might well have triumphed in this goal had it not been for his assassination by those who could not (or cared not to) understand either him or the dogs of war that would be unleashed if they allowed his shaky regime to be shattered. Tran Van Don, who for a time served as foreign minister for the Republic of South Vietnam, summed up his government's attitude toward Lansdale: "He was a great help. . . . He was a good friend to Vietnam."[1]

"Fortunately," Lansdale later recalled, "there wasn't a lot of attention given to my activities [in either the Philippines or in Vietnam] and there wasn't [always] a journalist with space in American papers looking over my shoulder."[2] He summarized his activities in both countries by writing that, among other things, "I acted as sort of a catalyst to bring together some solutions to problems with American experts who could help."[3]

When Lansdale finally returned to the United States in early 1957, he was posted to the Department of Defense where he worked for both the Eisenhower and the Kennedy administration. He held the impressive title of Deputy Director, Office of Special Operations, Office of the Secretary of Defense. As such he became an overseer of clandestine agencies he had once worked for. He directed policy on counterinsurgency matters for the Army, Navy, Air Force, and the National Security Agency. Lansdale brought onto his staff individuals trained by Air Force Special Operations, the Navy SEAL program, or those who were veterans of the Army's Special Forces. He warned against the Bay of Pigs but later headed Operation Mongoose, a committee set up to determine the best way to overthrow Fidel Castro. He traveled on advisory missions to Venezuela, Mexico, Panama, Bolivia, Peru, and Brazil. And he returned occasionally to Vietnam to check on its ailing health.

Almost made ambassador to Vietnam by President John F. Kennedy in early 1961—a move blocked by Dean Rusk at the State Department—Lansdale was not posted there again until 1965 when President Johnson named him an assistant, with ministerial rank, to Ambassador Henry Cabot Lodge. His job was to supervise pacification operations in that troubled land. He remained until 1968, at which time, worn-out and sick, he retired from further government service. He lived quietly in McLean, Virginia until his death.

He knew thousands of people but had few neutral acquaintances. He made friends and he made enemies by his single-minded dedication to people in the Third World. Those who knew him either were devoted to him and his work or despised him as an interfering ignoramus. His victories grew out of his ability to convince foreign leaders to act in ways supportive of their own populations. He did not do this for personal gain nor even solely on behalf of the U.S. government which he served. He did it because he believed it was *right*. He argued endlessly that leaders should do those things which would draw people to support their own governments rather than some handy insurgency—simple things that those governments should already have been doing as a matter of course, but weren't. Lansdale would have readily admitted that such an attitude made him an idealist, a dreamer, but he would have pointed out that there is nothing wrong in so doing as long as he was willing to spend his energy to provide earthly foundations for those castles in the air.

It was Lansdale's vision that others on this planet might also come to have rights under government as did the citizens of the United States. (He regularly insisted that those who worked with him refresh their ideals by re-reading the Bill of Rights and the Declaration of Independence.) His favorite Founding Father was Tom Paine. Benjamin Franklin had once written: "Where liberty dwells, there is my country." Paine had rejoined: "Where liberty dwells not, *there* is my country!"[4] Like Paine, Lansdale chose to work in areas of the world where constitutional liberties and privileges were at a premium or nonexistent, in the hope that, by his efforts, people there might come to a better life and governments with which he worked might become more responsive and responsible. He chose Asia because he liked it, was fascinated by it, and because that was where Cold War competitions, occasionally flaring into open combat, then simmered.

People of embattled areas were always Lansdale's primary concern. In America, an average man was known as "Joe Smith." In the Philippines, he was "Juan de la Cruz," while his Vietnamese counterpart was "Nguoi Thuong Dan." People on the land, who faced terror from insurgents and indifference or worse from their own governments, were the real losers in modern-day conflicts.

Lansdale even had real concern for insurgents and a great deal of sympathy for their goals. He was at one with his old friend, Magsaysay, who once said, "When a man is prepared to give up his life to overthrow his own government, he must first have suffered greatly." Lansdale was likewise in agreement with Magsaysay's position that "those who have less in life must have more in law."[5]

Lansdale simply wanted embattled peoples to achieve something better than most communist-inspired movements could offer. The *only* governments capable of providing people with real opportunity for improving their lot in life, he believed, were those founded on the concept that men possessed certain unalienable rights. Lansdale believed in America's charter documents which guaranteed such rights. The "liberty of individual men," he once stated, "is our really precious, fundamental belief." He and other Americans abroad were responsible for acting "in the spirit of our own most precious beliefs."[6]

He was not wrapping himself in red, white, and blue bunting; he was trying to establish a course of action for himself and others based solidly on American principles. America's own government, he knew, was born during an insurgency. "The Continental troops at Valley Forge, the officers and men under Marion, Greene, or Wayne would have found much that was familiar to them in the motivation of . . . modern [insurgent] toops, in the[ir] use of propaganda, in the covert political organs so reminiscent of [our own] Committees of Correspondence, the Committees of Safety, and in the support of our Continental troops by farmers and shopkeepers with food, money, and hard military information."[7]

The common combat ground of the Cold War struggle, Lansdale repeatedly pointed out, "is among the people at a village or rice paddy." A soldier manning a shovel at a rice paddy dike or offering a helping hand to villagers of his own country provided a bulwark against subversive insurgency. He called such deeds "civic action" and insisted they were as old as military history itself. The few real successes enjoyed by the West in the years since the end of World War II, Lansdale believed, "have been possible only when the armed forces of free men sincerely applied this cardinal principle." That moral law, he insisted, was too important to be ignored inasmuch as citizens of a nation caught up in an insurgency viewed the army as an inseparable part of their own government. Thus any deed "which makes the soldier a brother of the people, as well as their protector," was a worthy one. When troops acted appropriately, government was strengthened. When they did not, guerrilla influence increased.

Lansdale recalled earthy examples. He asked others to put themselves into the shoes of beleaguered peoples. "How would you react if soldiers stole your chickens or pigs or personal belongings—maybe roughing you up and having sport with your wife or daughter in the process? How would you react if political leaders posed as men of integrity, but you saw them living high on the hog, buying property and jewelry and expensive cars— all on a low government salary—and thus obviously hoggishly corrupt?"

Honesty and integrity were essential if Juan de la Cruz and Nguoi Thuong Dan were to support their own endangered governments. No amount of official rhetoric and propaganda could overcome a stolen chicken or a carelessly driven jeep. It was by observing the actions of their leaders' soldiers that Joe Smith, Juan de la Cruz, and Nguoi Thuong Dan came to know the real intent of those in power. Before beginning any course of action, leaders always needed to ask themselves first: "What will the people's reaction [be] to this proposed action?"

It was imperative for leaders to insist on the rights of their own citizenry and to at least begin to repair the rotten spots in the political and social fabric of their nations, "and do so with sincerity." When not serving as a protector while fighting insurgent bands, a national army must be a brother to its own people. There must be no assassinations of political opponents, no death squads, no pillaging from villagers, no torture, no hasty imprisonments, no midnight disappearances, no surly intolerance of one's own people at roadblocks or during country-side sweeps. A responsive and responsible government would insure and control the behavior of its own soldiers and use the army and all other appropriate means to improve the lives of its citizens.[8]

Lansdale hammered away at the need for wide-ranging social operations by the army, the need for officers to supervise troop behavior closely, for the wisdom of treating civilians in military hospitals who had accidentally been caught in and wounded by combat's crossfire. He even argued that insurgent enemies be offered "a fair chance at rehabilitation" if they surrendered or were captured, for they also were part of a nation's people.[9] There was, he believed, no other real answer. If rebels obtained popular loyalty and a governmental army secured for itself an overwhelming superiority in tanks, planes, artillery, and num-bers of soldiers, that government would still ultimately fall. In all his years of teaching, this may have been Lansdale's most important contribution to a proper understanding of the basic nature of people's wars.[10] In 1965, Mary McGrory, correspon-dent for the *Washington Star*, wrote Lansdale that she believed he had summed it all up. "I saw McGeorge Bundy the other night, and told him that of all the Vietnamese policies I had heard expounded, yours was the only one that made sense to me. I told him that while I had never recovered from the initial shock of learning from you that counterinsurgency is [only] another word for brotherly love, I was all for it."[11]

Perhaps not. Perhaps he only sought an efficient way to deal with insurgencies. He argued that America did not know how to do so. In Vietnam, the U.S. relied mostly on inordinate use of firepower, whether artillery or bombs. More munitions were

expended by the U.S. war machine in that small country between 1965 and 1973 than had been used by all sides in all
theaters of World War II. Lansdale saw the folly of this and
wholeheartedly agreed with the precept that the best weapon
to use against a guerrilla is a knife; the worst is an airplane. The
second best is a rifle; the second worst is artillery. And, of
course, the U.S. primarily relied on airplanes and cannons
during its years of struggle in Vietnam. Tactical doctrines sufficient for World War II or Korea were no longer going to work.
If U.S. flag officers could not understand this simple fact,
Lansdale said, then they should be "promptly retired to take up
basket-weaving or anything else truly suited to [their] talents."
Indiscriminate use of firepower, Lansdale argued, "might well
provoke a man of good will to ask, 'just what freedom of what
Vietnamese are we helping to maintain?' "[12]

All too often, Lansdale charged, U.S. generals concentrated
on eliminating enemy forces by firepower alone. As a consequence, the very people we were supposedly helping suffered
grievously. Civilians, trampled in combat by a large conventional force, endured "plainshirted hell" as they tried to go
about their daily lives: fields trampled, crops ruined, harvest
stores destroyed, homes burned, animals wantonly slaughtered,
wives and daughters raped, sons tortured and murdered as
insurgent "suspects." How, he wondered, could *any* government which approved of such actions expect to receive loyalty
from those so treated?[13]

Lansdale developed these ideas during the years he describes
in this autobiography. He does not, however, tell all in his book;
he closes his account much too soon. He ends his story with his
return from Saigon in early 1957 after having spent three years
as a close adviser to Ngo Dinh Diem. Much that he accom-
plished during his years abroad and everything he saw in later
times would remain unvoiced by him. But he tells a great deal.
It would be difficult to find a more readable non-fiction work
than his *In the Midst of Wars: An American's Mission to South-*

east Asia. It is a moving account of his activities both in the Philippines and during his first assignment to Vietnam. Largely anecdotal, his tale is full of compassion for the Asians with whom he worked and reveals his genuinely humane character. He writes also of adventures which tug at the heart—and manages to do all this simultaneously. In earlier days, because of his exploits, some thought of him as America's latter-day T. E. Lawrence of Southeast Asia, a title which he obviously never sought but which he richly deserved.

His story is filled with tales of bravery, tenacity, poverty, revolution, and war as seen through the eyes of this master of sub rosa intelligence work. *In the Midst of Wars* is, however, more than Lansdale's account of his own adventures. This epic attempts to provide the reader with a first-hand account of how *Asians* saw the events which filled their lives and determined their destinies in the years following the Second World War. Writing with real modesty and with the clarity of a true patriot's insight, Lansdale draws us into the backwaters of Asia almost as if we were participants. His thoughtful recounting of events shows us appropriate forms for American activity to take in Third World countries, lessons that were learned the hard way in the Philippines and never quite learned at all in Vietnam. The American government then ignored those few insights as the conflict in Southeast Asia escalated and the tiny band of Americans assigned there were augmented by hundreds of thousands of troops and bureaucrats, military and civilian. For this reason alone, *In the Midst of Wars* is worth reading.

Lansdale did not bring forth this autobiography easily. He long resisted the notion of writing it. Beginning about 1964, however, publishing houses occasionally contacted him, interested in publishing an account of his experiences in the Orient. He invariably refused. It was not until long after his return from his second mission to Vietnam (1965–1968) that Lansdale finally decided to write about his Philippine and Vietnamese experiences and signed a book contract with Harper & Row. He began work on these memoirs in 1970 and assiduously wrote page after page as facts and events flashed through his memory. It was a more wearying process than he had imagined when he agreed to tell his story, but finally, by July 1971, he could promise a friend that the book's publication date was to be in the spring of 1972.

In the Midst of Wars appeared in February 1972 and immediately attracted favorable reviews. Chester L. Cooper, who had been a White House assistant on Asian affairs during the Johnson administration and who had written his own book on Vietnam, *The Lost Crusade*, described Lansdale as one who was "intensely loyal" to those with whom he had worked. "[H]is friends can do no wrong. A mist of nostalgic affection sheathes his heroes." The book, Cooper wrote, was a reflection of Lansdale's own personality; a "contained and modest" story by a "laconic" man that recounted "exciting and colorful events." Cooper noted Lansdale's successful work in the Philippine elections of the early 1950s. "He should have quit while he was still ahead. . . . Poor Colonel, poor Vietnamese, poor us. If we had known then what we know now!"[14]

Peter Arnett, an Associated Press reporter who spent eight years in Vietnam, wrote a review for the *New York Times*. He called Lansdale "an idealized cold-war warrior" with "bravery, boldness and common sense" whose "legendary exploits and style became the model for the scores of young American operatives dispatched [to Southeast Asia] by various departments and agencies." Arnett was dissatisfied, however, by Lansdale's account, for, he said, even after 386 pages, Lansdale "remains as elusive as the legends" about him. The memoirs, Arnett wrote, were "like reading a history of the American Civil War that ends with the first election of Abraham Lincoln to the Presidency."[15]

Richard Critchfield, correspondent for the *Washington Star* at the height of the Vietnam conflict, called Lansdale "a fabled figure" and a "legendary Asian hand." *In the Midst of Wars*,

Critchfield wrote, was a "discreet" and "invaluable historical document and an exciting adventure story." Critchfield reported that "like the author himself, [the story is] rugged, humorous, compassionate, baffling, naive and a little infuriating." Critchfield believed Lansdale "was perhaps the best senior American official to serve his country in Vietnam."[16]

The review in the *Christian Science Monitor* would have delighted the heart of any author. Saville Davis, a special correspondent for the newspaper, listed some of the many ways others regarded Lansdale: "a folk hero, a military miracle man and a wrecker of United States policy." He was, Davis said, "a man who carefully chooses his adversaries at home and abroad and spares them no form of verbal demolition. Meanwhile he pours affection on anyone with a sense for people." The book itself, he wrote, was a "thriller." "It never preaches, barring a few paragraphs at the end. It explains by narrative, by one intensely gripping episode after another. It rocks you back in your chair, takes your breath away, reports crisp dialogue that is faster and more powerful than bullets, leads you through the most personal moments of guerrilla war and agony." No one, Davis believed, knew Asia like Lansdale. He had learned his lessons in the Philippines and honed his skills in Vietnam. Thus he was able to determine what was wrong with the American role in Vietnam long before the United States became militarily involved there. "He told us and told us and told us and only a few would understand." Since no one listened, "[w]e brought not liberty . . . but new-old forms of political repression, terror and tyranny. This was a people's war and we ourselves destroyed the only relationship—to the people—that could have enabled us to win. An artificial big-army war obsessed us and riveted our attention . . . and the real war went unnoticed."[17]

Sherwood Dickerman, who had five years' experience as a foreign correspondent in Southeast Asia, believed Landale did not tell all he knew in his book: "[T]here are grounds for suspecting that he may have omitted more than he put in."

Dickerman called Lansdale "a warmly sentimental man toward Asian friends, and a quick-study improviser and promoter." The book itself, Dickerman wrote, was "a period piece of the cold war, a nostalgic memoir." He described Lansdale as both "ingenious and ruthless" and "idealistic and courageous." He was "the most influential single American in Southeast Asia and certainly the most controversial."[18]

Jonathan Mirsky, on the other hand, used the opportunity to review Lansdale's book as a way to vent an unprofessional splenetic diatribe which grew from his leftist persuasions. His essay in the *Saturday Review of Literature* (it could not be called a review) mercilessly castigated Lansdale. Director of the East Asia Center at Dartmouth College, Mirsky charged that Lansdale's book "from the cover to the final pages . . . is permeated with lies." Whatever page one turned to, "the accounts are likely to be lies." It was, he wrote, contemptible for Harper and Row to "foist such a package of untruths on the public." No good thing was to be found in this publication and Mirsky warned those who traveled within his circle to be wary and spend their money on another title.[19]

In later years Lansdale enjoyed telling how, two weeks after the appearance of Mirsky's essay, he received a telephone call from the head of the Philippine-American Women's Association in Washington, D.C. "We all read that wonderful review of your book in the *Saturday Review*," she said, "and rushed out and bought copies." He added that perhaps he should have sent Mirsky a thank-you note.[20] Yet twelve years later Mirsky's unjustified charges still stung Lansdale. Those bitter words had been inspired, Lansdale reflected, by the fact that "I didn't admit that I was a chief CIA agent out in the Far East. . . . I was writing the history I saw and the hell with what I really was. It didn't matter too much about my position, in a way."[21]

Mirsky missed an essential point: Lansdale *could not* reveal the entire story of many of the events in which he had been a player. He was an honorable man. He came from a generation where one's pledges counted as heavy responsibilties, and Lansdale had long since been sworn to secrecy. William Colby once wrote that he "could not be accepted as an intelligence officer until I signed the secrecy agreement (which binds me still) that stated I would not reveal, without the CIA's authority, any secrets I would learn while working for the Agency."[22] Author Philip Burnett Franklin Agee has called that oath "permanent, eternal and universal."[23] And Lansdale felt bound by his pledge.

At our first meeting he set forth a caution to me: "Before we get started, I want to say something. I'm concerned about a biography [because of] my connections with CIA. . . . I gave my word years ago."[24] Two years went by during which he avoided answering many of my questions. Finally he opened up. "I checked with Bill Colby," he said, "on an old oath we both took some years ago. . . . And he kindly called upon some of the CIA folks to back up his judgment. They all voted with him. So I will now admit publicly that I served with the CIA, as an Air Force officer on regular Air Force pay, on volunteer duty, for the years 1950, 1951, 1952, 1953, 1954, 1955, and 1956. Just those years, no more."[25]

Those years enumerated by Lansdale were precisely those which he wrote about in his autobiography. Given his pledge of secrecy, the surprise is not that there is much missing from that story, but rather that he was able to tell as much as he did. Given the circumstances under which he had to write, he told a remarkable story and Mirsky's charges were unfair.

Indeed, what makes *In the Midst of Wars* so remarkable is that it clearly reveals Lansdale's honesty. It shows how quiet and unadorned was his pride. Nearly devoid of ego and empty of both caprice and enmity, Lansdale somehow manages to keep himself in the background. He is not the story itself. He is only a player in a greater drama. His capacity to do this is a tribute to his character, just as *In the Midst of Wars* is a tribute to those men he advised in an age long ago and far away.

In private letters to friends, Lansdale was open and unabashed about what he had done. Long ago, he had written his friend Peter Richards, in Manila, "I am never about to write the truth of some past events—the way they turned out made nice history for the nations involved and I'm happy to keep history in the fiction class."[26] He was acknowledging that information then available was incomplete. In a word, without his inside information, contemporary accounts were "fiction." Now he had done what he thought he would never do. But even his account did not relate the whole story of many events he had witnessed and in which he had participated. "Of course I tell some white lies in it," he admitted to friend Peter Richards. "Not just to protect some friends, but mainly to give Asians some sorely-needed heroes from among their own. I have a hunch it will bring some knowing chuckles from you. Yet, there's a lot of hirtherto [*sic*] untold history in it which is accurate enough to ease my conscience."[27] What 'white lies'? They consisted of downplaying his own role. To his friend Bo Bohannan, Lansdale confessed, "Our friends come out smelling like roses, untainted and heroic in it and against a proper background. As you know from long ago, I decided that Asia needed its own heroes—so I've given them a whole bookful of them, with us/uns merely being companionable friends to some great guys."[28] He also told Bohannan: "We [must] give all the credit to the Filipinos who were doing this. It is their fight. They are risking their lives."[29] To newsman and author Robert Shaplen, Lansdale observed, "The Phillipines is hard up for decent heroes and I am not about to aid and abet Magsaysay's detractors."[30] There were those, Lansdale wrote, who "simply cannot conceive of an Asian being a real man in his own right."[31] Lansdale wanted to show how wrong-headed such views were, and so he wrote his autobiography to reveal the stories of two such men. If that was lying, we should all be so guilty.

Why did he downplay his role? We have all read many first-hand accounts where authors have overstressed their own importance. So often they seem to be saying: "Without me the results would have been far different." Lansdale disagreed with such self-styling. "I haven't talked about things. . . . I haven't gone around saying, 'I did this [and I did that].'"[32] What Lansdale's critics failed to see (because the proud can seldom see beyond their own egos) is that he was a truly humble man. He would rather listen than speak, see than be seen, reach out than grasp. He would rather let a deserving person in the Third World receive credit where it was due rather than to claim it for himself when he might have easily done so.

Emma Valeriano, a prominent Filipina and widow of a long-time Lansdale follower, once recalled for me this quiet side of Lansdale's nature. He was, she said, always low-key, letting others exploit ideas he planted. Asians loved him because he always acted out of great respect for their dignity. He never ordered anyone to follow a course of action; he rarely even suggested. She described his manner of offering advice: "He would sit quietly . . . listen to you talk." Then he would sum up in his own words and with his own emphasis what had been said. "Suddenly you are getting a revelation. You think, 'Oh my God. Why didn't I think of this?' I am getting the light. Then I made my own judgment. Where did that come from? From myself? But he helped! That's why I would trust a man like him."[33] It was an attribute beyond Mirsky's ken.

This is enjoyable reading for all those who like adventure, and essential reading for those who must govern our nation and determine what future American strategy will be in unconventional settings.

—CECIL B. CURREY

NOTES

1. Tran Van Don, *Our Endless War: Inside Vietnam* (San Rafael, CA: Presidio Press, 1978), pp. 60–61.
2. Edward G. Lansdale lecture on military history, University of South Florida, Tampa, Florida, 19 November 1984.

3. Letter, Edward G. Lansdale to Robert Shaplen, 30 May 1965, Correspondence, U.S. Department of Defense, Office of the Secretary of Defense, Box 40, Lansdale Papers, The Hoover Institution for War, Revolution and Peace, Stanford University, Palo Alto, California. Hereafter cited as USDOD, OSD, LP, THIWRP.

4. Quoted on p. xxxi, *infra*.

5. Quoted from the reminiscences of Manuel Manahan, a former newsman and Philippine Senator; a longtime associate of both Ramón Magsaysay and Lansdale. Interviewed in Manila by the author on 25 July 1985.

6. Edward G. Lansdale, "The US Military in Non-Military Warfare" [Lecture] and Memorandum, "The EUCOM Cold War Seminar," [Oberammergau, Germany, 20 October 1959], Speeches, Writings, Notes/Miscellany, USDOD, OSD, Box 43, LP, THIWRP.

7. Edward G. Landale, "The Free Citizen in Uniform" [Lecture], Army Civil Affairs School, Ft. Gordon, Georgia, 1 November 1960. Mimeographed. 7 pp. THIWRP.

8. *Ibid* and Edward G. Lansdale, "The Insurgent Battlefield" [Lecture], U.S. Air Force Academy, Colorado, 25 May 1962. Mimeographed. 9 pp. THIWRP. See also Edward G. Lansdale, "People's Wars: Three Primary Lessons" [Lecture], Air War College, Maxwell Air Force Base, Montgomery, Alabama, 15 January 1973, printed in *Vital Speeches of the Day*, 1 April 1973, pp. 357–361.

9. Edward G. Lansdale and others, "Counter-Guerrilla Operations in the Philippines, 1946–1953" [Seminar comments], U. S. Army Special Warfare School, Ft. Bragg, North Carolina, 15 June 1961. Mimeographed. 74 pp. THIWRP.

10. "The Insurgent Battlefield."

11. Letter, Mary McGrory to Edward G. Lansdale, 23 November 1965, Correspondence, Senior Liaison Office, United States Embassy, Box 54, LP, THIWRP.

12. "People's Wars: Three Primary Lessons."

13. Edward G. Lansdale, "Two Steps to Get Us Out of Vietnam," *Look Magazine* (4 March 1969), pp. 92–98.

14. *The Washington Post*, 15 March 1972.

15. *The New York Times*, 9 April 1972.

16. *The Washington Star*, 26 March 1972.

17. *The Christian Science Monitor*, 6 April 1972.

18. *The Washington Post 'Bookworld,'* 19 March 1972.

19. *Saturday Review*, 1 April 1972.

20. Letter, Edward G. Lansdale to Peter C. Richards, 15 April 1972, Richards Collection. Mr. Richards, who has saved his correspondence with Lans-

dale over a number of years, kindly consented to allow me access to his files when I interviewed him in Manila, 23 July 1985. Hereafter cited as RC.

21. Edward G. Lansdale interview by the author, 15 February 1984.
22. William E. Colby and Peter Forbath, *Honorable Men: My Life in the CIA* (New York: Simon & Schuster, 1978), p. 81.
23. Philip B. F. Agee, *CIA Diary: Inside the Company* (Suffolk, England: Penguin Books, Ltd., 1975), p. 21.
24. Edward G. Lansdale interview by the author, 15 February 1984.
25. Letter, Edward G. Lansdale to the author, 8 January 1986.
26. Letter, Edward G. Lansdale to Peter C. Richards, 14 January 1964, RC.
27. *Ibid.*, 23 July 1971, RC.
28. Letter, Edward G. Lansdale to C. T. R. 'Bo' Bohannan, 18 July 1971, Bohannan Collection. Mrs. Dorothy Bohannan, wife of the deceased 'Bo', allowed me to consult her voluminous files of correspondence dating back many years when I used her Manila home as my research headquarters during the summer of 1985. Since her death, those files have been relocated to THIWRP.
29. *Ibid.*, and interview with Edward G. Lansdale, 12 November 1985. See also C. T. R. Bohannan, "Revisionism in Philippine History," an address to the History Department, University of the Philippines, Manila, Republic of the Philippines, 17 September 1979. Lansdale Personal Papers. General Lansdale's widow, Patrocinio Yapcinco Kelly Lansdale, kindly allowed me access to her husband's papers which remained at his home at the time of his death. They have since been relocated to THIWRP.
30. Letter, Edward G. Lansdale to Robert Shaplen, 30 May 1965, Correspondence, USDOD, OSD, Box 40, LP, THIWRP.
31. Letters, Bert J. Talbot to Edward Lansdale, 18 November 1954, and Edward Lansdale to Bert Talbot, 21 January 1955, Correspondence, USDOD, OSD, Box 41, LP, THIWRP.
32. Edward G. Lansdale interview by the author, 12 November 1985.
33. Emma Valeriano interview by the author, 26 July 1985.

ACKNOWLEDGMENTS

My rueful thanks go to Bob Shaplen, Al Ravenholt, and Cass Canfield for pushing me into writing an account of these years and to editors Gene Young and Ann Harris for keeping me from being too garrulous. My heartfelt thanks go to Reggie Miskovish who came through some unexpected combat as my secretary in Saigon only to find her spare time in the U.S. taken up with typing early drafts of this book and to my daughter-in-law Carolyn Lansdale who typed the final drafts with one eye on the children (my grandchildren!). Although I relied mainly on my personal notes and letters to refresh my memory, special thanks go to those who helped me pin down some names and places that had grown dim: Ev Bumgardner, Ellsworth Bunker, Dolf Droge, Mym Johnston, Sam Karrick, Pat Kelly, Hank and Anne Miller, George Peabody, Rufe Phillips, Joe Redick, Poling Valeriano, Jack Wachtel, and Rudy Winnacker. And most of all, my affectionate thanks go to my wife Helen for her understanding and help during the months it took to write this book.

PREFACE

When a man leaves home, he sometimes travels more than mere physical distance. This happened to me in the middle years of the century when the U.S. government sent me to help our Asian friends in the Philippines and Vietnam cope with wars of rebellion and insurgency. I went far beyond the usual bounds given a military man after I discovered just what the people on these battlegrounds needed to guard against and what to keep strong. The needs are so universal in today's world that I decided to share the story of those days with others. Hence this book. The narrative is quite personal, told the way I remember it.

You should know one thing at the beginning: I took my American beliefs with me into these Asian struggles, as Tom Paine would have done. Ben Franklin once said, "Where liberty dwells, there is my country." Tom Paine had replied, "Where liberty dwells not, there is my country." Paine's words form a cherished part of my credo. My American beliefs include conviction of the truth in the precept that "men are created equal, that they are endowed by their Creator with certain unalienable Rights" and in the provisions of our Bill of Rights to make that great precept a reality among men. Along with other Americans, I feel a kinship with Thomas Jefferson when he declared, "I have sworn upon the altar of God eternal hostility against every form of tyranny over the mind of man." These are principles for an American to try to live by wherever he goes, even two centuries later. Thus, I endeavored to practice my beliefs among embattled people abroad.

I dedicate the book to all my loved ones, my family, and those who fought the good fight by my side.

—EDWARD GEARY LANSDALE

Virginia, 1971

ACRONYMS

BCT	Battalion Combat Team
BOQ	Bachelor Officers Quarters
BUDC	Barrio United Defense Corps
CAO	Civil Affairs Office
EDCOR	Economic Development Corps
GAMO	Groupe Administratif Mobile (Mobile Administrative Group)
HMB	Hukbong Magpapalaya ng Bayan (Peoples' Liberation Army); also called Huks
JUSMAG	Joint U.S. Military Advisory Group
MAAG	Military Assistance Advisory Group
MIS	Military Intelligence Service
MNR	Movement for National Revolution
MSS	Military Security Service
NAMFREL	National Movement for Free Elections
OB	Operation Brotherhood
PCAC	Presidential Complaints and Action Commission
PNS	Philippine News Service
TRIM	Training Relations Instruction Mission
VNQDD	Viet-Nam Quoc Dan Dang (Vietnamese Kuomintang)

★ ★

CHAPTER

ONE

TO MANILA, 1950

U SUALLY A MAN goes to war as he enters life—in an undignified manner. Hannibal is famed in history, but reflect on what
it must have been like to have been a foot soldier in his army,
walking behind all those elephants across the Alps! Modern-
day journeys to war, with their human cargos crammed into
air, sea, rail, or truck transports are hardly less undignified.

So my September 1950 trip to a war in the Philippines, the
Huk Rebellion, cannot help but be memorable for me. The
experience was so utterly different from the ordinary lot of
a military man. I was forty-two years old at the time, a lieutenant colonel in the United States Air Force. (My promotion
to colonel came some months later.)

I rode to the scene of conflict sunk down in a pillowed lounge
chair aboard a Pan-American Clipper, a Boeing B-377 Strato-
cruiser that cruised between fifteen and twenty-five thousand
feet above the water. Some unknown benefactor in the travel
section in Washington had decided to hurry me to my destination, bypassing the delays of military traffic, which at the
time was concentrating on getting troops to Korea, and sending me to the Philippines by U.S. commercial carrier. It was

before the days of jet transports with their great loads of passengers and speeds that have made the far reaches of the world so commonplace. The Pacific still was a mighty ocean, not a pond, and the airlines treated each trip as an honored event. Clipper flights were all one class, strictly first. So I went to war in luxurious ease, past the fairy-tale cloud formations of the mid-Pacific, amid obviously wealthy passengers who chatted of business and social affairs awaiting them in the Philippines. None mentioned the war that was raging there or even asked me questions that would let me modestly admit that, yes, I was going to the war.

My orders were plain. The United States government wanted me to give all help feasible to the Philippine government in stopping the attempt by the Communist-led Huks to overthrow that government by force. My help was to consist mainly of advice where needed and desired. It was up to me to figure out how best to do this. If funds or equipment was needed, I was to remember that the United States was straining its resources to meet the war needs in Korea and that any requests from me would have to compete against higher-priority demands. As a military officer, I was being attached to the Joint U.S. Military Advisory Group (JUSMAG) in the Philippines by the agreement of both governments, although my advisory work wasn't necessarily to be limited to military affairs. After ninety days I should have run dry of all the advice I was capable of giving and should have returned home again. The subsequent stretching of those ninety days into years of work wasn't envisioned.

Thus I rode to war on that September 1950 flight to the Philippines. As we came in for the landing at Nichols Field (recently renamed Manila International Airport), a lady passenger exclaimed, "My, but everyone's in such a hurry! I thought this was a lazy tropical country." I looked over her shoulder at the scene on which she was gazing. It was the circumferential road around Manila, with dusty clouds billow-

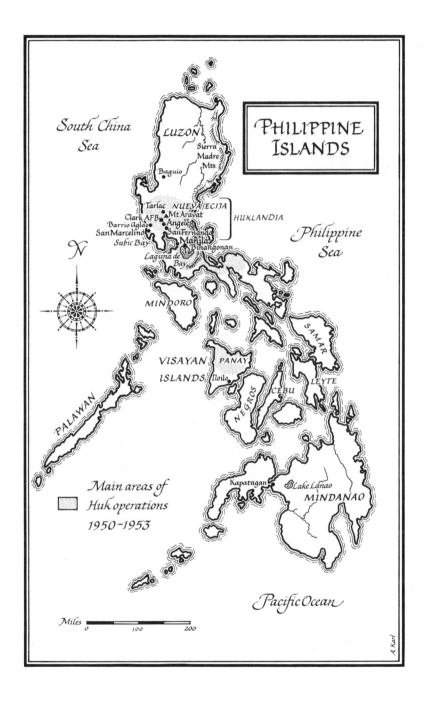

South China
Sea

PHILIPPINE
ISLANDS

LUZON

Sierra
Madre
Mts.

Baguio

Tarlac
Clark AFB
Barrio Aglao
SanMarcelino
Subic Bay

NUEVA ECIJA
Mt Arayat
Angeles
San Fernando
Manila
Binangonan

HUKLANDIA

Philippine
Sea

Laguna de
Bay

N

MINDORO

VISAYAN
ISLANDS

PANAY

Iloilo

SAMAR

LEYTE

CEBU

NEGROS

PALAWAN

Main areas of
Huk operations
1950-1953

Kapatagan

Lake Lanao

MINDANAO

Pacific Ocean

Miles
0   100   200

A. Karl

ing up from heavy trucks bumping and lurching through the holes and over the ridges of its surface. Lordy, I said to myself, they haven't yet finished paving highway 54.

My journey to the Philippines wasn't a chance one. It was a natural one, foregone. Events had shaped the itinerary over the past decade, with my own life-line becoming entangled in a larger skein.

In 1941 news of the attack on Pearl Harbor had caused me to quit my position with an advertising agency in San Francisco and join others in volunteering to defend the country. I served with the OSS for a time, then became an army intelligence officer. The end of World War II found me in the Philippines, a major and the chief of a group known as the Intelligence Division of the staff of the G-2, Armed Forces/Western Pacific. War's end brought a stampede among our temporary soldiers to go home. When my turn came, I discovered that I didn't want to leave. My eyes had been opened to the world outside my own country, to the new contentions brewing in that world, and to possibilities for an American in military service that I hadn't imagined in my civilian life. There was a strong appeal for me in the U.S. military's part in the creation of democratic institutions in postwar Japan and Germany. There were examples all about me in the Philippines of what a previous generation of American military men had done there, including the remarkable establishment of a countrywide public school system open to all. I decided to stay in the military for a close-up share in whatever happened next. This decision led to my remaining in the Philippines until late 1948, with my wife and two sons joining me for the last two years. I became deputy G-2 of the army command.

By 1947, frictions between Filipinos and the dwindling contingents of American soldiers had developed into an ugly situation, and I was appointed as the command's public information officer, with orders to resolve the problem. Quick gathering of firsthand facts and prompt use of them soon led to more understanding between all concerned; harmony returned. The work brought me close to journalists, politicians, and other opinion-makers in the Philippines. While all this was happening, my application for a commission in the brand new U.S. Air Force was accepted. The world was entering the air age. I had concluded that there would be more elbow room for fresh ideas in the air force than in the older military services. I was commissioned as a captain, United States Air Force, in 1947.

Military intelligence duties had opened the way for a rare education about the people, the life, and the land of the Philippines. Since modern armies need thorough information about conditions on the battlegrounds where they fight, as U.S. forces did in the Philippines during World War II, the G-2's office at our headquarters held a treasury of reports about the country, reports whose contents I had to master for my daily work. Then, at war's end, I gave my intelligence group the task of sorting through what we already knew and obtaining further facts about conditions in the Philippines, not only the physical aspects resulting from the long Japanese occupation and the fierce combat of the liberation, but also what had happened to the social structure. I checked many of the reported facts by traveling among the people throughout the islands that make up the Philippines, talking with hundreds upon hundreds of them, seeing for myself how things were. I was treated with endearingly warm hospitality and became acquainted with many families as a guest in their homes, from urban mansions to one-room *nipa* shacks in the rice paddies. After months of work, about a dozen volumes of current facts had been compiled. With the permission of the U.S. government, I gave copies of these reports to the Philippine president and his cabinet who were struggling to restore public services in the war-damaged country. Other copies went to those who were directing U.S. assistance programs in the Philippines. The reports were simply part of the multiple American efforts to help the Filipinos prepare themselves for their day of independence from the U.S., July 4, 1946.

Another of my duties was to do my share of helping the Philippine armed forces prepare for separation from the U.S. military, of which they were a part until June 30, 1946. My own chores concerned the military intelligence services, their organization, staffing, training, and equipping. Conferring day after day with members of Philippine intelligence groups on the sensitive problems they would face in the future, relaxing with them in their homes, and taking field trips with them brought not only friendship, but also anecdotal insights into the human ingredients that were shaping the ongoing history of the Philippines. Some of these ingredients were extremely lively. The years of war had brought many weapons to the Philippines, available for the picking from fallen soldiers on the battlegrounds or in raids on military stockpiles. An upsurge of banditry plagued the country after the wartime armies departed. Although all the illegal gunmen roaming the countryside were loosely termed "dissidents" at first, the label soon came to be used to describe just one group of them, the Huks.

A Huk (pronounced "hook") was the short name for a member of the Hukbong Bayan Laban sa Hapon, or People's Anti-Japanese Army. The "army" was a guerrilla organization formed in March 1942 by the Communist party of the Philippines for the avowed patriotic purpose of fighting against the Japanese forces then occupying the Philippines. Twenty-nine-year-old Luis Taruc became its commander. Taruc was a tailor by profession, an idealist who had spent more of his time working for the Socialist party than in his tailor shop and who had become a member of the political committee when the Socialist and Communist parties in the Philippines merged as the Communist party in November 1938. Initially organized as five squadrons of 100 men each, operating in the rice paddies and sugarcane fields north of Manila from mountain bases, the Huks were successful in recruiting many others to join them and in extending their operations into other areas of Luzon. U.S. and Philippine authorities, as well as Huk leaders themselves, told me that Huk forces had increased to about 10,000 by March 1943.

Their success was due in part to political enterprise, in part to expert guerrilla training. Politically, the Communists created a clandestine civil administration in the towns and barrios (hamlets) of provinces where their forces operated. Its base structure was the BUDC (Barrio United Defense Corps) with a membership of five to twelve persons in each barrio, depending upon its size, which carried out recruiting, intelligence collection, supply, and civil justice. Initial guerrilla training was given at training camps, known as "Stalin University," by Chinese veterans of the Communists' 8th Route Army from the mainland. Later, the Chinese became disenchanted with the amateurishness of the Filipinos and formed an all-Chinese force of their own, the Overseas Chinese 48th Detachment of the Huks (known locally as the Wachi), which operated independently: this Chinese force amounted to six squadrons of 200 men each and stayed close to Manila in Bulacan and Laguna.

The main Huk forces, emboldened by their full ranks and by the aggressive example of the Chinese, started attacking Japanese garrisons, patrols, and convoys, as well as waging a war of attrition against the puppet constabulary. The Japanese Imperial Army retaliated in the spring of 1943, putting the Huk stronghold of Mount Arayat under siege for ten days and killing or capturing many of the Huk leaders. The remaining Huks went underground and reorganized for a more tightly controlled political effort. Their guerrilla efforts henceforth seemed aimed mostly at reinforcing political control. American and Filipino leaders of other guerrilla forces on Luzon in those days later told me that the Huks were more interested in expanding their territory than in fighting the enemy; there were many Huk clashes with other guerrilla forces. Our intelligence community estimated that, out of the 25,000 killed by the Huks during World War II, only 5,000 were Japanese.

When U.S. forces pushed across Luzon toward Manila in February 1945, they found that Huk leaders had proclaimed themselves governors of three provinces. President Osmena of the Philippine Commonwealth, who traveled with the U.S. forces, refused to recognize the local Communist administrations. Taruc and other Huk military leaders were arrested by the U.S. Army's CounterIntelligence Corps but were later released. Embittered, the Huk forces formally disbanded at war's end, the men joining a tightly disciplined veterans' association. They refused to give up their weapons and secreted them.

The year 1946 should have been one of jubilation in the Philippines. World War II, in which it had been one of the battlegrounds, was over. Independence from the United States came in a generously friendly fashion, with money in the treasury, with political and social institutions administered by experienced Filipinos, and with advanced codes established for democratic behavior designed to give the citizenry the utmost benefits of self-rule and cooperative economics. Seemingly, everything for which the Filipinos had sacrificed and suffered during the past four years of savage occupation and liberation could at last become a reality. Instead, 1946 saw the outbreak of another war in the Philippines, the Huk Rebellion.

Deep down, the basic cause of the war was the impatience of some of the Communist leaders to gain control of the Philippines. If they hadn't set out to overthrow the government by force, there wouldn't have been a war. (Even the Communist Politburo in the Philippines recognized this after the military defeat of the Huks; in secret deliberations in 1953, it judged the "armed struggle" to have been a mistake and decided to take up the "legal struggle" again, with more patience than before. The "legal struggle" involved the use of politics to advance the cause, mostly under the guise of deceptive political "fronts" backed up by strong-arm coercion.) As 1946 began, the Communists were using the "legal struggle," with their military veterans giving it muscle by organizing goon squads to keep the citizenry in line. The Politburo established itself clandestinely in Manila and engineered a "front" with militant labor and farm groups. Six Huks, including their military leader, Taruc, were elected to Congress but were not allowed to take their congressional seats because of charges of fraud and terrorism in their election. Taruc and the others went back to the hills, reactivated the Huk guerrillas, and set out to conquer the Philippines by force. There were attempts to settle Huk grievances peacefully, some rather melodramatic, but they failed. Guerrilla warfare broke into the open two months before Independence Day in 1946, with a Huk ambush that killed ten national policemen. Before 1946 ended, Huk guerrillas were attacking police posts, ambushing, killing, kidnapping, robbing, burning homes and fields, and impressing new recruits by force in areas they dominated.

As the fighting developed, I was one of those designated to report to the U.S. government on what was happening. Faced with having to refine the mass of raw data coming into our headquarters, I began traveling around the troubled areas by jeep for firsthand checks on what was being reported. The United States assumed a neutral position as a matter of policy, stressing that the Philippines now was independent and must be left alone to solve its own problems. So I stuck to the role of neutral observer, talking to men on both sides of the fight and getting to know the people living on the battleground. After months of such visiting, I came to know the provinces of central Luzon, which the Manila press dubbed as "Huklandia," about as well as an American could. It was a period of intense education for me, sometimes scary, sometimes sad, sometimes funny.

One of the humorous moments concerned the Huks' motivational agitation, which contained strong doses of anti-Americanism along the usual Communist line. One day, while driving on a back road in Pampanga province, I came upon a political meeting in a town plaza. A Huk political officer was haranguing the crowd, enumerating their troubles with crops, debts, and share in life, blaming all ills on "American imperialism." Impetuously, I got out of the jeep from where I had parked it at the edge of the crowd, climbed up on its hood, and when the speaker had paused for breath I shouted, "What's the matter? Didn't you ever have an American friend?" The startled crowd turned around and saw an American in uniform standing up on his jeep. I had a flash of sobering second thoughts. I kicked myself mentally for giving in to such an impulse among hundreds of people living in hostile territory. But the people immediately put me at ease, they grinned and called hello. The speaker and many of the townspeople clustered around me, naming Americans they had known and liked and asking if I was acquainted with them. I teased them with the reminder that these folks they had known were the "American imperialists" they had been denouncing. They assured me that not a single one of them was. It was a long time before I could get away from the gossipy friendliness.

Aside from "Down with American Imperialism!" the Huk rallying slogans were "Bullets Not Ballots," a vengeful motif for the unseating of the Huks elected to Congress, and "Land for the Landless" to appeal to the tenant farmers who made up the bulk of the population in the areas of Huk operations. On the surface, none of these slogans should have been attractive enough to prompt people into risking their lives for the Huk cause. I could understand the convenience of having a remote and faceless target, such as "American imperialism," as a scapegoat for life's frustrations; it didn't answer back. But the Philippine Constitution, electoral code, and the laws on agrarian affairs were models of enlightened social thinking. They offered a better deal than the Huks did. The trouble came, of course, because it was fallible human beings who had to make these laws and codes work as perfectly as intended, and human emotions tend to get in the way of achieving perfection. Ambition, venality, indifference, and other human motivations had deprived many of the people in "Huklandia" of their fair share of what the written words had promised them. The inequity made "Huklandia" a breeding ground for discontent, which the Huks were skilled enough to exploit. Under the pressure of present injustices, it became irrelevant that Huk leaders were striving to make a future ruled by more ruthless men than those in the government they hoped to destroy.

During this period I experienced another memorable personal moment with the Huks. Just before my family arrived to help make our home for a while in the Philippines, boastful Huks told me how much they knew about me. They gave me the date, church, and performing minister of my marriage years before. They named the precise minute of the day, hospital room numbers, and doctors' names for the births of my sons. I was impressed because most of this information was not noted in U.S. government records filed about me, and certainly not in the Philippines. Somebody had gone to a lot of work to get these facts. Soberly, I decided on extra precautions for the protection of my family from then on. In later years, they stayed home while I went to the Communist battlegrounds. From the continuing threats, broadcasts, and news publications of the Communists about me through the years, I gathered that I had been wise to protect my family from terrorism this way.

Departure from the Philippines in November 1948 aboard an army transport bound for the United States brought an unusual scene at the pier, where a hundred or so Filipino friends heaped flowers upon my family and me and embraced us as the Philippine Constabulary band marched out on the pier next to the U.S. Army band and surprised me with a serenade of my favorite Filipino songs. It was a heartwarming sendoff for an American major and his family, unforgettable. It puzzled the other passengers. As we sailed off, a group of them asked me, "What in hell did you do to deserve that?" I shrugged my shoulders. How do words tell the inner feelings of human affection? My work had taken me among thousands of Filipinos. I cared about them as individuals and they responded with friendship. It was that natural and that simple. This has happened to other Americans in the Philippines and elsewhere abroad. Perhaps they, too, have run into doubting Thomases, a breed who have long plagued me with their disbelief in elementary cause and effect in human relationships.

By coincidence a change in the name of the military arm of the Communists was made as I was leaving the Philippines. The new name was Hukbong Magpapalaya ng Bayan, or People's Liberation Army. The former nickname "Huks" was still used, although both the Politburo and the Philippine government agencies started referring to these armed forces as "HMB."

In the United States, I was assigned to be an instructor at the U.S. Air Force's Strategic Intelligence School in Denver, where I was given the task of lecturing on economic intelligence. After preparing and giving one series of lectures, I was dismayed to learn that some of my superiors had concluded that teaching was my true calling. While they acted to fix me in a career as an air force educator, I sought ways to get into a more active life. Friends at headquarters in Washington responded. I was detailed to staff work in Washington, on cold war problems. It was 1949 and the United States was beset with knotty situations abroad of a type which we never had had to face before. The move to Washington coincided with my promotion to lieutenant colonel.

I found that most of my staff colleagues in Washington were focused on the moves of Stalin and on the Soviet strategy of manipulating the urban intelligentsia and proletariat into undertaking revolutions in countries friendly to us; Soviet concepts of guerrilla warfare showed the influence of World War II, when the Soviets had used partisans as adjuncts to conventional armies. A minority of us focused on Mao and the Chinese concept of a poor man's war that would start with rural farmers as guerrillas, a bucolic force that would become a conventional army as it met with success until, finally, it would be able to swallow up the cities and complete the conquest of a country. Mao's thinking was what I had experienced firsthand among the Huks in the Philippines. Of course, the objective of both Moscow and Peking was the same—to make the world Communist. Each saw the United States as the main stumbling block to that end.

I kept up with the news from the Philippines. It was filled with reports of Huk successes. Towns had been looted and burned. Constabulary barracks in six provinces were being attacked frequently. Ambushes on the highways were becoming commonplace, as were kidnappings and murders of local leaders in the provinces. Visitors from the Philippines gave me details of current events and conveyed to me a sense of the fear that was spreading over the island of Luzon from the reign of terror.

Among the visitors with whom I talked was Congressman Ramon Magsaysay, the chairman of the National Defense Committee in the Philippine House of Representatives, who was in Washington conferring with the U.S. Congress about Filipino veterans' benefits. A husky, intense man, his restlessness evident in his foot-jiggling, Magsaysay confided to me his worries about the current morale of Filipino soldiers. It was sinking under the combination of physical and psychological attacks, the latter perniciously erosive since the Huks pictured the Philippine government as totally corrupt and told the soldiers they were suckers for risking their lives to defend it. In several meetings with Magsaysay, I elicited his ideas about coping with the Huks and bettering the government effort. His ideas were infused with a practicality about the use of troops against guerrillas and a compassion for the people on the land, which stemmed from his own experiences as a successful leader of guerrillas in World War II, in areas where Huks now were operating. Impressed, I brought him together with a number of high-echelon policy formulators in Washington. They too were impressed.

Mindful of the part played by Americans in the recent Greek struggle against Communist guerrillas, I talked to U.S. leaders about giving similar help to the Philippines. This was in the spring of 1950. Few U.S. officials wanted even to think about going through another experience such as Greece, although they admitted that the Philippine situation seemed to be worsening. It was suggested that I draw up a modest plan for simple measures that could be added to the U.S. military and economic assistance already being given to the Philippines. I went to work on a plan for an input of less conventional actions against the political-military tactics of the Huks.

One aspect of this plan was the concept of giving the Philippine armed forces a capability for psychological warfare; other than a few speeches by the president, the Philippine government was almost voiceless against the skilled psychological attack of the Huks. This led to my organizing a seminar on psychological warfare at the Pentagon; the participants were persons I could find in the Washington area who had had wartime experience in psywar (as we called it) and Philippine military officers undergoing training in the U.S. whom the military attaché at the Philippine embassy could talk into visiting Washington on their own. We had no funds to support the seminar, just an available conference room in the Pentagon and much goodwill. We met for two days. I didn't know it at the time, but this was to be the extent of my own formal education in psychological warfare.

Reports from the Philippines continued to be full of bad news. A request came in from President Quirino of the Philippines for my services as an adviser on gathering intelligence about the Huks; my earlier help in the Philippines had been remembered. Now there was a dire need for better and quicker collection of tactical information about an enemy who kept popping up in surprise attacks and then disappearing again. The request was being checked against my concept of doing more to help than just advising on intelligence matters, and messages were being passed back and forth to Manila, when the Korean war broke out. Thus it wasn't until the end of August that I met with the vice chief of staff of the air force, General Nathan Twining, and with Livingston Merchant, the assistant secretary of state for Far Eastern affairs, and learned for sure that I was going to the Philippines. Orders were issued. They caught me in the midst of personal problems.

I recently had bought an old house in Washington and had set out with axe, crowbar, saw, and hammer to remodel it myself in off-duty hours. My wife had sold our home in California and arrived in Washington with our sons just as I received orders to go to the Philippines. She was appalled at the sight of our new home in Washington, in which I had only progressed as far as chopping down walls to make larger rooms and ripping out the plumbing for modernizing. Standing in the shambles, I broke the news that I was leaving within hours for the war in the Philippines. It wasn't the most pleasant moment of my life. We stayed that night in a hotel, while I located plumbers and carpenters who could make the house livable. My departure left the family stranded among a confusion of sawhorses, lumber, and plumbing fixtures, only faintly reassured by my pledge never to attempt remodeling a house again.

Perhaps the vivid memory I carry of the luxury of the flight to the Philippines flowed from my guilt about the condition in which I had left that house. It was close to playing hooky, to go to war.

NOTES

Mount Arayat. Mount Arayat, where Huk forces fought the Japanese and later fought the Philippine Constabulary, has a long history of guerrilla use. Previous bloody battles there were fought by Philippine guerrillas against a colonial Spanish army in the nineteenth century and with the U.S. Army during the so-called Philippine Insurrection. The guerrillas lost these earlier battles.

COMMUNISTS. The Communist parties in the Philippines and in Vietnam had almost twin beginnings. After organizational struggles in the 1920s, each managed to straighten out its internal affairs sufficiently to meet the standards set by the Third International or Comintern. Each with about fifteen hundred card-carrying members at the time was recognized formally by the Comintern in 1930.

Chapter Two

LEARNING ABOUT THE ENEMY

MANILA MIGHT HAVE BEEN posing for a travel poster on that tropical, sun-filled day I arrived in 1950. I squinted into the glaring brightness. I wanted to take in every possible inch of the familiar scene as a staff car drove me from the airport through the heart of the city to its eastern outskirts and the headquarters of JUSMAG (Joint U.S. Military Advisory Group), where I was to be stationed.

The capital city of a republic of twenty million people and seven thousand islands seemed to be just as I had left it two years before. Most of the city's one million inhabitants were showing how alive they were that day. Streets were crowded. Jeepneys darted jauntily from lane to lane in the busy American-style traffic, giving a dancing rhythm to the swaying passengers of this imaginative Filipino jitney adaptation of a U.S. Army jeep. People along the sidewalks were laughing and happy. Everywhere radios blared at their top decibel output, in raucous contest with neighborhood radios, equally loud, tuned to different stations in a happily generous electronic democracy. It made a bright and brassy welcome for me. Yet wasn't this a city ringed by a war? It didn't show. The people of Manila seemed as unaware of reality as were my fellow travelers on the flight from the United States.

JUSMAG added a touch of suburbia to the peaceful picture. It was located just outside the city proper in a housing development for upper-middle-class families. The housing tract itself had several score of homes built at the end of World War II to a uniform design, frame two-story buildings and one-story bungalows set in wide lawns along winding roads. A dozen or so houses at one end were surrounded by a wire fence topped by a strand of barbed wire. This segregated area was the JUSMAG compound where the American officers lived. Close by were the JUSMAG headquarters offices, which made use of the building that had housed the land development company. The staff car drove me through the gate of the JUSMAG compound, past a sentry box from whose shaded interior a Philippine Army soldier peered out more in idle curiosity than in military alertness and along a road to a two-story house. The driver helped me lug my heavy baggage, mostly full of equipment and technical manuals which I had scrounged in Washington, into the empty house. He explained that the building was to be the billet for my team and me.

The rest of that day and all of the next were filled with protocol duties. I reported in at the JUSMAG headquarters, meeting General Leland Hobbs, the chief, who gave me a warm, friendly welcome and assigned me to advisory duties on military intelligence. Since this was the service initially requested of me by President Elpidio Quirino, courtesy demanded a call upon him, which in turn demanded a prior call upon the U.S. ambassador. I met with Ambassador Myron Cowen, who introduced me to his embassy staff; they briefed me on their views of the situation in the Philippines. President Quirino surprised me; when I called upon him at the appointed time, he was presiding at a cabinet meeting. I was asked to "come right in and sit down." He and his officials briefed me about how *they* saw the situation. Absent from this cabinet meeting was Ramon Magsaysay, who had been appointed secretary of national defense the week before, on September 1. I recalled his visit to Washington as a congressman and his ideas on operations against guerrillas, and I congratulated the president on the appointment. President Quirino explained that Magsaysay was "in the field" and hoped that I would see him soon; perhaps I could give him some help. After this presidential meeting, I drove out to the headquarters of the Armed Forces of the Philippines at Camp Murphy, on the outskirts of town, where I called upon General Mariano Castaneda, the chief of staff, as well as officers of the General Staff. They too briefed me about conditions in the Philippines.

In other words, my first hours in the Philippines in 1950 were spent with most of the top officials of a country that had been independent for just four years and with the top local officials of the country that had given this newly independent nation its tutelage in self-rule. All were full of news about the threat the Communist Huks posed the infant nation. Yet, curiously enough, Philippine and American officials barely mentioned the political and social factors in briefing me. They dwelt almost exclusively on the military situation. It was as though military affairs were the sole tangible factor they could grasp, like shopkeepers worried about going bankrupt and counting the goods on shelves instead of pondering ways to get the customers coming in again.

I was told the grisly details of recent military actions, the disposition of troops, and diverse stories about the enemy. The main encounters of the past days had been within easy driving distance from the capital, ranging from the outskirts of town to about eighty miles to the north. Lesser activities were reported in areas just east of the city and to the south. A major part of the government forces had been concentrated in a ring around Manila, as well as in the larger towns of the threatened provinces, obviously a defensive posture, a back-to-the-wall position. However, the ingredients were available for far more dynamic action on the part of the government than what was being done, even in a strictly military sense. In the spring of 1950, the Philippine Constabulary (the national police force which had carried the brunt of the fighting against the Huks until then) was transferred from the Department of the Interior and made a part of the Armed Forces of the Philippines, under the Department of National Defense. This brought the strength of the armed forces up to 50,000 men. With this change, the armed forces were given the task of coping with the Huk Rebellion. There were enough men to do the job if their spirit and tactics so dictated.

A new organizational concept opened up possibilities. This was the BCT or Battalion Combat Team. Before the spring of 1950, the government had defended towns and highways with company-sized units of constabulary, combining a number of these companies whenever it attempted an offensive action against the Huks. Spring 1950, just before my arrival, saw the start of the first ten BCTs. A BCT was an infantry battalion with more firepower and manpower than usual at the time; it consisted of three infantry companies of 110 men each, a heavy weapons company, a reconnaissance company with armored cars, a headquarters and service company, and a battery of artillery. Each BCT, as soon as it was formed and trained, was made responsible for a zone in the provinces. The first BCTs went into the provinces immediately to the north of Manila, some being given responsibility for a half or a third of a province, others for a whole province, depending upon the situation and the estimated capability of the troops. The idea was that a BCT wouldn't sit around and wait for the Huks to come to them but would actively seek them out and engage them, making guerrilla life prohibitive for the enemy.

Organizing to get things done is one thing. Having an army do them successfully is something else again, and this takes leadership. The military leader of the Philippine Armed Forces was a conventional constabulary officer, General Castaneda, the same man who had been leading the downhill governmental struggle against the Huks. It seemed obvious to me that his tactics wouldn't change. When he went on the offensive, he favored a ponderous encirclement of an area where Huks were reported to be, using a "sweep" by infantry to tighten the circle into a smaller "killing ground," upon which artillery would then open up, delighting all who loved noisy fireworks. The fact that the mobile, elusive Huks would dodge out of the slow-moving encirclement early in the game and then watch the fireworks from a safe distance didn't seem to matter. The thunder and flashing of artillery apparently was a satisfying government end in itself, with the troops trudging happily back to their camps afterwards while headquarters announced some plucked-out-of-the-air number of enemy casualties. It was showmanship, but it wasn't defeating the Huks.

The other top leader in the military family was the secretary of national defense, Ramon Magsaysay, the civilian politician who had been in office only a week. Although he had fought as a guerrilla against the Japanese, his credentials for anything beyond politics were far from being accepted by the military professionals. In terms of prestige, the largest office suite at headquarters was occupied by General Castaneda. Magsaysay had given up the customary secretarial office in downtown Manila and had moved to the military headquarters but had had to argue hard to be given even a small office over the ballroom in the Officers Club. I stopped by his office, but he wasn't there. His staff said he was out inspecting units. He was on my "must see" list. In my own assessment, he had qualities sorely needed in the fight against the Huks. He knew the fears and frustrations of guerrilla life from firsthand experience; he was close to the people both from his daily work with the electorate as a congressman and from the days when he managed a bus company in territory that was now the Huk battleground; and he had a firm grasp of current military affairs from his tenure as chairman of the House National Defense Committee, which position he had relinquished the previous week.

In my protocol calls, the Huks were mentioned frequently.

They emerged as shadowy, cardboard figures in the commentary of top officials. Their numbers were put at "about a thousand" or "not more than five thousand." Although the Huks were pictured as bandits roaming the countryside, or as men posing as farmers in the fields who would take up weapons they had hidden and ambush lone vehicles whenever the chance arose, there was an underlying tone of fear in the descriptions of the officials that indicated there was much more to the Huk threat than was contained in those simplistic views. Certainly, I sensed baffled anguish in their voices as they described some of the more savage Huk attacks. The atmosphere in which officialdom lived in the capital city struck me as oddly unreal, as though they hated to admit out loud that they were being penned within the town by the enemy all about it.

The flavor of unreality was heightened by one American official with whom I talked. He told me solemnly that he believed there were only a hundred or so Huks, all of whom lived in Manila. According to his theory, the Huks would commute by bus into the countryside for their forays and ambushes, returning to town afterward. He hinted mysteriously of connivance when I asked him how such bus passengers could pass freely through the many military checkpoints on roads leading into the city. I avoided him and his nonsense after that. Information about what was actually happening was foggy enough without making it foggier.

My visits with the Philippine intelligence services brought me into a more realistic world. They showed me their "enemy order of battle" lists and maps, including photos of many of the Huk commanders. There were gaps in the information they had acquired in the past months, with much hard work and risk. Some of it wasn't as up-to-the-minute as they wished. Still, they had compiled an impressive amount of data, and I admired the blunt honesty of their evaluations of these data. When I asked them why so many of the top officials had different notions about the Huks, they shrugged their shoulders in puzzlement. They said that they kept the top officials informed regularly. I concluded that the value of the intelligence services was being badly underrated by those making governmental decisions. It was a situation worth correcting. My first step toward doing so was to tell President Quirino what was available.

Intelligence officers also confirmed that the Huks were still practicing the iron discipline and Pavlovian self-criticism that I had noted in previous years. Iron discipline was the harsh punishment, including death, peremptorily meted out by Huk squadron officers for infractions of guerrilla rules. Vivid in my own memory was the case of a teen-age Huk recruit whose commander made him hunt down and kill his closest boyhood friend, who had sneaked off for an overnight home visit without permission; the killing was done before the eyes of the boy's family, who had told me about it. It made the teen-age recruit an outlaw to his former neighbors and cemented him to the Huk ranks permanently. Self-criticism took place in sessions held by the Huk political cadre. Each member of a squadron would stand up before his comrades and, exhibiting shame, would publicly confess to his incorrect dialectical thoughts or deeds. The sessions were held after each combat action and did much to condition the resoluteness of individuals for the next attack.

The numerical accounting given me by intelligence officers was sobering. There were well over ten thousand armed men in the Huk forces, and the Communist leadership was making an energetic effort to increase this number. The people in the provinces close to Manila, particularly those just north of the city, were being induced to support the guerrilla Huk army as their own. The Huks spoke of these people as "the organized masses" and depended upon them for food, money, shelter, and information about government forces. Their number ran into many thousands. At the top, directing this whole effort, was a disciplined group of Philippine Communist party officials, the Politburo. Prominent among the Politburo members were two Stalinists, the Lava brothers, as well as Huk Commander in Chief Luis Taruc and a number of others. All of them had successfully eluded capture, despite continuing efforts to locate them.

Some days after this initial briefing, the Philippine intelligence services received an amazing windfall of detailed information about the Huks. I will tell about this windfall in its proper place. For now, the point is that the information given me by the intelligence services turned out to be sharply conservative, even though it painted a blacker picture than had the top officials. The Huks were stronger at that moment than any of us knew.

The briefings in official circles left me unsatisfied. They failed to answer some pertinent questions. What caused a Huk youngster to kill his brother Filipino in the government ranks? What would make him stop doing this? The government's answer was to kill, disable, or capture him. Wasn't there something beyond this? Even more germane, why were so many citizens supporting the Huk effort to destroy a government founded under a constitution which stated that it was to be fully representative of these selfsame citizens? Coercion of these citizens by terror couldn't be the sole answer. There had to be something else. The Huks followed Mao's dictum about guerrillas behaving towards the people as though they were the "water" in which the guerrilla "fish" swam and kept alive. Was this, then, the reason for so much popular support of the Huks? Why didn't people support the government forces instead?

In the following days, I spent every moment I could searching for clues to the answers. I started in Manila, seeking out journalist friends for private talks about conditions in the Philippines. I found that publishers, editors, columnists, and reporters whom I had known as an ebullient and outspoken fraternity were now strangely nervous and uncharacteristically reticent as we talked about the situation. Little by little, I obtained their views. The gist of what they had to say was ugly. They told me that the

Quirino government was rotten with corruption; that it had won the 1949 presidential election by extensive fraud ("even counting the birds and flowers in Mindanao as votes"); that the president's brother Tony had a staff of thugs to scare the critics into silence; that Magsaysay might be an exception—a "good" man in the government—but would be powerless to change an entrenched officer corps in the army; that arrogant behavior had caused the military to be hated and feared by the people; that Huk "atrocities" were matched by what the government was doing; that there were bright men among the Huk leaders; and that the Huks were going to win before long. Each journalist begged me not to quote him by name.

Among these friends was a publisher whom I had long felt to be among the best-informed men in the Philippines. I asked him why everyone seemed to be so afraid, even in private conversations. At the time, the two of us were alone in the middle of the living room—the *sala*—of his home. We were seated close to one another. I had spoken in hushed tones so that my voice wouldn't carry. He looked startled at the question and shook his head no. Silently, he got to his feet, beckoned me, and walked out of the door. I followed him quietly. He walked away from the house to the farthest corner of the garden, a patch of darkness behind some bushes. He waited until I came close to him. Then he spoke to me in angry whispers. I had alarmed him by asking about the fear. Anybody could have bugged his place with a hidden microphone or have had a listener under the window of the room. In addition to himself, he had a family who could be kidnapped or killed. Hell yes, he was afraid of Tony's goons. Hell yes, he was afraid of the Huk trigger squads. And hell yes, he was afraid to talk to me because the security of American offices, such as those at JUSMAG and the embassy, was a sour joke. I probably would write a report which General Hobbs and Ambassador Cowen would put in their safes. He himself knew people associated with the Huks who could have my report out of those safes almost immediately. He offered to get any top secret paper I desired from those safes, at a cost of only one hundred pesos.

Troubled by what I'd learned, I gave the significant highlights to Ambassador Cowen and General Hobbs without disclosing the names of the journalists with whom I had spoken. They were skeptical about the reported insecurity of their offices but agreed to changes in their security procedures and the combinations of their safes. Later, when I had to keep private files at the office, I picked the safest storage space at JUSMAG, the liquor locker of the JUSMAG staff. It was guarded zealously. Tamper-proof file boxes, I found, fitted snugly into the empty wooden cases for shipping scotch and bourbon. Steel straps around these cases made them look new again. My name stenciled on top made the cases my individual property. Such storage procedure wasn't in any security manual, but it was practical.

What the journalists in Manila had told me was bad enough. Worse awaited me in the countryside. I decided to find out what the local people thought of one of the "atrocities" recounted to me in official briefings. There had been a Huk attack on a military post, Camp Makabulos, and its 11th Station Hospital on the outskirts of Tarlac, some seventy miles north of Manila, on August 26, 1950. Aside from a handful of headquarters clerks and guards, the camp's personnel consisted mainly of doctors, nurses, and patients. Two hundred Huks under Silvestre Liwanag had swarmed suddenly into the hospital area, killing twenty-three of the military and seven civilians who were visiting the hospital. Some of the patients, lying helpless on hospital beds, had been hacked to pieces by bolo knives and bayonets. Nurses had been raped. The camp had then been set on fire as the Huks departed with their loot of medical supplies and money from the pockets and bedside tables of their victims. It was a repugnant story, a shameful act even for guerrillas.

Philippine military men, of course, spoke angrily as they told me about Makabulos, and some had a faraway look in their eyes as if they could see themselves wounded in the future,

lying helpless on a hospital bed and vulnerable to such savagery. This unsettling thought seemed to be the point the
enemy had tried to make by the attack.

I drove to Tarlac and stayed a night with friends, where I
met and talked with a number of the townspeople. I brought up
the subject of the August 26 attack on Camp Makabulos. They
talked about it readily, speaking of the Huks with considerable
admiration. I had been ready for reactions of horror or fear,
not admiration. It was a rude jolt.

The townspeople told how the Huks had infiltrated Tarlac,
singly or in small groups, during the day. Some had hidden in
the movie theaters, sitting out the daylight hours by watching
the same movie over and over again. Others had hidden with
families and friends, having secret but joyous reunions replete
with food and drink. After dark, the Huks came out into the
streets of the town and took it over. They requested the people
in polite and friendly terms to go inside their homes and stay
there, since there was to be some shooting against the lackeys
of the government and they didn't want any of the people hurt.
With Tarlac occupied and the townspeople snug in their homes,
the Huks then attacked Camp Makabulos and the 11th Station
Hospital. They also broke into the provincial jail, freeing forty-
seven prisoners. The camp commandant of Makabulos lived in
town with his family. He was seized by the Huks, taken out
into the street in front of his home, made to kneel, and then
was shot to death. His wife and children had cried, but they
were unhurt, shut away in the house.

As I heard these stories, my own emotions were stirred and
I expressed them. I was among friends. How could they blindly
admire murder and rapine? The army and constabulary men
lying in the hospital had gone there initially with wounds
suffered in the defense of the people. The camp commandant
and his family had been their neighbors for months. The Huks
had perpetrated an outrage against the very people themselves.
It was a cruel hoax to portray such murderers as heroes.

I was given sharp retorts. I had been away in the States and had not seen the many callous actions of the government and its troops against the people. The soldiers weren't the defenders of the people. Anything but. Yes, the commandant was a neighbor, but hardly anyone had known him. His friends were the soldiers at the camp, not the townspeople. Maybe he and the wounded at the camp shouldn't have been killed that way, but they represented something despotic and would have been killed eventually anyway. It was a government of the privileged few, not of the people. The troops protected only these few and made war on the people. Look at what happened in towns where the troops sought out the Huks. The people were the ones who got hurt. Look at the way farmers were losing everything they possessed through high rentals, decisions in the land courts that always favored the landlords, the usurious moneylenders who charged farmers mounting interest on the original small debts of their fathers. The townspeople had gone to the polls in 1949 and voted for representatives who could change all this. What had happened? Nothing. They had been cheated. The election had been rigged, bringing the corrupt to power. Of course the people were joining and helping the Huks. The Huks were right. The only thing left for the people to do was to use bullets, not ballots, to get a government of their own. It was going to happen, a sure thing. The Huks truly represented the "wave of the future."

So spoke the people seventy miles up the road from the government offices in Manila. Their words left me somber. I started to sort out what I had been learning since my return to the Philippines. Government officials talked of reestablishing "law and order," yet seemed blind to injustice in the administration of the law and the prejudicial imbalance of the order they desired. The people wanted to be governed by their own (whom they were starting to believe the Huks to represent) and were blind to the type of rule the Huks were planning for the time after they assumed power with the people's help. It would be a government by another and tougher "privileged few," dictating their own form of injustice, backed by even crueler force than the people had yet seen. Surely the principles I believed in, the rights of man as a free individual, lay in between such harshly jumbled social and political terrain!

I left Tarlac early in the morning for Manila. I drove past *karitons,* the small carts pulled by the half-pint horses of rural Luzon, loaded with farm produce on their way to market. At the market old women had started charcoal fires at the roadside and were baking the morning *bibingka* in fresh banana leaves. I stopped for one of these delightful cakes. As I was eating, a local lawyer whom I knew drove up and yelled a hello. I invited him to join me.

Over the *bibingka,* I said I had heard he had become a politician. "No sir, not me," he disclaimed, "never again!" He told me about his campaign for Congress the year before, adding with a laugh that the Liberals (the party of the Quirino administration in power) had taught him that he knew nothing at all about political arithmetic. "I'm laughing," he told me, "but it is really a sad story. They didn't even let my poor old mother vote. I know that she went to the polling place and cast her ballot. I know, too, that I'm her favorite candidate and that she would have voted for me. She told me that she did and mother never lies to me. Even more, I know that I cast a ballot for my favorite candidate, myself. Yet, when the tally of the vote was published, there I was with only one vote chalked up against my name! Wouldn't you think they would have had the decency to give me at least two votes? I'll never forgive them for robbing my mother of her vote!" Since I knew that my friend was one of the most popular young lawyers in central Luzon, noted for his legal help to the farmers, his ironic message was loud and clear. Probably the thousands of votes cast for him were "lost" before the tallies were counted.

I drove on into Manila. Just beyond the Rizal Monument on the North Road within the city's outskirts, I noticed a jam of buses and trucks stopped at the side of the road where the local police had a checkpoint. Policemen were talking to the drivers. Money was being handed over by the drivers, a little unofficial and illegal tribute they paid to enter the city. I had seen this collection of *pabaksak* often before and knew that the police split the take among many of their comrades to pad out their meager salaries. On this morning, the scene took on added significance. What must the people be thinking about all those in uniform representing authority!

There was a sudden blast of a police whistle. Startled, I paid belated attention to my driving. A traffic policeman had just changed his signal at the intersection. I jammed on the brakes, stopping a couple of feet inside the intersection. As pedestrians walked around my car, the traffic cop stepped off his platform in the center of the intersection and strode over to me, his face dark with anger. "Just because you are a big shot in the States," he shouted, "you aren't a big shot here. You didn't stop when I told you! You Americans think you can get away with anything here, drive any damn way you please!" I held up my hand to hush the tirade. "Officer," I told him, "thank you for calling me a big shot. I admit that I'm wrong. I guess I just wasn't paying attention. I goofed." The policeman and I looked at each other. I couldn't keep a rueful smile off my face; as a proponent of decent law and order, I was setting a lousy example. The policeman looked down at his feet for a moment, then back up at me with a grin. "Okay," he told me. "Just drive carefully after this." The onlookers were grinning, too. The policeman walked back to the center of the street and changed the signal to "Go." I drove on, with a wave and a thank-you smile for him.

That trip out into the country and back again into the city seemed light-years away from the official briefings I had been given.

NOTES

TEAM. In nearly all my work in Asia, I had a team of assistants helping me. At this point, in 1950, Captain Charles T. R. Bohannan and First

Lieutenant A. C. Ellis were my assistants, while Helen Jones of the JUSMAG staff, a former guerrilla and a friend of long standing, served as our secretary. Later, as there was need, others joined this team. In subsequent operations in Vietnam, a sizable number of Americans became members of my team at different periods, although the largest group at any one time was a dozen. All were volunteers, each gifted with one or more skills particularly needed to cope with situations posed by irregular conflict. They made up a considerable fraternity of individualistic Americans who helped the people in Asia against the tactics of conquest developed by Lenin and Mao. Some of them appear in this book. I regret that there isn't room for stories about them all.

HELEN. My secretary at JUSMAG, Helen Jones, had been my secretary years before when I was Deputy G-2 at PHILRYCOM, the U.S. Army command for the Philippines and Ryukyus. One day a navy officer had visited my office and caught sight of her, a small and very feminine woman tapping rapidly on a typewriter with a long cigar jutting out from her mouth. The navy officer asked me excitedly if I knew who she was. "She's my secretary, Helen Jones," I told him. "No, no, no, that's not what I mean," he replied. He then told me the story of how his aircraft had been shot down by the Japanese north of Manila, and had crash landed in a rice paddy. He dragged himself and his broken bones away from the wreckage. Japanese troops had appeared in the distance and started toward him when Helen Jones and her band of Filipino guerrillas arrived at the wreck. Helen patted him on the head with a "There, there, sonny boy, we'll get you out," just as Japanese mortar shells exploded close by. Helen and the guerrillas got him on an improvised stretcher and rushed him away to safety. After telling me this, the navy pilot gave Helen a hug and kiss. I had no chance to tell him that I knew of her guerrilla days and knew also that President Truman had awarded her the Medal of Freedom for her services.

★ ★

CHAPTER THREE

WITH MAGSAYSAY

I SPENT THE WORKING HOURS of the day I returned from Tarlac at armed forces headquarters, delving into the problems and potentials of the intelligence services. Captain Bohannan of my team was with me. We both had many friends among the Philippine intelligence staffs. "Boh" had arrived in the country initially as a combat infantry leader during the 1944 liberation, operating a scouting force behind enemy lines, and had stayed on in the postwar years as a counterintelligence officer, falling in love with the people and the islands. In our work with military intelligence officers that day, some mutual conclusions were reached. The Military Intelligence Service (MIS) needed upgrading, with infusions of funds, personnel, and new methods, as well as ways to make top officials pay more attention to its reports. The new military units being placed in the Huk fight, the BCTs, were going to need detailed, high-quality information about the enemy in their areas; thus a combat intelligence school should be started without delay to train the S-2 (intelligence) personnel of the BCTs in the most effective ways of collecting, evaluating, and using information about guerrillas. Boh thought of giving further support to the field efforts by

establishing district offices of the MIS, manned by agents familiar with the local scene. I promised to help sell the idea to top
officials. Boh and the MIS officers got to work promptly at drawing up organization and manning charts for this new concept.

It was nearly evening by then. I decided to try once again
to see Magsaysay and walked over to the Officers Club from
the main headquarters building. Inside, the vast ballroom was
empty and gloomy in the gathering dusk, a glow of light at
one end coming from the stairwell leading upstairs to the card
room which Magsaysay used as his office. As I started climbing
the stairs, I could hear the thump of running feet. When I
neared the top of the stairs, gasps and heavy breathing became
audible above the sound of running. Somebody was muttering
"sonnamabeech" over and over again. I wondered momentarily
if Magsaysay had turned his office into a gymnasium. I arrived
at the top of the stairs, walked into the former card room, and
stared at the amazing sight.

A civilian unknown to me was running around the room as
fast as he could, dodging between desks and chairs. Magsaysay
was in hot pursuit, swinging his big fist at the man every time
he got close. The "sonnamabeech" was coming from Magsaysay.
He saw me standing in the doorway and paused for a moment.
His victim capitalized on the break, jumped through a window
onto the nearby roof of the big portico at the front of the club,
went scrambling down it, and leaped to the ground. He looked
up at the window he had jumped through and yelled, between
his panting, "Hey, I was only joking! Can't you take a joke?"
Then he ran to his parked car and drove off. I shook hands with
Magsaysay. "The sonnamabeech tried to bribe me!" he said.

At the time, Magsaysay had just turned forty-three. He was
about my height, a bit huskier than I, and six months older.
I already knew that we shared things in common; each of us
was the second son in families of four boys, although he had
sisters and I didn't, and we each had worked for a living while
going to college in the lean years of the depression. Afterward,

Magsaysay had stayed with Try-Tran, one of the largest bus transportation companies in the Philippines, where he had worked as a mechanic while in college. He became shop superintendent, finally earning enough to marry Luz Banzon, whom he had courted while in college. Later, he became branch manager for Try-Tran in San Antonio, in his native province of Zambales. The Japanese attack in World War II had started near his home, with a bombing raid on the U.S. base and its radar installation at Iba, Zambales. The Japanese bombers next attacked Clark Field, across the Zambales mountain range.

After helping the U.S. forces with transportation until the surrender in neighboring Bataan, Magsaysay became a guerrilla against the Japanese occupying forces of his home province of Zambales. Commissioned as a captain, he served initially as the guerrilla unit's supply officer and was known by his guerrilla nickname of "Chow." Later, Colonel Gyles Merrill of the U.S. Army, who was directing guerrilla operations in that sector of Luzon from his sickbed in a mountain hideout, appointed Magsaysay as commander of the Zambales unit. As commander, he led the guerrilla attacks that cleared the area, destroying Japanese aircraft parked at their base at San Marcelino so that the liberating XI Corps of the U.S. Army could land at Subic Bay virtually unopposed. General Charles Hall of XI Corps appointed Magsaysay military governor of Zambales. In April 1946 the people of Zambales elected him to the Philippine House of Representatives by the largest majority in the province's history. In Congress, he became chairman of the House Committee on National Defense and subsequently, as chairman, went to Washington on a successful quest for help from the U.S. Congress to aid Filipino veterans—hence our eventual meeting in the U.S. capital.

After we talked in Magsaysay's office in the former card room, he invited me for a potluck dinner in his small bungalow on Arellano Street in the Singalong District, the home he had built for his bride when he had been shop superintendent of the bus company. There were no street lights in his neighborhood. Around the corner from his home was a sidewalk *sari-sari,* a small shop selling groceries and soft drinks, dimly lit by several pungent *tinghuy* lamps with their wicks floating in coconut oil held in the half-shells of coconuts. An unusually large number of people were clustered on the sidewalk around the shop. In the dim light, I could see that several of the men had long hair flowing down to their shoulders. This was the mark of a guerrilla; haircuts are hard to come by when a man is on the run.

At the house I met Magsaysay's wife Luz and their children, Teresita, Milagres, and Ramon Jr., for the first time. Luz welcomed me with a quiet smile. I was struck by her poise. She seemed unruffled by a sudden extra guest for dinner, and a foreigner at that. Yet there was a touch of tension in the atmosphere of the home, apparently unconnected with me. Luz gave her husband a look, the silent communication of a wife, and both left the room. Shortly afterwards, there were arrivals at the front door, Magsaysay's youthful aide Lieutenant Jerry Palaypay and two of Magsaysay's former guerrillas from Zambales. They told me, softly so that the children wouldn't overhear, that there were a number of strangers, armed men in the neighborhood. Magsaysay came in while we were talking; Luz had just informed him about the strangers. Palaypay and the former guerrillas took food out to the front steps and mounted guard there while the rest of us sat down in the dining room. I ate thoughtfully. Clearly, Magsaysay and his family were entirely too vulnerable to attack by a Huk trigger squad in that crowded Singalong neighborhood. The Philippines could easily lose its new secretary of national defense right at the start of his campaign against the Huks, who already were alert to the dynamic qualities he was bringing to his new role.

After dinner Magsaysay and I talked about the physical security of his family and himself. I suggested that he shift to quarters at Camp Murphy, where there was housing for staff officers and families within the protected compound. Magsaysay replied that he planned to, but that all the quarters were occupied and that he wasn't about to order any family out just to make room for his. A number of new houses were being constructed at Camp Murphy, and he would move into one of them when it was finished. Meanwhile, he could protect his family himself. He patted the .30-cal. paratrooper's carbine lying next to him on the couch.

I asked him if he had thought of what he would do if Luz or the children were kidnapped by the Huks while he wasn't home. In such a case, he would be hard put to concentrate on being the type of secretary of national defense he was set on becoming. Magsaysay scowled darkly and told me in angry tones how he would hunt down such kidnappers. This, I said, was exactly what I'd meant; his secretarial chores would go hang while he became a hunter.

Meanwhile, I was reviewing in my mind the safety factors of government housing in the metropolitan area outside Camp Murphy. The housing that was safest and closest to the headquarters at Camp Murphy was the JUSMAG compound where I lived. I mentioned this out loud to Magsaysay, adding that my two staff companions and I had just moved into the last available house in the compound. The compound was guarded by the Philippine Army. The Filipino staff at my house consisted of handpicked former guerrillas. As a temporary measure, I could move out of my bedroom and double up with someone else while his family used my room, if we could squeeze sufficient cots into it. Finally, we concluded that Luz and the children could take a brief holiday in the safety of her family home in Bataan, while Magsaysay moved in with me. Two cots would fit easily into my bedroom.

When I left the Magsaysay home that night, I drove over to see General Hobbs. Propriety required his permission, as the commanding general of JUSMAG, for me to have such a guest in the house he had just assigned me. He agreed wholeheartedly. In fact, he called Magsaysay on the telephone and offered to move somebody out of a house for the Magsaysay family. I was standing next to him at the telephone and volunteered to move my own group out, but Magsaysay overheard this and said he preferred to let the arrangement stay as planned. By the next day I had a roommate, Ramon Magsaysay, who quickly asked me to use his nickname of "Monching."

He opened a new dimension in my life. He was full of nervous energy, tapping a foot impatiently as he thought over a course of action, and passionately intent on the entire range of problems which the Huk Rebellion had brought to the Philippines. I had been getting along with little sleep. With my new roommate, I got even less. Each night we sat up late discussing the current situation. Magsaysay would air his views. Afterwards, I would sort them out aloud for him while underscoring the principles or strategy or tactics involved. It helped him select or discard courses of action. We grew accustomed to revealing our innermost thoughts to each other. Each of us had a deep yearning to bring peace and justice to the Philippine people. A sound start would have to be made toward these objectives. Between present circumstances and the achievement of our goals lay the Communist party and its guerrilla army aggressively dominating the scene, the ills in Philippine society that provided soil for rebellion to flourish, and a government military force that we felt was largely out of touch with reality or with the people it must defend.

The first night we sat up talking about the armed forces of the Philippines. Magsaysay described the clique-ridden officer corps; the growing inclination of troops to go on the cautious defensive or to remain in their barracks and thus leave the Huks to move around ever more freely; the corruption he suspected in the current military supply system; and his unsatisfactory attempts to get General Castaneda and the General Staff to change the whole system of military activities into something more dynamic, less hidebound and leisurely. As he talked, his eyes flashed, his fist pounded on his cot, his feet jiggled, and his voice became fuller. This was a man furious over what needed doing and was not being done.

I had a mental picture of such an angry man talking to officers in the field, out where the enemy was most active. I voiced this to Magsaysay, asking him if he was getting any results from inspecting the combat units. "No, not really," he said. He explained bitterly that the headquarters staff insisted on being kept informed of his movements into combat areas, citing their concern over his personal safety as the reason. After all, he was a civilian official, not a soldier, wasn't he? When he arrived at a unit, he would find that officers had been tipped off about his coming, had everything tidied up, and had their stories ready for briefing him glibly about the local situation. Dammit, he just knew that the rosy picture he was being given wasn't true. After listening to Magsaysay, I commented that as secretary of national defense, he had ample authority to visit units in any manner he personally desired, including surprise inspections if he wished. A smile lit his face at this.

I finally got to sleep at about four in the morning. It seemed that my head had barely warmed the pillow when I was shaken awake by Magsaysay. I looked at my watch. It was only a little after four-thirty. "Hey, what's up?" I asked my new roommate. "You'll see," he told me. "We're going to the provinces." I was still half asleep while we drove over to the Camp Murphy airstrip, rousted out pilots, and then took off in two L-5 light liaison aircraft, follow-the-leader style with Magsaysay in the lead. He wouldn't tell me where we were headed, saying that he would direct his pilot. Airborne, we headed north. The first hints of dawn were starting to lighten the sky. Oh well, I said to myself, the national anthem says that the Philippines is the "land of the morning, child of the sun returning."

We were well up into Nueva Ecija, one of the sorely troubled provinces of central Luzon, before we went in for a landing, tandem fashion. We came down in a rough field next to the highway, amid the withered stalks of last season's corn crop.

Magsaysay told the pilots to guard the aircraft while we went into town. He and I walked over to the empty highway. The town was out of sight down the road. We started toward it, a Filipino in a vividly colored sport shirt and farmer's straw hat, an American in khaki uniform and air force blue cap. A huge truck van came grinding our way along the highway from Manila. Magsaysay thumbed, the universal hitchhiker's sign, and we rode into town aboard the truck, getting off at the town plaza with warm thanks to the driver. The sun was up now, and the night coolness had left the air. An old man hobbled out of a house into the plaza, leaning heavily on a stick. Magsaysay greeted him and asked directions to the local constabulary headquarters.

At the constabulary headquarters, we found only a sergeant dozing at a desk. Magsaysay gave a shout, awakened him, and then asked him to have the commanding officer report in, pronto. "What! At this time of the morning?" The sergeant was incredulous. He blinked his eyes and looked more sharply at the civilian in the sport shirt. "Who says so?" Since I was in uniform, I spoke up and told the sergeant that the sport-shirted civilian was the new secretary of national defense, Ramon Magsaysay. I introduced myself. The sergeant threw us a hasty salute and dashed out the door. Magsaysay and I looked around the headquarters room. It was in disarray, showing signs of negligence. The gun rack, filled with rifles, was unlocked, a tempting target for the Huk guerrillas in the neighborhood.

I looked out the door and saw a plump captain trotting across the street, puffing, buttoning up his uniform as he came, the sergeant three paces behind. I told Magsaysay over my shoulder who was coming. There was the thump of a gun butt on wood. I spun around. Magsaysay had taken two rifles from the gun rack. He tossed one to me. "Quick, get behind the door," he whispered urgently. We moved quickly to positions on either side of the door. The captain burst into the room, his eyes try-ing to accommodate to the gloom after the bright sunlight outside. Magsaysay thrust the muzzle of his rifle into the captain's back. "Stick 'em up!" he shouted. The captain raised his arms.

The sergeant had paused in the doorway, startled. I motioned with my rifle for the sergeant to put his hands up too and to move over next to the captain. He obeyed. The two of them stood, arms raised, while Magsaysay lectured them angrily about running so slovenly a military post in the midst of an area where the enemy was active. We might well have been Huks who could have killed every soldier there. By now, a number of the soldiers in the unit were peering in at the scene. Magsaysay had the captain and sergeant put down their arms, told the gathering military unit who he was, and then spoke bluntly about how he expected them to behave from now on, starting off, "Boys, I don't know how you've managed to stay alive so long. . . ."

Afterward, he proposed that we walk the captain home. I was looking forward to getting a morning cup of coffee at last. At the captain's house, his wife offered us coffee. "No, thank you," replied Magsaysay to my dismay. "I just want to know if you won or lost at Mah-Jongg last night." The wife smilingly admitted that she had won "a little." Magsaysay said he had suspected that the captain and his wife were staying up all night playing Mah-Jongg, night after night. Mah-Jongg and poker sessions were all too common in military families, and it was the women who usually insisted on playing. "Look at your husband. He's so sleepy and tired that he wouldn't be able to think or lead his troops if the Huks showed up here suddenly. And you and I know that that's just what they might do. Your Mah-Jongg is going to wind up with all of you having your throats cut! Your husband was once a good officer. Now he's a nothing. No, he's a liability, because the people in this town look to him for protection and he can't give it to them!" Magsaysay announced that he was putting a stop to this right now. They could start packing, because they were moving as soon as he could get a new officer there to replace the captain. He was adamant about this in the face of the wife's tears, although he confessed to me later that staying firm was a harder task than he had expected.

We returned to Manila. At the house I rustled up some coffee and breakfast for the two of us while Magsaysay was on the telephone to headquarters, arguing with General Castaneda about a replacement for the hapless captain. He came away from the telephone angry, for Castaneda and his staff were resentful of a civilian's interference in such military affairs as who was to command where. Castaneda had grudgingly agreed to transfer the captain, however, after Magsaysay had lost his temper. Magsaysay glared down at his breakfast plate of eggs and pushed it away. "I don't want this," he told me. "Okay, don't eat it," I replied. I was busily reading the morning papers which I'd stacked up on the table before us. "Hey, I know what I want," he said suddenly. "Have you got any canned corn?" Startled, I put down the newspaper and helped him find a can of corn in the kitchen larder. That was his breakfast.

That first surprise inspection, carried out in so unorthodox but meaningful a way, set the pattern for many others that followed it. I became accustomed to the sudden departures for unknown destinations, the effective unmasking of something wrong. I learned to stick a toothbrush and razor in my pocket, since often days would pass before we returned to Manila again. I was tempted to wear the toothbrush in a buttonhole, recalling a British officer's account of Lee's troops moving along the road to Gettysburg; each man had a toothbrush stuck in a buttonhole, the only uniform item among them. However, I was a latter-day American; our military had learned to put roomier pockets in the uniforms. On the other hand, the air force uniform at the time was hardly suitable for running around in rice paddies and mountain jungles with the infantry. Bohannan wisely had brought along his own preference in clothing for tropical combat, a mixture of army and marine corps gear. I borrowed from him for these field trips.

In Asia people know that the mouth and the ear were invented long before the printing press, the camera, or the radio. They are accustomed to passing news from person to person by means of conversation. News travels in this gossipy fashion over great distances quickly and in the Philippines is known as the "bamboo telegraph." The early fall days of 1950 found the bamboo telegraph full of news about Magsaysay's surprise visits to unlikely places, as well as the consequences of each visit. The troops in the field started behaving as though the secretary of national defense might show up on the scene at any moment to praise or chastise them for what they were doing. Even government officials felt the effect. The postmaster of a provincial town once told me that Magsaysay had made him an honest man. "Every time I have the drawer open with all that stamp money in it and start getting tempted to help myself, I get to thinking that that damn guy would take that moment to show up and catch me!"

On one visit to troops who were in a hot fight with the Huks at the moment, a light tank had clanked to a stop, its supporting fire failing the infantry for an attack. Magsaysay squeezed in next to the tanker checking the engine, his old skills as mechanic and shop superintendent for the bus company resurging. He found the trouble. Faulty spark plugs. He took them out and examined them closely. They were old and worn out. The tank had just been delivered to the Philippine Army, brand new, by the U.S. Someone must have removed the new plugs and swapped them for secondhand ones at a neat profit. Magsaysay would have killed the perpetrator on the spot, but I argued for getting all the facts and then making the regular course of justice really work. He swore explosively but then sent his aide to put the chief of ordnance under house arrest until the facts could be checked out. Another time it was a patrol in the jungle, with the men limping as they moved along. Magsaysay had them sit down and show the bottoms of their locally made combat boots. The soles were worn through. Somebody had substituted cardboard for leather, and profited. Magsaysay went after the quartermaster like a tiger.

The inspections and Magsaysay's rapid corrective actions had a considerable impact on the armed forces. Not all of it was beer and skittles. He was stepping on toes, ruffling egos, and hurting the pocketbooks of some powerful people. I could see a developing crisis. The armed forces of the Philippines were getting the leadership they needed if they were ever to win out over the Communist Huks and save the constitutional government, but it was coming in a form that wasn't in the books, with a civilian instead of a military commander. Magsaysay would have to be on very solid footing if he were to keep up the pace. I discussed the situation at length with General Hobbs, since the JUSMAG chief in the Philippines was a unique U.S. military official, not only representing the U.S. Joint Chiefs of Staff but also officially the military adviser to the president of the Philippines. Hobbs agreed that Magsaysay deserved support and pleaded his case with President Quirino and General Castaneda. I added my own arguments in less formal meetings with the two.

President Quirino finally gave Magsaysay the required authority, in the form of a presidential memo. He could relieve officers for just cause. He could recommend officers for combat promotions or enlisted men for combat commissioning, on the spot. He could order the holding of courts-martial to try anyone within the military establishment who investigation indicated was doing something dishonorable. This authority was considerable. In the hands of the wrong man, it could spell ruin. Magsaysay knew this fully. I believe he honored the trust given him.

Step by step, Magsaysay carried out a housecleaning of the military establishment, ridding it of unjust favoritism and of slovenly and corrupt practices. It was a shaping-up that the military commanders themselves should have undertaken but hadn't. Apparently their friendships with brother officers and their conventional habits had blinded them to the need. The change in the military, however, proved to be one of the critical factors in the defeat of the guerrilla Huks. Without such revolutionary leadership, the struggle might have bogged down into one of those protracted conflicts which come to depend for solution upon a horrible attrition of human and material resources, ending when one side collapses from exhaustion. Eventually, General Castaneda and some of his cronies, most of whom were trusted friends of President Quirino and other prominent politicians, were retired. The move was emotion-charged, bitterly fought over. Yet it was done.

One time, when feelings were running high in the Philippine Army over the changes in how the war was to be fought, Magsaysay and I visited troops who were fighting the Huks in the Bataan mountains just south of Subic Bay. We caught a ride back to Manila that night aboard a Philippine Navy destroyer escort which was transporting General Castaneda and his staff. As last-minute interlopers, Magsaysay and I refused to take stateroom bunks away from them so we curled up on the deck to sleep. I awoke in the night to find one of Magsaysay's bodyguards standing over me, a submachine gun in his hands. He whispered that Castaneda and some of his staff were below in the wardroom, drinking. A mess boy had brought word that Castaneda had taken his pistol out and was boasting that he was going to come up and shoot me as the interfering bastard behind all the changes being made. The bodyguard had been set to shoot it out with Castaneda, wild-West style, over my sleeping body. I told him to keep watch over the sleeping Magsaysay, and I went below to the wardroom. Castaneda and several others were there, drinks in hand. I could see that his pistol was holstered. I suggested that he might give me a drink, since I'd heard he was going to shoot me and it might be my last one. He laughed, poured me a drink, and said he wasn't going to shoot me although I deserved it. We had known each other too long, so he would wait, since somebody else was bound to shoot me sooner or later. Over drinks, we thrashed out our differences verbally for an hour, his companions scowling at me all the while. Then I went back up to sleep on the hard deck. When I awoke, we were in Manila.

Another incident, about the same time, further rubbed the raw wounds of the conventional Philippine military establishment. It took place at a Promotion Board meeting of the Philippine armed forces, where Magsaysay was asked to approve recommended promotions and forward them to President Quirino. Magsaysay looked over the list and saw there wasn't a single combat officer on it. He asked about the criteria used and was told that the recommendations were based on seniority and the accumulation of good reports each year on the efficiency of the officers.

At this point Magsaysay lost his temper. He angrily noted for the board that the armed forces were in a war with the smaller Huk forces, and it didn't look as if the armed forces were winning. If every man in the armed forces went out that day and killed or captured one Huk, the war would be over. He grabbed the top recommendation on the pile and read the officer's name aloud. "How many Huks has he killed?" he asked. The answer was "none." While board members were describing the splendid noncombat duties performed by the officer, Magsaysay tossed the recommendation back, refusing to consider him for promotion "at this time." The remaining recommendations were reviewed in the same manner. All were turned down.

Magsaysay's grim arithmetic placed a sorely needed value upon good combat service. Within the relatively small family of the Philippine armed forces, it brought a significant uplift in morale among those who were getting shot at daily. They realized that they had a boss who would go to bat for them.

With Magsaysay living at our house, the number of Filipino visitors to the JUSMAG compound increased greatly. Apparently there had been only a trickle before, mostly men who had come in for nighttime poker sessions with some of the American residents. Now there was an almost constant procession of staff officers, day and night, for conferences with Magsaysay. Some of the new visitors told me that they had never expected to be invited into the compound, which had been nicknamed "the country club" by Filipinos, because of the apparently relaxed lives that Americans lived in the comfortable houses behind the well-kept lawns and gardens.

There were some unwelcome visitors as well. The Huks had learned of the presence of our house guest and had sent in trigger squads from time to time in the small hours of the morning, to assassinate him. I found out later that I too was on the list. Our household comprised an informal combat team, with someone always on alert guard. Huk trigger squad visits were firmly discouraged. We tried to be quiet about these skirmishes in the suburban setting, but we must have made too much noise. A delegation of resident officers called upon General Hobbs, stating that our occupancy of quarters in the compound was endangering families in its other houses, and it requested that we be moved out. General Hobbs replied shortly that a war was going on in the Philippines and if they were concerned about the safety of their families, the families could be sent home to the United States; my house guest and team were to stay. Relations with some of my American military neighbors were frigid after this, although others went out of their way to be friendly and helpful.

Our house in the JUSMAG compound also witnessed the birth of an ideal way for American advisers to be of help in a counterinsurgency. It began in so natural a fashion that I didn't realize at first that a pattern was being set that I was to follow thereafter. Philippine staff officers calling on Magsaysay at the house were treated hospitably while they were waiting to see him, usually having coffee in the *sala*. Often one of the people on my team would pass the time of day with these waiting officers and, of course, talk shop about the war. We discovered that some of them had been doing a lot of thinking on their own about the situation and in this informal atmosphere they would really express freely their views on what was going wrong and would suggest changes. Sometimes our own friends from combat units in the field would stop by to say hello, while in Manila, and would join in the conversations we were having with waiting staff officers. Usually they added details and ideas from their own current experiences to whatever topic was being discussed. The desk officers from the headquarters staff and the combat soldiers, encouraged by the warm interest and contributions of us Americans, would find themselves exploring all possible ideas. From time to time, Magsaysay would sit down and join us too.

Initially, I thought of these conversations among passing visitors as a sort of "Grand Central Station" phenomenon, since they took place in a busy waiting room. In fact, my team dubbed our *sala* Grand Central Station. Then we realized the impromptu discussions were turning up so many realistic insights and constructive ideas that they deserved to be held on a better basis. I hosted a series of "coffee klatsch" gatherings at the house, inviting the most thoughtful of the staff officers and combat commanders who had already visited there. Gradually others were included, as my teammates and I met people with ideas who were working hard in their different ways to defend human liberty in the Philippines, and asked them to participate. Thus veterans of the guerrilla resistance in World War II, journalists, civil specialists in government bureaus, and community service leaders gave some leavening to the mixture of military men. Any single coffee klatsch was kept to about a dozen people, so that guests could sit comfortably close and share in the conversation. The relaxed informality helped keep the talks free and flowing.

Among the notable undertakings that developed from the coffee klatsch sessions were the provision of gratis legal assistance by Philippine Army Judge Advocate lawyers to poor farmers in cases before the land courts; a ten-centavo rate on citizen's telegrams to the secretary of national defense, the daring Scout Ranger teams, and the EDCOR (Economic Development Corps) program to give surrendered Huks a new chance in life. Among the more mundane projects discussed were the reward system used to purchase thousands of unlicensed firearms at large among the people, which firearms were left over from World War II fighting (purchase would prevent their acquisition by the Huk guerrillas), and payments for information leading to the capture or death of principal Huk leaders.

The entry of Judge Advocate lawyers into land court cases was part of the effort to eradicate the causes of rural support for the Huks. Prior to this, a poor tenant farmer would often find himself alone in court against a rich landlord with his lawyer and become too confused by the legalities of the proceedings to plead his case adequately under laws intended to provide equitable justice. Now, with an army lawyer by his side, the tenant farmer began to be treated with the fairness due him. Given back their dignity as men, the farmers lost the temptation to help the Huks pull down the whole system. The system was shown to be good when it was made to work properly.

The ten-centavo telegram gave Juan de la Cruz, the John Doe or man-in-the-street of the Philippines, a voice at the top level of the military establishment. The government post office ran a commercial telegraph and radio net throughout the country and agreed to deliver one-page telegrams from any citizen to the secretary of national defense at this rate (less than $.05 U.S.), which even the poorest could afford. Magsaysay asked the people to wire him about both good and bad things they saw government troops doing, as well as anything they wanted to tell him about the Huks. He formed a special staff section headed by Colonel Jose Banzon (who recently had returned from duty as an observer in Vietnam), answerable only to Magsaysay, to receive these messages from the people, check contents for truthfulness, and initiate whatever follow-up action was required. The people responded hesitantly to the appeal at first, unsure of how much to trust Magsaysay and a bit apprehensive of retaliation by those they reported on. But as prompt actions followed the first telegrams sent in, the word spread that the people really were being made partners of Magsaysay in the fight. The trickle of telegrams became a flood.

The concept of the Philippine Scout Rangers was a coffee klatsch contribution by a young Filipino captain who had graduated from West Point, Rafael "Rocky" Ileto. His idea was to set up small teams of volunteers, each made up of an officer and four men, who were to be given intense training in jungle warfare, scouting, and survival. After training, each team would be sent to a remote area to make contact with the enemy— either keeping the enemy under close observation until detailed information was gathered or eliminating him by ambush or surprise attack. The choice would be left to the team's on-the-spot decision. Magsaysay immediately took to the idea and put Captain Ileto in charge of the program. Soon a Scout Ranger team was attached to each BCT. The parceling of the Scout Rangers among the BCTs proved to be a provocative seeding of the morale of the armed forces.

The volunteers in the Scout Rangers were no shrinking violets. Coming back from their hazardous patrols and their contacts with the enemy in remote hideouts, they would boast about their exploits while relaxing with the soldiers of the BCT; the talk made the enemy seem less fearsome and even started shaming the troopers into emulating the Scout Rangers. If the Scout Rangers had remained a separate elite unit, in the manner customary in more conventional armies, their exploits would have meant little to other soldiers. It would have been a case of "let those nuts do it—that's what they're paid for." However, with a Scout Ranger team living and operating with a BCT, its men set immediate examples for the soldiers of that BCT.

One morning, for instance, I visited a BCT camped near the

"Zig Zag," the twisting climb of highway across the mountains from Bataan and Subic Bay to the central lowlands of Pampanga where exhausted American and Filipino troops had passed in 1942 on their "death march" after defeat on Bataan by the Japanese. On that historic ground, I talked to the BCT troops about the latter-day war in which they were engaged. Huks were close by, the troops said. While we were talking, the Scout Ranger team attached to the BCT came in from a two-day patrol in the surrounding jungle. The rangers began to tease the BCT troops about having seen them the night before, allegedly protecting the highway by driving along it fast in trucks, the BCT soldiers hunkered down in the back of the trucks "like rabbits." A whole Huk squadron could have been hiding next to the road without the troops seeing them. Some protection! The BCT soldiers were silent after this teasing. I left them and drove on to Subic Bay. That night, I drove back across the "Zig Zag," nervously alert as the dark jungle growth pressed in against the highway, hiding Huks in ambush for all I knew. I came upon soldiers walking along the shoulder of the road and stopped to talk to them. They were the BCT troops with whom I'd talked that morning. I noticed other troops in among the trees, moving parallel to the road. Apparently the BCT troopers were out to show their Scout Rangers that *they* knew how to conduct a real patrol too. I wished them well and drove on.

The EDCOR (Economic Development Corps) program grew amid the ferment of early ideas in the coffee klatsch sessions, although it didn't get off to a formal start until December 1950. Since it owes some of its life to these sessions, it will be described here with the others, even though the events noted in the next chapter intervened chronologically before the inauguration of EDCOR. It lay close to the heart of the campaign against the Huks and was cited by many of them as their main reason for surrendering. (Of the overall total of 25,000 Filipinos who fought in Huk ranks in the 1950–55 period, Philippine

Army records show that 6,874 Huks were killed and 4,702 were captured, while in the same period *9,458 Huks surrendered!* The remainder stayed at large.)

In our first coffee klatsch, we opened up the subject of the socioeconomic ills that caused people to join the Huk ranks, and then we pondered what to do about such people if they could be induced to surrender. Something more enlightened than prisoner-of-war or criminal prisoner status seemed indicated. There was general agreement that rehabilitation, including the opportunity to earn a better life, would be ideal, perhaps on one of the remoter islands. The subject was discussed for days. In one session Magsaysay reminded us of what he had done for Tomas Santiago, alias Manila Boy, a minor Huk follower who had approached Magsaysay with the intent of killing him, only to lose heart and surrender. In the prisoner stockade Santiago had begged for a chance to redeem himself; he was a carpenter and could make some furniture for Magsaysay if given tools. Several other prisoners overheard the plea and asked for an equal chance. Magsaysay turned down the offer of personal furniture for himself but staked them to a modest sum for woodworking tools and lumber, had them incorporate as a business firm, and let them bid on making furniture for the army. They won a competitive bid and soon were boasting to other prisoners that they had started making a profit and that "capitalism" was both exciting and rewarding. Other prisoners began asking for the same opportunity.

Magsaysay had a contingency fund for use at his discretion, but most of this money had been earmarked for the purchase of loose firearms and the rewards for Huk leaders. However, enough was left over for one or two other pilot projects. The money itself had been raised by popular donations in a massive "peace fund" campaign in the Philippines, led by Vice-President Fernando Lopez; toward the end of 1950, I was told that about 2 million pesos, amounting then to nearly a million U.S. dollars, had been collected. (Because of some strange quirk of human nature, critics have tried to give me credit for furnishing these "peace funds" to the Philippines, picturing me as a Wall Street type with bloated money bags, buying my way through life. This is a slander on the many thousands of Filipinos who dug into their pockets to contribute these funds. Theirs is the full credit.)

The concern about the Huks who surrendered, the thought of the Manila Boy private enterprise making furniture in the prisoner stockade, and the availability of money from the peace fund for a pilot project joined spontaneously with still another idea presented by Colonel Ciriaco Mirasol at a coffee klatsch, a plan for placing army trainees on mechanized farms to learn both military and agrarian skills. The final EDCOR concept emerged rapidly after this, with Magsaysay an enthusiastic contributor to the ideas that blossomed forth. Magsaysay would undertake to obtain land that was judged to be in the public domain, ready for homesteading. He then would grubstake a group of settlers on this land, the settlers being retired or nearing-retirement soldiers and their families along with former Huks who were neither indicted nor convicted by civil courts and who desired to be "reeducated in the democratic, peaceful, and productive way of life." The grubstaking would consist of six to eight hectares (fifteen to twenty acres) of land to each family, a house, a *carabao*, farm implements, and seeds. Successful homesteaders who truly improved their land would then be given legal title to it. It would be a start toward dimming the Huk rallying cry of "land for the landless."

EDCOR was formally established on December 15, 1950, as a responsibility of the Department of National Defense, with Mirasol in charge. On February 22, 1951, the first EDCOR farm was established on sixteen hundred hectares (nearly four thousand acres) of land at Kapatagan, Lanao, on the island of Mindanao, far south of Manila and the Luzon battlegrounds. Magsaysay, Mirasol, a detachment of troops, surveyors, and I went to Mindanao and looked over the area. It was lush, virgin jungle several kilometers inland from the sea, reached by an abominable muddy track of a road. A few small farms lay along this road, with rich-looking soil and reportedly abundant crops. While troops were clearing a campsite and putting up tents, I listened to Magsaysay and Mirasol envisioning the future. They pointed out where the town site and a sawmill would be located and talked about milling boards from the trees as the jungle was cleared and building a community hall to shelter the first settlers. They spoke of building a chapel, a school, a dispensary, a mess hall, and a town hall which would be used as EDCOR headquarters. Listening to this amid the thick growth of the jungle, with the huge trees towering over us, I thought blackly that by the time the place was readied for the first settlers, the war would be over and with it the pressing need for the army to engage in a pioneering effort such as this. How wrong I was!

By that May, the site at Kapatagan was ready for its first settlers, with the road in shape, a hundred or so hectares cleared, the sawmill operating and the community hall and a dozen rude houses built. Retired military personnel, their families, EDCOR technicians and their families, and fifty-six Huk surrenderers, some with their families, along with household goods, cattle, and supplies, were loaded aboard an LST in Manila. This modern Noah's ark began its long voyage down the chain of thousands of islands to the big southern island of Mindanao. Magsaysay flew south and boarded the LST on its final day at sea, taking some of this staff and me along. Sailing those last hours with the settlers, I became involved in an incident which came to illustrate in a very human way just what EDCOR meant to the combatants in the Huk campaign.

Aboard the LST, I saw a young settler glare at me and then quickly turn his head away. This was strange. My curiosity aroused, I kept a discreet eye on him during the voyage. He moved around from group to group, singling out individuals for earnest conferences. I mentioned this to one of the EDCOR technicians. "Oh, yes, I know about him," the technician replied casually. "He's a nut, one of the Huk prisoners. He thinks he can get the others to join him in starting a Huk group where we're going. I don't think he's having much luck." His offhand revelation hit me hard. It would be savage irony if the whole bright EDCOR dream and all the hard work being done to make it a reality turned out to be simply a clandestine opportunity for the Huks to expand their movement into Mindanao. I told Magsaysay about the Huk and his recruitment attempts, adding that it looked as though the security screening of Huk settlers was somewhat lacking in thoroughness. Magsaysay went over to the Huk and had a long talk with him.

Then he rejoined me at the rail, and we looked out over the sea and discussed the Huk. Magsaysay admitted that the man had used all the Communist clichés about social injustice and corruption in government, had disputed Magsaysay's glowing account of farming in Mindanao, and clearly felt that he and other Huks were just going to a new type of jail. The Huk had noted bitterly that he was the last remaining male in a family, consisting only of his mother and sister. His father had died not long ago, worn out by the inequities of tenant farming, leaving debts that the young Huk could barely pay the interest on, let alone pay off the principal. A rotten system! Magsaysay had concluded that the Huk, despite his youth, had sounded as though he were beyond rehabilitation. Sadly, Magsaysay had told the Huk that he would be returned to the prisoner stockade in Manila.

When the LST nosed ashore at the Kapatagan landing, a hundred people were grouped at the landing waiting to greet the new arrivals. There were engineer troops in fatigues, who had been working on the EDCOR project, and farm families from the area who were curious about their new neighbors. It was a small party which seemed even smaller against the backdrop of tall jungle trees. They waved, jumped up and down excitedly, yelled, and waved crude signs lettered with greetings to the new settlers. A three-piece band of drum, bugle, and tuba played lustily off-key. As we came ashore and the welcomers moved forward to greet us, dogs scampered around the edge of the crowd and barked at us. Amidst the clamor of music, shouts, and barking dogs, the faces of the welcomers were alight with pleasure at seeing the newcomers. It struck me suddenly that they must have felt lonely in what they believed to be a spot at the end of the world. The scene was touching.

Later, as the new arrivals climbed into trucks and looked about at the lush growth, our renegade Huk settler ran up to Magsaysay and pleaded that he be allowed to stay. He said that it was all different than he had thought it would be, that Magsaysay and the army really seemed to be sincere. He had never imagined that papayas could grow as big as those he saw there. Please, he implored, he wanted to stay. I watched the Huk and Magsaysay, wondering if the Huk had really caught the contagion of the welcomers' enthusiasm. Magsaysay frowningly explained that EDCOR was only for those who honestly wanted a fresh start in life, not for those who wanted to bring their old troubles to a new scene. The Huk pleaded harder. If he earned the title to a farm at EDCOR, he would be the first man in the whole history of his family ever to own his land. If Magsaysay would give him a second chance, he would like to bring his mother and sister down from Luzon, make a new home for the family. Please! At this, Magsaysay relented. He agreed that the Huk could stay provided he proved his sincerity. In a couple of weeks, Magsaysay would visit here again. If the EDCOR officer reported that the Huk was doing his share of the work and was behaving himself, then Magsaysay would take him back to his home town in central Luzon. There, he could tell the people about EDCOR, as well as help his mother and sister prepare for the move to Mindanao. There were tears in the eyes of the young man as we left.

Two weeks later, Magsaysay visited EDCOR, heard good reports about the Huk, and flew him back to central Luzon. The young man offered to speak about EDCOR not only to the people of his home town but in other towns where the Huks had been active. Magsaysay agreed and the Huk spent the next days in a dozen towns of "Huklandia," sounding like a combination evangelist and president of the chamber of commerce. He admitted openly that he had been a Huk but now felt that being a Huk was wrong. He would stretch his hands, fish-story style, to show how gigantic the fruits and vegetables grew in Mindanao. He boasted that he was getting a house and would soon be the owner of an eight-hectare farm. When his speaking tour was finished, the Huk and his family, with their meager possessions, went to Mindanao and their new life at EDCOR.

A month later, Hank Lieberman, who was then covering the Far East for the *New York Times,* flew over from Hong Kong to report on the Huk campaign in the Philippines. I was at Kapatagan, marveling over the vast clearing that had been done, the streets of new homes and the classes of children in the rough schoolhouse, when Lieberman arrived. He questioned everyone in sight, then came over to me. He was disappointed. The people he had interviewed seemed to be happy, full of their daily accomplishments. None of them seemed ever to have been the enemy, he said, looking at the way they got along with one other in evident friendship. Was there actually any single person at EDCOR who had been a real Huk, who had fired a shot in anger at government troops?

I pointed out the former Huk renegade to Lieberman, explaining that I knew with certainty he had been a hard core Huk. Lieberman talked to him for a half hour or so. "You s.o.b.," he said to me bitterly, when he returned. He drank a mug of coffee with his back turned to me. I asked him what was wrong. Lieberman explained in deliberate tones that he was a professional journalist, which meant he was an honest and responsible reporter who was not about to be taken in by one of my propaganda agents. Even when I told him the whole story, he remained skeptical. The Huk had been too enthusiastic about his new farm and the possibilities for the future for anyone who hadn't known the man before to believe that he once had been an enemy.

At about this time, Huks were showing up at BCT camps and offering to surrender. As they did so, they would ask how soon they could get a farm at EDCOR! EDCOR, which at the time had settled only fifty-six Huk surrenderers, had become a favorite topic in the Huk camps despite countermeasures taken by the Communist political cadre to stop the talk. The EDCOR dream was too appealing to be erased by dialectics.

News of EDCOR spread. Visitors from the mainland of Asia started asking to see "the EDCOR" as though it were a tourist attraction comparable to the Banaue rice terraces or the live volcanoes such as Mayon or Hibokhibok. Among the visitors in 1951 were British officials from Malaya where another war against Communist guerrillas was raging. We had long talks, comparing the problems of the two campaigns and the various solutions being attempted. The British visitors pressed questions about EDCOR, asking especially for details of the electric power plants. My saying "Oh, yes, there's an army generator at Kapatagan" didn't satisfy them. The British had moved masses of people out of the trouble areas in Malaya and had placed them in hundreds of "new villages," each surrounded by fencing and barbed wire for defense and population control, which held substantial housing, new roads, schools, town halls, and good water supply. The people had been bitter about the enforced move from their old homes in guerrilla-infested areas. Now they were complaining that the "new villages" didn't have electric lights, "like EDCOR in the Philippines"! The British officers found it hard to believe that EDCOR was only one small pioneer settlement and that it included only fifty-six former Huks. "But everyone talks about it so, there must be more!" they protested. In Mao's analogy of the guerrilla fish swimming in the water of popular masses, the British "new villages" dealt with the "water." EDCOR initially dealt with the "fish."

A second EDCOR farm community was established in another area of Mindanao the following year, and a third in 1954. Meanwhile, EDCOR officials had been looking at the island of Luzon, where Manila and the main Huk battlegrounds were located. In 1953 an EDCOR settlement was started there about a hundred miles north of the northernmost limits of enemy operations. Also, in a dramatic action, EDCOR picked the most destitute barrio of San Luis, Pampanga, which was the home town of Huk "Supremo" Luis Taruc, and offered its residents a chance to homestead new land just across the river from their old homes if they would help the army prepare the area. The town lay at the very heart of the battlegrounds, some thirty miles north of Manila. Most of its sons had made up the original Huk force. The town and its socioeconomic challenges long had beguiled us at coffee klatsch sessions. When its residents and the government forces started working together, the Huks lost their last vestiges of having a "mass base." The end was in plain sight for them.

The "new land just across the river" from San Luis was the noted Candaba Swamp, a great soggy lowland that is drowned for half the year and that makes a watery barrier across the fertile central valley that runs north from Manila to mountains a hundred miles away. Similar to the bayous of Louisiana, highways cross it on dikes and bridges. Huk squadrons were expert at losing pursuing troops by taking to the swamp. So geography added to the drama of the barrio's move from San Luis. With the volunteer help of residents, the army cleared and drained the new area for habitation and farming. As the emerging land dried, farm lots were surveyed, new housing and a school built, fresh water wells dug, and a bridge built across the river linking the new and old barrios. The army moved all the residents of the old barrio to the new one and helped them with seeds and agricultural advice. The community of new landowners bustled into successful life, a pointed example of what the people and their government should be able to accomplish when the will is there.

My last EDCOR visit was in 1959 while I was serving on the staff of the President's Committee to Study the U.S. Military Assistance Program, headed by William H. Draper, Jr. At that time EDCOR officials told me that titles had been issued on practically all the farm lands, that the initial grubstakes largely had been repaid, and that the EDCOR communities were a healthy influence on the security and stability of the whole areas where they were located. The EDCOR farms had a population of 5,175.

NOTES

BREAKFAST. Once, when I teased Magsaysay about eating canned corn for breakfast, he told me the story of his meeting General Hall's XI Corps when it arrived at Subic Bay during the World War II liberation. Magsaysay had gone out in a rowboat to meet the incoming navy task force and troop transports, to tell them not to open fire at the shore since his guerrillas already had cleaned out the Japanese defenders. After his conference with the American top brass, he was invited to breakfast in the ship's wardroom. A mess boy asked him what he would like to eat. Looking around the table, Magsaysay saw bowls of oatmeal, pushed aside untouched by the Americans, and realized he was hungry for some, not having tasted oatmeal since the 1941 Japanese invasion. He asked the Americans at the table if they were going to eat their oatmeal. Hell, no, they told him, we're tired of the stuff. To their astonishment, he had them pass the bowls along to him and ate oatmeal until he was stuffed.

★ ★

CHAPTER Four

POLITBURO CAPTURE

THE MOST INCREDIBLE of the many dramatic events in the Huk campaign happened in the fall of 1950. I was introduced to it in a casual, offhand way by Magsaysay one evening. We had been relaxing after dinner, reflecting on the difference between the peace we had envisioned during World War II and the lack of peace we had found in the postwar era. For a time we sat in silence. Magsaysay broke it by commenting softly that there were perhaps a million other supporters involved besides those actually in the Huk ranks. Did I believe that Huk organizers now had as many as a million Filipinos in their "mass base," supporting them actively? He himself found it hard to believe, yet that was what one of the leaders of the other side had told him, a man who was the number four or five man in the Philippine Communist party. He had sounded very positive about that figure. He hadn't been boasting. Just the opposite. This leader apparently was heartsick over the direction that the Huk armed struggle was taking and over the glibness of the dialectical justification for the violent bloodletting. He felt caught up in a nightmare and was in despair because a Communist victory seemed historically inevitable.

I sat up and looked hard at Magsaysay. "Is this true?" I asked him. "You have been talking with one of the enemy leaders?" I couldn't believe my ears. Magsaysay nodded. I plied him with questions.

The Huk leader he had talked to was Taciano Rizal, a grand-nephew of Dr. Jose Rizal. (Rizal was perhaps the greatest national hero in the Philippines, a novelist and the inspiring leader of the revolt against Spain at the end of the nineteenth century who was executed by a Spanish firing squad in 1896. The family name would be priceless to the Philippine Communists, much as Washington's name would be in the United States.) The grandnephew Rizal apparently had become disaffected with fellow members of the Politburo some time ago and had spoken of this to a politician who had the ear of President Quirino. Quirino had passed the information along to the Military Intelligence Service, but no action had been taken; the tip looked as false as many others, since there was no one listed in their known information files under the name of Rizal or his alias "Commander Arthur." Rizal had demanded that he be met by a ranking official, alone, unarmed, and in the dead of night, at a place of Rizal's choosing in the Tondo district of Manila. It was the hangout of gangsters and racketeers. The setup had a bad odor to a professional, suggesting a kidnapping or murder for political gain. Magsaysay was told about Rizal by President Quirino on the day he was sworn in as secretary of national defense and had acted on the tip that same night. He had met Rizal, alone, unarmed, at midnight, in a house in Tondo, and had talked to him for two hours. Jerry Palaypay, Magsaysay's aide, and a driver had waited outside in a car.

Magsaysay believed that Rizal was sincere in wanting to leave the Huk movement. Although Rizal had been scathing about the immorality of the Philippine government, he was also bitterly disillusioned by what he had seen of the Politburo's direction of the Huk conflict. He wasn't seeking a pardon when he surrendered; he asked that he be tried in court for his actions exactly as any other Politburo member would be. He was ready for any punishment, including death or life imprisonment. Magsaysay's recital was convincing to me. Rizal sounded as though he were one of those idealists who had embraced communism as others embrace a religion. Breaking away must have been a soul-searching decision, with his feeling of guilt leading to the wish for punishment.

Magsaysay was to see Rizal again the following night, so we sat up late discussing the situation. Rizal had mentioned that there had been a physical split in the Politburo, half of its members remaining in the city of Manila and known as the Politburo "in," the other half joining the Huk forces in the field and known as the Politburo "out." The latter were of prime interest to me, since they were giving direct political leadership to the guerrillas. I recalled the Filipino guerrillas of World War II and the compelling attraction the arrival of a U.S. submarine held for them. Perhaps the Huk guerrilla leaders would find the reputed arrival of a Soviet submarine equally irresistible. Through Rizal, we could get credible word to the Huks of the arrival of such a submarine and use it as the magnet to draw Huk leaders to a rendezvous, where we could capture them. I asked Magsaysay to put it up to Rizal and then went to work to try to "borrow" a U.S. submarine which could be disguised and used for the operation. Rizal was agreeable but said we had only one week to do it since the other Politburo members were becoming entirely too suspicious of him and his credibility was waning. Bohannan and I started practicing Russian phrases, so we could pose as Soviet deck officers, and I strove to convince U.S. authorities to lend me a submarine for the enterprise. We completed a detailed plan, including convincing "bait." If the leaders of the Huk combat forces could be picked up in one fell swoop, the war would be close to over.

My pleas to U.S. officials to lend me a submarine for a couple of days seemed only to arouse their suspicions that I had gone insane. The frustrating result was that I didn't get the submarine and had to give up the plan. This left the Manila members of the Politburo "in." Rizal refused to inform on them to Magsaysay but did let slip a clue as to how they might be located. Communications between Politburo members were conveyed about the city by a woman courier delivering baskets of food; hidden in the baskets were secret messages for distribution to the members. If she was followed and her stops were noted, the location of Politburo members would be discovered! The practice of having such an identifiable link between the top members of a clandestine group, such as the Politburo, hiding in Manila, was hard to believe. Still, implausible as the clue sounded, it might be true. The Military Intelligence Service (MIS) was assigned the task of keeping the woman under surveillance. They soon had the information we needed.

In the early morning of October 18, 1950, twenty-one MIS raiding teams were poised around the houses that had been located. Armed with search warrants, they acted simultaneously; 105 persons were arrested, including most of the members of the Politburo "in." Nearly five tons of documents were seized, files of past activities, minutes of policy meetings, and the detailed plans of the Communists. Weapons, radio transmitters, typewriters, and mimeographs were found with the papers. It was a dramatic blow that left the enemy crippled but not knocked out. There still were Communist leaders active in the countryside who could assume the work that had been carried on by the captured Politburo members. Charges of sedition, treason, and rebellion were filed. The consequent trials lasted for three years before the Politburo members, including Rizal, were convicted and sentenced. Eventually, Rizal's role in the capture of the Politburo became public.

The documents, including minutes of meetings, revealed that the Huk movement had been reaching its high point just at the time that Magsaysay had taken charge of the fight against them and when I had arrived in the Philippines to help. A strategic plan for the seizure of national power had been initiated, calling for the fall of the government and the establishment of a Communist state by May 1, 1952. Party membership was to go up rapidly from 10,800 to 172,000; organized masses were scheduled to number nearly 2.5 million by mid-1951. Huk forces presently numbered only 15,000 men, but were being expanded into thirty-five divisions of 3,329 men each for a total of 116,515 men. In order to expedite this growth, selected Huk leaders had been sent into regions far beyond the old operational areas which had been named "Huklandia," for recruitment and readying of new forces. Most of this expansion was on the island of Luzon, where the present fighting was going on, but further to the north and to the south of the battle area. One of the leaders had also gone to the Visayas, the middle islands of the Philippine chain, and was reporting some success in getting new recruits. Thus, along with our jubilation over the capture of the Politburo in Manila, there was the sobering recognition that the enemy was a better organized, more potent force than had been imagined.

The reaction shook top government circles. On top of the shock of finding a secret, rival political leadership existing in the capital city, there was an awakening to the fact that the government had scanty legal resources for coping with Huk violence. The law permitted an apprehended person to be held no longer than six hours without formal charges. What *fiscal* (district attorney) would deem it feasible to charge a captured Huk with treason, sedition, or even murder within the six-hour limit he had in which to examine the evidence and expect to get a conviction when the case was tried in court? A growing list of *fiscals* and judges who had been murdered, kidnapped, or had their homes blown up after threats by Huks in court underscored the need for thorough proof before making charges. Unless there was strong evidence present at the time of capture, prosecutors were inclined not to prefer charges. Many a Huk, captured when alone, was released at the end of six hours.

Three days after the capture of the Politburo, with its attend-
ant legal problems, President Quirino issued Proclamation 210,
which temporarily suspended the writ of habeas corpus in cases
of sedition, treason, and rebellion. His action was provided for
in the Philippine Constitution when the nation faced insurrection or rebellion but had not been acted upon until that moment. I was gravely concerned over this abridgment of rights
and found that Magsaysay shared my views. We concluded
that the suspension of the writ of habeas corpus should be put
on a rationally temporary basis, with restoration being made as
soon as reality permitted. We defined on maps the exact boun-
daries of those zones in which Huks were employing terror to
make a mockery of justice, as the limits within which Proclamation 210 was to apply. Inspection procedures were put into
effect to ensure that prisoners were not mistreated in custody.
An evaluation system was created by Magsaysay's staff so that
when a zone became free of terror the writ of habeas corpus
could be reinstated promptly. Magsaysay discussed with President Quirino these proposals for the implementation of the
proclamation and received his approval. A year later peace had
come to most troubled areas and the writ was restored.

The capture of the Politburo in Manila seemed to provoke
new excesses from the Huk enemy. There was an outburst of
holdups, house-burnings, murders, and kidnappings and an increase of guerrilla attacks by Huk squadrons against military
units, with the added touch of grenades tossed at wounded
soldiers being evacuated to the hospital by jeep. There was a
Jesse James flavor to one of the robberies, when Huks held up
the Manila Railroad at Binan and took $76,000 worth of loot.
A dairy farm near Manila was raided by the Huks, who demanded money from the two young American owners, Mr. and
Mrs. John Hardie, and then murdered them and their fore-
man, Donald Copuano. The purpose behind the Hardie attack
apparently was simple terror, to make other unarmed civilians

living in the suburbs fearfully compliant to the demands of the Huks. Those murdered at the Hardie farm had devoted their lives to supplying fresh milk to the children of Manila.

One Huk attack touched Magsaysay deeply. The night of November 25, 1950, about a hundred Huks raided his home town of Barrio Aglao in Zambales. He had lived there as a boy and would duck away from official duties whenever he could for a few hours of rural peace among those living in the barrio. Nearly every man, woman, and child in the barrio was a personal friend of his. In their raid, the Huks killed twenty-two of the barrio residents—men, women, and children—kidnapped ten others, and burned down thirty-four houses.

The news of the Aglao attack reached Magsaysay in Manila during the small hours of the morning of November 26, at about the time the Huks were pulling out of the barrio. We rushed to the scene. At Aglao, the ugliest face of war was showing. Smoke rose, timbers still aglow, from the burned houses. Bodies lay strewn over the ground. Most seemed to have been hacked to pieces by bolo knives. Survivors knelt, weeping, by the scattered heads, arms, hands, feet, and torsos of those they had loved. We were told the size of the Huk force and that it had quit the barrio at 0230 hours, withdrawing eastward toward the Zambales mountain range. Troops had arrived on the scene shortly before we had. Former guerrilla comrades of Magsaysay, armed with shotguns, knives, and pistols, came into the barrio as the news spread to nearby towns. We all took off after the Huk force. We were more like a posse than a military unit in pursuit of the enemy.

By midafternoon it was apparent that we weren't going to catch up with the enemy that day. Negrito tribesmen in the mountains, friends of Magsaysay from guerrilla times, emerged shyly from the jungle growth and informed us that the Huks were still far in front of us. They were making good use of the head start. I put a sympathetic arm across Magsaysay's shoulders and reminded him that he was no longer a guerrilla major.

Despite the horror of Aglao, there were other attacks taking place elsewhere. He was needed back on his appointed job as secretary of national defense instead of in pursuit of one small enemy group. Magsaysay stared off in the distance, thinking silently of his burdens, then shook himself as if coming out of a bad dream. He said softly, "It musn't happen again, *ever.*" He ordered the pursuit to continue until every last one of the Huks in the attack on Aglao was accounted for. His brother Jesus Magsaysay and other former guerrillas present swore to see this through, and we returned to Manila, heartsore and weary.

The memory of Aglao stayed with Magsaysay. In the nights immediately following, vivid nightmares would tear him from his sleep; and once he rose from bed and dressed himself for battle, seizing his paratrooper carbine, stuffing his pockets full of ammunition, and asking me to hurry up and join him. I knew there had been no urgent message by telephone or courier. He insisted that the Huks were attacking another town, killing women and children, and it was hard for me to convince him that he had dreamed it all.

Yet Aglao brought him something more than bad dreams. His concern for the plight of the people of "Huklandia" mounted, and he made more field visits, dropping in on the barren *nipa* shacks of the poorest families, peering into the cooking pots to see their meager fare. From these field visits, where he was coming to know the troops and the people so well, he would go directly to cabinet meetings in Malacanang, the presidential palace in Manila. He wasn't aware of it at the time, but he was starting to reflect the needs and feelings of the people and the troops when he attended the cabinet meetings, subconsciously becoming their spokesman. It set him apart from the other government executives and made them increasingly uneasy about him. His anger at the status quo was mounting.

Some days after the Aglao attack, newly built housing became available at Camp Murphy. Magsaysay moved into a small house designed for junior officers, and he, Luz, and the children picked up their family life again. Later, after General Castaneda vacated it upon his retirement, the family moved to the more palatial residence of the chief of staff. Magsaysay and I visited frequently and continued to share the surprise inspections in the field. Luz often added a pleasant surprise to these trips from which we benefited. We were both forgetful about money and all too often would discover that we didn't have a peso between us when we shopped at a *sari sari* to buy a can of corned beef or salmon for a shared meal. Luz, knowing her husband's habits well, took to hiding money in his clothes for just such emergencies. We started eating more regularly on our provincial jaunts.

★ ★

CHAPTER Five

PSYCHOLOGICAL ACTION

I HAD A LIFE full of other endeavors in those fall days of 1950. Psychological warfare was one of them. At the time I arrived in the Philippines, the Huks clearly outmatched the government in the use of this weapon. The government supported its operations with occasional speeches by the president and other political leaders, together with press releases, but combat psychological warfare, or psywar as we called it, was practically unknown in the military establishment. Against this skimpy government effort, the Huks recognized the value of psywar and made it their major weapon.

The Huks followed the Communist practice of building their strategic psychological campaigns around slogans, which were produced by the Politburo after lengthy deliberation,' each being seen as a significantly important factor in the shaping of the struggle. Since the Huk movement's earliest recruiting efforts were among tenant farmers, their main slogan in the early years was "Land for the Landless." When the presidential election of 1949 evoked cries of fraud among the electorate, the Huks took up the slogan of "Bullets not Ballots." There were lesser slogans as well for tactical use. Although every man in the Huk forces had responsibilities in carrying forward the psychological work, the Huks had an organizational structure for this work as well. Each Huk military unit had a political officer. He not only was a propagandist but also was in charge of the morale of the men in his unit, giving constant lectures to the men to increase their political stability, as well as holding the self-criticism sessions mentioned previously. The Huks also had civilian agitation-and-propaganda units, known as agitprop cells, which operated more secretly among the population, mostly producing and distributing propaganda leaflets or conducting whispering campaigns.

At my suggestion Magsaysay created a psychological warfare division as part of his own staff, instead of in the General Staff where officers still were dubious about the need. It was named the Civil Affairs Office (soon known as CAO or "cow"), to encompass the larger mission I envisioned for it: it would not only perform combat psywar but would also improve the attitude and behavior of troops toward civilians—those masses whose loyalty is the imperative stake in a people's war as waged by the Communists. I helped organize CAO and a school to train personnel. Many of the graduates were assigned to BCTs. Each BCT had a CAO section which operated directly under the BCT commander but which also maintained liaison with its parent staff division in Magsaysay's office. It wasn't too unlike the enemy's organization, where political officers in Huk squadrons were in touch with the Politburo.

Thus, along with psychological blows at the enemy, CAO set out to make the soldiers behave as the brothers and protectors of the people in their everyday military operations, replacing the arrogance of the military at highway checkpoints or in village searches with courteous manners and striving to stop the age-old soldier's habit of stealing chickens and pigs from the farmers. As a descriptive term for this brotherly behavior, I dubbed it "civic action." The name stuck and later was adopted by armies in many countries. The Philippine Army's legal assistance to farmers in land courts, the new start in life given residents of San Luis, and the care of civilian casualties in military hospitals were all part of civic action. The fraternal activities in the Philippines were sharply different from programs in other countries labeled "civic action" but actually using soldiers as cheap labor in public works projects remote from the expressed needs of the people.

Troop commanders were not always willing to undertake civic action with their soldiers because they viewed this action as "political" and therefore outside their military domain. To persuade them to try it, I pointed out that one reward of brotherhood was the willingness of people henceforth to talk more openly with the soldiers. If a commander were to practice civic action honestly and thoroughly, I guaranteed that it would increase his unit's "raw take" of tactical intelligence by 100 percent in a week. It often took less time than that.

Conventional military men think of combat psywar almost exclusively in terms of leaflets or broadcasts appealing to the enemy to surrender. Early on, I realized that psywar had a wider potential that that. A whole new approach opens up, for example, when one thinks of psywar in terms of playing a practical joke. We all know that many people risk their lives and safety to paint slogans and appeals on walls in forbidden territory, motivated as much by anticipation of the antics of their outraged enemies as by ideology or patriotism. Low humor seems an appropriate response, somehow, to the glum and deadly practices of Communists and other authoritarians. (I recall a case in Europe once, when militant youths were to partake in a massive street demonstration. The Communist party had followed the book, systematically placing its cadre to incite the demonstrators into acts of violence. Police and military forces were ready to prevent this with tear gas, rifles, and bayonets. But bloodshed was avoided. A ribald benefactor brought out cauldrons of hot chocolate and coffee and invited the would-be demonstrators to share his brews—which he had laced generously with a powerful laxative. The militants found themselves with more urgent business to attend to than street brawls.)

When I introduced the practical-joke aspect of psywar to the Philippine Army, it stimulated some imaginative operations that were remarkably effective.

To the superstitious, the Huk battleground was a haunted place filled with ghosts and eerie creatures. Some of its aura of mystery was imparted to me on my own visits there. Goosebumps rose on my arms on moonless nights in Huk territory as I listened to the haunting minor notes of trumpets playing Pampanguena dirges in the barrios or to the mournful singing of men and women known as *nangangaluluwa* as they walked from house to house on All Saints' night telling of lost and hungry souls. Even Magsaysay believed in the apparition called a *kapre*, a huge black man said to walk through tall grass at dusk to make it stir or to sit in a tree or astride a roof smoking a large cigar.

One psywar operation played upon the popular dread of an *asuang*, or vampire, to solve a difficult problem. Local politicians opposed Magsaysay's plan of moving more troops out of defensive garrisons to form further mobile and aggressive BCTs, and in one town the local bigwigs pointed out that a Huk squadron was based on a hill near town. If the troops left, they were sure the Huks would swoop down on the town and the bigwigs would be their victims. Only if the Huk squadron left the vicinity would they agree to the removal of the guarding troops. The problem, therefore, was to get the Huks to move. The local troops had not been able to do this.

A combat psywar squad was brought in. It planted stories among town residents of an *asuang* living on the hill where the Huks were based. Two nights later, after giving the stories time to circulate among Huk sympathizers in the town and make their way up to the hill camp, the psywar squad set up an ambush along a trail used by the Huks. When a Huk patrol came along the trail, the ambushers silently snatched the last man of the patrol, their move unseen in the dark night. They punctured his neck with two holes, vampire-fashion, held the body up by the heels, drained it of blood, and put the corpse back on the trail. When the Huks returned to look for the missing man and found their bloodless comrade, every member of the patrol believed that the *asuang* had got him and that one of them would be next if they remained on that hill. When daylight came, the whole Huk squadron moved out of the vicinity. Another day passed before the local people were convinced that they were really gone. Then Magsaysay moved the troops who who were guarding the town into a BCT.

Another combat psywar operation used the "eye of God" technique, which I had heard about when it was used at the siege of Caen, and from its use by spotter aircraft-'oudspeaker tank teams in World War II in Europe. The idea was to get exact information about the enemy and then broadcast it through loudspeakers in combat situations, making individual enemy soldiers feel that they couldn't hide from an all-seeing eye and had to follow the directions of the broadcasts. In the siege of Caen, a German officer would be told by name that he was the next to die because he refused to surrender and moments later an artillery shell would hit his house or headquarters. In the air-tank technique, the loudspeaker tank would call out to German soldiers hidden in defensive positions but visible from the air, claiming to see individual soldiers, describing what they were doing at the moment, announcing that they didn't have a chance, and telling them to come out and surrender. Both examples made effective use of fresh combat intelligence about the enemy.

The only equipment that the Philippine Army had for making broadcasts to Huk guerrillas under combat conditions was a handful of U.S. Navy loud-hailers (bull horns), designed for use by beachmasters in amphibious landings, which I had scrounged in Washington and brought with me. I had planned for them to be used by infantry, but it was found that they could be used from the light liaison aircraft assigned to BCTs, when flying at low altitudes. (Colonel Napoleon Valeriano, who commanded the 7th BCT, almost lost his teeth discovering this. On his first attempt, he shoved the bull horn out of the aircraft's window, ready to yell a message to people on the ground below. The aircraft's slipstream slammed into the belled mouth of the bull horn, pushing the whole thing back violently, practically down his throat. He thus learned that the bull horn had to be pointed away from the slipstream.) I had distributed this equipment to each of the first BCTs formed. One day, a Philippine officer made use of the bull horn, the light aircraft, and the "eye of God" technique in an unusual way, thanks to his BCT's collection of detailed information about the enemy.

On this day a Huk squadron was being pursued by an infantry company from a BCT, which had not been able to make contact with the elusive guerrillas. The officer went up in the aircraft to see if he could spot the Huks from the air. He saw them, and he saw also that his troops were hopelessly behind in their pursuit. Frustrated, he looked around in the aircraft for something to throw at the Huks below him—and found a bull horn stowed behind the seat. Inspiration came. Through the bull horn he shouted down at the Huks below, telling them that they were doomed because he and his troops knew all about them and soon would catch them. He cudgeled his brains for what the BCT's intelligence officer had told him about this Huk squadron, and he remembered some of the names on its roster. He called down to the Huks by name, pretending to recognize individuals. As the aircraft made a final circle, the bull horn sent his amplified voice down with these parting words: "Thank you, our friend in your squadron, for all the information." Then he flew away chuckling over his final broadcast. The BCT found out later that the mention of a mysterious "friend" in their ranks had aroused the Huk's darkest suspicions of one another. Three of them were singled out and executed on the spot. The words had inflicted as many casualties on the enemy as troops could have done in a running fight.

The name of this technique, "the eye of God," reminded me of the ancient Egyptian practice of painting watchful guardian eyes over the tombs of the pharaohs. The painting was stylized to give the eye a baleful glare to scare away grave robbers. Recalling its appearance, I made some sketches until I recaptured the essence of its forbidding look, and I handed over the final drawing to the Philippine Army with suggestions for its use. It was mainly useful in towns where some of the inhabitants were known to be helping the Huks secretly. The army would warn these people that they were under suspicion. At night, when the town was asleep, a psywar team would creep into town and paint an eye on a wall facing the house of each suspect. The mysterious presence of these malevolent eyes the next morning had a sharply sobering effect.

Two evils practiced by the Huks were curbed to some extent by technical means. One was the nasty habit they had of throwing hand grenades from ambush onto jeeps carrying wounded soldiers. The other evil was the Huk practice of buying ammunition from corrupt suppliers on the government side. I took up the problem with the Philippine Army's intelligence and research chiefs. Once we found the Huk's clandestine channel of supply, I asked them if contaminated ammunition could be made and inserted into the stocks being delivered secretly to the Huks. They agreed. After weeks of work by the two chiefs, wounded soldiers started reporting they had heard grenades going off in roadside ambush positions—exploding right in the hands of Huk ambushers. Incidents of attacks on the wounded declined sharply. Meanwhile, government combat troops reported a curious new phenomenon on the battlefield. Huk rifle barrels were exploding from the use of faulty ammunition. It came as small surprise that the illicit sale of ammunition to the Huks ground to a halt. Dirty tricks beget dirty tricks.

One of the contributing causes of social unrest in the countryside, which the Huks had been exploiting, was the load of debt which many families carried. Usury made an already bad situation worse. When a tenant farmer was barely able to pay the interest on borrowed money, much less make an appreciable dent in the principal he owed, and this condition went on for years, that farmer was ripe for revolt against the system that had put him in such a fix. I felt that some relief might be possible through the liberalizing of rural credit. Magsaysay had strong feelings on the subject and started to press for the creation of an enlightened government-sponsored system of rural credit, while I worked on the shorter-range problem of getting some immediate relief. I turned to friends in the Chinese community to enlist their help, because the Chinese owners of small shops throughout the country were the traditional sources of credit to those with little or no tangible collateral.

I broached the subject of possible Chinese help in liberalizing agrarian credit with a trusted friend, Go Puan-seng, who was publisher of the leading Chinese daily newspaper in Manila, the *Fookien Times*. He brought me together with a number of the leaders of the Chinese community to discuss the problem. The talk soon turned to their own gripes. The Chinese themselves were a minority suffering from abuses. Filipino racketeers exploited them while Philippine law enforcement agencies were unsympathetic to their plight. The payoffs were so large that Chinese merchants felt that they had to increase their profit margins in order to stay in business. In other words, they were willing to help in the agrarian problems, but how about including them among the persons also deserving "social justice"?

A story told by Go Puan-seng at the Chinese gathering opened the way for a suggestion I offered that would bring the Chinese leaders and Philippine officials together in a friendly enough atmosphere to start them toward some answers to their differing problems, Go Puan-seng remarked that few people seemed to obey Philippine laws anymore, although he would have to make an exception of a few Americans known to him. The night before he and his wife had been driving home from a party. It was late and the boulevard was almost deserted, so they drove fast and overtook a car that was moving at a sedate pace. They passed it, glancing over to see who was going so slowly. The couple in the car were General and Mrs. Hobbs of JUSMAG. Go Puan-seng slid down in the seat fast, hoping that he wouldn't be recognized, for he realized that the other car was keeping to the legal speed limit while he was breaking the law. Imagine, he said to us all, these Americans keep the law even when nobody is looking! On a practically empty road, at night! When the laughter died down, I asked whether the Chinese leaders would be willing to have an American such as General Hobbs host a meeting between them and Philippine officials? They responded enthusiastically. I promised to see if it could be arranged.

The next day Ambassador Cowen and General Hobbs agreed to my suggestion of having Hobbs act as the American *amicus curiae*, the friendly third party. A week later, the first of a series of meetings between Philippine government officials, led by Magsaysay, and the leaders of the Chinese community took place in Hobbs' office. Gradually, mutual understandings were established and healthy starts were made in actions against racketeers who preyed on the Chinese and in the moves of Chinese bankers to ease the credit situation in the provinces.

Magsaysay undertook further efforts as well. In his travels around the provinces, he noted that Filipinos were envious of the Chinese for making more money than they. He would explain that the Chinese worked harder because they stayed healthier than the Filipinos. They drank tea, which they had made by boiling the water first. Filipinos drank contaminated water and became ill, unable to work hard. Magsaysay urged the people to join together and put in a community well to get pure water for their town or barrio. Army engineers helped in these well-digging projects whenever they could. Then one of the Chinese bankers, Albino SyCip, started a movement to raise funds to donate wells to poor communities. The wells were given the name "Liberty Wells." The first hundred wells donated were paid for almost entirely by funds raised in the Chinese community, although wealthy Filipinos joined in later with contributions to keep the program growing throughout the provinces.

My most frustrating project in the Huk campaign was the attempt to give the Philippine Army the flexibility of using airborne troops. In operation after operation, the slow-moving infantry approached reported Huk positions, only to find that the guerrilla enemy had slipped away. There was an urgent need for a faster way to place troops on the battleground, and the most feasible system at the time was to have troops jump in by parachute. A battalion of such troops could be delivered quickly in behind the enemy, where they act as the "anvil" while the slower-moving infantry on foot could be the "hammer," with the Huks caught in between. Magsaysay liked the idea, and JUSMAG concurred and put it up to Washington. The Pentagon said it had neither instructors nor parachutes available. Both were filling priority demands from the war in Korea.

With my three months of temporary duty coming to an end, I went back to Washington for consultations about the Huk campaign and was given orders to return to the Philippines and finish what had started out so well. I used every spare moment of the Washington visit to get the necessities for a Philippine airborne battalion. General George C. Marshall, who then was serving as secretary of defense, heard about my efforts and gave me his personal support. His backing was magic in the Pentagon. I got parachutes for a full battalion. Also, I got what I most wanted, instructors who were experienced in the "smoke jumping" techniques of making parachute landings in the giant-tree forests of the American Northwest: they should be able to train Filipinos in jumping in the jungle.

A Philippine airborne battalion of volunteers was formed and trained. There was an opportunity to use them when two squadrons of Huks set up camp on the tip of a peninsula.

Government forces planned an amphibious assault on the Huk camp from the sea. I urged that the airborne battalion be dropped at the neck of the peninsula to block off a Huk retreat. At that moment the U.S. Army airborne officers serving with JUSMAG in various administrative positions woke up to what I was proposing and vetoed it strongly. The main basis for their veto seemed to be that I was an air force officer and therefore couldn't possibly have anything to do with an army operation. They would not believe I could know anything about conditions on the proposed drop zone even though I was the only one among them who had gone on foot over the ground where the operation was to take place. In turn, they convinced Philippine Army commanders that my proposal was foolhardy. The airborne battalion wasn't used, the amphibious attack went ahead as scheduled, and the Huks took one look at the approaching armada and scampered away, with nobody to stop them.

Time after time, other opportunities rose to use the airborne battalion and were scuttled. I wondered if the American and Filipino airborne officers had left their brains and balls behind the first time they had jumped out of an airplane. Magsaysay, running the war on a shoestring, worried about the jump pay and other luxury expenses of the airborne battalion. I waited until there was one more balking at an operation and then suggested to Magsaysay that we scratch the airborne idea. He said, hell yes! So I collected the parachutes and returned them to the U.S. Army as promised. Magsaysay sent the battalion into the hills to fight the Huks on foot.

Two years later, when I was visiting Indochina, French paratroopers begged me for details about Philippine airborne operations against the Huks, saying that they had heard many favorable stories about the imaginative and successful actions. I was tempted to invent some stories for them, but my conscience won out and I admitted the sorry truth. Perhaps it was well that I did so. They had their own gripes about the way top French commanders used airborne troops, jumping them in by air to be the support battalion in an operation, when they might better have arrived on the battleground by truck. Our mutual candor cleared the air. We put our heads together on ideas for airborne operations against the Vietminh. I had a chance to pass these ideas along the next day to the French commander in North Vietnam, General René Cogny, and I later heard that they had been adopted.

The churches, clergy, and laity of organized religion were targets of the Huks, especially the Roman Catholic church and the native evangelistic Iglesia ni Kristo (Church of Christ). The Huks sought followers among the same masses who were the churchgoers, so the confrontations were frequently savage. A number of Catholic parish priests were casualties in this strife, and congregations of the Iglesia ni Kristo going to church reminded me of paintings of the Pilgrims in early-day America, with a father guarding his wife and children by carrying a shotgun or rifle under the crook of his arm. Worried about the antireligious acts of terror by the Huks, I decided to bring together church prelates and army operational planners to see if the military could provide effective physical protection. Ideas could be exchanged about enemy threats in precise locations and measures undertaken to thwart these threats.

Plans for easing the guerrilla pressures against the Catholics were worked out readily with Papal Delegate Emilio Vagnozzi, who was well acquainted with the rationale of unconventional warfare from his observations of Italian resistance activities in World War II. Our first talk together was distinguished by its candor. Peter Richards, a close friend of mine, had brought the two of us together. He managed the British news service, Reuters, in Manila and was an exceptionally shrewd observer of the Philippine scene. Our frank and informed knowledge of the hazardous situation in the parishes of central Luzon made rapid and constructive planning possible.

My meeting with the executive of the Iglesia ni Kristo, at which similar arrangements were made, was set up through one of the church's lay leaders whom I had known for several years. The executive founder and organizer of the Iglesia ni Kristo was Bishop Manolo. Manolo's name slipped my mind when requesting my friend to arrange a meeting for me, so, instead of naming a name, I asked if he could get me an appointment "with the head of your church." He was dumbfounded, his mouth agape. Puzzled, I explained gently that I couldn't recall the man's name at the moment. My friend looked even more astounded. Then I asked him point-blank, "What is the name of the man who is the head of your church?" My friend promptly replied, "Why, it's Jesus Christ, of course!" I was still scarlet afterward when Bishop Manolo's name popped back into my memory and I could make a more mundane request of my friend.

A group of American evangelical missionaries in the Philippines had established a radio station on the northern outskirts of Manila, known as the Far Eastern Broadcasting Company. These missionaries made and distributed receiving sets which were tuned in only to the broadcast band of their own transmitter. The sets were loaned to willing people in the barrios of the countryside and supplied with fresh batteries if the recipients gathered in neighbors to listen with them. The broadcast programs were sermons, hymns, and inspirational messages. In talking with the director of this missionary enterprise, John Broger, I discovered that they had a daily audience of thousands, spread throughout the danger-laden areas of Luzon where the Huks were operating—including some barrios which government officials didn't dare to visit. Through Broger, Magsaysay and other leaders were given air time to broadcast to this rural audience, explaining the ethics that motivated government actions and asking the people for understanding. It was a unique way of communicating with people in the Huks' own backyard.

The capture of the Politburo in Manila had given the Military Intelligence Service a heady boost in morale, and moves were made to give it an even more dynamic role in the struggle. I had heard reports from Europe about a massive influx of Communist agents into Western Germany and elsewhere just before the completion of the Berlin Wall and the fencing of the borders of Communist states. Hundreds of the Communist agents had been apprehended, but it was believed that hundreds or even thousands of others had succeeded in their disguise of simple refugees. I brought up the subject with Magsaysay and Colonel Ismael Lapus, the chief of MIS, suggesting that this bold Communist move in Europe might be worth translating into an MIS operation against the Huks. The Huks were trying hard to recruit manpower for their ranks. Why not train a large number of volunteers as agents and make them available for Huk recruitment? Once in the Huk ranks, they not only could collect information for passing secretly to the government but also could work to induce the rank and file to surrender. My suggestion was accepted with enthusiasm.

There were a surprisingly large number of volunteers for this risky service. They were trained singly or in small groups and, before the end of 1951, a considerable number had been infiltrated into Huk ranks. Some of them were outstanding and started rising rapidly in the military command structure of the Huks. I recall one painfully awkward moment when two of these MIS agents among the Huks were selected by Guillermo Cappadocia, the Huk leader who was trying to create a new Huk front on Panay, one of the Visayan Islands far south of Manila, as trusted lieutenants and were assigned by him to murder Magsaysay and me. The two agents saw us secretly to tell us of their mission and urged that Cappadocia and his force be eliminated; they were getting fed up with posing as Huks. Plans were made and Cappadocia was killed in an ambush. Cappadocia's deputy took command and asked the two staff officers if they had any ideas of what to do next. "Why, yes, we do," they replied. They revealed that they were MIS agents and placed him under arrest. They then talked the men in the units into surrendering to nearby army troops. Their action saved many lives. The following day, Magsaysay and Colonel Ismael Lapus of MIS went unarmed to a secret meeting with remaining Huk leaders in the Visayas and arranged the surrender of further Huk forces on Panay. The Huk threat in the Visayan Islands dwindled.

Several days before the end of Cappadocia and his guerrilla force, I had spent a brief holiday on the island of Panay at a friend's farm, sleeping in the grass under the trees and swimming at the nearby beach. Fishermen and schoolchildren visited the farm, finally winding up their visit by singing some of the local folk songs. I had taken out a harmonica and accompanied them, then played some of the songs currently popular in Manila. It was a happy, relaxing interlude in the war for me, lounging about on a tropical island, barefoot, dressed only in a pair of shorts. The day after I returned to Manila, the Huk guerrillas appeared in the neighborhood hunting for me, saying that they had heard that I was around there somewhere. The people admitted that an American had been there but had left the day before. They didn't know his name. "Well," said the exasperated Huks, "was he an air force colonel?" The neighborhood people said they doubted it, because this American played their own songs on his harmonica for them. If the American was a colonel, then he must be a colonel in the Salvation Army! The Huks left, angry and frustrated.

N O T E S

CAO. The Civil Affairs Office of the Department of National Defense was first established in 1950 as the Psychological Warfare Staff division under Secretary Magsaysay, headed by Colonel Carmelo "Mike" Barbero. Barbero became the G-1 (personnel director) of the Philippine Army in Magsaysay's first shake-up of the military establishment. The staff division's name was changed to Civil Affairs and Captain Jose Crisol (soon promoted to major) was put in charge. Crisol had been an instructor in English literature at the Philippine Military Academy. Ebullient, witty, and ambitious, Crisol took to his new task as does a hungry man to a big dinner.

CIVIC ACTION. Of course, my concept of having soldiers behave as the brothers of the people wasn't original. The U.S. Army has a long history of similar civic action, from the opening of the West and protection of settlers in our country to such endeavors in foreign countries as the founding of public school and public health systems. In "wars of national liberation," civic action is a compelling necessity for countering the "socialist comradeship" of Asian Communist guerrillas with the people. The fundamentals of this Communist practice are summed up in the "three great disciplinary measures" and the "eight noteworthy points" of the Chinese Communist 8th Route Army as publicized by Mao Tse-tung.

★ ★

CHAPTER Six

1951 BY-ELECTION

THE CLIMAX of the Huk campaign in the Philippines came in
1951. It continued savagely for months and years afterward, but
the back of the Huks' "armed struggle" was broken in November 1951, and they became weaker and weaker thereafter. The
reason was fundamental. The people and the armed forces were
truly joined together that November. Once the civilians and
the military united, the Huks were left outside the national
family. In effect, this event added a noteworthy footnote to
Mao's dictum that the people are the water in which the guerrilla fish swim. The Huks became fish out of water.

But in the early months of 1951, this dramatic turning point
that was to occur in November seemed highly unlikely. The
struggle was furious with both sides on the offensive. The Huks
were following their master plan of the previous summer, which
was to take over the government by 1952. Apparently they
were not weakened by the capture of the Manila members of
their Politburo; I began to wonder if the government had done
them an unwitting favor by eliminating some of their bureaucratic overhead. There were daily attacks and ambushes. Selected Huk leaders were pushing north and south of their old

battleground in Huklandia to stake out new operational areas on the main island of Luzon, just as Cappadocia had attempted to do in the Visayan Islands. However, most of the 1951 fighting was on the old battleground in the provinces just north of Manila.

It was at this very moment, when the enemy's expectations were at their highest, that Magsaysay's domination of the government forces became magnificently evident. He roamed the battleground by sedan or jeep (at times with his driver and aides, but sometimes alone with me taking turns at the wheel), visiting his combat troops and talking with the farmers and townspeople on the battleground. He became a familiar figure to the troops, a burly and energetic civilian wearing a floppy straw hat and a vividly colored aloha sport shirt who seemed always to turn up on the scene almost magically when the going got rough, his eyes spotting the details of the situation at once, and quick words following to praise the deserving or to correct the wrong. Some soldiers who had shown unusual qualities under fire were promoted on the spot; some who had been cowardly or negligent were relieved of duties promptly and sent to face investigation and trial.

These informal, unannounced visits by Magsaysay gave a tremendous boost to the morale of his troops; their leader, near the very top of the government, was with them in the field, instead of sitting around in some safe and distant office playing at being a big shot. They responded by an increasing initiative against the Huks. By the summer of 1951, the Huks were showing the strain of the constant attacks. Their safe places, where they had rested up after an attack, were disappearing. They started abandoning their casualties when they retreated after battles.

My memory of those first months of 1951 is a blur of events: Magsaysay placing his paratrooper carbine so he could grab it quickly as we drove into ambush terrain on provincial roads (he was a crack shot, firing the carbine from his hip gunslinger style); burnt out buildings after a Huk raid; the dead bodies crumpled in the fields; tired troops moving along the trails; a company commander lamely explaining why he didn't go to the rescue of a nearby town which was attacked one midnight; the wife of a sergeant who fought alongside her husband defending an outpost; the slowly spreading smiles on the faces of captured Huks as they realized they were out of the fighting; and, always, the pleas of farmers and townspeople to Magsaysay for help. Amid this blur, though, I do remember the morning of my birthday in February. I celebrated it by driving Magsaysay to visit a Pampanga sugarcane central (plantation) about thirty miles north of Manila, where an ugly little scrap was taking place between a BCT and the Huks. The combatants were hidden from view in the miles-long fields of cane. The Huks had been cornered and blocked in the cane and were thus forced to choose either surrender or death. Most of them surrendered.

We drove to this fight through a provincial morning heavy with the sweetness of mango blossoms, past high school youngsters playing softball in a clearing, onto a dirt trail where I hit a ford across a deep stream driving too fast, slapping up a great cascade of water which conked out the engine. From the dense and tall greenery of the sugarcane surrounding us came the close-by din of rifles and automatic weapons. Magsaysay popped under the hood and wiped dry the carburetor and spark plugs, while I stood guard, wondering if the closest firing was friend or foe. Both sides used U.S. weapons. Then we drove on to the command post. I suggested to the BCT commander that he use a bull horn to tell the Huks they were cornered and call on them to surrender. While the amplified voice was booming this message into the cane field, a farmer walked into the post and began to tell Magsaysay about how frightened his family and other civilians were at this sudden battle in their midst. I stepped back to take a picture of the two of them talking and only then noticed that the farmer's back was dark with blood from a shoulder wound. We put him in a jeep with some wounded soldiers and off they went to the hospital. The sounds of combat died away as Huk guerrillas wandered out of the cane, hands up in surrender. It was over. We returned to Manila and the work awaiting us there. What a way to spend a birthday!

The 7th BCT under Colonel Valeriano added another element to the fighting that year, by grouping volunteers in its "Charlie" Company and training them to pose as a Huk squadron in enemy-controlled areas. They lived in a jungle camp, barefoot, eating with their fingers out of community bowls, letting hair and beards grow, dressing as Huks, learning the pat phrases of dialectical materialism, and singing the enemy's songs. Trained and ready, Charlie Company moved into the field and mingled with real Huk squadrons, able to get close enough in their disguise for surprise combat, often hand-to-hand. The only bad mauling came from a neighboring BCT which hadn't been told of the disguise and took them for Huks. A month later, the Huks retaliated against the Charlie Company ruse by disguising one of *their* squadrons as a 7th BCT company. On its first operation, it ran afoul of 7th BCT troops whose suspicions were aroused when these men in 7th BCT uniforms didn't know passwords or countersigns. After a brisk fire fight, the disguised Huks pulled out. They had retreated a couple of kilometers when they met Charlie Company returning to its camp. It was evening, dusk turning to dark. Each side took the other to be their true comrades. Joyously, they shouted greetings and rushed together—only to discover that supposed friends actually were the enemy. There was a sudden scramble of fighting and then both sides broke away; the confusion of identities had made the encounter too unnatural for the combatants. Use of deception on this scale gradually was dropped by both sides after this encounter, as each started using tighter safeguards against being fooled.

The fateful actions of November 1951, which determined the outcome of the struggle, began for me much earlier than that.

While in Washington obtaining parachutes with the help of General Marshall, I had met the members of a special staff of senior officers who were assisting him with his tasks as secretary of defense. One of them was General Harry Malony, a Greek and Latin scholar as well as a combat division commander who was noted for his political acumen. I had told General Malony about the Huk campaign, including the Filipino belief that the 1949 presidential election had been fraudulent and how the Huks had exploited these feelings. There was to be a Philippine election in November for some congressional seats and for provincial governors; if this coming election were fraudulent, the progress that government forces had been making in gaining the people's help against the Huks would be undone. Malony launched into a fascinating description of the problems encountered in attempting to insure honest balloting in international plebiscites. He knew ways of policing elections to keep them free, as well as the nature of the tricks pulled by protagonists. It was a nutshell course in political realities.

Upon my return to the Philippines, I found Magsaysay and some of the guests at our coffee klatsch sessions gloomy about the political party scheming already underway for the November elections. A fraudulent election would shake the people's faith in the government, wasting the sacrifices of the Philippine Army over past months. I told them about General Malony's tactics for keeping elections free and reminded them that the Philippine Commission on Elections had been established by the Constitution as an independent entity, above party or political administration, to control conduct under the Philippine Election Code. The Commission on Elections was handicapped by not having enough assistance, yet was empowered to request such assistance from government and citizenry. Magsaysay and the others had to figure out a way to get that assistance for the commission this coming November.

During the late spring and early summer of 1951, there were many long discussions and some concrete plans. In midsummer the plans were quietly put into operation without informing the political party leaders, one of whom was President Quirino. Quirino was away from the country; after having visited Johns Hopkins Hospital in Baltimore for an operation, he had taken an extended vacation in Spain. The action phase started with a formal request by the Commission on Elections to Secretary of National Defense Magsaysay asking for the assistance of the military establishment in the forthcoming elections. Further, a group of public-spirited citizens (the just-formed National Movement for Free Elections, known by its acronym of Namfrel) and a group of newspaper publishers (the directors of the Philippine News Service or PNS) also had been asked for help by the commission. For my part, I did my best to awaken American interest in the importance of these Philippine elections by talking with visiting U.S. officials and journalists, by enlisting the active support of U.S. Ambassador Myron Cowen, and by writing to U.S. policy-makers in Washington.

Some of the Filipino politicians were of the "old fox" school. Their early tutelage had been in U.S. politics, from which they had gleaned the tricks known to American political machines in local and national elections and to which they had added many cunning maneuvers of their own devising. There was potential violence, too, since some political leaders were wont to use goon squads for physical coercion of voters or their opponents. However, the sudden emergence of the unified campaign to hold a genuinely free election in 1951 caught them by surprise. Philippine Army troops guarded public meetings to guarantee free speech and later patrolled the vicinity of polling places to prevent harassment of voters and electoral officials. The polling places themselves were guarded by high school and college ROTC cadets, who were often taken to the precincts by army transport or by the members of Namfrel; and the latter also served as poll-watchers under the direction of the Commission on Elections.

Leading U.S. publishers sent foreign correspondents to cover the election, so that a correspondent of a noted American publication was an eyewitness at each of the major potential trouble spots, inhibiting any tricksters by his presence. In Washington, Secretary of State Dean Acheson made a speech underscoring the devout concern of Americans for the freedom of the democratic process in the world and wishing the Philippine electorate well. In the Philippines, Ambassador Cowen courageously traveled an ambush-prone highway into the heart of Huklandia and spoke at a Namfrel mass meeting in Pampanga about the meaning of a free election among people who wanted to keep their freedom.

On election day in November 1951, the army's civil affairs officers helped Namfrel volunteers encourage voters to go to the polls, while the army transported and guarded ballot boxes until the final official count was completed in each provincial capital. PNS correspondents obtained the unofficial tally at each precinct as the balloting closed and reported this by radio (often over the military network) to PNS in Manila, where newspapers and radio stations immediately announced the unofficial tallies to the public, forestalling any large-scale, secret manipulation later of the votes in ballot boxes. Out of a total of about five and a half million registered voters, some four million voted; this was a million more voters than in the previous election. The honesty of the election was attested to by the rueful fact that most of the candidates who were elected belonged to the opposition party!

The military's role in safeguarding the franchise brought about a curious incident which I witnessed on the afternoon of election day. An hour before the polls closed, I had visited the deputy chief of staff, Colonel Jesus Vargas, who was running the military's electoral assistance program and who was on the list for promotion. While I was with him, he answered a phone call, his face growing distressed as he listened. He muttered, "Just a minute," put his hand over the mouthpiece, and turned to me. He said that a "very highly placed person" was his caller and was demanding that he pull troops out of guarding the precincts in Caloocan—a populous Manila suburb—immediately, or else Vargas would never become a general. What should he do? I reminded him that as a soldier he had taken an oath to "preserve and defend the Constitution." How he honored his oath was strictly up to him. He thanked me, took his hand from the mouthpiece and said into it slowly and distinctly that he was going to keep the troops in Caloocan until the polls were closed and the ballot boxes were safe. He then hung up and grinned at me. I shook his hand. Later, I told Magsaysay about the incident, and he went to work to protect the officers and men from political retaliation. Vargas got his promotion to general and continued his fine career.

The obvious honesty of this 1951 election had a dramatic effect on the population. It underscored the fact that, under the Constitution, the government belonged to the people and that changes could be made without resort to violence. The election also fractured the morale of the Huks, due in part to a series of events among them which had been provoked by a secret operation I initiated. An opportunity arose to let me pay them back in their own psychological coin, and I took it.

MIS agents had located a Huk agitprop cell in Manila. I asked MIS to hold off arresting members of this clandestine group immediately and, in the waiting period, to introduce some propaganda material into the cell's communications which, hopefully, the members then would adopt and use as their own. Based upon my foreknowledge of steps being taken to make the election honest, I felt that the Huks could be provoked into opposing the election for their old—and now false—reasons. I wrote a strongly worded, fake Huk directive asking all Huk adherents to "Boycott the Election!" The fake directive cited the arguments to be used, including the frauds of the past and the certainty that the 1951 election would be no different. It was typed on a captured Huk typewriter on captured paper, with authenticating identification, and secretly placed into Huk propaganda channels, via the agitprop cell.

In the following days, the Politburo and the whole Huk apparatus adopted the slogan of "Boycott the Election!" and carried out a vigorous campaign using the arguments I had provided them. Then came election day and its shockers for their side: the huge turnout of voters and the clear evidence of honest ballots. The government forces, the press, and the citizen volunteers in Namfrel publicly called to the attention of the Huks and their sympathizers how wrong had been their predictions about the election. Ballots, not bullets, were what counted! If the Huk leaders could be so wrong this time, then in how many other things had they been wrong all along? Why should anyone follow them any more? The Huk rank and file started echoing these sentiments, and Huk morale skidded. Groups of Huks began to come into army camps, voluntarily surrendering and commenting bitterly that they had been misled by their leaders. Well, it was true enough. They had.

The real lesson of the November election, of course, was that a vigilant and determined citizenry could choose, under the Constitution, the government it wanted without resort to the violence advocated by the Huks. Now the people knew this. There was a great uplift of spirits throughout the country as the election news became known, and, with it, the people overwhelmingly changed their minds about the government soldiers. This one glowing effort at civic action apparently was the clincher, because the troops were treated as heroes by the people for the rest of the Huk campaign.

I saw evidence of this again and again in my travels through the provinces. The most amusing example was a sight I saw in Huklandia the day after election. A truck convoy of troops had stopped on the road near a town, to let the soldiers get down on the side of the road and urinate. As customary in hostile territory, they kept their weapons handy, while guards stayed with machine guns mounted on the trucks, fingers on the triggers and nervously alert for any surprise attack. Just then, with loud and joyous cries, the town's inhabitants came rushing out of the houses and ran up to the soldiers, greeting them, hugging them, slapping them on their backs, and thanking them for the free election. The lads in uniform took it like soldiers.

When I saw that incident of the townspeople and the troops, I was en route to a meeting with Magsaysay who had asked me to join him in the 1st Military Area, which covered what then was the main part of Huklandia. I found him at the area's military hospital, going from bed to bed, talking with wounded soldiers. I noticed that a group of civilians had clustered around a bed in the corner, in which an old man lay. The doctors told me he was a farmer, dying of bayonet wounds in the chest and stomach. The crowd around him was his whole family. Would I like to go over and see him? I declined. The family was obviously deeply grieved, and it was no time for a stranger to intrude into this biblical scene, the old patriarch leaving the world surrounded by his loved ones.

But the old man must have seen me looking at him, for his oldest son came over and told me his father had asked "the American" to visit him. As we walked over to the old man, the son explained what had happened. His father had insisted that all the eligible voters in the family should go to the polls and vote, which they all had done. That night, Huks had come to the house and had requested some rice, their usual "tax" which they had collected from the family before. The old farmer had gone to the door and told the Huks to go away. His family would give them no rice, would no longer give support to the Huks, were through with violence. When they heard this, the Huks had bayoneted the old farmer and had left him mortally wounded in the doorway. The family had brought him to the military hospital, but he was beyond help and was dying.

I stood beside the family at the bedside. The old man looked into my eyes and spoke softly, his strength almost gone. He said that he wanted to talk with an American before he died, which would be soon, because an American would understand. He had wanted social justice for his family and had been proud when one son had gone off to join the Huks to fight for this ideal.

He had given the Huks food and money in the past. Yet, in Tuesday's voting, the old man and his family had gone to the polls, actually to give democracy one last chance at being deserving of their allegiance. He had found that democracy was still alive. Every man he had voted for had won. At this, he had sent word to his son with the Huks, telling him to leave the Huks and come home. Then, last night when the Huks had come for the "tax," he had refused to pay and they had stuck bayonets and knives into him. "What I did was right," he said, his voice almost a whisper. Moments later, he died.

NOTES

NAMFREL. The National Movement for Free Elections (NAMFREL) was formed initially by Terry Adevoso, Jaime Ferrer, and Frisco Johnny San Juan, all of whom had been national commanders of the Philippines Veterans Legion. All too had fought against the Japanese occupation in World War II as members of Hunters ROTC Guerrillas, a group of college students who idealized democracy and freedom. Ferrer became NAMFREL's director. Later, San Juan organized volunteers from Hunters ROTC veterans into the founding membership of Freedom Company, which aided in work I encouraged in Vietnam.

★ ★

CHAPTER

SEVEN

PHILIPPINES 1952–53

AND INDOCHINA 1953

THE HUKS HAD SEEN themselves as "the wave of the future."
The wave evaporated in 1952. With dwindling support from
the people after the November 1951 election and with growing
disaffection in their ranks, the Huks withdrew most of their
forces from their old heartland in the provinces just north of
Manila. They sought remote areas where they could hide out
to rest and ready themselves for a return to the struggle. Small
groups scattered far into the north. However, the main body of
Huk troops and their most loyal followers went south, detouring
around Manila by climbing up into the jungled mountains of
the long cordillera called the Sierra Madre that comprises the
eastern backbone of the island of Luzon. There, in forbidding terrain, they set up camps, a new main headquarters, several training schools for intensified political indoctrination, and a series
of "production bases" to raise food. These were fields hacked
out of the jungle and planted mostly in upland rice, corn, and
camotes, or yams.

The Huks should have been safe enough in this area to catch
their breath after the 1951 maulings. Few lowland Filipinos
ever had attempted to penetrate it. It was too wild. Although

96

I had explored much of Luzon by jeep in past years, often far away from roads, I knew only small strips and patches of this wilderness. As the Huks moved into it in 1952, I was reminded of other soldiers who knew it all too well. Two of them were Americans whom my friend Go Puan-seng, the Chinese publisher, had told me about. He and his family had fled the Japanese invasion, had hidden out on a mountain ridge of the Sierra Madre and had never been found by the Japanese. One day in early 1942, two American soldiers stumbled into his camp, emaciated, exhausted, uniforms in tatters, but with rifles still clutched in their hands. They had been part of the defense line which had tried to stop the Japanese landings on the eastern coast. Overrun by the enemy, cut off from the roads, the two had started for Manila over the mountains. Now, weeks later, they were almost in sight of their goal. While feeding them, Go explained softly that the U.S. Army no longer held Manila and suggested that the two remain with him. When they asked where the army was, he took them to a vantage point from which they could see Manila Bay and, beyond it, in the far distance, the hills of Bataan where there were flickers of light from explosions. He explained that all that was left of the U.S. Army was on that peninsula, under siege by the enemy. The gaunt Americans stared at the sight. Then they thanked him for the food and his offer that they stay with him, but turned and wearily set off for Bataan. "We know now, more than ever, that we are needed," they told him.

In this same tangled fastness through which the two Americans had clawed their way from the coast in 1942, the Huks now were hoping for a safe haven ten years later. Magsaysay and the Philippine Army didn't let them have it. The BCTs moved up into the mountains and went after the Huks. The fighting of 1952 became that of army patrols pushing ever deeper into the jungles, keeping going until endurance and food reached the danger point, driving the Huks away from their production bases and camps, forcing them into a starkly fugitive existence. The jungles were too thick for supplying the government troops by air. The hardships were cruel on both sides, but the army could replace tired troops with fresh ones and the Huks couldn't. Huk casualties and desertions kept mounting with every encounter. The Huks were caught by surprise again and again as the army kept up its relentless pressure. The number of prisoners captured increased. By late summer of 1952, only a small remnant of the Huk forces still remained in the field. It was a drab contrast to Huk dreams of a triumphant takeover of the government in Manila that year.

Among the prisoners taken by the army was an American Communist, William Pomeroy. He had married a Filipina several years older than he, a woman who had been a long-time member of the Philippine Communist party. The Pomeroys had gone into the Sierra Madre with the Huks, she as a political leader and he as an instructor at "Stalin University." An army patrol had made a surprise raid on the Sierra Madre camp where they were, sending the Huks into a wild rush for safety. Pomeroy started running, lost his glasses, and myopically ran smack into a tree, knocking himself out. The watching troops couldn't help laughing as they walked over, picked him up, and made him a prisoner. Typically, Magsaysay had a talk with Pomeroy and then wrote a letter to Pomeroy's mother in the U.S. reassuring her about the well-being of her son as a prisoner. Pomeroy's wife had run in another direction during the raid but was also captured. Unlike Pomeroy, who talked freely to his captors, she refused to speak a word. Later, they were sentenced to life imprisonment for "rebellion complexed with murder, robbery, arson, and kidnapping." After serving ten years of this sentence, both were pardoned, and Pomeroy was deported to the United States.

In the summer of 1952, with the momentum of the Huk campaign firm, Magsaysay felt that he could safely leave the country for a brief time. He visited the U.S. and Mexico. I accompanied him. We stopped at El Paso for an overnight visit with his World War II commander, Colonel Gyles Merrill, for whom Magsaysay had an abiding respect and affection, and we sat up most of the night reliving the old guerrilla days. Then we went on to Washington, where Magsaysay requested U.S. help in equipping his forces, principally with bulldozers, road graders, and similar machines for use in military civic action projects. In New York there were meetings with publishers and editors, to strengthen their interest in the nature of the campaign against the Huks. (The most detailed article about the campaign had been written in 1950 by Robert Shaplen for *Collier's* magazine; updating was needed.) In Mexico City Magsaysay was the principal speaker at the convention of Lions Clubs International, explaining his doctrine of offering the Huks a choice of either "all-out friendship or all-out force," as well as the enlightened role a government must take for the prevention or control of Communist-led insurrections, by keeping the government and the people on the same side. The Lions Clubs of California responded with a drive to collect millions of dollars worth of agricultural equipment for the Philippines, to help provide a meaningful follow-up to the military campaign.

The Washington visit gave me a brief taste of family life again, of householder's cares (both the roof and the basement leaked in that remodeled house of mine), and of meetings with U.S. officials. I tried hard to convince them that the campaign against the Huks was in its final stage and that it was time for me to leave the Philippines. My arguments fell on deaf ears. They seemed to find my descriptions of what the Philippine Army and people were doing to be incomprehensible in terms of the warfare they knew, such as the war in Korea. They were skeptical about the remaining campaign being only a routine mopping-up exercise, for which any advice from me would be redundant, and sent me back to the Philippines. I left Washington depressed. There had been too little grasp by senior American officials of the fundamentals of people's warfare as waged by Asian Communists. Korea, with its old-fashioned positional

warfare, had misled them about what Mao had taught and practiced to win China. Yet guerrillas in other Asian countries, in
Latin America, and in Africa were heeding Mao's lessons from
China. They were bound to make problems with which U.S.
officials would have to cope over the years. How could they
cope if they didn't understand? Unknown to me at the time,
this same question was to haunt me over and over again for the
rest of my service to my country.

Back in the Philippines once more, I slid easily into the daily
life of visits to combat areas with Magsaysay, of operational
planning sessions on military intelligence, psywar, and civic
action, and of visits on my own among the people. Changes
were afoot that fall in the Philippines, so subtle that I became
aware of them only gradually. The first indications I noticed
were at Magsaysay's home. Magsaysay and his family had
moved into a large house in the armed forces' headquarters area
at Camp Murphy. I would visit him early each morning for a
quick talk about current affairs. If there was an urgent situation
in the provinces, we would go out for a firsthand look. If not, I
would leave him and take care of my other duties.

During these morning calls, I noticed that there were a growing number of people patiently waiting to talk to Magsaysay
each day. Mostly, they were people from the small towns and
farms of the provinces who had problems and were seeking his
advice or assistance. Magsaysay would be at the breakfast table,
often still in his pajamas, receiving them one by one as he ate,
a line of people leading from his place at the table back through
the other rooms of the house, out the front door, and along the
street.

Eventually, this line of daily visitors grew until it became two
blocks long—a formidable sight to greet Magsaysay as he got
out of bed and went in to have breakfast each morning. I would
have a cup of coffee with his family and his aides, awaiting a
free moment with him, and thus couldn't help overhearing what
the people were saying to him. Their pleas, questions, and com-

ments ranged far beyond the normal purview of a secretary of national defense. I realized that, to the people, Magsaysay rapidly was becoming *the* government, *the* leader who cared about what was happening to them and who would try to right any wrongs.

Much the same thing started happening to him in the countryside as well. True, there had been an unusual rapport between the people and Magsaysay all along. But something further developed in the fall of 1952. I first encountered it one day when Magsaysay and I had visited troops in the mountains skirting the eastern side of Laguna de Bay, the thirty-seven-mile long inland sea south of Manila, and had stopped at the fishing town of Binangonan on our return. While Magsaysay was talking with fishermen about using their boats to carry supplies to the troops, the townspeople started gathering around. I could hear calls from the street to those inside the houses, "It's 'The Guy'! He's here!" The Guy? I hadn't heard this nickname for Magsaysay before. A dense throng surrounded him, the women pushing in close to Magsaysay to touch his clothes shyly with their fingertips, almost as if for good luck, the fingering of a favorite charm. Magsaysay grinned bashfully and said hello to them. There was a quick response from the hundreds of people crowded about him, laughs, shouts of welcome, and well wishes. Amid this happy din, we made our way to the car. As we drove away, I reflected on what I had seen. The upsurge of emotion had startled me. The words "charisma" and "adulation" came to mind, but they seemed too tame. These people had lived too close to the dangers of guerrilla terrorism, were too mindful of cruel retaliation, to show their feelings openly toward a government leader unless there was some compelling motivation. Clearly the people were discovering that they had their own champion in their midst and wanted him to know it. In the following days, the people in other towns reacted in the same way. The practice became widespread.

While the government troops were fighting and dying in the

final phase of the Huk campaign and while the people were awakening so vibrantly to the presence of Magsaysay, the administration in Manila did a foolish thing. At a gathering of leaders of the Liberal party, the party in power, plans were made for the presidential election scheduled for November 1953. As with most secrets in Asia, this secret soon leaked out and became the choice topic of conversation in coffee shops, in field messes of the military, and at family dining tables. The Liberal party, angered over their losses in the by-election of 1951 and mindful of how they had won in 1949, planned to establish even tighter control over the polls than they did in 1949 and thus make certain that they remained in power. The president, of course, would run for reelection. He also told his cronies that Magsaysay was a comer, a man whom he looked upon fondly, almost as a son. Magsaysay should be considered as a possibility for the Liberal party's list of candidates for the Senate. He would be a good boy and do the party's bidding. With the disturbances from the Huks almost at an end, the country would return to normal times again. The *status quo ante bellum* could be reestablished.

Now, this bit of political planning would have gone almost unnoticed in ordinary times. It was within the political tradition. But there was nothing ordinary about the waning days of 1952. There had been too much violence and change in past months for any sensible person to believe that the clocks could be turned back now. Even so, I was unprepared for the wave of highly charged emotional reaction that came as word of the Liberal plans spread around the country. The body politic looked as though it were about to run amok en masse. Citizens told me dramatically that if the Liberals cheated in another election it was the end of the country. Soldiers talked savagely about stopping their fight against the Huks and taking to the hills to fight as guerrillas themselves against the government. Some of the latter feeling rubbed off on Magsaysay. It was evident that he had reached the nadir in his disenchantment with the administration. He said darkly one day that "everyone" was talking about going to the hills to fight the government and that his place would be with "everyone," not with the government. He reported caustic stories about the free-loading trips of politicians abroad and about the many pairs of shoes their wives bought while abroad and then sneaked past Philippine customs officers. President Quirino came in for personal cudgeling, too. He had used five thousand pesos (about $2,000 U.S.) of government funds to buy himself a bed. Wasn't it obvious that the politicians were callously indifferent to the plight of the people?

My heart was with those who were angry over the parasitical nature of so many of the "in" people of Philippine society, but change had to be effected through the ballot box and reforms under the Constitution, not by widening the strife of the Philippines into a genuine civil war. I found myself arguing patiently with Magsaysay and the others about the importance of their making the democratic processes work correctly, if they were ever to realize their dreams of what the Philippines should be. The only written guarantees they had were in the Constitution and Electoral Code, which would be destroyed if they set out to destroy the government. Didn't they see that?

Magsaysay found his personal answer. Unknown to me, he started meeting secretly with leaders of two opposition political parties. It was a strange combination, since each of these men had strong presidential ambitions himself. They were Jose Laurel and Claro Recto of the major opposition party, the Nacionalistas, and Lorenzo Tanada of an idealistic opposition group, the Citizens party. On November 16, 1952, these four signed a pact. The Citizens party was to merge with the Nacionalista party. At an appropriate moment, Magsaysay was to resign from the cabinet, sever his membership in the ruling Liberal party, and become a Nacionalista. At the Nacionalista convention, Laurel, Recto, and Tanada would exert every effort to win the Nacionalista nomination for Magsaysay and then undertake a "Great Crusade" to elect him president in November 1953.

On the evening of November 16, after signing the pact, Magsaysay visited me and told me about it. My main concern, as I heard the details, was whether or not Magsaysay had had to compromise his own beliefs. He assured me that he had made no deals for political payoffs. It actually was to be a crusade to achieve decent government, nothing else. He asked me about American reactions. I told him that Americans who knew him would be enthusiastic about his running for the presidency. U.S. official policy, though, would certainly be nonpartisan and I would have to abide by it despite our friendship. Perhaps the U.S. could encourage the holding of a free election, as was done in 1951. If so, all Magsaysay needed to do would be to campaign hard. He could win an honest vote.

News of the secret plan started leaking out all too soon, though Magsaysay kept away from cabinet meetings and made himself practically inaccessible. I was surprised to hear my name included in the rumors as having given Magsaysay three million dollars for his campaign. The rumormongers certainly didn't know the tiny budget of government and personal funds on which I was operating. I was close to being flat broke. In the midst of all this political hubbub, I concentrated on writing a plan for safeguarding the integrity of the 1953 election.

By January 1953 the official American family was changed considerably from 1951. There were a new president and a new cabinet in Washington and a new ambassador in Manila. I took my plan for U.S. support of nonpartisan safeguards in the 1953 election to the American embassy and went over it with Admiral Raymond Spruance, now the ambassador, and with his counselor of embassy, William Lacy. They endorsed it and helped with my request to visit Washington, where I hoped to get it approved by the new policy-makers there. Spruance and Lacy were aware of how far outside military affairs I was straying, but they also understood the necessity of a fair election if the campaign against the Huks was ever to be finished. Their warm backing was priceless to me in getting sympathetic hearings at State and Defense, along with the support of Admiral Arthur Radford, then chairman of the Joint Chiefs of Staff. Spruance was probably the most professionally respected navy officer of World War II, and Lacy was a career diplomat who came to Manila from years in Washington at the policy and decision level. I arrived in Washington in late January and made the rounds of talks with policy-makers. My proposal for helping the Philippines safeguard the election was approved.

Some of the civilian officials and military officers with whom I talked in Washington were not too happy over what I was proposing as a military man. They failed to grasp the political nature of "people's warfare," such as the Huks had attempted to wage. I found myself quoting Mao Tse-tung to them, from one of his lectures to military officers in a Yenan cave classroom early in World War II. Mao had said: "There are often military elements who 'care for only military affairs but not politics.' Such one-track-minded officers, ignoring the inter-connection between politics and military affairs, must be made to understand the correct relationship between the two. All military actions are means to achieve political objectives while military action itself is a manifested form of politics." I would note that it didn't matter that Mao had cribbed his lecture from Sun Tzu, Clausewitz, and Lenin. Asian Communist doctrine currently was heeding Mao's words in its warfare, and we, on our side, had to learn to be more flexible in meeting it.

Further, I would point out, Americans too have an ideology. It sees man as a free individual, graced with spiritual values from which come human rights. It is in keeping with what Paul of Tarsus wrote to the Corinthians nearly two thousand years ago: "Where the spirit of the Lord is, there is liberty." When we Americans give of our substance to the people of other countries, we should give as generously of our ideology as we do of our money, our guns, our cereal grains, and our machinery. In sharing our ideology while making others strong enough to embrace and hold it for their own, the American people strive toward a millennium when the world will be free and wars will be past. In my proposed course of action in the Philippines, use would be made of our ideology in helping the Philippine people fulfill the promise of their own laws and form of government, not in imposing something strange and different upon them.

After my plan for a free election was approved, I made use of accrued leave for a vacation with my family. While I was loafing with them on a Florida beach, the political situation in Manila came to a head. At a cocktail party on February 27, President Quirino commented to reporters about Magsaysay: "He knows nothing about affairs of state, or how to conduct them. He is only good for killing Huks!" These remarks made front-page news in next day's Manila newspapers. Magsaysay sent his formal resignation to Quirino, noting that "it would be futile to go on killing Huks while the Administration continues to breed dissidence by neglecting the problems of our masses." Magsaysay was out, but not yet running, for he would have to await nomination by the convention of the Nacionalista party in April before he could really start his presidential campaign. President Quirino appointed a new secretary of national defense, Oscar Castelo, the judge who had tried and sentenced the Politburo members after their capture in 1950.

When the news from Manila came into Washington, Secretary of State John Foster Dulles asked me to cut my vacation short and call on him immediately. He told me that Carlos Romulo, the Philippine ambassador in Washington, was moving reluctantly toward informing the U.S. that his government was about to declare me persona non grata. Politicians of the Liberal party were angry over my "meddling" for freedom of the polls in the 1951 election, which they had lost. Dulles reminded me that he had given his word in approving my plan and would support me as far as humanly possible. But nothing could be done if I were excluded from the Philippines, so I was therefore to return to the Philippines immediately, by the least obvious way, and try to keep from getting too much attention. If things got too hot, he would arrange a visit for me to Indochina or Malaya where I could do a study for the U.S. government and await a cooling down in the Philippines. Meanwhile, he would try diplomatically to avoid receiving an official document about me from the Philippine government.

Two days later I arrived at Clark Air Force Base in the Philippines aboard a C-119 cargo aircraft that had given me a lift from Okinawa, to which I had made my way from Washington. My head aching from the din of the engines in the nearly empty cargo hold in which I had ridden, I thanked the pilot for the ride to the U.S. base. Then I lugged my baggage around some parked aircraft toward a side gate—and walked right into a big crowd of Manila journalists who were interviewing the commander of U.N. Forces in Korea; he had stopped off at Clark for a brief visit! The reporters grabbed me. They said that President Quirino was talking about "p.n.g.-ing" me (that is, declaring me persona non grata) and that the Liberal party leaders in both houses of the Philippine Congress were pressing for investigations of my conduct. One of the reporters, bless him, asked if I were going to Indochina. I refused to answer and grinned. There was a wise nodding of heads over having guessed my destination. Rod Nazareno, the UPI bureau chief in Manila and a long-time friend, helped me extricate myself, then gave me a lift in his jeep to Manila sixty miles away. He kept his promise not to reveal the fact that I had returned to Manila.

The next several days were painful ones. I briefed Ambassador Spruance and the new JUSMAG chief, General Albert Pierson, about my visit to Washington and the instructions from the secretary of state, in which the chairman of the JCS had concurred. Pierson was adamant about my leaving JUSMAG immediately, since my presence there was embarrassing to him, and announced to Manila reporters that I no longer was a member of the JUSMAG staff. Angry but belated messages came in from Washington over this news. They were too late. Officially, I was orphaned and needed a home. I found one, in the office of the historian, 13th U.S. Air Force at Clark, thanks to General John Sessums who commanded the 13th. I quietly arranged the rental of a room in Manila and of a small *nipa* house in the town of Angeles near the U.S. base, as well as taking a room in quarters on the base. I expected that I might have to move around from one to another in case of trouble.

These expectations were realized. Tony Quirino, the president's brother, had had himself recalled to active duty as a lieutenant colonel in the Philippine Army and had organized a special command in the Military Intelligence Service, manned by strong-arm thugs whom he had recruited as "agents." They got on my tail a couple of times while I was driving in Manila and made their intentions plain. I was to be shipped home in a coffin. There was one wild nighttime chase all through Manila before I eluded them, in which my mind was busily inventing gadgets needed by the pursued, such as one emitting an aerosol cloud of black paint which would cover the pursuer's windshield. The inventions remained imaginary; I had no time in which to construct such gadgets. Despite their continuing attention to me, these thugs never discovered my living places.

In the following weeks, I met with citizen's groups as they planned in detail how to get out the vote, watch the polling for the Commission on Elections, and publicize the electoral activities of all parties and candidates. Namfrel (the National Movement for Free Elections) used volunteers from the Philippine Veterans Legion to create an organization in every precinct of every province throughout the country, and other civic groups joined them to swell this volunteer force a hundredfold over its size in the 1951 election. Newspaper publishers and editors also . organized for more thorough coverage than in 1951, including means for radio communication if use of the military nets was denied them. The ham radio operators of the

Philippines took part in this operation. While these preparations were being made, the Nacionalistas met in convention and nominated Magsaysay as their presidential candidate amid tumultuous enthusiasm. The Liberal party met and nominated Quirino as their candidate for reelection. Carlos Romulo, home on consultation from his ambassador's post in Washington, had a falling-out with Quirino and, when Vice-President Fernando Lopez found himself in the same plight, the two formed a new party which they named the Democratic party; it was made up mostly of defectors from the Liberal party and was financed by wealthy sugar planters and refiners. As Magsaysay, Quirino, and Romulo started campaigning for the presidency, the administration got caught up in the electoral race and forgot to file formal papers for my expulsion.

By the end of May, the tenor of the political contest was established. Magsaysay was determined to stump personally in every city and town in the country and kept up an amazingly vigorous schedule that exhausted his staff; his campaign song, the catchy "Magsaysay Mambo," became the number-one hit tune of dance bands and I heard it being played, sung, whistled, and hummed every place I went. The song was so immensely popular that some of the Liberal politicians fighting Magsaysay complained to me that they couldn't get away from "the damn thing," even their families and servants were whistling or singing it. President Quirino contented himself with a few appearances in Manila and let his vice-presidential candidate, Jose Yulo, go on the hustings for him elsewhere. Yulo, Romulo, and Lopez followed the time-honored custom of making long speeches belaboring their opposition, in contrast to the brief remarks of the ground-covering Magsaysay. As crowds fell off, Romulo and Lopez eventually gave up campaigning, disbanded their Democratic party, and helped Magsaysay.

On June 20, 1953, with progress in the Philippines going well, I was able to accept an invitation to join a small U.S.

group headed by General John W. "Iron Mike" O'Daniel which stopped at Clark AFB en route to Indochina. In Saigon the group was to meet with French General Henri Navarre, for any counseling he wished and to examine his needs for resources. Navarre arrived in Saigon shortly before we did, assuming command over all the forces fighting the Communist Vietminh guerrillas in the Associated States of Vietnam, Cambodia, and Laos. The visit of about six weeks gave me a unique introduction to the affairs of Indochina, at the height of French power, in a savage war that had been going on since 1946.

Some of the French officials had demurred about my last-minute inclusion in the O'Daniel mission (apparently they saw me as a dangerous revolutionary), but General Navarre welcomed me graciously. He was devising details for a grand plan for winning the war and asked me for thoughts on unconventional operations, such as intelligence, psychological warfare, counter-guerrilla maquis, and pacification. He agreed that I required a firsthand look, so I traveled throughout the three Associated States visiting headquarters, combat areas, training camps, and local political groups involved in pacification. I had only a smattering of French so I relied heavily on interpreters, sign-language, and a pocket dictionary. The people were strikingly different from the Filipinos, but the guerrilla methods of the Communists were all too familiar.

Vietnamese told me of their history. In brief, these high-spirited people had been under Chinese rule for a thousand years and under French rule for a hundred years, with nearly every one of those years marked by struggles for independence. At the end of World War II, the Vietnamese had declared their independence from the feeble hold of Vichy French administrators. The Communists under Ho Chi Minh were participants and set about eliminating their political rivals in a bloodbath which the survivors never forgot nor forgave, even though the world at large remained ignorant of it. The Communists held the power when the French Army returned in 1946. Fighting broke out between the Vietnamese and the French, and Ho took his forces to the hills to enter into "protracted conflict" with the French, who captured and held the cities and towns.

The majority of the Vietnamese, still hungering for independence, had no side to join. They were opposed to both the Communist Vietminh and the French. As the war raged around their families and homes, they gave lip service to whichever side was locally dominant, in order to stay alive. When French Union forces ravaged the countryside trying to destroy the Vietminh guerrillas, the resentful people joined the Vietminh to get revenge. Later, when the French increased measures of Vietnamese self-rule and promised an independent Vietnam, nationalists started joining the fight against the Vietminh in ever-mounting numbers. By the time I visited Vietnam in 1953, millions of Vietnamese had taken a definite stand against the Vietminh.

I was amazed at the hundreds of forts I saw in Vietnam, ranging from big complexes of bunkers and trench systems to little *Beau Geste* movie set forts that housed a squad, a platoon, or a company. Totally unlike the Philippine Army's campaign against the Huks, most of the French Union forces were manning static defense positions. Frequently, most of the countryside had been left to the enemy. There was a Vietnamese Army and large forces of local Vietnamese militia, both with a liberal sprinkling of French soldiery to train, advise, administer, and even command them. The Vietnamese civil administration reflected this same mixture. There were French administrators and advisers throughout the governmental structure. It struck me that French paternalism was turning over the controls of self-rule too slowly and grudgingly to the Vietnamese to generate any enthusiasm among Vietnamese nationalists. I didn't see how Navarre was going to win, unless he made radical changes to get the Vietnamese nationalists much more deeply involved. They needed something worth risking their lives for. I said as much. French officials reacted as though they thought I was going to undertake radical changes myself and appeared glad when I left Indochina.

Plain arithmetic was pertinent to any scrutiny of the struggle in Indochina. The best estimates I could get from French officers and neutral observers put Vietminh strength at somewhere between 300,000 and 400,000 men. (Oddly enough, General Vo nguyen Giap who commanded the Vietminh was equally offhand about numbers in his writings later, speaking of "hundreds of thousands.") From captured documents and other evidence, I deduced conservatively that there were about 335,-000 men in the Vietminh regular army and in its local militia, and perhaps a million civilians helping them actively, including villagers impressed into forced labor as porters of supplies. Against them were arrayed some 433,000 men of the French "Forces d'Extrême-Orient": 233,000 in the French Expeditionary Force of 177,000 regulars and 56,000 *supplétifs* (native militia in the French command) and 199,500 men in the Associated States Forces (of which the Vietnamese Army had over 100,000, a big growth over its start in 1949). Whatever the true figure of the enemy's strength, the numbers were too close to a one-to-one ratio for conventional forces to have any realistic hope of defeating guerrilla forces. Even imaginative unconventional campaigns required a better ratio. In Malaya it took 65,000 troops and police to defeat 8,000 guerrillas. In the Philippines it was 50,000 troops and constabulary against 15,000 guerrillas.

Some memories of my Indochina visit have stuck with me. There was the hasty trip to a foreign legion outpost on the Plaine des Jarres in Laos to observe a sudden Vietminh invasion of the area—only to discover that the Communist invasion had been called off when the French preclusively bought up the opium crop in the region and thus denied it to the enemy. (Ever since, I have noted wryly how Communist military forces of the North Vietnamese or Pathet Lao become most active in that region every year at opium harvest time. The opium now pays for many of their battalions and divisions.) There was General Navarre briefing us about his plan for moving troops into the countryside against the enemy, apparently talking from notes hidden within the palm of his left hand; I wondered if the notes had been written on a postage stamp. There was a formal call on Norodom Sihanouk in Phnom Penh, the king turned prince, who had given up the throne shortly before to become prime minister of Cambodia. It was the only time I ever met this plump playboy. (Years later, he made a movie in which he as the hero bested a villainous American spy who was a caricature of me. Evidently he loved fantasy.) Also, there were the stories told me by French volunteers who formed maquis, or guerrilla bands, among the mountain tribes of how Chinese Communist divisions had gone into border provinces of North Vietnam to "pacify" the region by denuding it of every living human being. (I couldn't get into the area to verify the stories at firsthand, but I noted that several years later the Chinese Communists reportedly pacified Eastern Tibet in identical fashion.)

I left Saigon eager to get back to the more soluble problems of the Philippines. I had little notion that I ever would see the troubled people of Indochina again.

NOTES

AMERICANISM. Among documents on proletarian military science captured at "Stalin University" was a syllabus for a lecture on the history of the Philippine Communist party. It gave lavish credit to Asians for helping found the party, among them the Indonesian Communist Tan Malaka (alias Elias Fuentes when he posed as a Filipino in 1925) and various Chinese encountered in Canton (in 1920) and in Shanghai (in 1928) by Filipino founders Isabelo de los Reyes, Dominador Gomez, Crisanto Evangelista, and Antonio Ora. In the margins of the syllabus were handwritten notes, probably by American Huk Pomeroy, protesting that American Communists deserved credit too! Harrison George (actually William Janequette of San Francisco) had been the man who encouraged the Filipinos to go to Canton. Earl Browder of the American Communist party had met with the Filipinos in Shanghai in 1928. American Communist James Allen (alias Dr. Sol Ouerbach) persuaded President Quezon in 1938 to pardon Communist leaders who had been jailed. Funds from the U.S. had supported the Communists in the early days.

READERSHIP. When talking with editors and publishers in New York in 1952, I told them of Huk esteem for American journalism. Nearly every Politburo member was a regular reader of *Time* magazine and the American-owned *Manila Bulletin*. The English-language, American-edited *Manila Times* was another favorite. Lower-echelon Huks read the Tagalog daily, *Bagong Buhay*, published by Manuel Manahan.

COUNTRY TEAM. Bill Lacy organized the first U.S. "Country Team" in Manila in 1952. It was composed of U.S. military commanders and directors of U.S. civilian agencies in the Philippines and met weekly under the leadership of Ambassador Spruance. Lacy said he had borrowed the idea from the American embassy in Iran, whose officials later told me that *they* had adopted the team idea from the American embassy in Moscow. Soon, nearly every American embassy around the world had a similar Country Team of U.S. officials.

NAVARRE PLAN. In essence, General Navarre's 1953 plan for the war in Indochina, was to cut down on the number of places to be defended and to use troops freed from these defensive duties to form sizable striking and reserve forces which would seek out the enemy and destroy him. Increasing use of the new Vietnamese Army would be made, with the Vietnamese acting as commandos in battalion-size forays. The Vietnamese Army was to be increased to fifty-four battalions in 1953, permitting French Union troops to start returning home. Years later, the Johnson and Nixon administrations adopted strikingly similar U.S. plans for the war in Vietnam.

★ ★

CHAPTER Eight

THE 1953 PRESIDENTIAL

ELECTION

In LEAVING SAIGON, I had stayed up the whole of the last night to write papers and reports, finishing the last of them on the flight back over the South China Sea. It was well that I had done so. The clamor of Philippine affairs engulfed me the moment I landed again at Clark, where friends met me and brought me up to date. Thoughts about the struggle in Indochina gave way to the onslaught of news about the struggle in the Philippines. I was told about plots to assassinate Magsaysay, the use of thugs to intimidate political workers, the location of a shipment of a million fake ballots printed in Hong Kong and secreted in the Philippines in readiness for stuffing ballot boxes, and the surreptitious moves of political bosses to gain control of the electoral machinery.

One of the Namfrel volunteers chided me the next day for having taken a vacation from the Philippines, when so many of my friends were risking their lives for the ideal of holding a free election. Didn't I know that thugs were bombing the homes of Namfrel volunteers? I asked him to forgive my absence during the past weeks. If he and the others wished, I would move in with the families and share the dangers. The arrangement

115

seemed to buck up morale. I didn't get bombed, although I became the target for some shooting, once at point-blank range with a .30-cal. rifle while I was in my car. Incredibly, the bullets missed me.

In the final three months of the 1953 presidential election, the people of the Philippines lived a magnificent chapter of their history. There were countless acts of quiet, dogged courage. Hired bands of thugs attempted to break up political rallies, but audiences refused to be intimidated. Once, at a Magsaysay rally in Mindanao, local constabulary troops in an armored car, apparently under the orders of an administration politico, aimed .50-cal. machine guns at the audience while thugs moved through the crowd toward the stand to rough up the speakers. The audience was composed mostly of Moros, the Mohammedans of the southern Philippines, who have a long history of being fierce warriors. The men in the audience sent the women and children home, expelled the thugs, turned and faced the muzzles of the armored car's machine guns while getting their own weapons in hand, and called over their shoulders to the speaker (Magsaysay's vice-presidential running mate, Carlos Garcia, was at the microphone) to keep on talking. Many of the Moros had given up their traditional kris, the tough "flame sword" that could hack through a rifle barrel, in favor of .45-cal. pistols or hand grenades as part of their costumes. The potential shoot-out was stopped by the arrival of Magsaysay who, unaware of the trouble, invited the constabulary troops to have lunch with him. They accepted eagerly, apparently overjoyed to get out of the hornet's nest they had stirred up.

Other audiences in the Philippines behaved less dramatically but just as firmly. One crowd in Bulacan, just north of Manila, refused to disperse even when thugs opened fire on them; the awed thugs dispersed instead. In Negros, one of the Visayan Islands in the middle of the Philippine chain, unarmed Namfrel workers disarmed one thug who was threatening to kill them and gave him the tar-and-feather treatment. Lacking proper ingredients, they dipped him in molasses and rolled him in bagasse, the refuse from crushing sugarcane. Negros is one of the world's great sugar-producing areas.

The Namfrel volunteers worked unarmed, heeding my counsel that the electorate could establish the rule of law in its most meaningful form only if they didn't resort to the rule of the gun. I was in daily touch, advising and encouraging these workers. Nearly every civic organization in the Philippines, such as the Veterans Legion, Catholic Action, the Jaycees, Rotary, and the Lions had volunteers with Namfrel toward the end of the campaign. The League of Women Voters and the Committee for Good Government (formed by a handful of Jaycees) worked closely with Namfrel. When armed thugs started a campaign to break up political meetings of opposition candidates by force, all the foremost World War II guerrilla leaders met and publicly pledged full support for the aims of Namfrel, thereby informing the thugs that they were incurring the enmity of these hard-bitten fighting men. Teletype operators and clerks at the Bureau of Posts who handled telegrams and radiograms spotted evidence of skulduggery in some of the messages of political bosses and passed this information to those working for a free election, who exposed them to public view in the press.

This great host of volunteers had for guidance a handy reference booklet published and widely distributed by Namfrel. It detailed the provisions of the Electoral Code, listed the known ways that ward bosses would attempt to circumvent them, and suggested counteractions to keep the code in force. (The Namfrel booklet and the lessons I learned in 1953 come to mind every time I hear a statesman proposing that a conflict in some country other than his own be solved by the vote of the people who are pawns in the conflict—without also proposing a realistic way of supervising such a plebiscite. The usual vague suggestion that an 'international body" could do this doesn't take into account the dirtiest sort of ward politics that come into play in any plebiscite for high stakes. The conscientious and decent person likely to be asked to serve on such an international body would probably be incredibly naive about the gutter tactics to be found in countries around the world. Making an election reflect the true will of the citizenry is perhaps the most difficult task human beings ever encounter.)

The main effort in the 1953 election campaign was to motivate political bosses and their henchmen toward good behavior by penalizing bad behavior. One potent instrument used for this was exposure of political activities through the public press. A henchman had a valid excuse to duck out of underhanded work ordered by his boss, because "the whole world would know if I tried to cheat." Initially, it was thought that the established newspapers and radio stations could perform this function throughout the campaign. Owners, publishers, editors, and station managers agreed. The jointly owned Philippine News Service (PNS) hired more than three thousand extra local journalists from among volunteering school teachers, priests, and public-spirited citizens, many of whom had served in the Allied intelligence network of the resistance against Japanese occupiers in World War II. PNS also formed fourteen mobile teams of reporters, photographers, and radio technicians to cover regions where political terrorism was expected. The Commission on Elections issued official press cards to this huge PNS staff. In addition, U.S. newspapers and news magazines sent nearly fifty foreign correspondents to the Philippines in the final days of the campaign. Their mere presence and the U.S. publications they represented were powerful inhibiters of malpractice.

But the political bosses struck back. Owners and publishers were subjected to strong, coercive pressures. Their newsprint supply was threatened; advertisers dropped out because of fear of governmental sanctions and of direct threats against their persons and properties. Since President Quirino had granted pardons, at the height of his campaign for reelection, to a group of notedly vicious thugs in the national prison, and journalists then learned that these thugs had gone right to work under the direction of the president's brother Tony, the threats of violence against the public press were chilling. It was time to put a contingency plan into operation. This was the rebirth of the most famous of the underground Philippine newspapers issued during the Japanese occupation, the *Free Philippines.* Survivors of the death, imprisonment, and torture which the Japanese had dealt out to the staff of this newspaper re-formed in 1953 under the leadership of their wartime publisher, Manuel P. Manahan, and offered to put out as many issues as necessary. Manahan, who in 1953 was the publisher of the leading Tagalog daily, *Bagong Buhay,* was one of the directors of PNS who had committed that news-gathering organization to the free election cause. He, too, was a survivor of Japanese torture and imprisonment. Freedom was dear to him.

The *Free Philippines* of 1953 was an eight-page tabloid, printed secretly. There were seventeen issues between September 28 and November 17, with an average run of 100,000 copies. The copies were passed from hand to hand. They had an enormous readership throughout all the provinces. A copy of each issue was placed surreptitiously on the desk of the president moments after it came from the press. Similar mysterious deliveries were made to other political bosses. The paper must often have spoiled their breakfasts, since the front page often reported details of their secret meetings to plan actions to control the electoral machinery. The *Free Philippines* reported frauds in voter registration, once bringing a group of voters to Manila from central Luzon for a press conference as proof that they were alive and not "deceased" as town clerks claimed when denying them the right to vote; nearly 12,000 names were restored to the rolls. In Mindanao two municipalities with a total population of 5,080 persons showed 10,935 names on their registration lists!

Skulduggery exposed in the *Free Philippines* included the ominous transfers of honest constabulary commanders from big vote areas and their replacement by more pliable commanders, large-scale distribution of ink eradicator to henchmen who had access to the polls, an excess one and a half million ballots run off at the Bureau of Printing (which the Commission on Elections then impounded), the smuggling of millions of counterfeit ballots from Hong Kong and the subsequent fires that destroyed them, the police records of gunmen in the employ of local politicians who had requested firearm permits for their employees, and the plans for terrorizing poll-watchers in community after community. Morale-lifting stories were also published about those working for a free election, including reports on the acts of volunteer legal teams in freeing Namfrel members arrested on charges of "subversive activities" (which actually were activities upholding the Electoral Code).

There was violence in the 1953 election. An attempt was made to assassinate Magsaysay in the city of Iloilo, in the Visayan Islands in the center of the Philippine chain, by two of the vicious characters released from the national prison. For once, word of the plot arrived too late for early remedial action. A radio warning to Magsaysay's staff brought the agonized response from them that Magsaysay had stopped his motorcade from the airport when he saw the immense throng of people waiting along the streets to cheer him and impulsively had jumped out of his car. He was now walking along the street toward the plaza where the rally was to be held, and thousands of people swarmed around him. Thousands more awaited him in the plaza. He would be easy prey for assassins hidden in this sea of people. Later, word came that Magsaysay was safe. The would-be assassins had been caught. They had lost their nerve. As they came close enough to shoot Magsaysay, they realized that they could never get away afterward; the crowd would literally tear them apart. One of them said, "It's the first time in my life I was afraid to shoot."

The new chief of JUSMAG, General Robert M. Cannon, met with Ambassador Spruance and me to talk about possible misuse of the Philippine military establishment in the election. Most of the Philippine military men were proud of their role in keeping the 1951 election free and were balking at a sudden rash of orders moving constabulary officers around. (The constabulary had the duty of transporting ballot boxes from precinct to provincial capital and then safeguarding them until a final, official count was made. As custodians, subject to the orders of their officers, the constabulary had a highly sensitive role. Some officers were vulnerable to the enticement of quick promotions or other rewards.) After our meeting General Cannon sent his American officers on inspection rounds of all Philippine military units in areas of potential election trouble. The inspections continued through election day until the final tally of the vote. Although some politicians decried his "meddling," virtually the entire rank and file of the Philippine armed forces welcomed this U.S. military presence. General Cannon was showered with warm thanks.

The result of these months of work and risk was a free election. The Philippine people made their own laws work for them, and so they expressed their true political choice in 1953. When the registration lists had been cleansed and non-registered citizens had been listed, the total came to 5,603,000 registered voters. This was nearly every eligible citizen in the country! On election day more than four million people went to the polls. The final tabulation announced by the Commission on Elections showed that Magsaysay received 2,912,992 votes and Quirino 1,313,991. It was a landslide victory for Magsaysay.

He was exhausted from his energetic campaign. He had stumped in every city and town, and in almost every barrio of the Philippines. In keeping with U.S. policy, I had avoided associating with him in the campaign. (Oddly enough, my absence in his campaign didn't prevent gossip that I was present at Magsaysay's side during much of it. People swore that they

saw me on the platform with him, including the time when I
was in Indochina. Later, Magsaysay confessed to me that he
had generated some of this gossip himself, believing that the
idea of his closeness to Americans would help in his election.
He aided the image by having his aide Manuel Nieto grow a
mustache like mine. Nieto, of Spanish ancestry, could pass for
an American.)

With the election over, I accepted Magsaysay's invitation to
join him for a rest at his father's farm in Zambales province,
where we both unwound from the tensions of the recent past.
Laziness, sleep, skinny-dipping in a nearby river, fish-fries and
corn-roasts on its bank, and nightly serenades by neighbors
with their guitars and *bandurrias* (the 15-string musical instrument of the old Philippines) soon worked their restorative
magic. Rested, the two of us settled into our old, familiar
routine as we discussed the reforms and programs he intended
to carry out as president. He would expound his ideas, and I
would ask questions to be certain that he had considered the
alternatives that awaited his decision. The decisions themselves
were his alone to make. Meanwhile, politicians seeking office
and favors descended upon us; while they were closeted with
Magsaysay inside the house, his family and I would sit on the
front porch of the farmhouse and idle away the time. The many
requests for appointments to office nettled Magsaysay, who
told me that dozens of people were being pushed for each
cabinet job and the other appointive posts. I suggested he
list his own criteria for each position and use this list as the
basis for his appointments. His electoral majority had freed
him to choose the best men and go his independent way.

When we were discussing governmental reforms, I had suggested that Magsaysay remember the success he had had in
setting up direct communication with the people, via the ten-
centavo telegram, while he had been secretary of national defense. Magsaysay was enthusiastic about adopting this for
his presidency. He created a new office, the Presidential Com-

plaints and Action Commission, which soon was widely known by its acronym of PCAC (pronounced "peacack"), and appointed Manuel Manahan, who had revived the *Free Philippines* underground newspaper and who had sparked the PNS election coverage, to be its first chief. PCAC brought the people and the President into a real partnership. Ten-centavo telegrams, letters, and visitors to PCAC ran into hundreds daily, covering the whole spectrum of governmental affairs from the behavior of minor clerks on up to what was really happening on major public works programs. With Magsaysay's strong backing, PCAC would go directly to responsible officials, investigate thoroughly, recommend remedial action when necessary, and later follow up and check on compliance. Public servants became just that, employees of the people. (Years later, I learned that Scandinavian cities have a similar post in government, the ombudsman. In 1953 in the Philippines, I thought we had invented something as useful to mankind as fire or the wheel.)

I planned to return home to the U.S. shortly after the inauguration of Magsaysay as president on December 30. I had finally convinced U.S. officials that my mission in the Philippines was completed. The Communist Huks had been defeated politically and morally, as well as militarily. If the Philippine people kept the premises of their Constitution alive, as they had just demonstrated that they could, the scattering of Huks left could only exist as outcasts. (Indeed, Luis Taruc, the Huk military commander, surrendered a few weeks later.) Vice-President Richard Nixon, who visited Manila shortly after election day, had agreed about the end of my mission in a private session with my team and me. He relayed this opinion to the policy-makers in Washington.

Asians have been liberal in dubbing me with nicknames over the years. The Indian ambassador in Manila added to the list in 1953 when he commented to the press that the election results "should cause a certain American colonel to change his

name to 'Lanslide.'" This comment gained wide circulation
in Asia and even was picked up in the British press.

When Magsaysay was inaugurated at the end of December
and held open house at the presidential residence, Malacanang,
it reminded me strongly of the cartoons and stories of Andrew
Jackson in the White House. The public went wild. Vast
throngs of citizens at the Philippine inauguration actually tore
the clothes from Magsaysay's back as he made his way to the
stand. After he was sworn in, he threw open the doors of
Malacanang and invited everyone to come for a visit. They
came by the thousands, the well-clad and the barefoot, jamming into rooms of state, bedrooms, offices, and kitchen, eating
picnic lunches on the lawn, their children taking turns jumping
up and down on the costly bed of President Quirino, which
Magsaysay had moved out into the yard. On New Year's Day,
the Magsaysay family tried to greet all callers personally but
had to give up, worn out, by early afternoon. A total of 80,000
people visited Malacanang that day!

This exuberant scene of democracy triumphant was a fitting
way to mark the close of my mission and to return home.

NOTES

FREE PHILIPPINES. The board of editors of the underground *Free Philippines* was composed of Manuel Manahan, J. C. "Johnny" Orendain,
and G. R. "Gumsy" Alba. M. Aragon was news editor and C. Foronda
was business manager. A host of volunteers gathered news and wrote
stories for it anonymously. Some of the staff confessed to me that they
thought they were going to be killed by goons or security guards of
politicians for this work. None were. One of my most cherished possessions is a bound volume of the 1953 editions, which they presented to
me as "salesman extraordinary of democracy."
PCAC. The Presidential Complaints and Action Commission (PCAC)
ended with Magsaysay's death during his presidency. Its first chief,
Manuel Manahan, devoted full time to PCAC, and as a result his
publishing affairs suffered; so Magsaysay let him return to private
business. Frisco Johnny San Juan succeeded Manahan as PCAC chief.
After Magsaysay's death, the two were among a large group who
formed a third political party and ran Manahan for President unsuc-

cessfully. Today, Manahan is a senator and San Juan is a congressman.

NICKNAMES. Asians were prone to tag me with nicknames, not all of them known to me. Three I was quick enough to catch in the Philippines were "Bigote" (Tagalog for "mustache"), "Eagle" (from my initials "EGL"), and "Brod" (from the way a friend said "brodder" for "brother"). The Vietnamese dubbed me with the names of beneficent or cunning animals, including certain dragons and foxes, although to my face I often was "Elder Brother." In the Philippines I had given myself the mocking title of "Feather Merchant" and later used this when I had medals made up by refugee silversmiths and awarded them to individuals whom I felt had helped the Asian people in unassuming ways. (W.T.T. Ward, 13th Air Force Historian, served as secretary for these awards.)

Chapter Nine

ASSIGNMENT: VIETNAM

AFTER THREE AND A HALF YEARS of heavy drama in the
Philippines, I was ready for a change of emotional fare. Even
the prospect of paper work in a Pentagon cubicle, if need
be, acquired an attractiveness I hadn't thought possible. But
such a change was not to be. Shortly after my return to
Washington in January 1954, I was told to get ready to go
to Vietnam. Go I did and stayed in Vietnam until the end of
1956, living in the middle of a brawling and passionate bit
of history that turned the nation's fate upside down. It wasn't
an ideal place for a rest cure.

I got the news about my going to Vietnam in a Pentagon
meeting of State and Defense officials where French military
supply needs in Indochina were being discussed. Before it
closed, Secretary of State John Foster Dulles voiced his expectations that Vietnam soon would be given a greater degree of
independence by France and that when this happened, the
U.S. could help the Vietnamese directly instead of channeling
aid through the French. Hopefully, with assistance, the free
Vietnamese could achieve self-rule and self-protection in the
foreseeable future. Dulles turned to me and said that it had

been decided that I was to go to Vietnam to help the Viet-namese much as I had helped the Filipinos. Defense officials added their confirmation of this decision. I was to assist the Vietnamese in counterguerrilla training and to advise as neces-sary on governmental measures for resistance to Communist actions. Ambassador Donald Heath in Saigon and General John W. "Iron Mike" O'Daniel, who was being given com-mand of MAAG/Indochina (the U.S. Military Assistance Advisory Group), had requested my services. Their requests reinforced the Washington decision. I wasn't to leave for Vietnam immediately, but soon.

I broke the news about Vietnam at home, saying that I probably would have a couple of months to get ready. But even that was not to be. That same night I had a telephone call from Ramon Magsaysay in Manila. He asked me if I could return to the Philippines for a few weeks and help him with his programs for agrarian and governmental reforms. I explained that I had to prepare for my next assignment, including learning a foreign language, and was certain to be very busy the next few weeks. Perhaps, I could visit him in the spring. Since it was past midnight in Washington, I assumed that he was telephoning me from his luncheon table in Manila and sug-gested that he take a postprandial nap while I went back to sleep in Washington. He hung up. However, he called again on subsequent nights with the same request. Then, one night, I didn't get a call from Manila. I got one from the Pentagon in-stead. Magsaysay had telephoned President Eisenhower and had asked him directly if I couldn't be sent to Manila for a few weeks. That did it. The Pentagon was cutting orders. I was to depart immediately. Yes, yes, yes, I could come back to Washington and prepare myself for duty in Vietnam. Mean-while, go to the Philippines!

I packed hurriedly. While I was cramming piles of clothing into my luggage, I received a telephone call from my brothers in Los Angeles. Mother had just died. We were a close, affectionate family and the news hit me hard. I changed my flight plans for a stopover in California to attend her funeral. It was a sad reunion, and I was in a deeply somber mood as I flew on to Asia.

The weeks passed quickly in the Philippines, and work helped to dull my grief. There were long sessions with Magsaysay and his officials, going over the moves they planned for social and economic actions, and the ways to gain legislative support for the new president. Also, I often drove out into the provinces to see for myself what was happening now that peace had returned. There was a new, visible bustling joy for life in the countryside, evident in the faces and attitudes of the people in the barrios. I was grateful for this chance to learn what the end of the long struggle against the Huks had come to mean for these people. Now they had hope of rewarding lives again. Only a handful of Huks were still at large, living fugitive existences far from their old haunts. The Huks simply had no reason for being now that the people had an effective government of their own. The Philippines seemed full of new promise. Before I quite realized how time was passing, it was late May.

A radio message from Washington ended this interlude. I was to "proceed without delay by first available transportation" to Saigon. There would be none of the promised time to return to Washington and prepare myself for this new duty. I gathered that events in Indochina were moving toward a climax and that the U.S. wanted me on the spot for whatever occurred next. The radio message ended with a personal touch that neither the clerks at the message center nor I had seen before in official orders. After the string of abbreviations and budget citations normally given in orders, the message closed with "God bless you"!

Several hours later I was on my way to Saigon aboard the "first available transportation," an amphibian aircraft from the 31st Air-Sea Rescue Squadron at Clark Air Force Base. The pilot and crew had offered me a lift, if I didn't mind some extra hours of flight time while they patrolled the South China Sea. The added time suited me fine. It gave me a chance to reflect on what lay ahead and to wonder why there was such a rush about getting me to Vietnam now. I sat on a bucket seat, shaking gently with the aircraft's vibrations, sipping coffee from a paper cup, and mulling over the situation.

I had been told that I was to help the Vietnamese help themselves. As far as I knew, this still was almost impossible for an American to do. The French ran Vietnam as a colony, with a minimum of Vietnamese self-rule. Chief of State Bao Dai was in France. His appointed prime minister and government in Saigon had French administrators and advisers throughout the ministries and bureaus. These French officials were highly sensitive about their colonial prerogatives and weren't about to let any outsider such as an American get close to their Vietnamese charges. It was true that France had said that Vietnam was independent (the Bay d'Along Agreement of 5 June 1948, the Agreement with Bao Dai of 8 March 1949, and the French Declaration of 3 July 1953). But the French issued and controlled Vietnam's currency, ran the national bank, customs, foreign affairs, armed forces, and police, and had a host of French officials placed throughout the administrative system. The French high commissioner for Vietnam, not Bao Dai, was the real authority. Was the shock of Dien Bien Phu and the conference at Geneva causing a change of status? I simply didn't know.

The French defeat at Dien Bien Phu had shown that Asians could beat Europeans decisively in battle. Back in January 1954, at about the time that I was attending the Pentagon meeting, the Vietminh moved forces into the mountains surrounding a series of forts which the French had started building the previous November, astride Route 41 in the valley at Dien Bien Phu. The French command, noting the arrival of the enemy forces and apparently bemused by thoughts of Verdun and the Maginot Line, decided that here was the place where the enemy could be lured out onto the killing grounds before the guns of the forts and be slaughtered by the thousands—with the result that the Vietminh would give up their war. The French sent more men to Dien Bien Phu. So did the Vietminh. In March the Vietminh starting attacking. During April their attacks, now incessant, were pressed savagely home. The Vietminh had massive new artillery to smash down French resistance, and observation from the higher ground allowed the Vietminh to make their fire accurate—a factor evidently and fatally ignored at the start by the French command. Finally, during the night of 6 May and early morning of 7 May, the Vietminh came swarming into the demolished French forts, where bitter fighting continued into the next day. At 4:45 in the afternoon of 8 May, the French commander radioed a farewell message, saying that Dien Bien Phu had been overrun by the enemy and further resistance was impossible. The decisive battle of the war had indeed been fought, but with an ending different from that expected by the French generals.

On that same day, 8 May, delegates from the warring sides were opening a conference in Geneva to talk about ending the war in Indochina. Sponsors of the conference were the British and the Soviets, who were present together with the French and the Vietminh. The United States had representatives there as "observers." Other participants were Cambodia, Communist China, Laos, and the State of Vietnam (the Saigon government). From the press accounts I had been following, the delegates at Geneva seemed to be wrangling so angrily that it would be many days before they could agree on anything at the conference table, if ever. (However, the conference did succeed finally, with agreement on a cease-fire and accords on 20 July.)

What did all of this mean to the millions of non-Communist Vietnamese I was supposed to help? They were a vital part of the stake at the Geneva Conference. The French defeat at Dien Bien Phu must have meant to them that the French would go home soon, and I presumed that this made them happy in their yearning for independence. But what was going to happen next to these millions of Vietnamese? Was I going to be able to help them? I couldn't answer my own questions. They were still nagging me when we landed at Tan Son Nhut, Saigon's airport.

It was late afternoon when we taxied over to the military side of the airport, where I wrestled my baggage to the ground and thanked the crew. An American mechanic working on a C-47 transport parked nearby was just finishing work and offered me a lift into town in his jeep. We set off through the streets, while I took in the scene avidly. After all, I was to be a part of this from now on. Saigon, with its tree-lined streets and red-tiled roofs, seemed more relaxed and carefree than it had been during my visit the summer before. Maybe I read this on the faces of people in the teeming traffic around us. Most of them seemed anxious only to get home to dinner after their day's work. Cyclists swarmed down the streets, some pumping away on pedals, but most with small motors putt-putting them along. Here and there whole families balanced themselves before and after papa at the handlebars. Mixed into this melee were tiny taxicabs, jeeps, and ancient open touring cars which the Saigonnais then used as jitneys to and from the suburbs. The only reminders of a country at war, other than the uniforms worn by so many of the people, were an occasional military truck with an African colonial soldier driver and now and then a French military dispatch rider, helmeted, crouched over the handlebars, zig-zagging through the sluggish traffic on his motorcycle.

My destination was the house of General John W. O'Daniel on Rue La Grandière in the heart of town, where I was to report in to him. I arrived just as he was sitting down to dinner. He gave me a warm welcome, offered me a spare bed for the night, and asked me to share his meal. Iron Mike O'Daniel was a soldier's soldier, combat wise, a bulldog look to him. The summer before, when I had served on his mission, he had

N

CHINA

17TH PARALLEL

LAOS

THAILAND

Hue

Tourane
(Danang)

QUANG
NGAI

Bong Son

BINH
DINH

Qui
Nhon

CAMBODIA

VIETNAM

Dalat

Loc Ninh

Phnom Penh

Mekong River

Nui ba Den Mt.

Bai Trai

A. Karl

Bassac River

PLAINE
DES JONCS

Tay Ninh

Saigon

Mekong R.

Nha Be

Rung Sat

Long Xuyen

Cai Von

Go Cong

Long Hai

Cai Son

Cantho

Cap St. Jacques
(now Vung Tau)

PHU
QUOC

Long My

Soc Trang

South China
Sea

Gulf of
Siam

Camau

Baclieu

CAMAU

CONSON

Miles

0   50   100

SOUTH VIETNAM
1954–1956

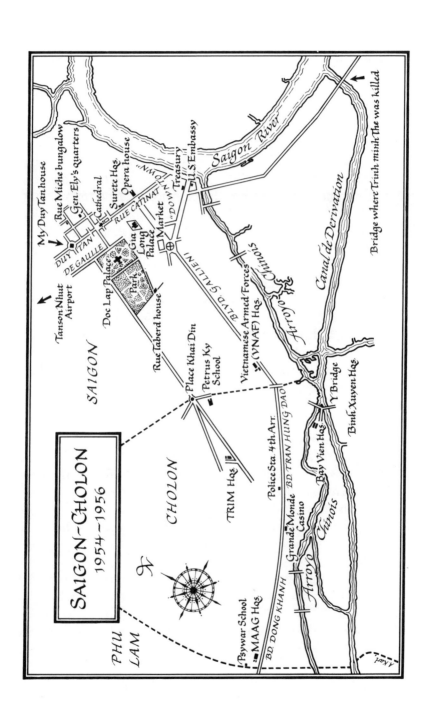

SAIGON–CHOLON
1954–1956

SAIGON

CHOLON

PHU
LAM

My Duy Tan house
Rue Miche bungalow
Gen. Ely's quarters
Cathedral
Surete Hqs.
Opera house
Treasury
U.S Embassy

Saigon River

"N'M'O"

"DOWN"

DUY TAN
DE GAULLE

RUE CATINAT
Market
Gia Long Palace

Doc Lap Palace
Park

Tanson Nhut Airport

Rue Taberd house

Place Khai Din
Petrus Ky School

BLVD. GALLIENI

Vietnamese Armed Forces
(VNAF) Hqs.

Arroyo Chinois

Canal de Derivation

Bridge where Trinh minh The was killed

Y Bridge
Binh Xuyen Hqs.

Arroyo Chinois

TRIM Hqs.

Police Sta. 4th Arr.

Grande Monde Casino

Bay Vien Hqs.

BD TRAN HUNG DAO

Psywar School
MAAG Hqs.

BD DONG KHANH

Arroyo Chinois

A Kari

been a three-star lieutenant general. Now he wore the two
stars of a major general. When the post of chief of MAAG/Indo-
china became available, the U.S. looked for a major general
to fill it, to fit the protocol of a rank junior to the French commander in Indochina. O'Daniel asked to be demoted, in order
to serve in Indochina. U.S. authorities gulped at this unorthodox request, but finally gave in. En route to Saigon,
O'Daniel had stopped briefly at Hong Kong to buy some necessities. Rather than undergo the ceremonies expected of a visiting general, he had borrowed insignia from a lieutenant colonel
on his staff and had worn it for his hasty shopping chores. A
mild diplomatic fuss had been kicked up by this incident. It
was the main conversational fare at the dinner table that night.

We talked for a time and then went to bed. I fell fast asleep.
The next thing I knew, I was being shaken awake by O'Daniel.
Fuzzily, I became aware of him standing beside my bed in
pajamas, and of a terrific racket. There was the constant roar
of gigantic explosions somewhere not too far away. Gusts of
hot air beat at the wooden shutters on the windows, setting
them dancing and banging. I stumbled out of bed and helped
him open the shutters. We peered out into the night. The great
violence was taking place on the outskirts of town, near the
airport, where the French had an immense ammunition dump.
Our guess was that Vietminh sappers had raided the dump
and started it exploding. A telephone call confirmed the guess.
The roaring went on and on. After listening to the explosions,
I said there was nothing an American could do about coping
with the problem and excused myself, to go back to bed. Now
I knew that a war was still going on in Vietnam.

As May turned into June, I worked at settling myself into
the local situation. I still could find no evidence of why I had
been sent to Vietnam in such a hurry. With time to spare, I
sought out acquaintances with Vietnamese military men, with
the townspeople of the Saigon metropolitan area, and with

the unique religious sects of Vietnam. There were more mundane matters too, such as finding a place to live, an office other than my hip pocket, and some transportation of my own.

Space was at a premium in crowded Saigon. I found a room at a BOQ, temporarily vacant while its regular occupant was away on leave. I had been posted to Saigon as an assistant air attaché so that I could work readily with both the ambassador and the chief of MAAG, but there wasn't a vacant desk, table, chair, or file in the air attaché's tiny office. As for transportation, I was told that none was available for me. I took to bumming rides with others or to getting around town in *cyclos*, Saigon's version of the rickshaw, in which the passenger sits in a carriage seat in front a few inches off the ground while the cyclist pedals or motors his wheel behind. A *cyclo* ride, in which the passenger feels he is acting as the front bumper of the vehicle, is a fast way to get the adrenalin flowing when going through Saigon's crowded streets. As I rode in *cyclos*, I noticed that the U.S. aid to the war had been generous. It seemed to me that every last French officer and enlisted man was driving around town in his own American jeep.

My pique at the lack of a vehicle became overwhelming on the night of the first diplomatic reception I was to attend. It was a dress-up affair given by Prince Buu Loc, the Vietnamese prime minister, at Gia Long Palace. Resplendent in white uniform, I walked to the palace and stopped on the sidewalk in front to take in the scene. A line of automobiles was entering the gates and moving slowly up an incline to the front doors of the palace, where an honor guard presented arms in salute to each arrival. I was damned if I was going to saunter into the reception as the only guest on foot. A crowd of Vietnamese stood watching the arriving procession on the street next to me in front of the palace. Among them were several *cyclo* drivers, resting on their vehicles. I picked out one, clad only in a pair of undershorts and otherwise bare except for sandals on his feet, and hired him to drive me to the palace entrance.

He and the onlookers wore big grins as the *cyclo* joined the line of entering automobiles. Pumping hard on the pedals, my cyclist managed to get us up the incline to the entrance, where I solemnly paid his fare while the honor guard stood at a rigid "present arms."

Inside the palace, I went through the receiving line and right into an ambush of angry American officials. They informed me that they had never been so embarrassed in their lives. How dared I lower the prestige of the United States of America by arriving in such a manner? I replied that it was the only vehicle available to me. If they were worried about prestige, let them assign me a car. General O'Daniel came up at this point. He had greatly enjoyed the sight. MAAG had just received a few 2-CV Citroëns, he said, and since I was so hard up, he was assigning one of them to me. Thus I got my own transportation. The 2-CV was an ugly little tin can, its seats made from wide rubber bands, but I loved it.

General O'Daniel escorted me to courtesy calls on Dr. Phan huy Quat, the defense minister, and on General Nguyen van Hinh, who commanded the Vietnamese armed forces, telling each that I was to be an informal liaison officer for him and would give them any help possible. Quat and I discovered that we had met each other in Hanoi the summer before. Like many Vietnamese medical men, he had gone into politics, although he continued to practice medicine from a small clinic in his home. (Vietnamese governments always seem to have some doctors and dentists in prominent positions.) We got along well with each other, despite his few words of English and my scraps of French. General Hinh was the son of a former Vietnamese prime minister, taller than most of his staff officers, a handsome ladies' man with a French wife, who held a regular commission as a colonel in the French Air Force. We had met before, during a brief visit he made to Manila during the Huk campaign. Hinh plied me with questions about Magsaysay, saying that he admired him and that he had found another admirer in Nasser with whom he had visited recently in Egypt. I did my best to answer his questions, finally staying for dinner to tell him more at the table.

Dr. Quat had suggested, and General Hinh agreed, that I might give some help to the G-5 staff division of the Vietnamese Army. G-5, which was known as the 5th Bureau, was the army's propaganda and information organization. Apparently the French had paid scant attention to it and wouldn't mind an American assisting in what they saw as a minor enterprise. (G-1, Personnel, and G-2, Intelligence, were headed by French officers at the time, while G-3, Operations and Training, as well as G-4, Supply, were filled with French advisers.) G-6, Special Operations, was a French activity, with a nominal Vietnamese chief. I never knew of any French officers connected with G-5, Psywar. Thus, thanks to the defense minister and the chief of staff, I became the unofficial adviser to Captain Pham xuan Giai, the chief of the 5th Bureau. It brought me directly into the psychological operations of the Franco-Vietminh war that continued on its savage way while the delegates of the warring sides argued at Geneva.

G-5 appeared to be far ahead of what the Filipinos had in their civil affairs organization for the Huk campaign. There were a large headquarters staff, three armed propaganda companies in the field, a staff of artists and writers, a radio unit broadcasting daily programs to the troops from the government radio station in Saigon, access to major printing facilities, and combat psywar equipment, such as portable sets for voice amplification, of a quality far superior to anything I had known. What was lacking, fundamentally, was a real purpose to which all this talented manpower and fine equipment could be directed. True, G-5 was attempting to induce enemy soldiers to surrender and was passing along information about current events to the troops of the Vietnamese Army; but G-5 had a heavy political handicap. Vietnamese in uniform were teamed with the soldiers of French colonial forces, fighting a Communist enemy amongst a population yearning for independence from France. The Communist enemy continued to pose as the only true nationalist force in Vietnam and, though this camouflage had worn thin during the long war, the enemy kept its psychological lead over the Vietnamese Army.

Initially, I gathered that Captain Giai thought that because I was an American, I had come in the role of Santa Claus. He promptly composed a shopping list of U.S. equipment that he would like to have. I suggested that we could make better use of our time together, since he already had more resources than I had realized. Wouldn't he prefer to use them in such a way that he would double or triple the results? Once this was done, then we could consider whatever new equipment would be needed. Giai asked what I had in mind. I then offered to teach some combat psywar techniques, as well as how to conduct word-of-mouth campaigns, if G-5 would undertake the basic mission of changing the behavior and attitude of Vietnamese Army troops toward the people. Arrogance and cupidity were far too prevalent in military dealings with the people. A prouder military tradition for the Vietnamese Army would be that of protecting the people. G-5 could help establish such a tradition. After some hesitation, Giai agreed to take up the proposal with General Hinh. Hinh approved, and we went to work to make it succeed.

A school was established for military psywar training, using a curriculum that I outlined which detailed ways to improve the relationships between the troops and the people. Radio programs, posters, leaflets, bulletin board newspapers in troop units, playlets written and enacted by G-5 personnel, prepared lectures for commanders to give their troops, the Arellano brothers' movies showing the people's reactions to good and bad troop behavior in the Philippines, and a soldier's handbook prepared by the U.S. Information Agency were used in this attempt to change the pattern of behavior. Success was spotty. Hungry and ill-paid troops still stole chickens, pigs, and rice during military operations. Advice alone could not change this. It would take some new direction from the top and more adequate physical provisions for the troops for true change to take place. This meant dealing with the never-never land of French sensibilities, since the French were in actual control of the Vietnamese forces. I started an educational effort with the French staff officers I had met. They found my ideas alien and suggested laughingly that I take up smoking opium instead.

Officials in Washington heard of my work with G-5 in an odd way. Captain Giai and some of his officers had been fascinated by my descriptions of how word-of-mouth techniques could give psychological support to troop operations. They asked for details, thinking especially of using them in North Vietnam, where the Vietminh pressures were particularly heavy at the time. Among the suggestions I gave was the spreading of a three-part story implying the presence of a Chinese Communist division in one locality near the border (Chinese troops were roundly hated in most of North Vietnam). The G-5 officers made notes as I described the methods to be used and thanked me. I forgot all about it in the following days. Then, one day, I was told in an embassy meeting that a query had arrived from Washington, asking about the truth of reports that three Chinese Communist divisions had crossed the border into North Vietnam. Since General O'Daniel and I were flying to Hanoi for a visit later that day, would we please check on the truth of these reports? In Hanoi I asked about the reported Chinese Communist divisions crossing the border. There were big grins in answer. The Vietnamese Army's armed propaganda company operating in Tonkin had used my story-spreading technique. Instead of hinting at just one Chinese division, they had decided to make it three. The technique worked, they told me. Nearly everyone believed the story and reports were flooding the military intelligence collectors! Ruefully, I wrote an explanation of what had happened and turned this into the embassy upon my return to Saigon. Officials in Washington let it be known subsequently that they did not appreciate the joke.

Behind the façade of French provincial buildings and colonial life on the main thoroughfares of the Saigon-Cholon metropolitan area lay the real city, a densely-packed complex of Vietnamese hamlets. It was almost like a conjuring trick. Down alleys and byways past the concrete and stucco of office buildings, shops, and villas there were the hidden hamlets, throbbing with an intense life of their own, with thousands of people crowded into wooden dwellings along a block or two of dirt lanes. A total of perhaps a million people inhabited these hamlets in Saigon-Cholon, out of the sight and ken of those on the paved thoroughfares. Few foreigners, except for groups of police, ever visited these hamlets. They made up a nearly secret city of timeless Vietnamese ways within a surface city that had taken to foreign modes.

I found the inner city when I tried to learn what "social action committees" were. There had been vague references to them at diplomatic gatherings, but nobody seemed to know much beyond the name. Rob McClintock, the counselor of the American embassy, finally started me on the way by introducing me to the minister of social action and labor. This minister introduced me in turn to his "man for social action," Nguyen van Hanh. Middle-aged, portly, wearing coat and tie, Hanh looked the obsequious bureaucrat as he responded politely to the introduction. But when I asked if I could visit some of these committees and see what they were doing, his face lit up eagerly and he seemed another person. The minister invited me formally to go along with Hanh and learn what he was doing. With that, Hanh grabbed me and pulled me along with him as he left the office. It was clear that his portliness came from muscle, not fat. In rapid French, he told me about the social action committees, and my halting translation gave me only the general drift of his words. We took off on a round of visits to committees, Hanh insisting on leading the way on a motorcycle while I followed closely behind in the 2-CV Citroën.

About a hundred social action committees had been formed in the metropolitan area of the capital and its suburbs. Each committee served a "quarter" or neighborhood. A committee used self-help to stimulate the residents of a neighborhood to improve their lives there. Thus, educated residents conducted night schools to teach the illiterate how to read and write, taking the biggest house in the neighborhood for their schoolhouse. Residents formed a neighborhood watch to guard against arson and thievery, with volunteers taking turns. Other projects included community hygiene (via pit latrines), public works (building up a proper main lane through the community and hanging lanterns from the houses along it to furnish public lighting at night), and utilities (which seemed to consist mainly of trying to get water and electric power from the city mains into the community). Committees were elected at neighborhood meetings by voice vote. Hanh organized the meetings, explaining the benefits to the residents of setting up such a committee, and then conducted the election. Hanh said he had never held an election by secret ballot because too many of the people were illiterate and couldn't write names down on ballots. I suggested that even illiterates could draw a symbol on a ballot, such as a cross, a circle, or a triangle, and he agreed enthusiastically.

The following days found me visiting neighborhoods with Hanh in every bit of spare time I could squeeze in, as he held meetings to explain the workings of a "social action committee" and then the mystery of the electoral process "American style" (with a gesture toward me to show the people what an American was). Hanh and I would be loaded down with the large ballot box, a simple wooden box with a slot cut in its hinged lid and a hasp fastener, and a supply of scratch pads and pencils. A declared candidate would take a sheet from the scratch pad, painstakingly draw his own idea of an appropriate symbol on it, and then hold the symbol up for all to see as he made his speech about why the people should elect him.

Poll clerks, usually elderly women who seemed to be the actual authorities in each neighborhood anyhow, would be selected by voice vote. They would pass out the "ballots," a sheet torn from a scratch pad, and pencils. People would mark the ballots as privately as they could in the crowd, hiding behind backs, squatting on the ground and bending over to screen their markings, or else ducking into nearby houses. Then all would line up and walk past the ballot box, each pushing his folded ballot through the slot on the lid while the sharp-eyed poll clerks watched. When all the residents had voted, the poll clerks would open the box and tally the ballots, as the whole neighborhood pressed in around them to watch. A great noise of cheers, laughs, and exclamations rose up when the electoral results were announced.

Not all my time was spent in helping military psywar and neighborhood social action. I needed to know much more about the history of Vietnam and the functioning of its government. Books and other written material on these subjects were scarce, although excellent books on Vietnam began to be available in Saigon the next year. Most of what I learned came to me orally through questioning knowledgeable Americans, Vietnamese, and Frenchmen. Increasingly, I was awed by the complexity of this small country in the southeast corner of the Asian mainland. Its people were amazingly resilient, with little sign of weariness after years of a war which was continuing unabated while delegates talked of peace in Geneva. What was their heritage?

Vietnamese scholars told me proudly that the Vietnamese, as a people, were five thousand years old. They spoke of the Vietnamese kingdom in southern China, which lasted for three thousand years until it was destroyed in 333 B.C. Other scholars said the people had come out of China, reaching present-day Vietnam at the end of the third century B.C. All agreed that there was a Chinese conquest of Vietnam in 111 B.C.

The next thousand years were marked by one rebellion after

another. In A.D. 938 the Vietnamese won their freedom in a war and defended it in subsequent wars against the Chinese, repelling one invasion by the Mongolian hordes of Kublai Khan in 1284. In the following century, the Vietnamese fought wars with the Chams and the Khmers, winning the rest of the territory that makes up modern Vietnam. Warfare continued through the centuries, both against Chinese invaders and between internal factions. French troops first appeared in 1858, taking the seaport of Tourane, and by 1862 were in such dominance that the Vietnamese ceded territory to France. Subsequent years saw many rebellions against the French, including a great nationalist uprising in 1945 just before the end of World War II (sponsored by the Japanese occupying forces); a brief spell of freedom marked by Communist reprisals against nationalists; and then the Franco-Vietminh war which had started on 19 December 1946 and was still going on.

Millions of Vietnamese were under the control of the Communists, whose political cadre had established a civil administration under the guns of their guerrilla forces. There were also many millions of Vietnamese under the rule of the French-sponsored nationalist government—the government that I was supposed to help when it became feasible. It was headed by Bao Dai, the chief of state, whom many people called "Emperor." He did not live in Vietnam. Instead, he stayed on the French Riviera, ruling his domain by radiograms and letters to his prime minister in Saigon and to his chief agent, Nguyen De. The prime minister was charged with running the government, which consisted of a number of ministries and bureaus in Saigon, with branch offices in Hanoi, and he had to listen not only to the wishes of Bao Dai (and Nguyen De), but also to the French High Command in Indochina. There were French officials in all the ministries and bureaus, many of them still performing executive duties although they were in the process of switching over to advisory roles.

Vietnam, like ancient Gaul, was divided in three parts, North, Central and South. Each of these regions had its own Vietnamese governor. Each region was further subdivided into provinces, with a province chief for each. Further, each province was subdivided into districts, with a French or Vietnamese district chief as its administrator. Throughout the country, French Union forces (including the Vietnamese Army) were waging war against the guerrilla Vietminh enemy. Often, local military commanders were the de facto bosses of government as they undertook measures and actions affecting the welfare and livelihoods of the population living in combat zones.

Below this governmental structure in the cities, the regions, the provinces, and the districts were the villages and the hamlets of the villages where the agrarian population lived. By custom, the emperor's rule ended at the village boundary. Although there were many twentieth-century forces at work to change the archaic customs (among them the Communist organization men who were setting up structures for authoritarian rule), there still existed a definite schism between the administrative apparatus of the central government and the traditional administrative apparatus of the rural villages. These villages were ruled by village councils, made up mostly of elders who had gained the respect of their neighbors for being wise and honest men. The village system might seem simplistic, but actually it was highly practical, able to undertake many complex tasks within the tradition-bound customs of thousands of years.

The Vietnamese nationalists, confronted by the changes being initiated by the Vietnamese Communists, made a belated move to change the structure of administration in January 1953, by holding elections for municipal and communal councils in the larger population centers controlled by the French forces. Although only about a million people voted out of a total population of about twenty-five million, these elections at least were a start toward self-government by the non-Communist Vietnamese majority. The elections had helped strengthen and polarize Vietnamese sentiments for a form of independence from France that would be different from that proposed by the Communists, whose performance had disillusioned so many patriots since 1946. Anti-Communist Vietnamese nationalism, which had been smoldering since the betrayals by the Communists nearly a decade before had led to the slaughter or imprisonment of a great many nationalists, caught fire again in these January 1953 elections. Most of the Vietnamese who were elected had devoted their oratory to the cause of independence for Vietnam.

Prime Minister Tam, who held these elections, eventually paid a price for them. He was a French citizen and Vietnamese nationalists deemed him too much of a French puppet (and too corrupt) to fit the Vietnamese ideal for which the nationalists were now openly yearning. Bao Dai, from his Riviera palace, dismissed Tam and asked his cousin, Prince Buu Loc, to become prime minister and to form a new government in January 1954. Buu Loc created what he called a "government of technicians." It was this government with which I was becoming acquainted. (I did not deal with the Ministry for Democratization, whose officials totally ignored reality in their dreams of creating a Shangri-la in Vietnam overnight.) Nearly all the ministers and bureau chiefs told me that they were simply "caretakers." Evidently something new and better in government was expected soon.

I managed to travel to each region of the country that June. During visits to the North, I renewed acquaintance with Vietnamese politicians in Hanoi and Haiphong whom I had met the previous summer. Mostly, they were members of the two oldest nationalist political parties, the Dai Viet and the VNQDD (the Vietnamese Kuomintang or Vietnam Quoc Dan Dang). None of them admitted party membership to me at that time, although some did later when I had come to know them better. Initially, I sorted out their affiliations by listening to gossip. These groups were alien to an American's idea of political parties, since they were clandestine, revolutionary organizations composed of three-man cells and run by a secret directory. Their tutelage in politics had come during the French colonial regime, a regime they were striving to get rid of to make Vietnam independent. Members risked both arrest by the French as subversives and murder by the rival Communists. Party discipline was necessarily strict. Considering the conspiratorial nature of these and other nationalist political parties, I couldn't help wondering if they would be able to function constructively in an open society, once Vietnam actually became independent.

In Central Vietnam, at Tourane, I took part in an abortive attempt to rescue four Americans captured by the Vietminh when they had sneaked away from the air base at noon to swim at an off-limits beach. The rescue attempt, by jeep and a foreign legion light tank, ended when an elderly Vietnamese woman we met on the road told of seeing the Americans, clad only in swim trunks and wincing as they walked barefoot over the rough ground, burst into tears as they were brought before the inhabitants of her village. The bearded legion sergeant commanding the tank spat on the ground, said that he wasn't going to risk his tank trying to rescue such softies, and took his tank back to Tourane. Without fire support, the rescue try had to be abandoned. (The Americans were among other prisoners turned over at war's end.)

In the South, I became acquainted with the sects, unaware that they were soon to involve me in deadly drama. Two of the sects, the Hoa Hao and the Cao Dai, were indigenous religions with a million or so adherents each and with their main centers in the agrarian provinces west of Saigon. The third sect, the Binh Xuyen, was a social organization numbering tens of thousands in the Saigon-Cholon metropolitan area, whose leaders had won control of the criminal underworld. I was struck by the medieval warlord image all three sects conveyed. Each had its own armed forces complete with generals and battalions, its own political parties, and definite territories which it dominated. Nearly all the sect forces were in the pay of the French Army as *supplétifs* (militia). The one exception was a dissident Cao Dai group of guerrillas under Trinh minh Thé, who held a territory near the Cambodian border; they fought both the French and the Communists. When I expressed interest in visiting them, French officers told me to have nothing to do with such "monsters."

My first guide in trips to the sect territories was every bit as colorful as the sect leaders we saw. He was Colonel Jean Leroy, leader of a Catholic guerrilla group called the Unités Mobiles de Défense des Chrétientés. Short, wiry, and intense, he apparently combined the most forceful characteristics of his French father and Vietnamese mother. Meeting him at his house in Saigon, I noticed the fortress look of the place with its barbed wire barriers, the sandbagged machine gun positions in the yard, and heavily armed troops at every vantage point. Leroy explained blithely that he had moved recently into Saigon, had liked the house, and had forcibly ejected the family that owned it. Now the owners were showing up at the house with lawyers and police to get it back—and Leroy was daring them to start a fight for the house if they had the guts to do so.

In the capital city itself, I bumped into one more piece of Vietnamese reality. I had heard stories from French and Vietnamese acquaintances that Bao Dai had run short of funds for his fun and games on the Riviera and had sold the position of chief of police for Saigon-Cholon to the boss of the underworld, "Bay" Vien (General Le van Vien), for forty-four million piastres (then about $1.25 million U.S. at the official rate). Bay Vien commanded the Binh Xuyen sect forces, levied a take on commercial traffic into and out of the city, and ran the city's gambling casinos, houses of prostitution, and opium trade. This sordid transaction was made possible by the final initialing on June 4, 1954, of the Franco-Vietnamese treaty giving Vietnam the independence from France that had been announced the year before. Legally, as the chief of state of an independent nation, Bao Dai could act as he pleased. The sell-out of the police to the boss gangster came close to killing off the infant country in the following months. I saw some of the first fruits of this deal in an incident I will long remember.

It happened one night when I was in my room at the BOQ attempting to read local French newspapers with the aid of a translator's dictionary. I heard the telephone ringing in the hall a few doors from my room. It kept on ringing and I finally got up and answered it. "Allo! Allo! Allo!" I shouted into the instrument in the manner worthy of the temperamental local telephone system. From the instrument gushed an excited American female voice, in accents of the Deep South, asking, "What are all these strange soldiers doing shooting around the house?" Baffled, I started asking questions. I learned that three American girls, secretaries at the American embassy, were living in a small house a few blocks away. At the moment, all of them were hiding under beds, from which position the telephoning was being done. In the background, I could hear a burst of submachine gun fire and then the boom of an explosion. The voice on the telephone said there seemed to be a battle going on in their yard and in the street in front of their house. "Y'all come over and help us. You hear?" I drove right over.

A company of troops in the green berets of the Binh Xuyen were in combat posture along the street and in the yard. The target of their bursts of submachine gun fire was a two-story house just behind the bungalow where the American girls lived. A hand grenade came sailing out of an upper window and landed in the street, causing a wild scramble for safety among the attackers. After seeing that the girls were safe and cautioning them to stay put behind the protection of the bungalow's walls, I sought out the Binh Xuyen commander. I finally translated the gist of his words. He was trying to arrest somebody inside the house. We must have been observed talking, for with that, a voice shouted out of the house that the people inside would only surrender to the French officer, not the Binh

The Manila Times

Luis Taruc, the Huk leader, giving a political lecture to his bodyguards in a central Luzon hideout, 1948.

Near Subic Bay, 1950: Philippine military leaders meet in schoolyard during an operation against the Huks. *Left to right:* General Calixto Duque; Secretary of Defense Ramon Magsaysay; General Mariano Castaneda, chief of staff; and General Pelagio Cruz of the Air Force.

Lansdale

Lansdale

Magsaysay in L-5 liaison aircraft, 1950, on one of his surprise visits to combat areas in the fight against the Huks.

Lecture during training of "Charlie" Company, 7th BCT, to prepare them to pose as Huks.

Ellis

Signal Corps, AFP

7th BCT troops resting during approach along gulley to mouth of Biak-na-Bato caves where Huks were holed up.

Manila, 1950: The author and Magsaysay in house in JUSMAG compound.

Ellis

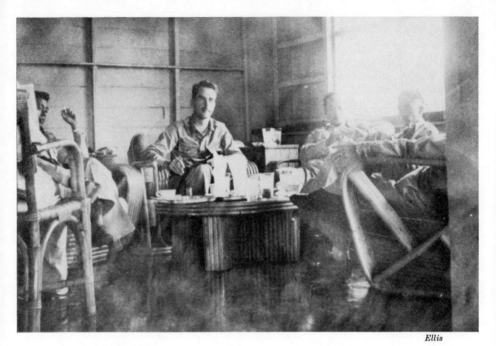

Ellis

Manila, 1950: Typical coffee klatsch at house in JUSMAG compound.

Lansdale and Magsaysay in central Luzon, January 1951.

Ellis

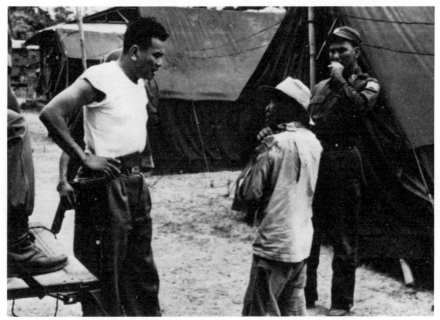

Lansdale

Ramon Magsaysay at field headquarters talking to a farmer wounded in a fight in a sugarcane field in February 1951.

Coffee klatsch in Manila, 1951: Philippine civilian and military officials meet with Colonel Wendell Fertig *(center)* who led guerrillas on Mindanao during World War II. Author, elbows on knees, sits between Fertig and Major Jose Crisol, chief of Civil Affairs Office.

Ellis

Lansdale

Ramon Magsaysay with his mother and father at the family farm in Castillejos, Zambales Province, 1951.

Kapatagan, Mindanao, 1951: A walk down the street of the almost completed first farm community of EDCOR; Magsaysay, with measuring rod, in lead. Author, to his right, is carrying on conversation with Colonel Mirasol, project director, to Magsaysay's left.

Signal Corps, AFP

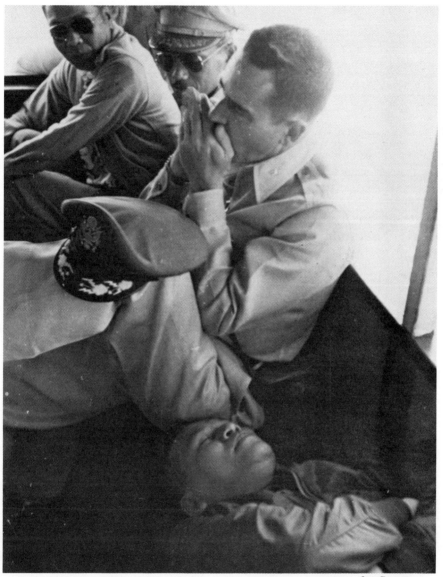

Jose Banzon

Harmonica lullaby by Lansdale, aboard a launch off the coast of Cagayan de Oro, Mindanao, March 1952. Defense Secretary Ramon Magsaysay is dozing in foreground; behind them are Anatolio Litonjua of Manila *Times* and Colonel Tirso Fajardo, commander of IV Military Area, Philippines.

J. P. Redick

First meeting with Trinh minh The at his guerrilla headquarters, Nui Ba Den, 1955. Le khac Hoai at right.

General Hinh makes Hoa Hao rebel Ba Cut a National Army colonel during the Diem-Hinh struggle.

Vietnamese Army

Vietnamese Army

"Operation Giai-Phong": Troops of National Army's 31st Division entering a Binh Dinh village. One result of this "national security action": young people returned from the hills.

"Operation Giai-Phong": Colonel Kim starts distribution of 2,000 tons of rice to a hungry population.

Vietnamese Army

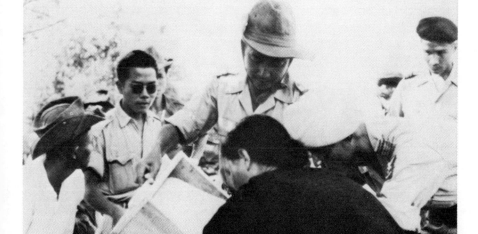

Vietnamese Army

April 1955: Decision in Saigon-Cholon.

Tran Hung Dao Boulevard, Cholon, April 1955: Government troops moving to secure area of fire, after Binh Xuyen forced firemen away.

Vietnamese Army

Operation Brotherhood International

Cesar Climaco, director of "Operation Brotherhood" in Saigon, organizing a boys' brigade to clean up part of the city destroyed during the Binh Xuyen fighting. Note presence of Ngo dinh Diem in upper tier.

Saigon, fall 1954: Ambitious men meet with Prime Minister Diem to give him proposals which would let them divide the rule among themselves, elevating Diem to a figurehead. General Nguyen van Hinh of the Vietnamese Army on left; Diem in white suit facing camera. On right is General Le van "Bay" Vien of the Binh Xuyen. With back to camera is Bao Dai's friend Nguyen van Xuan, a brigadier general in the French Army and a former president of French Cochin China. Diem broke off the talks shortly after this photo was taken.

Lansdale from Diem

Operation Brotherhood International

"Operation Brotherhood" Clinic, Camau, during "Operation Liberty."

Prime Minister Diem being greeted by the people of Qui Nhon just after the Communists had left the port city in 1955.

Lansdale from Diem

Lansdale from Diem

Saigon, 1955: General J. W. "Iron Mike" O'Daniel lays a wreath at tomb of Unknown Soldier in square in front of Saigon's City Hall at the opening of the first national convention of the Vietnamese Veterans Legion. Behind and left of O'Daniel is Prime Minister Diem, who laid the first wreath.

At 1955 ceremony in Saigon. *Front row, left to right:* General "Iron Mike" O'Daniel, U.S. Ambassador Frederick Reinhardt, Prime Minister Diem. Author is removing cap.

François Sully—Black Star

Lansdale from Diem

Saigon, 1956: President Diem, Mme. Nhu, and Prime Minister U Nu of Burma. Noting U Nu's Burmese garb, Diem wore the traditional mandarin clothing of Vietnamese high officials.

Lansdale from Diem

Weekend at beach cottage near Long Hai, Vietnam, 1956: Diem *(center)* talking with Mme. Nhu.

President Diem in visit to mountain people, Ban Me Thuot, 1956.

Lansdale from Diem

Official U.S. Air Force Photograph

Major General Lansdale at retirement (1963).

Xuyen! I looked around. Not a French officer in sight. Evidently I must be lucky Pierre. After laborious talk in my atrocious French, arrangements finally were made. The Binh Xuyen withdrew and let me take custody of the prisoners, a man, his wife, and two children. From their hurried pleas, I made out the words "military" and "army," so I put them in my car and took them to General Hinh's house in Cholon. They were clearly glad to arrive safely at the Vietnamese Army commander's home.

It was then that I learned the cause of the wild scene at the girls' bungalow. Having come into possession of the police in the capital city, the Binh Xuyen were setting out to rid the police force of all those members who had been too effective in fighting crime. The good cops were being cleaned out. The man I had rescued was a Sûreté detective. General Hinh and the Vietnamese Army gave safe haven to him and to scores of other experienced detectives and policemen by establishing a new intelligence and investigative organization, the Military Security Service or MSS, and by enrolling these highly qualified refugees in it. The highest-ranking Vietnamese in the Sûreté under the French, Mai huu Xuan, was one of the refugees and was made a general in the Vietnamese Army and put in command of MSS.

What was most memorable about this event was not the formation of a new military organization but the way a man had defended his home and family by using hand grenades. I tucked it away in my mind as something useful to know. A man could stay safe behind walls and keep a company of troops at bay with hand grenades tossed through windows or doors. From then on, I kept a supply of grenades in my own living quarters.

As the end of my first month in Vietnam was drawing to a close, I sat up one night to evaluate my situation. I had been sent to help the Vietnamese help themselves, at such time as this became possible. Clearly, though, the French living in Vietnam seemed not to have heard of the granting of independence. Their possessive attitude toward the Vietnamese remained as strong as ever, evoking strong French emotional responses whenever an American came near one of "their" Vietnamese. The French High Command, still directing a war against the Vietminh, continued in tight control of Vietnamese nationalist military forces. There still were French officials throughout the Vietnamese government, giving advice in tones that sounded strangely like orders. A Swiss journalist said, "The French are like a man giving up his mistress. He knows the affair is over, but he hates it when he sees his mistress ride by in the big car of a rich man she has just met." I gathered that we Americans were the rich newcomers.

There were many millions of Vietnamese who were non-Communist and who supposedly had reached the point of starting to govern themselves in some way other than the Leninist system. Their fate was one of the major stakes being considered at the international conference at Geneva, and I expected that they would be given a chance for *tu do,* or liberty. In their family life, the Vietnamese respected the Confucian ethic. Yet in the nation, the Confucian ethic seemed to be absent—as witness the sale of the police to the gangsters in the capital city. How could the free Vietnamese ever govern themselves effectively when their top leadership flouted the ruling personal ethics of the citizenry, when the subtle subversion of the Communists was loose in the land backed by military force, when paternalistic French coddling kept the Vietnamese from learning by doing on their own, when nationalist political parties insisted upon retaining their clandestine character, and when there were so many feudal satrapies dividing up the people and the countryside?

I suddenly understood why somebody had enlarged the travel orders sending me to Vietnam with that tag line of "God bless you."

N O T E S

TARUC. Luis Taruc, the Huk Supremo, surrendered to the government in large part due to the moral suasion in negotiations carried on for over seven years by a friend who maintained contact with the Philippine president. (I had helped establish this relationship originally with President Roxas and it continued with his successors.) The actual surrender was made at the last moment by chance through another man, Benigno Aquino, a young reporter with the *Manila Times*, who later went into politics, becoming governor of Tarlac Province and then a senator.

DIEN BIEN PHU. I was told a strange sequel to the battle of Dien Bien Phu in talking with French survivors after their release from Vietminh prison camps. The Vietminh selected French prisoners to return to this battleground for a reenactment of the fight in front of cameras, so that official movies could be made of the battle. When the actors arrived, the battleground was under water! At the time of the battle, Communist General Giap had ordered new channels cut for the streams in the surrounding mountains, to flood the lowlands. When the rains came, the French fortifications might as well have been at the bottom of a bathtub with the taps flowing fully. Thousands of lives would have been saved if the Vietminh had only awaited the coming of the rain. Evidently the political need for a quick victory made the Vietminh forgo waiting for a victory through hydraulics.

VIETNAMESE. I follow the practice of most Vietnamese and use a person's given name when speaking of him, even Ngo dinh Diem. Ask a Vietnamese about President Ngo and he would probably be baffled, although he would recognize President Diem's name. Yet Ngo was the family name. Dinh was the name designated by the family for the generation in which he was born. In social writing Vietnamese hyphenate their names, usually with the initial letter of the middle name in lower case. For ease in reading in English, I have dropped the hyphen from names, along with the Portuguese diacritical marks used by Vietnamese as pronunciation guides.

CANDY. Social action committee elections in the Saigon-Cholon neighborhoods acquired a festive air when Hanh and I invited Pat Byrne and Anita Lauve to watch several of them with us. The girls were foreign service officers in the political section of the American embassy. Noticing the great number of children who would gather to watch the proceedings, the girls brought large jars of hard candy and passed them around among the youngsters. The elders, not to be outdone in hospitality, invited us into their homes for tea.

REGIONALISM. The three stripes on the Republic of Vietnam's flag represent the country's three regions, the North, the Center, and the South. My Vietnamese friends insist that the people in each region have markedly differing characteristics. They see the northerners as essentially hard-working and practical, the central Vietnamese as intellectual and aristocratic, and the southerners as fun-loving and easygoing. Significantly, most of the modern leaders have come from Central Vietnam, among them Ngo dinh Diem, Ho chi Minh, and Nguyen van Thieu.

SECT FORCES. The irregular armies of the sects, as well as most of the troops who fought against the French with the Communist Vietminh, were started on their military life by the Kempeitai—the political police of the Japanese Army. After the fall of France to Germany in 1940, the Japanese had moved into Vietnam under an alliance with the Vichy government and used the country as a base for operations against Singapore and other parts of Southeast Asia. When the tide of World War II began to turn against Germany and Japan, the Kempeitai selected a number of promising young Vietnamese and trained them secretly in Cambodia and Laos for guerrilla warfare. They became a secret native force under Japanese direction and surfaced on March 9, 1945, when the Japanese overthrew the Vichy colonial regime in Indochina. When the French returned after the war and announced on March 4, 1946, that they were assuming control again, the sect forces joined other Vietnamese in the Vietminh ranks to fight the French. The Cao Dai were in early Vietminh Regiments 7 and 8, whose political officer was Tran quoc Buu (later the noted and respected head of the Vietnamese Federation of Labor, well known to American AFL-CIO officials). However, the sect forces had violent quarrels with the Communists and soon left the Vietminh ranks. They continued to fight the French, but were gradually won over to the French side in a pacification campaign that skillfully used a combination of force and subsidy rewards.

HOA HAO. The reformed Buddhist sect known as the Hoa Hao (pronounced "wah how") was founded in 1939 and takes its name from the village where its founder Huynh phu So was born in 1919. Adherents refer to him reverently as "the Master" and speak of his demise in 1947 as his "disappearance"—a secret act by the Communists who were allied with the Hoa Hao at the time against the French but added the Hoa Hao leader's name to their purge list of potential rivals, lured him to a meeting, and murdered him. However the act is described, it made the Hoa Hao grimly anti-Communist from then on. In my 1954 visits to their region along the Mekong and Bassac rivers, the Hoa Hao were split into two main political parties and had two separate armies under rival Generals Tran van Soai and Nguyen giac Ngo, and three smaller independent military groups. The most energetic of the latter were guerrillas led by Le quang Vinh, nicknamed "Ba Cut" for a finger joint he cut off dramatically in a pledge to fight for Vietnamese independence. The first stories I heard about him were mostly concerned with the temporary marriages he arranged between his troops and village girls and a novel torture method he used for forcing farmers to disclose their hidden valuables—a steel nail pushed slowly into the victim's ear.

CAO DAI. The eclectic nature of the Cao Dai is shown by the sect's pantheon of saints at their Holy See in Tay Ninh—Jesus Christ, Buddha, Lao-tse, Confucius, Sun Yat-sen, Trang Trinh, and Victor Hugo. Founded in South Vietnam in 1919, the religion was organized as a formal church in 1925 by influential government contractors and civil servants (reputedly after an all-night session of ouija board reading and table rapping). In August 1941 Cao Dai leaders attempted to take advantage of the weak colonial rule of the Vichy French and declared an independent state. French troops occupied the Holy See and exiled the Cao Dai leaders to Madagascar, where they remained until 1946. In 1943 the Japanese secretly organized a Cao Dai army of 3,000 men, training some leaders as *Aspirants* or third lieutenants (lower than the lowest U.S. rank of second lieutenant), sergeants, and corporals— including men whom the French made generals four years later. This Cao Dai force helped the Japanese overthrow the Vichy colonial rule in March 1945, fought in the Vietminh against the French who returned in 1946, but broke with the Communists and joined the French against them in January 1947. The chief of staff of the Cao Dai Army, Trinh minh Thé, split away in 1951 with 1,500 men and formed his own guerrilla army, the Quoc-Gia-Lien-Minh (National Union) which fought both the French and the Communists.

BINH XUYEN. This nonreligious sect originated about 1940 as a social club or gang of day laborers and charcoal makers, taking its name from their home neighborhood in the southern outskirts of the city of Cholon and soon spreading into other parts of the city. The Japanese Kempeitai secretly organized, trained, and armed them as a military force, using them in the 1945 coup against the Vichy colonial regime. The Binh Xuyen joined the early Vietminh to fight against the returning French in 1946, but soon broke with the Communists, mostly because of quarrels over the powers of Le van "Bay" Vien, the Binh Xuyen chief, and Nguyen Binh, the Communist comander for South Vietnam. Ironically, both men were on the secret purge list of Ho chi Minh, who personally intervened to patch up their quarrel temporarily. Binh was liquidated shortly afterward, but Bay Vien escaped by taking his forces over to the French side. The French used the Binh Xuyen as a militia to help guard the capital city and its environs, as well as in operations to open the main highway from Saigon to the sea at Cap St. Jacques. As the chief of the native armed force in the nation's capital, Bay Vien developed rapidly into the combination role of the city's Boss Tweed and Al Capone.

★ ★

CHAPTER TEN

LAST HALF OF 1954

THE COURSE of Vietnam's history got a nudge and a shove toward new directions that summer of 1954. The nudge came from the appointment of a new prime minister, Ngo dinh Diem; he arrived in Saigon from France on June 25. The shove came from the conclusion of the international conference in Geneva, where the warring French and Vietminh signed an agreement on July 20 to end their hostilities in Vietnam and where, the next day, the representatives of the large and small nations present took part in a "Final Declaration" about restoring peace in Indochina.

I had little inkling that the new prime minister was going to make history or that we would become friends. As far as I can recall, I first heard his name when Ambassador Heath told me that Bao Dai was appointing Diem to form a new government. Heath had asked me what I knew about him. I knew nothing and offered to get what information I could from the Vietnamese. While waiting for Washington to send a biography of Diem, I visited my Vietnamese acquaintances and plied them with questions about the next prime minister.

To my surprise, I discovered that Diem was exceptionally well known by the Vietnamese and that people either admired him or disliked him. Few were neutral. All agreed that he was notably honest and had a strong character. Most of those with whom I talked felt that Diem was a great patriot, probably the best of all the nationalists still living, with an outstanding record as a wise and able administrator; some even asserted that he was far better known among his countrymen than was Ho chi Minh. (How did I miss learning this before? "You never asked," I was told.) Several who had good political connections tipped me off that the French government itself, not merely the French colonial office, had recommended Diem's appointment to Bao Dai, calling him the only remaining Vietnamese nationalist with sufficient status to rally all the non-Communist Vietnamese. A minority view held that Diem was mulishly stubborn, too aloof to be a good political leader, and should have obeyed his boyhood wish to become a monk. One man said he was an idiot, another that he was a coward.

The biographical sketch, when it arrived, supplied more concrete data. Diem was born in Hué on January 3, 1901, growing up in imperial court circles where his father was a mandarin or high official of the court. He graduated a year ahead of his contemporaries from the school for administrators and was governing a district at twenty-one (by the Vietnamese tally of age, which counts a newborn baby as one year old). He became governor, successively, of two provinces, and in 1933 Bao Dai made him minister of the interior—where he soon fell out with French colonial authorities who refused to consider his proposals for more Vietnamese autonomy. Diem quit the government and started working in his own way to make Vietnam independent.

Diem and his family were Catholics, deeply opposed to the ideology of the Communists. His older brother Khoi was killed by the Vietminh in 1945. Diem himself was kidnapped by the Vietminh, held prisoner in the mountains for a time, and eventually was invited by Ho chi Minh to join his government, which Diem refused. In 1950 Diem left Vietnam and stayed away (in Japan, then for several months in New Jersey with the Maryknoll Fathers at Lakewood, and then in Europe) until Bao Dai asked him on June 16, 1954, to become prime minister.

My curiosity whetted, I headed out to Saigon's airport on the morning of his arrival, planning to be among the diplomatic and official welcomers. Driving out the Rue Général de Gaulle, the main street to the airport, I was amazed by the crowds jamming both sides of the road. The population of this wartime capital usually was too blasé even to glance at dignitaries in limousines or at the martial passing of troop convoys and tanks. Yet here they were by the thousands, obviously waiting to see just one man. It was unexpected, because there had been little effort to get the people out on the street for a welcome other than the simple announcement that Diem was arriving that morning. On impulse, I turned off the street, parked my car, and joined the massed crowd along the curbstones.

Whole families were clustered together, children riding on backs or shoulders, clutching parental hands, or packed on the curbs. The carts with apparatus for crushing sugarcane were doing a land-office business selling their sweet juice. The people were animated, happy, in holiday spirits. An hour went by. Then another. And still another. The people were talking knowledgeably about the air schedule of flights from Paris. The flights were sometimes late. This had happened before. They stayed on in the hot sunshine of the late morning, still expectant, still happy.

In the distance we could hear a wail of sirens and the pop-popping of motorcycles. As the sounds grew louder, the crowds pushed forward, the better to see. Suddenly, motorcycles in a police phalanx came roaring by. Whizzing past the crowd and hugging a position just behind the motorcycles came a big black limousine, Vietnamese flags fluttering from holders on its fenders, windows closed, passengers invisible in its deep interior. Whoosh! Limousine and entourage were past. The crowds of people looked at one another in disappointment. Was that *him*? Did you see *him*? He didn't even see *us*! They broke up in a disgruntled mood. There were arguments. The "let down" feeling was something tangible, obvious. I got in my car and drove to the embassy.

There, I told Ambassador Heath of the crowd's reaction to the hurried, guarded entry of Ngo dinh Diem to the city. Whoever was advising him had clearly misread the mood of the people. Diem should have ridden into the city slowly in an open car, or even have walked, to provide a focus for the affection that the people so obviously had been waiting to bestow on him. Perhaps his advisers were afraid of the people, to rush him so into town behind a police escort. I wondered aloud what further errors of judgment Diem's advisers might be making. Then the thought occurred to me that perhaps he needed help, since he had been away from Vietnam and the Vietnamese people for years. I voiced this to Ambassador Heath, along with the suggestion that I note down some thoughts to give to Diem for his consideration. Heath told me to go ahead.

I spent the rest of that day and that night writing the paper. In it, I tried to distill what I had learned of the expectations of the people, in terms of how they were hoping he would act, and the main problems as they saw them. I followed this with a series of suggested actions which a leader could take toward solutions of the problems, step by step. One proposal was the integration of all military and paramilitary forces of Vietnamese non-Communists into a single national armed force, an action that should be started at once but be phased over weeks as political and economic factors were worked out. There were similar suggestions about bringing together the nationalist political groups in a reassuring manner, so that the more clandestine partisans would join in open participation in the body politic; suggestions about making the government more responsive to the people, about agrarian economics and reforms, about

encouraging the institution of public forums around the countryside, about veteran care, about public health, about making
the government more effective in the provinces, and about the
personal behavior of a prime minister who could generate
willing support by the majority toward accomplishing these
ends.

The sun was up by the time I finished the paper the next
morning. I showed it to Ambassador Heath and General O'Daniel. They felt that while its contents were well within the
limits of U.S. policy, our government could never think of
giving such a paper officially to a brand new prime minister.
However, if I made certain that Ngo dinh Diem understood
that the paper was a *personal* one, without official backing
from the U.S. government, why, I could go right ahead and
hand it to him. Because I wasn't sure how well Diem understood English, I got Heath's permission to take George Hellyer,
the U.S. Public Affairs officer who spoke fluent French, along
with me.

The small governmental palace where the prime minister
held office (the French occupied the main governmental
palace) was in a disorganized state when Hellyer and I arrived.
There were no guards to challenge our entry, no civil servants
to receive visitors. A few harried-looking people wandered
about a hallway from one office to another, clutching papers
and office supplies in their hands as though looking for a place
to sit down and start work. One of them told us that the
prime minister was upstairs. Upstairs we went. The hallway
there was empty. Noticing that one office door was ajar, we
pushed it open and stuck our heads in. It was a small office,
almost filled by a table piled high with papers. Seated at the
table was a middle-aged Vietnamese, who looked up at us from
a document he was reading as we entered. At first glance, he
wasn't very impressive. A rolypoly figure dressed in a white
sharkskin double-breasted suit, his feet were not quite touching the floor. He must be very short-legged, I thought. Intensely

black hair, combed strictly, topped a broad face in which the most prominent feature was high rounds of flesh over the cheekbones, as if they had been pushed up there by constant smiling. I met his eyes, lively and friendly, and suddenly he was a different person to me, the alert and eldest of the seven dwarfs deciding what to do about Snow White. Excusing the intrusion, Hellyer explained that we were trying to find Prime Minister Diem.

"I am Ngo dinh Diem," the man told us. We introduced ourselves hastily, and related the story of my watching his arrival from the airport and then writing a strictly personal, unofficial paper with some suggestions for his consideration. Diem asked us to sit down, took the paper I held out to him, donned glasses, and started to read. After a moment, he reached into a pocket and pulled out a small French-English dictionary of the type useful for shopping or in asking when trains are due—not in translating phrases concerning the political, social, psychological, economic, and military lifestream of a nation. I hastily suggested that Hellyer might translate the document for him. At Diem's agreement, Hellyer took my carbon copy, looked at it, moved it out to arm's length, and muttered, "Dammit, I can't read it without my glasses—and I don't have them with me!" Diem laughed, took off his own glasses, and gave them to Hellyer. Hellyer, with the borrowed glasses, was able to perform superbly as a translator. Diem listened intently, asked some searching questions, thanked me for my thoughtfulness, folded up the paper, and put it in his pocket.

Thus it was that I became acquainted with Ngo dinh Diem. We saw each other more and more frequently in the weeks and months that followed until we fell into the habit of meeting nearly every day. Our association gradually developed into a friendship of considerable depth, trust, and candor.

After Diem and I came to know each other a little better, I was invited now and then to share a family meal with him. A bachelor, Diem enjoyed such moments. Although he sat at the head of the table, as befitted his position as prime minister, mealtime was strictly family style. His older brother, Bishop Thuc, usually had the final, positive word on any subject under discussion. Thuc and Diem were both trenchermen when it came to eating, but Thuc usually finished first and would hold forth while Diem was still eating. Diem's younger brothers, Nhu and Luyen, with their wives, would add a pointed remark now and then, but spoke far less than Thuc or Diem. Nhu, who was looked upon as the intellectual in the family, would tend to expound briefly on his theory of why some current event had happened. Luyen, who was the family diplomat, would usually add some comment to soften the blunter remarks of his elder brothers. Mme. Nhu would speak right up, along with the men, to give her opinion, but Mme. Luyen was far more reserved, usually responding only to remarks addressed to her.

Other than at these infrequent family meals, I seldom saw Diem's brothers. I never met the youngest, Can, who lived with Diem's mother in Hué. Luyen and his wife soon went off to Europe; he later became ambassador to the Court of St. James's in London. Now and then, Thuc or Nhu would be with Diem when I arrived for a meeting with him, but they would excuse themselves after we exchanged greetings. I saw Nhu's children more often, since they had the run of the palace, and I often stopped for a brief game of cowboys and Indians with them. Once, when I had tumbled dramatically to the floor under their pointed finger "guns," there were gasps behind me. I looked up to see a group of diplomats arriving for a protocol call. They were staring at me deadpan, not a smile among them. The children and I thought the moment hilarious.

Several days after my first meeting with Ngo dinh Diem, a group of perhaps fifty U.S. military men arrived in Saigon and reported for duty at MAAG. Their arrival was in anticipation of a more active role by Americans in the training of the Vietnamese armed forces, an expectation based upon the recent final initialing in Paris of the treaty providing independence for Vietnam. Twelve of the new arrivals had been assigned as my "team." Soldiers, sailors, and marines, they had been selected for me by personnel officers in Washington who must have had a Korean-style conflict in mind and disregarded my own written list of requirements. They were an ideal crew for guerrilla combat, for blowing up things, for jumps behind enemy lines, and for sensitive intelligence work against Communist infiltrators, saboteurs, and terrorists. But none had an inkling of psywar, the one activity in which I already was helping the Vietnamese Army, nor did they know anything about military civic action as practiced in the Philippines or the subjects which I had outlined to the new prime minister as worth doing and with which we might be asked to assist.

The arrival of this team caused me to reflect wryly on the different values placed by our side and by the Communists on the unconventional aspects of revolutionary conflict. Staff officers who were steeped in the conventions of Western life had picked these individuals for me, evidently in ignorance of the actuality of a Communist "people's war" such as the Vietminh waged. On the other side, the best Vietminh teams were composed of personnel trained for political-military action in an isolated school, where their final examination was conducted personally, individual by individual, by Ho chi Minh himself— similar to what Mao Tse-tung had done in China. This personal involvement in turning out cold war professionals would be an alien concept to any of the Western leaders I know, none of whom had any real familiarity with the daily actions on cold war battlegrounds. After all, the presidents and premiers on our side had arrived on top by a different route than Communist leaders, who had clawed their way up through the harsh realities of revolutions. In this respect the Communists had the edge over us. Their leaders asked their field lieutenants to do tasks which they themselves had performed.

I still had no office, but I had been assigned a small bungalow on Rue Miche near the heart of town the week before. Gathering my team of newcomers at the bungalow, I described the situation to them. They were to be trainers in counterguerrilla warfare, but the French had yet to give permission for U.S. training of the Vietnamese in subjects known by the team. They would have to be patient and wait, as would the other Americans brought in to provide training. Only three of them responded when I asked for volunteers to help me assist the Vietnamese in military psywar. I assigned the others the tasks of finding a house or two in crowded Saigon where they could be billeted as a group, as well as means of transportation and similar necessities. Two could move in with me at the bungalow, which also would have to serve as our office for the time being. It then being lunch-time, I shared what food I had with them—a meal that all of them insisted later was the poorest they ever had. (I had stocked the bungalow with coffee, a quarter wheel of Swiss cheese, and some bottles of Algerian table wine, supplementing this with long loaves of French bread from the bakery across the street—an easy-to-prepare daily menu for a man living alone, as I had been.) It wasn't too surprising that one of the first acts of my new team was to find a cook for me.

Two of the newcomers were fluent in French, and I tagged them for my housemates. Navy Lieutenant Joseph Redick was an expert in countersubversion and small arms who had studied at the Sorbonne after World War II. Soft-spoken, professorial, and the deadliest shot on the team, he soon became my almost constant companion as an interpreter. Army Major Lucien Conein had served with the foreign legion until the fall of France in 1940, later joining the American OSS for work with the French Resistance; and near the end of World War II he had jumped into Vietnam to help guerrillas fighting the Japanese. A bull-voiced paratrooper, he taught me much about the 1944-1945 history of Vietnam, lessons which I had to pick out carefully from among sentences laden with some of the most colorful cussing I've ever heard and delivered in a powerful voice.

The Franco-Vietminh War was brought to an end at Geneva in July, after eight years of conflict and the loss of some 400,000 lives. When copies of the Geneva agreements and declarations arrived in Saigon, I borrowed a set for careful study. The Geneva conference had settled some problems but raised some others which would have to be dealt with in the future. As one of those who would be living on the scene where these future problems would exist, I felt that I needed to understand them thoroughly if I was to be of help.

The main Geneva agreement was not only concerned with a cease-fire. It also gave details on the phased disengagement of the French Union and the Vietminh forces. Vietnam was to be cut in two by a military demarcation line at the 17th Parallel, with the Vietminh to be north of the line and the French Union forces to be south of the line at the end of three hundred days. A timetable specified the withdrawals from designated areas. For example, Hanoi was to be cleared of French Union troops in eighty days, just as Vietminh troops were to vacate two areas in the South in the same period. Other transfers were noted for accomplishment by the end of one, two, and three hundred days.

The military demarcation line at the 17th Parallel was an act of traumatic surgery reminiscent of the division of Korea. It placed the major industries and mineral resources (anthracite coal, iron, and bauxite) of Vietnam under the dominance of Vietminh guns in the North and the major food production of Vietnam under the dominance of French Union guns in the South. In the North some thirteen million people lived in twenty-two provinces covering 62,000 square miles. In the South about twelve million people lived in thirty-nine provinces covering 65,000 square miles.

The twenty-five million people of Vietnam—who were the basic prize sought by both sides in the eight-year war—had no say in naming representatives at Geneva. Both the main contenders, the French and the Vietminh, actually had been playing the role of predators in Vietnam, arbitarily attempting to impose alien ways on subjects who were theirs by *force majeure.* To the Vietnamese people, the totalitarianism of Lenin was as foreign and as unpalatable as the colonialism of Paris. Only a minority of Vietnamese willingly accepted either of these foreign impositions, and they did so mainly for the age-old reasons of personal benefit or survival.

A separate declaration was made at Geneva that kept the people of Vietnam in mind. It added a further period to the timetable. The representatives of Cambodia, the Democratic Republic of Vietnam, France, Laos, the People's Republic of China, the State of Vietnam, the United Kingdom, and the United States of America took part. This declaration "recognized" the military demarcation line as temporary and stated that the people of Vietnam would choose their own future in general elections to be held in July 1956. This future was described as one in which the Vietnamese people were "to enjoy the fundamental freedoms, guaranteed by democratic institutions established as a result of free general elections by secret ballot." Prior to these elections, Vietnamese citizens could decide in which zone they preferred to live, the Communist zone or the Bao Dai-French zone.

The semantics of this declaration varied widely among the participants at Geneva. The Communists who subscribed to it had far different definitions of "freedoms," "democratic institutions," and "free general elections" from the definitions given these words in a free society. Even while the declaration was being written in Geneva, the "liquidation" of political opponents by the Communists continued in Vietnam, apparently as an activity which the Communists felt was nonnegotiable. These murders committed by Communist authority in Vietnam, numbering many thousands by the time of the Geneva Conference and many more thousands since then, have been ugly facts of life which the people of Vietnam have had to look upon at firsthand and have had to consider when interpreting the words of any promises given them.

After studying the Geneva documents, I concluded that a number of us in Vietnam had been sentenced to hard labor for the next two years. There were masses of people living in North Vietnam who would want to take advantage of the Geneva-given chance to move out before the Communists took over. They would not only need help in making the move, but ideally ought to be provided with a way of making a fresh start in the free South. Long stays in refugee camps would be as demoralizing and vitiating to these Vietnamese as such stays had been to refugees in Europe and the Middle East. If Vietnam actually was becoming independent from France, it was going to need the vigorous participation of every citizen to make a success of the non-Communist part of the new nation before the proposed plebiscite was held in 1956. Not only that, but who would want to forsake his family home for a long journey to a new existence in a camp? I saw that part of the hard labor ahead would have to include providing for the care and transportation of a great mass of migrants and then finding the means for farmers to start new farms, fishermen to move into new fishing grounds, artisans to locate new industrial employment. It would be a gigantic undertaking.

As though the refugee problem weren't difficult enough all by itself, another major question was posed by the Geneva agreement. Vietminh forces would be quitting areas in the South that they had dominated and ruled with a political apparatus. After the Vietminh authority quit an area, who would move in as a successor? The Vietnamese government didn't have enough experienced or trained public servants to fill this need in addition to taking over from French authorities elsewhere. Yet I suspected that Diem and other Vietnamese nationalists in the government would be strongly opposed to turning to the French for help in manning provincial organizations for administration, security, and public services: in Vietnamese eyes, this would be visible evidence that South Vietnam was still a French colony, not an independent country. Americans were out of consideration. The only large pool of manpower which was organized, disciplined, and presumably available to the government was the Vietnamese Army. It still was under French control, however, and was familiar with fighting enemy guerrillas with fair-sized units and artillery; it had no experience of moving into a territory to help set up government, perform public works, and provide police protection for the inhabitants. If the Vietnamese Army was to be used for so different a mission, it had a lot of habits to change and new skills to learn. Again, I foresaw that some of us would have to help with this task.

I talked these views over with Ambassador Heath and General O'Daniel, adding a suggestion that the U.S. military men at MAAG, who were still standing by awaiting a French agreement to help train the Vietnamese, had managerial skills worth putting to work in helping to plan the movement of refugees. The move would be similar, in some respects, to a massive transporting of troops. Initially, my ideas seemed startling, because government and relief agency officials were indeed thinking in terms of putting the thousands of refugees into camps similar to those set up after the recent exodus of Arabs from Palestine. I felt that plans should be made for moving and settling at least a million refugees, perhaps even two million. Also, I noted that the Vietnamese government was treating the problem as merely one more item on the long agenda of cabinet meetings. Prime Minister Diem should be persuaded to create a high-calibre refugee commission, with executive powers, to deal with this problem full time.

Messages flowed between the embassy and Washington on this subject over the next few days. Ambassador Heath and I talked to Diem, who was reluctant to grant so much authority to a separate refugee commission. I argued that he himself would hold the final executive power, since he would both appoint and relieve the commissioners, as well as approve or disapprove all program proposals. Finally, I asked him point-blank if he thought it prudent to force a million or so Vietnamese to remain under Communist control when they wanted to move out, just because of travel difficulties and poor prospects at journey's end. If this happened, they would be captive to the Communist will when the 1956 plebiscite was held. At this point, Diem gave in. He created a Refugee Commission immediately. Shortly afterward, Washington agreed that the U.S. would assist in the movement of the Vietnamese refugees from the North to the South, for humanitarian reasons.

Civilian and military teams of Americans went to work helping the Vietnamese Refugee Commission. Embarkation and reception camps were set up. Surveys were made of available public lands and resources for the final settlement of refugees in new homes. The U.S. Navy formed a task force of sea transports for the refugee move south. The French Air Force established an airlift. Voluntary agencies of a number of countries sent in supplies and personnel to care for the refugees. It became an epic migration. By the time it was over, about 900,000 Vietnamese had moved from North to South and had been settled adequately in new homes. (In the same period, about 90,000 moved from the South to the North, with most of them transported in Liberty ships under the Polish flag; the ships had been part of American lend-lease aid to the Soviets in World War II. The unkempt, rusty appearance of these ships undoubtedly frightened some Communist refugees out of making the voyage.)

As closely as I could estimate from later information about conditions in the North, perhaps another 400,000 people had made family decisions to move south but were intimidated from emigrating by local Communist authorities and by Vietminh troops. These troops stopped road and train traffic in some areas and closed off beaches to refugees who hoped to flee south by small boat. For months after the Geneva-designated period had ended, refugees emerged from the North, walking over remote jungle and mountain trails or using small boats. Over 100,000 additional refugees trickled south on their own.

I had split my small team in two. One half, under Major Conein, engaged in refugee work in the North. The other half stayed with me to help with other endeavors. I had created considerable interest and talk with my views about ways in which the Saigon government might fill the vacuum left by the Vietminh's political and administrative departure from various areas in the South. The subject stayed in the discussion stage, however, and no substantive action was taken. I did my best to learn what was happening in those areas and to get some preliminary planning done against the time when the decision was made to take action. I found out that a skeletal organization of political cadres was staying behind on a clandestine basis after the open withdrawal of the Vietminh. Further, huge quantities of weapons, ammunition, mines, grenades, and other materiel were being buried secretly by the Vietminh before they withdrew. The Communist forces didn't say goodbye when they departed but told the people "We'll see you again soon." This information from the countryside in the South hardly made happy news.

A touch of Philippine sunshine relieved what for me was a gloomy Vietnamese scene of people torn en masse from their homes, of Communists evidently stockpiling future battle-grounds for a continuation of their struggle, of the fractionalized nationalist body politic with its propensity for partisan secrecy, and of the heavy-handed presence of French colonialism continuing despite the avowed independence of Vietnam. The sunshine came in the form of a remarkable group of Filipino volunteers who made up the first contingents of an endeavor called Operation Brotherhood. This happy and hard-working crew had only one aim. They wanted to ease the suffering of their fellow Asians.

I was present when Operation Brotherhood was born. My ebullient Filipino friend, Oscar Arellano, made a duty visit to Saigon as vice-president for Asia of the International Jaycees (Junior Chambers of Commerce) and invited me to join him for dinner with leaders of the Vietnamese Jaycees. Arellano, balloon-shaped, energetic, an architect by profession, had participated in my Manila coffee klatsches and had organized one of the volunteer groups for the free election campaign of 1953 in the Philippines. The Vietnamese Jaycee leaders included a doctor, a dentist, and a pharmacist. During dinner they described their concern about the health problems posed by the refugees coming from the North and the dire shortage of Vietnamese medical personnel and resources for coping with these problems. Arellano caught fire as he listened to this talk. He said that there were many doctors, dentists, and nurses in the Philippines. If the Vietnamese Jaycees wanted their help, he would try to get some volunteers for service in Vietnam. Maybe the International Jaycees would support this project. There might even be teams of volunteers from other countries willing to help in Vietnam. In any case, he knew of Filipinos who would volunteer as soon as he told them of the need. The Vietnamese Jaycees listened with growing enthusiasm and, as we finished dinner, wrote out a formal invitation for the help of such volunteers.

Several weeks later the first contingent of Filipino volunteers in Operation Brotherhood (quickly nicknamed "OB") arrived. They were seven doctors and nurses. A clinic was established at the main refugee reception center in Saigon, and they soon were hard at work. Other Filipino volunteers followed this first group, as Jaycee chapters in the U.S. added contributions to funds raised in the Philippines, until 105 Filipino doctors and nurses were in Vietnam. Then, as the International Jaycees adopted the project, teams of volunteers from many other countries arrived and served in Vietnam. Operation Brotherhood treated some 400,000 Vietnamese patients that first year. Eventually, their free clinics were established in many areas of South Vietnam, not only where the refugees settled, but wherever there was great need for their services. Medical aid was augmented by lessons in hygiene, nutrition and home economics (including canning). There were even lectures on improved methods of agriculture; Filipinos showed Vietnamese farmers just south of the 17th Parallel how to raise fish commercially in fish ponds. The news of this undertaking spread across the demilitarized zone into the North, where leaders in Hanoi heard of it and asked their Red Chinese agricultural advisers to duplicate the feat. They were experts only on upland rice production and botched the attempt to build a model fishpond in the North.

The Communists paid other compliments to Operation Brotherhood, some of them dubious. The most amusing one was when Radio Hanoi broadcast an accusation that Oscar Arellano was a major general in the Philippine Army whom Magsaysay had sent to Vietnam to be my assistant. Arellano, as unmartial and kindly a civilian as I've ever met, moped for an hour after hearing this accusation but then chuckled at the zany absurdity of the charge. More sincere compliments, in the form of imitation, were the arrival in North Vietnam of "socialist comrade volunteers," a medical team of East Germans who established a hospital in Hanoi, and several public health teams of Czechs who traveled in the provinces of the North. I suspect that a million or so Vietnamese benefited from the attentions of the original volunteers on our side of the line and their emulators on the other side before these projects closed. Despite the foolish propaganda, it was a warmhearted and memorable moment in the cold war.

I continued my efforts with the Vietnamese to stress the problems arising in the southern provinces as the Vietminh forces withdrew into staging areas for their journey to the

North. I talked to Defense Minister Le ngoc Chan and to General Nguyen van Hinh about the subject and suggested the use of units of the Vietnamese Army to fill temporarily the administrative-security vacuum caused by Vietminh departures. I seemed to be talking to deaf ears. The top leaders of the Vietnamese defense establishment were preoccupied with concerns of more immediacy to them. Some of these concerns were reasonable, such as the daily load of chores connected with the transfer of Vietnamese forces from the North to the South. But their current major concern was over a haplessly irrational issue, which was kept hidden from me in its earliest stages and which I only found out by bluntly asking what was going on so secretly. Later, it became widely known. General Hinh was toying with the notion of overthrowing Prime Minister Diem!

Vietnam already had taught me that it was full of surprises. The emergence of Hinh's ambition at this particular moment was the lesson that clinched my education. He didn't have a prayer of being able to lead the Vietnamese nationalists. They looked upon him, correctly, as a French career military officer who had been placed and kept in command of the Vietnamese military forces by the French. There was a remote possibility that he could have served as prime minister if Vietnam had remained a French colony. But Vietnam legally was a colony no longer, and the status of French military leaders was scarcely a respected one after the French were defeated by Asians at Dien Bien Phu. I could only conclude, from the remarks of disgruntled French colonialists and military adventurers, that some of them probably had put Hinh up to planning a coup. Perhaps they thought that they could turn back the clock with such a move. Crazy!

Thus, at a time when South Vietnam was supposed to be starting its life as an independent nation while carrying out the heavy burdens imposed by the Geneva accords, a shallow melodrama elbowed its way onto the center stage of national affairs. As though to underscore the gaucherie, much of this melodrama was played in slapstick style. Those of us close to the principals on stage didn't know whether to laugh or to cry.

The affair apparently stemmed from personal antipathies between Prime Minister Diem, a straightlaced bachelor, and General Hinh, a married man with a considerable playboy life away from his family. The prime minister asked the general to move certain battalions. The general refused. The battalions, officered by militant nationalists, attempted to make the move on their own, but were blocked by special units brought in by the general. At this point the prime minister tried to dismiss the general, but the general refused to give up his command. Instead, he said that he thought that he would fire the prime minister and take over his job himself. General Hinh, asked about this, only smiled and showed me a cigarette lighter given to him by Gamal Nasser, who had come to power in Egypt by a military coup not long before. Nasser, said General Hinh, had the right idea. I said that Vietnam needed teamwork, not pranks, among its leaders. My advice to Hinh was that he stop trying to play the politician and start acting like a general. A few hours later, Prime Minister Diem was giving me his side of the controversy. My advice to Diem was that he stop trying to play the general and start acting like a politician.

The French High Command, which still had authority over the Vietnamese Army (including its pay and the promotion of its officers), didn't intervene. The melodrama continued on and on. Troops loyal to Hinh took over the national radio station in Saigon and began broadcasting attacks on Diem. The U.S. Information Agency attempted to retrieve the broadcasting equipment it had loaned to the Vietnamese government, equipment which was vital in keeping the station on the air, but couldn't get through the tanks which were surrounding the building. I managed to get an American friend of the Vietnamese military broadcasters into the building and gradually the attacks on Diem diminished.

One day, while the radio attacks were at their height, I visited the Defense Ministry. The anterooms were deserted. I could hear angry shouting in the minister's office so I pushed open the door. An incredible scene was taking place. Defense Minister Chan, all five feet of him, was standing erect behind his desk, with one hand in an open drawer. Facing him were three of General Hinh's cronies in the Vietnamese Army, aiming submachine guns at the bantam minister. My sudden entry broke up the scene. I suggested that the soldiers put down their guns and leave, which they did after grinning at me. Chan then pulled his hand out of the desk drawer, with a revolver he had hidden there. He told me that Hinh's men had come in to arrest him, to which he had replied that *he* was placing *them* under arrest. At this point I had entered. Chan was miffed that I had stopped his action. I told him that dead men don't make arrests and that he was lucky to be alive.

My relationship with Defense Minister Chan led to a strange piece of make-believe that was patched onto the melodrama taking place. Chan, a lawyer by profession, had clients among the Hoa Hao leaders, including the guerrilla Ba Cut, who had chopped off a finger joint as a vow to his cause. Chan had suggested that the two of us take a few days off some time and visit Ba Cut, but our busy schedules never permitted this. This suggestion of Chan's was my only relationship with Ba Cut at a time when some U.S. officials visited Saigon and were given a briefing at MAAG about the situation in Vietnam. General O'Daniel had invited several French staff officers to talk to the American visitors at this briefing session, which I also attended, taking a seat in the rear of the room.

One of the French officers at this briefing session gave a little talk about the unhappiness of the Vietnamese Army with Prime Minister Diem and said that the activities of Colonel Lansdale in trying to buy the loyalty of sect forces for the prime minister hardly were helping matters! Even at that very moment, he said, I was making a visit to Ba Cut in his guerrilla hideout, carrying a suitcase filled with millions of piasters with which I naively thought I could buy Ba Cut. Ba Cut planned to ambush me and grab the suitcase! The French officer paused at this dramatic point to let the audience savor the folly of so stupid an American. I broke the silence by standing up in the rear of the room and begging him to go on with the story. I wanted to know whether Ba Cut had killed me or not.

My spoiling the French officer's story never stopped its circulation. Apparently, French staff officers found the picture of a duped American too alluring. Some of them came up to me at diplomatic receptions and tried to unbutton my uniform to see the bullet wounds I supposedly had suffered. They would flush with anger when I implied to nearby guests that the attempts to unbutton my uniform must be evidence of homosexual lechery.

Meanwhile, General Hinh continued to boast that he was going to overthrow Prime Minister Diem. He would name a date for the event, then laugh uproariously when the day passed without its happening. On one such occasion, Ambassador Heath suggested that I might stop by Doc Lap Palace to see if the prime minister was all right. (The French had turned over Norodom Palace, the residence of the French high commissioner, to the Vietnamese prime minister on September 7, and it was promptly renamed Doc Lap or Independence Palace.) The palace was almost deserted, guards absent from their posts, none of the clerks scurrying as usual in the hallways. Prime Minister Diem was calmly working at his desk, surprised that anyone would be concerned over his safety. That evening, I saw General Hinh, who asked me how I had liked his riding on his motor scooter around the streets bordering the palace. I told him truthfully that I hadn't seen this feat, since I had been indoors with the prime minister, who had also missed seeing this. Hinh insisted that his coup threat and motor scooter ride had frightened Diem. I admitted that Hinh seemed to have scared almost everyone else except Diem.

Several evenings later Hinh invited me to dine with him

and his staff. His home was a beehive of activity, staff officers shouting into telephones, motorcycle messengers coming and going, and several unit commanders poring over maps of the Saigon metropolitan area. General Hinh blandly explained the hubbub by saying that his coup was set for the next morning. Thinking to slow him down on so disastrous a course, I commented that it was too bad, since an opportunity had come up to take Hinh and his staff officers for a brief visit to the Philippines. I added that I was leaving Saigon for Manila later that evening and apologized for the short notice. Wouldn't he like a visit to the nightclubs of Manila? Hinh answered regretfully that he would be busy but said I could take some of his staff officers for the visit. I picked his chief lieutenants. A hurried telephone call to General O'Daniel led to the loan of his C-47 transport aircraft for the trip. That night, I arrived in Manila with Hinh's closest cronies. I explained to Magsaysay why we had suddenly shown up in the Philippines and he arranged a week-long program for the Vietnamese visitors. I hurried back to Saigon alone. General Hinh told me ruefully that he had called off his coup. He had forgotten that he needed his chief lieutenants for key roles in the coup and couldn't proceed while they were out of the country with me. I never did figure out how serious Hinh was with his talk of overthrowing the prime minister.

The lengthy shenanigans of Hinh's coup threats were drawing to a close. Ambassador Donald Heath was leaving Vietnam, to be replaced by President Eisenhower's personal representative, retired Army General J. Lawton "Lightning Joe" Collins. The French High Command also was changing, and General Paul Ely, a thoughtful and highly respected soldier, arrived to become the new leader of the French Union forces. Ambassador Heath gave a number of farewell suppers and parties for his many French friends in Saigon, some of which I attended. At one of them Heath gathered a group of French military officers around him at the piano, told them that he knew most of the *chansons* popular in Paris, and offered to play the piano accompaniment for whatever they wanted to sing. There was a momentary silence while they were thinking of the kind of salon song that an American diplomat might know. In the silence, General O'Daniel boomed out to Ambassador Heath, "Do you know 'The Dog-Faced Soldier'?" Heath didn't. So O'Daniel and I sang, without accompaniment, this favorite song of the U.S. 3rd Infantry Division during the liberation of France in World War II. I'm afraid that our growly voiced rendition quashed any desire by the others to sing.

General Collins arrived in Saigon on November 8 and flew to Dalat the next morning for a conference with General Ely, who was resting at this mountain resort. Evidently the two agreed that it was time to end the Hinh melodrama. On November 19 Hinh handed over the command of the Vietnamese Army to General Nguyen van Vy, and departed for Paris. Joe Redick and I were the only Americans at the airport to say goodbye, a fact noted by the many French officers gathered at plane side for a farewell to Hinh. One group of these officers made some scathing comments about my presence. I told them cheerfully that I was looking forward to the pleasure of watching them depart from Saigon, too, before long; their heavy-handed humor had worn thin for me. General Hinh went on to Paris and a rewarding career in the French military establishment.

The lords of the Saigon-Cholon underworld, the Binh Xuyen, had become restive during the Hinh imbroglio. Unsatisfied with being masters of the metropolitan police, narcotics, gambling, vice, and the battalions of soldiers in their private army, they demanded that Diem give them a bigger slice of the government—say, a couple of ministerial portfolios. I met with the political advisers to Bay Vien, the chief of the Binh Xuyen, and suggested that it was time that the Binh Xuyen started considering how they would be recorded in the Vietnamese history books. Instead of being known as gangster overlords avaricious for power, why couldn't they act in ways that would earn the esteem of their fellow citizens and go down in history as benefactors? This suggestion was taken well, with the advisers telling me how Bay Vien and the other Binh Xuyen leaders had spent their boyhoods in poverty and would probably welcome ideas on how they could help the people. What did I have in mind?

I suggested that the Binh Xuyen figuratively beat their swords into plowshares. Their private army could lay down its weapons and, with equipment and material bought with the sale of their underworld enterprises, it might build a much-needed superhighway from Saigon to the sea at Cap St. Jacques (where the Binh Xuyen owned much property). The highway, as their donation to the country, could bear the name of the Binh Xuyen leader.

My highway proposal appealed to Bay Vien. I arranged a meeting between Bay Vien and Diem. After the meeting, an angry Bay Vien returned and took out his ire on the advisers; in fact, one of them was shot in the stomach at point-blank range. When I heard of this disastrous aftermath, I rushed over to Diem to find out what had happened in his talk with Bay Vien. Diem told me that the Binh Xuyen leader had made some sort of "silly" proposal about giving up his errant ways and using his resources to build a highway. "Yes, yes," I told Diem. "That's what I explained to you when I asked you to meet with him. So, what did you say to him?" "Why," replied Diem, "I said that I didn't believe him. I turned it down. After all, the man's a scoundrel." I was shocked by Diem's political obtuseness, and I told him so. He had failed to make use of a constructive solution to a vexing problem. The Binh Xuyen controlled an army and the police, backed by underworld funds. Instead of encouraging them to give up these things, he had earned their hatred. A gangster scorned is as deadly as the proverbial female. One day there would be hell to pay.

During my hurried visit to Manila with Hinh's chief lieutenants, I had talked to Magsaysay about the conditions under which Prime Minister Diem was working at Doc Lap Palace in Saigon, particularly the inadequacies of the military guard which was supposed to provide security for the palace. Magsaysay had agreed that, if Diem desired it, Colonel Napoleon Valeriano might be spared for a week in Saigon to advise on ways to improve security for the prime minister. Valeriano was Magsaysay's chief military aide and commanded the presidential guard battalion in Manila. Diem eagerly accepted, and Valeriano was invited to Saigon and soon tightened the security of Doc Lap Palace. When he went back to Manila, he took with him a group of Vietnamese Army officers for additional training with the Philippine presidential guard battalion.

Another Philippine Army colonel, Jose Banzon, had been in Saigon giving suggestions to the Vietnamese military. Banzon, who had run the ten-centavo telegram program when Magsaysay was secretary of national defense and who had been an enthusiastic participant in military civic action during the Huk campaign, was the Philippine military attaché in Thailand and was also accredited as a military observer in Indochina. He had a wide friendship among Vietnamese military officers and did considerable missionary work in pushing the concept of a closer and friendlier relationship between the Vietnamese Army and the people. Thus, when I learned from Diem that some units of the Vietnamese Army had moved into Long My after the Vietminh had departed and were attempting to "fill the vacuum," I asked Joe Banzon to accompany Rufe Phillips of my staff for a preliminary look at what was happening.

Long My is close to the Gulf of Siam far to the southwest of Saigon, a land of rice paddies barely above sea level. Banzon and Phillips returned from their visit to Long My full of praise for the Vietnamese Army's efforts to help the people by rebuilding bridges, roads, and other public structures. They also said the district probably had the world's biggest mosquitoes and that, despite its steamy tropical heat in the daytime, there was a damp chill in the air at night. There was dire need for mosquito nets and blankets. I took Banzon and Phillips in to brief U.S., French, and Vietnamese officials about the situation, Prime Minister Diem among them. I urged him to take a load of mosquito nets and blankets with him on a personal visit to Long My; as a leader, he needed to see for himself the conditions the people and the government were facing as the Vietminh withdrew. Diem took this advice and made the trip, getting around to some of the outlying farms along rivers and canals by rowboat. After talking with hundreds of farmers and soldiers on the scene, Diem became as convinced as I that a major governmental program was needed for reoccupation and rehabilitation of areas vacated by the Vietminh. The Long My visit was the first of many such visits he was to make in the countryside.

Of Christmas 1954 in Saigon, I remember only two things. One was the delivery of a gift for an American. The second was a search for Christmas carols.

The gift came by mail from William Bullitt, the noted American diplomat, who asked me to find and deliver it to a Vietnamese friend of his, Do van Bong. Bullitt, on a mission to France for his cousin Franklin Roosevelt in World War II, had suffered nearly fatal injuries in a jeep accident. Bong was a hospital orderly in the French Army at the time and had nursed Bullitt back to health over many months. He was easy to find. He had become the chief Vietnamese *planton*, or clerk, at the American embassy in Saigon, and I saw him frequently. Delivering Bullitt's gift to him and extending the season's greetings, it suddenly struck me that the two had known each other for a decade. It was about the maximum time that any American and Vietnamese had known each other. How newborn was this relationship between the two nationalities across the Pacific! The Christmas carol incident showed that these two nationalities could have clashes between their cultures. One day I asked Prime Minister Diem how Christmas was celebrated in Vietnam. It was treated as a holy day, he said, with the Christians going to church and observing the religious nature of the day quietly at home. No presents, no Christmas trees, no special dinners. The really festive time for Vietnamese came at Tet, the celebration at the beginning of the lunar New Year. This was when families gathered, gifts and greetings were exchanged, traditional meals were eaten, and great strings of firecrackers were shot off. When I pressed him further about Christmas, Diem admitted that he was quite fond of carols and hymns such as "Silent Night" which he had heard while he was abroad but which were almost unknown in Vietnam. This led to my suggesting that perhaps we could find some phonograph records of Christmas music and broadcast a special program on Radio Saigon. Diem said, "Let's do it!"

Diem checked the phonograph records at the palace and at the radio station, while I hunted through the record collections in the American community. We both came up empty-handed. Apparently there wasn't a single record of Christmas music in Saigon at the time. Hurriedly, I sent word to friends in Manila. Their package arrived the day before Christmas, and I rushed it to Doc Lap Palace. Diem was as eager as I to hear the music, and he set up a portable phonograph on the desk in his office while I tore open the package. On went the first record of joyous holiday music and out of the loudspeaker came "All I want for Christmas are my two front teeth"! The next record was "Rudolf, the Red-Nosed Reindeer."

I read hastily through the labels on the stack of records. They were all similar novelty tunes, most of them now happily forgotten. Diem sat next to the desk, patiently listening to the lyrics raucously delivered by the vocalists, a puzzled frown on his face. "Are those Christmas carols?" he asked me politely. I started to assure him that they were but then broke out laughing at the absurdity of this moment in Saigon and the disappointment on his face. It was the first time I had heard any of these songs. I had been away from home too long.

The last week of 1954 held signs and portents of change. On December 28 the Paris agreements finally were ratified, and the French government granted the total independence of Vietnam. In Saigon, French and American military men were working out plans to implement a December 13 agreement by the French that Americans could start helping soon in the training of the Vietnamese armed forces, through a combined French-U.S. organization. The latter was to be under the authority of French Commander in Chief General Paul Ely and under the immediate direction of the senior American military leader in Vietnam, General O'Daniel. The staff planners came up with a working title for the new organization, the Allied Training and Operations Mission, which lasted only until somebody realized that it would become known by the acronym of ATOM. The name Training Relations Instruction Mission (TRIM) was finally chosen. At my urging, the new military body concerned itself with utilization of the Vietnamese military establishment in the reoccupation of zones from which the Vietminh were withdrawing, as well as with more normal training work, and I was asked to join the organization when it was established.

Also, in the last week of 1954, it was confirmed in Paris that the French-owned Bank of Indochina would be abolished and that the government of Vietnam could manage its own banking affairs. The National Bank of Vietnam was established on January 1, 1955. The Vietnamese and French, at the same time, were coming closer to agreement on the question of the command and control of the Vietnamese armed forces. (Three weeks later, on January 20, 1955, the French agreed to turn over full control of the Vietnamese armed forces to the Vietnamese government within five months.)

As 1954 ended, the rhetoric said that Vietnam was an independent nation. There still was a large French Expeditionary Corps present in the country, however, and there still were many Frenchmen throughout the Vietnamese civil and military establishments, although most of them were stepping down from positions of executive authority to assume the role of advisers. The French presence was evident and heavy. At most, Vietnamese officials were getting sniffs, not deep breaths, of the air of freedom and independence.

NOTES

HISTORY. Some imaginative journalists have twisted the history of Vietnam to their own liking, baldly including the curious "fact" that I had been one of a group of American conspirators (the others being Cardinal Spellman and the Dulles brothers John Foster and Allen) who had forced Bao Dai to appoint Ngo dinh Diem as prime minister. Such stories make me wonder how historians can ever formulate a straight account of human events. I trust that my reporting of Diem's 1954 arrival in Vietnam will throw some light on the subject.

ROSSON. Among the U.S. military men who helped in the 1954–1955 refugee exodus was one man who made a respected name for himself a decade later as a U.S. Army division commander, first as chief of staff and then as deputy to the commander of U.S. forces fighting in Vietnam, General William Rosson. As a lieutenant colonel in 1954, he was in charge of the American military men assigned to refugee work. After being soaked one night in a tropical downpour while directing the unloading of a refugee transport, toting squalling infants and bundles of household goods in his arms from transport to the shelters, he told me that he had never cussed anyone so hard as he had me— for the bright idea of assigning military men to such work. I told him blandly that it was a good way to learn some truths about "people's war."

BAMBOO CURTAIN. There were many reports at the time about Vietminh actions blocking the exodus of refugees in the North. The most serious account I heard told of eight thousand refugees being halted by armed forces at Ba Lang in Thanh Hoa Province between Phat Diem and Vinh. The troops opened fire, killing, wounding, and stampeding the refugees. These reports were consistent with the Communist practice of keeping their populations in hand, behind the so-called Iron Curtain in Europe and the Bamboo Curtain in Asia, so I am inclined to believe them.

"OB." The Saigon Jaycees who helped Oscar Arellano create Operation Brotherhood were Dr. Wang Tsio-yong, Dr. Ho quan Phuoc, and Le thanh Nghe. In my first meeting with them in 1954, they showed me a photograph of a former American Jaycee who had visited them the year before, Richard Nixon, then vice-president of the United States.

PROPAGANDA. Jean Barre, a French journalist, helped General Hinh with propaganda in the squabble with Diem. His most telling line for Hinh to speak: "I admit that Diem is honest, but then so is my four-year-old daughter. Does that make her qualified to be prime minister?" Later Barre fled to Phnom Penh where he published a newspaper and wrote speeches for Prince Sihanouk. I have long suspected him of being the author of a 1957 canard that I plotted Sihanouk's assassination with Dap Chu'on, a Khmer patriot who died violently during a visit by Sihanouk's bodyguards. I never met nor had dealings with Dap Chu'on, although I wish I had, since he was beloved by the people of Cambodia. The weird assassination canard set me up as a straw man for Sihanouk to attack in his frequent tirades.

SHARPE. The American who braved the tanks and machine guns to enter the radio station, and then to modify the anti-Diem broadcasts of General Hinh's men, was Navy Lieutenant Lawrence Sharpe. Sharpe, a staff officer in the U.S. Navy task force transporting refugees, had entertained Lieutenant Nguyen van Minh in his home in the U.S.; the two had become warm friends. When I learned this, I asked the task force commander, Admiral Sabin, to transfer Sharpe to duty with me temporarily so I could bring Sharpe and Minh together. Minh was in charge of the radio station for General Hinh.

CHAN. After his service as defense minister, Le ngoc Chan became the Vietnamese ambassador to Tunisia. Currently he is his country's ambassador to the Court of St. James's in London.

DUC. The reoccupation of Long My by the Vietnamese Army was under the command of Lieutenant Colonel Duong van Duc who later commanded the pacification of Camau, was promoted to general, and served for several years as Vietnamese ambassador to South Korea.

★　★

CHAPTER ELEVEN

TRINH MINH THÉ

IF THERE WAS any single act of mine in 1954 that made tongues wag more than usual among French gossips in Saigon, it was my becoming acquainted with the legendary rebel guerrilla chief Trinh minh Thé. It struck them as scandalous that an American would meet with someone whom the French had outlawed. As a farm boy turned soldier who had raised his own guerrilla army in the cause of Vietnamese independence, Thé had had the temerity to fight both the French colonialists and the Communist forces. Worst of all, in the eyes of his enemies, he had achieved considerable success. When I first met him, French Union troops still were trying to hunt him down, as were trigger squads of the Vietminh. They wanted him dead.

My first meeting with Thé (pronounced "Tay") stemmed from a talk I had with Prime Minister Diem in the fall. The Hinh affair was at its height. Diem reminded me of my early suggestion that all the sect armies and guerrilla bands should be merged into the Vietnamese Army to make a single national force. Did I honestly believe that this was feasible, given the sorry state of affairs in the Vietnamese Army currently? If sect armies were integrated into the army, wouldn't this compound the troubles?

I admitted that military affairs seemed to be in a mess, although responsible French officials apparently were getting fed up with Hinh and his ambitions. Hinh apart, however, what choices did Diem have? There surely was a potential challenge to governmental authority if secular armies consolidated their regional fiefdoms. Any attempt to disband these armies would be full of forbiddingly complex political and technical hazards. Yet, with so many armed bands roving the countryside south of the 17th Parallel, Vietnam would remain in political chaos. There were only so many days allotted by the Geneva conferees for South Vietnam to get its house in order before a showdown vote in the proposed plebiscite. Diem would have to do whatever he could, whenever he could, and could not afford the luxury of waiting for the safest or most logical time to do it. A single, united army was a national necessity.

Diem looked at me for a few moments without speaking. Then he asked me softly if I had heard about Trinh minh Thé. I replied that I had, mostly from French officers who hated him and whose descriptions of him were hardly flattering. Diem said bluntly that he considered Thé to be a real Vietnamese patriot, the kind of nationalist leader whom he would need with him if non-Communist Vietnamese ever were to have a decent chance in the future. Diem told me of Thé's prestige in the West (that is, west and southwest of Saigon), and said that if it became known that Thé was supporting the government, it would weigh the balance of power heavily in Diem's favor. Diem's brothers Luyen and Nhu had been in touch with Thé's representatives in Saigon, and Thé was showing considerable interest in joining with Diem in the nationalist cause.

Then Diem asked me if I would deliver a personal letter from him to Thé. Since French forces were surrounding Thé's guerrillas, there were certain difficulties in Diem's having a face-to-face meeting with him. Being an American, I should be able to get to Thé personally, as he or his brothers could not. The main burden of the letter would be a proposal to integrate Thé's forces into the national army as soon as effective arrangements could be made. Surely I should be able to speak approvingly to Thé on that subject. Diem would leave the letter unsealed so that I could read it before delivery.

I admitted that I would like to deliver the letter and satisfy my curiosity about this controversial guerrilla leader by meeting him. The only difficulty that I could foresee was getting U.S. permission for the visit; it might take a few days. Diem replied dryly that it might take him a few days also to make the arrangements with Thé for my visit, since I would be the first American to meet him and Thé's guerrillas were rather rough on foreigners, as witness their present fighting with the French. Diem cautioned me to behave with some secrecy, fearing that the French would learn of the visit and perhaps ambush me or take other measures to prevent a meeting.

I discussed Diem's request with Ambassador Heath. We agreed that the support of Diem by Thé could make a critical difference in Diem's political position, probably opening the way to similar actions with other irregular forces in Vietnam. General O'Daniel was strongly in favor of integrating all the various military forces into a single national army. By radio, the matter was put up to Washington. A couple of days later, Washington sent an okay. I notified Diem, who told me that final arrangements were underway for the visit to Thé.

Two days later I set off for the meeting with five of my team of Americans who had asked to go along, as curious as I about seeing these Vietnamese guerrilla forces. We wore civilian sport clothes, as though for a day's outing. Some had hand guns tucked out of sight under their shirts. My own weapons were on the floorboard of the car, within quick reach. Accompanying us was a Vietnamese government bureau chief, to whom Diem had introduced me, dressed up as for a day in his Saigon office, in white sharkskin suit and black tie. He assured me nervously that he would set up the initial contact with the guerrillas. His nervousness was noted by some of my American teammates, who whispered that they didn't trust him. Our destination was a hamlet about a hundred kilometers (sixty-two miles) from Saigon, beyond Tay Ninh and not far from the Cambodian border. Driving west along Route 1 in the early morning sunshine, past the lonely watchtowers and little road-side forts sitting in the rice paddies, and then north on Route 22 through the Ven Ven and Tra Vo rubber plantations, I went over in my mind what I had been told about Trinh minh Thé and his guerrillas.

My knowledge was much too sketchy and came in two starkly contrasting versions. To the French he was the treacherously cunning monster who had murdered General Chanson in 1951 and had blown up a vehicle in front of the Opera House in Saigon in 1953, killing innocent passersby. To many Vietnamese he was a Robin Hood, a patriot who yearned for national independence, who had fought successfully against both the French and the Communists, and who had brought a tangible advance in social justice to the farm communities in his zone of operations. (Even some of the French officers who hated Trinh minh Thé admitted to me that he was surprisingly honest and fair with the people of his area.) Estimates of his guerrilla forces ranged from 500 fighting men up to an exuberant figure of 10,000. (Later, I learned that he had 2,500 men under arms.)

In subsequent days, more details of the life of this nationalist leader became known to me. He had crowded much colorful living into his thirty-two years. Leaving the family farm at twenty-one, he had joined other Vietnamese for training in guerrilla warfare at the secret camps of the Japanese Kempeitai in Cambodia and Laos. In 1945 he was an officer in the secret Cao Dai military company formed at the Lichinan shipyard in Saigon, and he participated in the Japanese-fomented coup against the Vichy French colonial authorities that March. When French Union forces returned to Vietnam after World War II, Thé joined other Cao Dai soldiers in the early nationalist Viet-minh resistance against the French. Sickened over Communist betrayals and purges, the Cao Dai left the Vietminh movement in 1947 and formed a militia under French auspices, to protect their religious communities. Trinh minh Thé became chief of staff of these Cao Dai armed forces.

His first notable military success was a strange sequel to the secret training he had received from the Japanese. In 1949 he formed twelve mobile platoons and undertook a lightning campaign against the Vietminh led by the Communist commander of the Eastern Zone, Nguyen Binh. He and Binh had been classmates at the Japanese guerrilla warfare school, where they had devised a plan of operations for South Vietnam. In the 1949 campaign, Thé realized that Binh was using their old plan, which he knew as well as Binh, and he acted accordingly. The Cao Dai mobile platoons caught the Vietminh by surprise and broke their units. (After this defeat Binh and his weakened forces were betrayed to the French. I heard that the betrayal was engineered by Le Duan at the request of Ho chi Minh, as part of a Communist purge.)

Fighting the Communists who threatened the Cao Dai was one thing, but doing it under the French banner became more and more distasteful to Thé. He felt that the Cao Dai should be part of the struggle for independence and not contribute to the French colonial system. In 1951 he left the Cao Dai armed forces and started a political-military movement of his own for national independence, called the Quan-Doi Quoc-Gia Lien-Minh (National Alliance Forces). Many Cao Dai joined him, including his father (who was a lieutenant in his son's forces) and four brothers; father and brothers later were killed in combat against the Communists. When French forces took the field against him, Thé adopted the unique tactic of reprisals against the actual French commanders whose orders sent the troops into combat against him. This led to the killing of General Chanson in 1951 and the explosion at the Saigon Opera House in 1953 (with top French commanders as the intended victims). Needless to say, French generals thought this tactic barbaric.

In 1952, Trinh minh Thé moved his Lien-Minh forces to the mountain of Nui Ba Den, fulfilling the widely believed prophecy of local soothsayers that "the Genius General of God" would one day come and live on the mountain. The mountain, which rises steeply and abruptly from the surrounding flatlands, is also known on the farmlands and rivers in sight of it as "the heart of the people." Thus it was a psychologically rewarding base for guerrilla forces, just five miles northeast of the Cao Dai seat in Tay Ninh city. Lien-Minh guerrillas were able to move easily to and from their base, despite the presence of French Union forces which attempted to block them, and in 1954 they extended their zone of influence southwest through the boggy, drowned lands of the Plaine des Joncs practically to the Mekong River.

Their dominance over a considerable amount of territory, for so small a number of armed men as reported, suggested to me that the Lien-Minh were adept politically as well as militarily. I was struck particularly by the affection the Vietnamese people expressed for them. Farm families voluntarily brought the traditional rice cakes at Tet, and huge mounds of these gifts were left at the edge of the forest for the guerrillas. Vietnamese soldiers in the French Union forces operating against the Lien-Minh would leave supplies of cigarettes and sugar, accompanied by notes saying "Sorry we are fighting you," when the French would break camp. "He's a *good* man," I was told over and over by Vietnamese when I asked them about the Lien-Minh leader.

On that fall morning in 1954, we drove along a rutted dirt road to the foot of the mountain Nui Ba Den and stopped near the hamlet of Bai Trai. The mountain loomed over us, trees and bushes thick along the mountain side of the road and rice paddies stretching out on the other side of the road. I was watching a group of children walking barefoot along a paddy dike when a group of guerrillas emerged silently onto the road from the jungle growth. One of them, whom I took to be a youth of high school age, no more than five feet tall and maybe weighing ninety pounds dripping wet, was in the lead. Wearing a faded khaki shirt and trousers, tennis shoes on his feet, weaponless, hatless, he looked as if he might be a guide sent to take me to his leader. He had a broad, infectious smile on his face, which brought one to mine as he reached out and shook my hand in welcome. He introduced himself. He was Trinh minh Thé.

This wiry youngster was the villainous guerrilla hated by the French! I couldn't believe it. His eyes alive with laughter at the look on my face, Trinh minh Thé suggested that we get off the road promptly since there were French Union forces nearby. We hid our cars in the jungle and took off on foot, Trinh minh Thé in the lead, scrambling almost straight up the slopes of the mountain over a vast slide of huge rocks that had tumbled down in some past era. After a long climb, we reached a small shelter hidden amidst a tangle of jungle. This was his headquarters. We entered the tiny, almost barren shelter and sat at a forester's homemade table. Despite a high school education, Trinh minh Thé spoke only Vietnamese, and had very little French and a smattering of Japanese. Since my French was sketchy too, our conversation required generous help from others.

With Trinh minh Thé was an exceptionally quick, bright, obviously well-educated civilian, Le khac Hoai (who later had a distinguished career in the Vietnamese foreign service). I had Joe Redick with me. The shelter was so small that my other companions had to wait outside with the Lien-Minh soliders. Our talk went the tortuous route of Thé's Vietnamese to Hoai, who translated it into French for Redick, who translated it into English for me, with my responses going back over the same route. Trinh minh Thé and I would look at each other, speaking mutely with our eyes and facial expressions, while our helpers struggled with the translations. I couldn't get over how young and boyishly merry a person he was to be either the notorious monster of the French or the famed patriot of the Vietnamese. I found myself liking him instinctively.

I gave him the personal letter from Ngo Dinh Diem, which he read carefully. Then he commented that he was an admirer of Diem, believing him to be a sincere, honest, capable man who might lead the Vietnamese nationalist cause to success. I nodded at this and then carefully asked Thé about his own political beliefs. He showed me a "declaration" which he had circulated in the surrounding farming areas where his troops operated, along with a series of documents, plans, and studies about the future of Vietnam. The declaration announced independence from French colonial rule and stressed the need of man for individual liberty, emphasizing that public justice should be designed to serve this need. His plans called for self-governing communities and included some sections with unusually mature, enlightened concepts for the agrarian economy.

Trinh minh Thé watched me closely as Hoai translated the documents and then made a comment in Vietnamese to Hoai. I heard the words "Magsaysay" and "Phi-Luat-Tan" (Philippines) as he spoke. Hoai translated, saying that Thé wondered what Magsaysay would think of these political ideas; Trinh minh Thé had followed the news of the Huk campaign and the 1953 elections in the Philippines and wanted me to know that my own association with Filipinos and events in the islands was known even in Tay Ninh. I replied that Magsaysay was indeed a champion of man's liberty and shared the beliefs that were expressed in the documents shown me. However, as an American, I must tell him that his declaration and documents had reminded me, deeply and touchingly, of some other people of bygone days, the Americans who had founded my own country. I sincerely hoped that he was dedicated to the principles shown me. Trinh minh Thé banged the table with his fist when this was translated to him and said forcefully, "That's what we fight for!"

We discussed the need for unity among Vietnamese nationalists, including the need for a single Vietnamese Army. He responded slowly and thoughtfully that perhaps there was such a need, but there were so many "bad elements" in the national army at present that a man who loved his country would find it almost impossible to be comrades with them in the ranks. However, he said, I could tell Diem that he and the Lien-Minh would pledge him their support. They would take care of Diem safely, if he was forced out of Saigon by General Hinh and "the other French officers." I assured him that I would take this word back to Diem and knew that he would be grateful for the pledge. I then asked him about his guerrilla forces. "Come on, I'll show you," he said. We left the shelter and went clambering down the mountain.

We visited platoon after platoon of barefooted men dressed in the *calicot noir* pajamas of the southern farmers, armed with a wide variety of well-kept individual weapons and even with crew-served weapons such as heavy machine guns and mortars. The platoons were scattered all over the jungly mountain, and, as we trudged from one to another, runners went past us swiftly, carrying French officer's shoulder insignia which the officers in the next platoon would don hastily as we appeared. I told Thé that it wasn't necessary for the officers to wear insignia as far as I was concerned. He laughed and said that the officers themselves had wanted to do this, but there was only the one set of insignia to pass around. I was most impressed with the obviously cared-for weapons the men were armed with, including a small-caliber semiautomatic pistol and what appeared to be .50-cal. machine guns. I asked him where he got such weapons. "We make them," was his reply.

Thus it was that he showed us the jungle workshops of the Lien-Minh, amazingly complete with forges, drills, lathes, and a variety of machine tools powered by diesel generators. The shop foremen and senior skilled workers were Chinese who told me that they had been fighting the Communists for years, had finally been driven from their homeland, and had gradually made their way to this southern area where again they had a chance to fight against a hated enemy. When I asked about the French, they spat on the ground angrily, their eyes glaring.

They were distinctly taller and huskier than the Vietnamese who were working alongside them and struck me as some of the most fiercely independent people I had ever met. With their long experience and skills, they would be formidable fighters. They showed me some heavy machine guns and some copies of U.S. M-1 rifles that were being completed. I asked about the supply of steel and was shown steel rails which the guerrillas had carried off from a railroad line. (The closest railroad was many miles away, running north from Saigon to Loc Ninh, and I never did learn the source of supply of these steel rails.) The Chinese also were manufacturing radio transceivers for the Lien-Minh.

As we walked along a path from the last workshop, one of the Lien-Minh pointed to a place on the path and laughingly related an ancedote. It seems that some French troops had arrived at that spot not long ago, hunting for Trinh minh Thé and his guerrillas. The Lien-Minh leader had ridden up to them on a bicycle and had asked them what they were doing. The French had taken him to be a village youth and called him "sonny" as they asked for information. He had misdirected them blithely. While this story was being told to me, Thé disappeared, to appear shortly afterwards riding a bicycle up the path to show me how he had met the French troops. When he rode up and stopped, we both burst out laughing. Although he was thirty-two, he did look remarkably like a teen-ager.

After promises to meet again soon, we parted. It was evening by the time I got back to Saigon. I stopped at the residence of Ambassador Heath and described the visit with Trinh minh Thé, then went on to the palace, where I gave Ngo dinh Diem the information about the pledged support of the Lien-Minh. Leaving Diem in a happier mood than I'd ever seen him, I drove to my quarters for a belated supper. People were waiting to see me. (At times, my house was reminiscent of a railroad depot, there was such a variety of people coming and going through the days and nights.) Among them was a French acquaintance. He told me angrily that my visit to that dirty, murderous so-and-so, Thinh minh Thé, was well known and that the next time I tried something like that I was going to be killed. I grinned and invited him to join me for supper, but he went stomping out of the house. Ah well, I thought, so much for secrecy in Asia!

Trinh minh Thé had invited me to visit him again at his guerrilla hideout on the mountain, so several days later I drove with Joe Redick to the same lonely spot on the road near Bai Trai hamlet. Again, there were children in the rice paddies along the road on the side away from the mountain. This time, they paid attention. Redick and I had stepped out of the car and were leaning against its front fenders, enjoying the morning sunlight and the freshness of the country air. Suddenly, rocks and sticks came whizzing at us from the children, and we heard angry shouts of "Phap" (French). Our civilian clothes, our French car bearing civilian license plates, and our obviously foreign looks had caused the children to take us for Frenchmen.

Trinh minh Thé and several of his guerrillas arrived at this moment, and the children scampered away. I said that it must be very sad to be a Frenchman in Vietnam at that time, particularly if one were one of the many French who felt a real affection for the Vietnamese, because even the children reacted so violently against them. My host looked puzzled, probably wondering why I was concerned at all over such a commonplace matter.

We dropped the subject in favor of other matters. This incident with the children in the rice paddy stayed in my thoughts in the following days, however, as contention arose between French individuals and me. I wisely didn't mention this to the French. They seemed to dislike me enough without my making it worse by telling them how sorry I felt about their predicament.

That evening, after my return to Saigon, several Hoa Hao

leaders called at my house. Among them was General Nguyen giac Ngo, a quietly dignified older man whom I hadn't met before and whose plain, open candor as he spoke had an appealing rustic honesty about it. Another leader, Colonel Lam thanh Nguyen, was a sharp contrast to Ngo. I had met this roly-poly man with the "gimmee" look in his eye before, at Soai's headquarters in Cai Von. Nguyen took me aside from Ngo and the other Hoa Hao leaders at my house to inform me that he was ready to make a "deal" with me, in return for money and weapons. I gathered that, with such help, he was ready to scramble over the bodies of other Hoa Hao and emerge as undisputed leader. I said I had no money or weapons for him or anyone else. He didn't seem to believe me.

Nguyen's proposal was symptomatic of the divisive ambitions of all too many Vietnamese leaders whom I'd met in Vietnam. It prompted me to ask him to sit with the others while I spoke to all of them "from my heart." I told the group my feelings about the position the people were placed in by the Geneva accords and the great need for unity among Vietnamese nationalists. They sat patiently while I made these remarks. Several of them told me afterwards that what I'd said might be all right for general consumption, but what about my "deal" with Trinh minh Thé? I had told him the same thing, I said. Some didn't bother to hide their skepticism. But General Ngo told me gravely, as he was saying goodbye, that he shared my beliefs and was ready to integrate the rest of his Hoa Hao forces into the national army, as he already had done with one regiment.

Later I talked to Ngo dinh Diem about the visit of the Hoa Hao leaders, suggesting that they were deserving of some extra attention by his government. The cabinet had been changed again, and the Hoa Hao's friend Chan was no longer the minister of national defense. Following a suggestion of mine, I had expected Diem to appoint Dr. Quat to this post, where he might have been able to bridge the gap between government and army. But Diem gave the portfolio to a businessman, Ho thong

Minh. I expressed hope that the new minister could concentrate on the problem of integrating all of the various Vietnamese armed forces into one national army.

Diem wasn't too sanguine about the possibilities of incorporating the sect forces into the national army, saying that it was up to the French to do this, since they controlled all the rival forces and were the only ones who could give them orders. He promised to discuss this with both the French and his new defense minister. Meanwhile, would I please give some help to General Ngo? I reminded Diem that I was firmly opposed to helping Ngo or the chief of any other private army. None of the sect armies should be made stronger.

Diem had a strange smile on his face as I said this. He held up his hand to stop me. "No, no, that isn't the 'help' I meant," he told me. "Nguyen giac Ngo is a very honorable person, the type of fair and honest man who is needed in Vietnam. But he is a military man, a shy man really, who doesn't talk much when he is with the people. What I ask is that you help him learn how to get along with the people, so that they will *love* him as he deserves. Will you do this? You can, you know." I was too astonished at this request to do more than nod my head yes, I'd try.

The following day, as I was making arrangements for another meeting with General Ngo, I received word that Trinh minh Thé was on his way to see me at my small bungalow on Rue Miche in Saigon. This was a real surprise. Here I had been making trips to Tay Ninh to see him, because the Diem government officials supposedly had found it too difficult to do so themselves, and now he jauntily was coming to town himself! I went out the front door of the bungalow to see if the generally quiet neighborhood was in its normal state. Rue Miche is a side street, usually empty of vehicles. This morning, there were jeeploads of men armed with submachine guns at each of the corners of the short block where I lived. Across the street was a sedan full of other armed men. One was a French officer whom

I had met previously. I walked across the street to him and asked, "What's up?" He had scowled as I was crossing the street, and his face darkened even more as he told me not to be cute with him. He knew that Trinh minh Thé was coming to visit me. When Thé appeared, he was going to get blasted out of existence just as he deserved. With luck, I'd be standing in the line of fire and get what I deserved also.

I thanked him for his honesty and started back across the street to my bungalow, wondering desperately how I could get a warning to Thé about the ambush awaiting him. As I reached the front of my bungalow, a small sedan came around the corner and drove slowly towards me. There were many eyes scrutinizing the occupants of the sedan, including mine. The driver was a small man, wearing nondescript khakis, an old hat pulled down over his eyes. The passenger on the back seat was a fat and prosperous-looking Vietnamese, dressed in a white sharkskin suit, fanning himself with a panama hat. The small sedan stopped in front of me. The driver popped out from behind the steering wheel and hurried around the car, the sandals on his bare feet slapping on the pavement, to open the rear door for the passenger. As the driver opened the door and stood aside, he raised his head and looked at me with a big grin. It was Trinh minh Thé, obviously enjoying the moment hugely! I quickly put out my hand to welcome the fat civilian passenger, started toward the house with him, then stopped and, in loud tones for the audience, told the driver to go around to the kitchen where there would be refreshment for him. The fat civilian and I went into the front door; up close, I noticed that he was trembling and sweating profusely. At the door, I looked around. The armed men were still in their ambush positions, still looking alertly down the street for the arrival of their intended victim. I was grateful that it seemed to be common knowledge that I had many Vietnamese visitors coming to my house, day and night. One unknown fat man hadn't aroused the watchers' curiosity.

Trinh minh Thé came into the house through the kitchen

door, laughing delightedly. He explained that his passenger was one of his friends whom he had brought along to act as interpreter. I commented that the French seemed well informed of his movements, even if they failed to capitalize on it because they were unable to recognize him when he was in one of their traps. I urged him to take more precautions, including a security check for possible informers among his staff.

Trinh minh Thé nodded, then changed the subject. His forces in the West had bumped into the forces of Ba Cut. Could I go to the Hoa Hao area, see Ba Cut, and arrange a truce? He himself was heading there immediately after leaving me, to take personal command of the operations, which had been carried out so far by his deputy Van thanh Cao. I suggested that he disengage from fighting with Ba Cut, since I had no quick way of either seeing Ba Cut or influencing him. There were French liaison officers with Ba Cut, but I doubted if they were responsive to orders from French headquarters, since they seemed to be playing some game of their own. They surely wouldn't listen to me. Trinh minh Thé nodded agreement, shook hands, slipped out the kitchen door, and drove away with his fat passenger. The ambushers kept their positions on the street until that evening, when they gave up in disgust.

Several days later Trinh minh Thé visited me again, riding up to the house on a bicycle. He told me the sequel to the fighting with Ba Cut's forces. He had attempted to disengage the Lien-Minh forces and negotiate with Ba Cut, but Ba Cut had refused to talk, pushing his forces instead into vigorous attacks against the Lien-Minh. So Trinh minh Thé had employed his fundamental tactic of "get the leader." He and a picked group of the Lien-Minh had infiltrated the Ba Cut forces and located Ba Cut who was directing operations against the Lien-Minh, surrounded him, and called upon him to surrender. Ba Cut answered the surrender call by a blaze of gunfire, which the Lien-Minh returned. Ba Cut and his immediate staff went down under the hail of bullets. Ba Cut had been shot through the neck

and chest and presumably was dead. With Ba Cut's men running to the scene, the squad of Lien-Minh slipped away to
safety. Shortly afterward, they were amazed to see a French
military helicopter arrive. Ba Cut was flown to a hospital. The
Lien-Minh had taken two days to locate the hospital and find
~ut about Ba Cut. He was still alive and would recover, thanks
to prompt medical attention from the French. For now, however, with Ba Cut a casualty, the fighting between his men and
the Lien-Minh had stopped.

Months later, on February 13, 1955, arrangements finally
were completed for the integration of Thé's 2,500 guerrillas
into the national army. A ceremony marked the event. Trinh
minh Thé and his Lien-Minh troops marched through Saigon,
along Boulevard Norodom, down Rue Catinat, across Rue
d'Espagne, to Boulevard Charner and the square at the Treasury. The troops wore the black pajamas of the rice paddy
farmers, faded now to a rusty gray, and cloth jungle caps with
stitched brims around the edges like turned-down sailor caps
or the old army fatigue caps, the only uniforms—or clothes, for
that matter—they had. Many of them were barefoot, although
those who owned rubber basketball or tennis shoes wore them
and marched in the outside ranks nearest the spectators to help
hide the bare feet of their comrades. The absence of heavy
boots made the march seem almost ghostly.

The thousands of Saigonnais who lined the curbs and sidewalks watched these troops swing by in their fast, nearly silent
long stride, and stared at them, not making a sound themselves. They seemed astonished that these were the fierce fighting men of the Lien-Minh of whom so many tales had been told,
It was a strange scene, that brilliantly sunny day, the well-
dressed city people lining the city street, the black-clad troops
flowing swiftly past them, the only sound the hushed slap of
their bare feet or rubber soles on the pavement.

Diem, his cabinet members, officers of the Vietnamese

General Staff, and a hundred or so foreign dignitaries sat in a grandstand on Boulevard Charner. I had been watching the march through the streets and slipped into a seat on one end of the stands, among some French and American officers, just as the Lien-Minh troops came into the boulevard and formed ranks for the ceremony. There was a murmur from the spectators around me, consisting mostly of pejorative remarks about the faded black pajamas and the bare feet of the Lien-Minh. One of the French officers behind me called out in a stage whisper, "Look at what Lansdale calls soldiers!" There were snickers in the grandstand. I turned around to the French officers sitting there. "Hold it," I said. "You French types were never able to beat them." An American near me asked what all that was about and who were these guys in black pajamas anyhow? I told him, in a voice loud enough for the others to hear, that they were guerrilla troops just in from the country and, being guerrillas, what was worth noticing was not their feet or their uniforms, but their weapons and their faces. These were what showed that these were men accustomed to combat, not parades. Each weapon was in prime operating condition, maybe a little battered-looking but ready for use. The men held their heads proudly, amused contempt visible on their faces as they returned the gaze of the well-dressed notables in the grandstand.

The Lien-Minh troops were sworn into the Vietnamese Army. Then Ngo dinh Diem administered the oath to Trinh minh Thé as a brigadier general and placed a Vietnamese general officer's cap on his head. The oath-taking was performed out on the square. When it was over, Diem and Thé came back to the grandstand, and Thé looked searchingly at the spectators. He saw me sitting over at one side and broke away from Diem, walking over, grinning, his eyes almost hidden under the visor of the imposingly large new cap. We exchanged salutes and I congratulated him. Diem had halted out in the square and was looking after Thé puzzledly, obviously wondering why he had gone straying off. Diem spotted me just then, a smile warming his face. He waved hello. I gave him the boxer's sign, arms over-head and hands clasped. The French behind me growled among themselves. Diem and Thé took their places in the grand-stand, and the Lien-Minh then went marching past them and out of the square. The ceremonies were over. The Lien-Minh, no longer guerrillas, were now part of the regular army. That evening they went out to their new camp, north of Saigon.

NOTES

Nui Ba Den. Nui Ba Den means "Black Woman Mountain." A decade later, when American troops came to this area, they were more romantic and called it "Black Virgin Mountain." Television cameras have shown combat on and near the mountain to audiences around the world a number of times.

★ ★

CHAPTER

TWELVE

EARLY 1955

THERE HAVE BEEN times when I wished I had the proverbial nine lives of a cat. The early days of 1955 were such a time. As a cat, I could have given up the life of those days and started a fresh one. However, I had to live the one I had. So while I was becoming acquainted with Trinh minh Thé, I also went ahead with my other affairs, most of which seemed to be full of fractious and complex problems.

I got off on the wrong foot with our new ambassador, General Collins. I encouraged a Vietnamese project that quickly stirred up the wrath of the bureaucrats. I welcomed some Filipino visitors to Saigon and discovered that they were the fore-runners of a group of eager volunteers, seeking guidance on how they could help the Vietnamese. I joined the combined Franco-American military training organization as a division chief, with a difficult mission to perform, only to find that the French had packed my staff with their intelligence agents who preferred to spend their time and talents in writing reports about me. To cap it all, the French clandestine service in Viet-nam presented our embassy with a long list of my alleged mis-deeds and invited me to a star-chamber session to answer the charges if I could. What a happy way to start the new year!

General Collins brought an aura of military precision to the meetings of the U.S. "Country Team" in Saigon, which previously, under the guidance of Donald Heath, had been friendly gatherings with much open discussion. J. Lawton Collins insisted upon a more disciplined format, calling for brief oral reports from each member, after which we would all shut up and sit there while he told us what the situation *really* was like and what each of us was to do about it until the next weekly meeting. He was very much the boss, to whom we were to respond with a yes sir or no sir, period.

Collins and I collided head on at the first Country Team meeting he conducted in Saigon. The underlying reasons for what happened, perhaps, lay in the extremely different backgrounds which each of us had brought to that moment of time in Saigon when we needed to work together to serve our country.

I had just emerged from the struggle against the Huks in the Philippines, with its heavy reliance upon the citizenry. It influenced me strongly.

Collins was from the world of "the big picture," the top management circles of Washington with their necessarily simplistic view of the complex problems of the world facing them daily, as they parceled out the exact quantities of men, money, and materials they deemed sufficient to cope with each demand. In such a world, semantics at that time seemed to be amiss, words often conjuring up false pictures to those using them. "Government," for example, connoted a somewhat mature organization of administrators who had been on the job for years and who had a stable place in the society, despite periodic changes of president or prime minister, as in the Americas or Europe. To apply this picture to what then existed in South Vietnam, where a small group of bureaucrats clustered in Saigon and issued orders mostly to one another in tragic ignorance of what was happening beyond the suburbs, could only lead to faulty judgments. Vietnamese society was still in the feudal Middle Ages. The Communists had found one way of breaking out. The nationalists would have to find another way or else succumb.

In his first Country Team meeting, Collins had outlined the priorities of our joint tasks ahead, among them helping to strengthen the effectiveness of the Diem government and to make drastic cuts in the manpower of the national army, for which the U.S. was footing the bill. When he had finished, I spoke up about the two matters I had been stressing before his arrival: the need for generating popular institutions in the body politic before the proposed 1956 plebiscite showdown with the Communists, and the importance of integrating the feudal, local armed forces into the national army before starting to pare it down. Collins told me firmly that I was out of order, that he was the personal representative of the president of the United States, that as the representative he had set the priorities, and that there was no need whatsoever to discuss them. Did I understand? I stood up and said, "Yes, sir. I understand. I guess there's nobody here as the personal representative of the people of the United States. The American people would want us to discuss these priorities. So, I hereby appoint myself as their representative—and we're walking out on you." I walked out of the meeting.

I went to the office of the counselor of embassy, close by the ambassador's office where the Country Team meeting was being held. Sitting there, I started making notes of the many affairs I would have to settle before leaving Vietnam, since I fully expected Collins to order me out of the country immediately. After a time, Randy Kidder, the counselor of embassy, came into his office and told me that the Country Team meeting was over. General Collins wanted to see me, at once. I went in to see Collins, who was seated at his desk busy with papers.

In fatherly tones he told me that he had been sadly disappointed in my behavior at the meeting. As a military man, surely I understood that there could be only one commander giving the orders. I agreed but pointed out that the situation we were in was neither simple nor cut-and-dried; we faced a highly complex one that needed a lot of thought and understanding before setting a course of action, there being an awful lot of future at stake. Collins replied that he had given a great deal of consideration to the selection of the priorities he had established for us. They were the giant rocks of the major problems besetting us. What I had brought up at the meeting were really only secondary pebbles.

I said that I sincerely wanted him to succeed in his mission to Vietnam, that his success would have meaning in the future of millions of people, and that I had hoped to help him. However, neither his success nor my help would be possible if we were to wear blinders and gags in the midst of a scene where so much was alien, unknown, or misleading. I was ready to be sent home or to stay, the decision being his. If I stayed, then I wanted to contribute information to the body of subject matter and data he would consider before making a decision. I understood that his nickname of "Lightning Joe" actually was given him by his comrades-in-arms for the speed with which he thought problems through and came up with solutions to them. Perhaps in Vietnam he could do some of this thinking out loud in private meetings with me and I could add whatever I knew, to illuminate the factors he listed as pertinent to whatever problem was being considered.

"Lightning Joe" smiled at this and said that this wouldn't be feasible. He explained that he often did his heaviest thinking after lunch, when he rested briefly in bed. Didn't he take a nap, since a short afternoon sleep was a custom in the tropics? No, he simply stretched out in bed, rested, and thought. "Good," I exclaimed. "I'll come over to your house right after lunch and join you in your room, sitting there quietly while you rest. If you want to talk, okay, we'll talk. If you just want to rest,

I'll not say a word. Let's find out if this will work." I excused myself and left hurriedly, since it already was lunch-time. There were people awaiting me at my house with whom I would have to deal quickly, then gulp down a bite of lunch and get over to the ambassador's residence. With a bit of rushing, I managed to arrive at his place just as he was finishing lunch. He grimaced when he caught sight of me and told me that he had no desire to try to rest with my hanging about.

"Come on," I urged. "Let's give it one try anyhow, now that I'm here." Reluctantly, he led the way to his room.

He stretched out on the bed while I sprawled in a chair at bedside. We spent the whole rest period talking. I told him of what I believed to be the shortcomings and strengths of Ngo dinh Diem, for Diem's aloofness from the people worried me. I described the chasm between the government in the capital and the fragmentary administration in the provinces and the even greater gulf between provincial administrators and the village people. There was a need for popular institutions through which the citizenry could start participating in public affairs. Ready-made instruments of government, such as the large army and the minuscule civil service, could be used to bring administrative services (and perhaps even political light) to areas of the countryside being vacated by the Vietminh under the Geneva accords. I described what I had found out about the thrill that villagers had felt in the early Vietminh days, when they first got a chance to sound off publicly in mass meetings and when some genuine land reforms were undertaken. Later repression had deadened this enthusiasm, but the Saigon government had never even attempted the beginning that the Communists made. It was *vital* to the outcome of the 1956 plebiscite challenge that the government make a sincere start, one that the people would understand and feel a part of.

Collins took me to task for misusing the word "vital" in this context. He told me of the many problems in Washington, the strictures on making more effective use of budgeted monies at this transitional stage of U.S. relations in Indochina, of the delicate nature of our assistance to the French while they were becoming involved more deeply with problems in North Africa and while their position in the Indochinese states was undergoing great change, and of the growing seriousness of the nuclear confrontation between the U.S. and the U.S.S.R. The political power plays of this confrontation deserved the description of "vital"; lesser matters certainly didn't. The need to work harmoniously with the French in Vietnam was "essential," even though this might become increasingly difficult as U.S. aid to them dwindled and French sensitivities increased. It didn't look as though the U.S. was going to finance the French struggle in North Africa, and there were ticklish questions of the U.S. armaments now in French hands in Vietnam.

After this long, hard talk, I looked at Collins. He appeared tired and I realized that he was still caught up in the circadian imbalance from his swift flight out of the time zone of Washington to the time zone of Saigon. His body and habits were telling him that he was in the wee morning hours of Washington. I apologized for having insisted upon our "skull session" when he would have been better off actually taking a nap, to adjust himself to Saigon time. He agreed. I beat a hasty retreat. On subsequent days we had further talks of a similar nature on a number of subjects. They often left me disquieted, as though each of us had been proceeding carefully and sincerely in two wholly separate worlds.

One answer to the question of what to do about the Vietnamese civil servants came from a visitor to my house. He was Kieu cong Cung, a short, husky, intense Vietnamese about forty years old. As had others, Cung simply arrived one day, introduced himself, said that he had heard that I was trying to help Vietnam and that he had some ideas of what needed doing. He had been an official with the Vietminh, but had quit in anger over the way that Communist bureaucrats had "contaminated" the movement for their own narrow ends. But what he had seen since of the Saigon bureaucrats filled him with dismay. They were an arrogant, slow-moving, undisciplined lot of paper-pushers, with no political convictions and interested only in their salaries. When the showdown with the Communists came in 1956, this Saigon gang would be an extremely weak reed to count on. He, Cung, wanted to teach these bureaucrats how really to serve the people. Maybe then the nationalist cause would have a chance in 1956.

Cung's eyes flashed with angry fire as he explained the reason for his visit. He flared up even more when I told him that he sounded merely as though he wanted a job with the government himself, as a sort of civil service czar, and that I wasn't the person to see for Vietnamese government jobs. Words exploded from him. He wasn't just a job-seeker. He didn't want to be a boss. In fact, he would be content if he could get some of his ideas accepted by some official who showed enough sense and guts to put his ideas to work. Then he would gladly go his own way and leave the government alone.

He was right that government service was overdue for change. It was sketchy in some regions and nonexistent in others. Some 80 percent of the government employes lived and worked in the Saigon metropolitan area and were city folk, typical white-collar workers. The Saigon government was finding it almost impossible to create capable teams of civil administrators to fill the vacuum in areas from which the Vietminh were withdrawing. If Cung had some practical ideas on how to change effete desk workers into rugged field people in a very brief time, I would do my best to try to get him a hearing with a government executive. He promised to work out a practical plan.

The next day I conferred with Americans on the public administration advisory staff of the U.S economic mission. They were busily planning the establishment of a National Institute for Administration in Saigon, which would give high-level instructions in classrooms to the most promising government employes. A contract was being let to Michigan State University to undertake this work, as well as to supervise a public safety program to prepare police for duty in rural areas. I listened as these Americans described the thoroughness of the program. It would be months before there were any results from such efforts. We didn't have time. I explained to them that the Geneva timetable would leave huge sections of the country barren of any public service, particularly between February and May 1955, because of Vietminh withdrawals. Not only would Saigon have to move into these areas, it would have to commence government service where it was sketchy or nonexistent elsewhere. The Geneva plan was to have the governments in the North and the South start discussions about the proposed 1956 plebiscite some time in July 1955. A year was little enough time to demonstrate to the people a nationalist government that was an acceptable alternative to what the Communists had shown them. This meant that, somehow, good government had to be established and working with some effectiveness throughout South Vietnam by July 1955. "Impossible!" they told me. They went back to planning the institute.

In early January Cung brought me a plan he had drawn up. It envisioned a training camp in the countryside, perhaps near Saigon. Increments of several hundred civil servants at a time would be given a crash course in how to work with their hands *in manual labor*. Upon entry to the training camp, they would doff their city clothes for the *calicot noir* pajamas of farm villagers. The pajamas were to be the only clothing permitted until they finished Cung's whole planned cycle. This cycle included not only political indoctrination, physical toughening, and learning to use tools at the training camp, but a further period of service in a hamlet or village. In the villages they would help the inhabitants build schoolhouses, roads, bridges, pit latrines, and similar public works, as well as help establish self-government. After a month of this, they would be judged on their ability to serve the people, and the successful candidates would be placed as administrators wherever needed (in coat and tie, if they wished). It would bring a useful government presence into the countryside quickly and produce civil servants, with some understanding of the real needs of the people, for staffing offices in both the capital and in the provinces.

The next time I saw Ngo dinh Diem, I told him about Cung. Diem was as intrigued as I by the idea of white-collar workers being trained as civil servants by first getting their hands dirty. He had heard of Cung and would ask his brother Nhu for more information, explaining that Nhu seemed able to get such data quickly. (It was the first time that Diem had admitted to me that his brother was running an intelligence service for him.) Later that day, while talking with the new Defense Minister Ho thong Minh, I learned that Minh not only knew Cung but was the one who had suggested that Cung come to see me. "A very able man," Minh said of him. Two days later Diem flew to Hué for a visit, inviting Minh to accompany him. Minh brought Cung along on the trip. The result was that Diem appointed Cung to get to work on the program, reporting directly to Diem but using office space in the Ministry of Defense where Minh could help Cung get started.

The program was given the name "Civic Action." I objected, pointing out that it would be confusing because the Vietnamese Army already was starting to use that name for *their* work to help the people. I was overruled. Diem had picked the name himself from what I had told him of military civic action in the Philippines. It was an even more fitting name, he thought, when applied to training bureaucrats to learn to serve the people. I shut up.

The Civic Action program was presented by Cung at a cabinet meeting, with an expression of hearty approval from Diem. A site for the training camp was found on the outskirts of Saigon. A recruiting drive was initiated to drum up volunteers from the ranks of the white-collar employes of all ministries. It flopped. Nobody volunteered. The consensus among the bureaucrats was that Cung was some sort of nut, wanting them to give up cushy jobs in the city to go out into the country and soil their hands helping people. Didn't he understand that they were educated men, not laborers? The outcry was so loud that I suggested to Diem that some judicious, selective firing of civil servants might be in order. He preferred handling the problem in another way.

Diem had been studying the future prospects of refugees from North Vietnam. I recall that he wanted some of the farmers to vary their crops from the traditional rice to the growing of kenaf for fiber and the raising of cattle, and he wanted the artisans to start new enterprises in the Saigon suburbs. Among the refugees were bureaucrats from Hanoi who were vying for high-ranking posts in Saigon bureaus and a number of recent graduates and students from the University of Hanoi. Diem saw the new Civic Action program as a ready answer to their importuning. He dragooned a group of the Hanoi bureaucrats ("So you want to serve in my government? I have just the place for you!") and called for volunteers from the university crowd, who responded enthusiastically. These refugees became the first cadre class for training at the Civic Action center.

Civic Action started its training and operations on a shoestring. Diem scraped up a small sum from his overextended budget. The U.S. economic mission was cautious about giving help to this program, despite my attempts to involve them in its planning and to remove myself from any connection with it. They offered only the minimum possible support after much pressure. Some of the U.S. administrators later confessed that they were afraid that it was some scheme of mine to flood the country with secret agents, of which they wanted no part. (Ironically, this echoed a Communist propaganda broadcast making similar charges.) The consequence of this niggardly support was that the Civic Action training program was a school of hard realism from its inception. The students exchanged their city clothing for the *calicot noir* pajamas of southern farmers and laborers the first day. They learned to work with their hands by constructing their own barracks and classrooms, while sleeping on the ground at night and attending the brief class sessions in the open air.

When the first Civic Action teams later reported to province chiefs for work assignments after graduation, many of the province chiefs refused to believe that these young men in black pajamas and with work-calloused hands were actually government administrators. As a result, most of the teams were kept idle in provincial capitals until Kieu cong Cung hit upon the idea of visiting each provincial capital himself, dressed like them in black pajamas. The sight of Cung, known to be a high government official in the confidence of Ngo dinh Diem yet garbed in workaday manner, was convincing. The teams were sent out into the villages. There, other troubles beset them. The strange accents of the northern dialect aroused xenophobia, never far beneath the surface in any Vietnamese village, and the Civic Action teams often were treated as aliens. The Vietminh stay-behind organization was quick to exploit this vulnerability. Rumors were skillfully spread about the dire ills these strangers were bringing to the villages. Vietminh guerrillas, who had been lying low, dug up their hidden weapons and went to work. Members of the Civic Action teams began to be murdered.

Hasty revisions were made in the Civic Action program. Most of the teams of northerners were switched to work in the new refugee communities where their fellow northerners were trying to start life over again. Southerners were recruited to man new teams, among them a number of promising young men from rural villages who were returned to work in their home districts after training. Finally, in the most dangerous zones, where guerrillas were on the prowl nightly, the Civic Action teams were brigaded with Civil Guard policemen and troop units, as the unarmed civilian component of such a force.

It is a sad commentary on the inhumanity of the long struggle in Vietnam that, after many years and changes of name, the original rationale behind the Civic Action program is still largely valid. Black-pajama-clad native cadre of what is currently called Revolutionary Development now go out to the countryside and work in the villages to help foster self-rule, self-development, and self-defense. The training they take is filled with memories of the youth who have gone before them and who met their deaths while trying to help their fellow men. Now the black-pajama cadre are armed in self-defense. The Communist leadership has put an ugly value on the merit of their work. One cadre killed is given the same high rating as one American killed, in listing merit for promotions and awards among the forces of the Vietcong and the North Vietnamese Army. The Communists established this equivalent rate in orders of March 15, 1967.

The doctors and nurses of Operation Brotherhood weren't the only Filipinos who caught the spirit of help for the Vietnamese in their predicament. A large group of Filipino veterans of the guerrilla fight against the Japanese and civilians, who served as volunteers in the Philippines' free election campaign of 1953, formed a nonprofit, public-service corporation in Manila in November 1954. They named their new organization the Freedom Company of the Philippines and described as its purpose "furthering the cause of freedom." They elected Frisco Johnny San Juan their president and included Magsaysay and me among the honorary members. I had met with the leaders of the new organization during my brief visit to Manila with General Hinh's coup lieutenants and had encouraged their enterprise. I felt that the presence in

Vietnam of such people, so visibly dedicated to the principle of man's liberty, would have a heartening effect upon Vietnamese nationalists.

When I mentioned the Filipinos of Freedom Company to Prime Minister Diem, I bumped right into the classical prejudices of Asia—a nationality tends to look down upon the people of neighboring countries. (In this respect, Southeast Asia is very much the Balkans of the Far East, seething with more ancient wrongs to be righted than even the black or white racial bigots of the U.S. could imagine.) With a grimace on his face, Diem told me that the Vietnamese didn't need the help of a bunch of orators and nightclub musicians (most of the dance bands in Asia at the time were made up of Filipinos). I reminded Diem of the Filipino doctors and nurses at work in Vietnam and noted that there was a woeful lack of trained Vietnamese in many other technical fields where the help of knowledgeable Filipinos would be invaluable. Diem said that he would have to sleep on it. I left it at that.

Frisco Johnny San Juan arrived in Saigon with a group of Freedom Company officials, to make a survey of ways in which they might be helpful to the Vietnamese. Since the Philippines hadn't recognized Vietnam diplomatically and had only one official in the country, military observer Colonel Jose Banzon, I suggested that he arrange a meeting for them with Diem. If Diem reacted favorably, then a contract might be drawn up between the Vietnamese government and the corporation for the services of the Filipinos. At their meeting, Diem became intrigued with the Filipinos' accounts of public service reforms in the Philippines, where San Juan had been active in modernizing the customs service and currently was serving as deputy chief of the Presidential Complaints and Action Commission. Before the meeting was over, a contract was signed between the government of Vietnam and the Freedom Company "to further the cause of freedom in Vietnam."

Later, both Diem and the Freedom Company officials asked

me separately for ideas on what the Filipinos might do. I told them both that Vietnam had greatest need of national institutions to start pulling the people together. Particularly important were institutions wherein the people could have a voice heard by the government. Since Vietnam was full of veterans from its years of recent warfare, how about a national veterans organization? Freedom Company had a number of elected officials of the Philippines Veterans Legion in it. San Juan himself recently had served as the National Commander of this legion. These Filipinos could help the veterans of Vietnam to form an organization of their own, with chapters throughout the country. Veterans would be inclined to speak up not only about their own needs but also about the affairs of their communities.

The idea was adopted. Freedom Company's first task in Vietnam was to provide guidance and encouragement in the founding of the Vietnamese Veterans Legion. The new organization earned funds by taking over the national distribution of newspapers and magazines. It soon had a booming membership of many thousands of veterans and set up chapters in nearly every province. Later in 1955 Freedom Company was asked to provide technicians to train Vietnamese soldiers in ordnance maintenance, vehicle repairs, the use of electrical equipment, and the running of quartermaster and other depots, and from time to time, it met Vietnamese requests for specialists in other areas.

After months of doing business out of my hip pocket in Vietnam, I was delighted to be assigned a formal office of my own in January 1955. Perhaps "formal" is too elegant a term. It actually was a little shed in the yard of MAAG headquarters in Cholon. Duckboards covered the dirt floor. Two bare light-bulbs, dangling from their cords, lit the interior. Folding chairs and field tables, and some open crates to hold files, completed the furnishings. The shed was one of several clustered around

the main building of the headquarters, which was an old
French colonial schoolhouse of cement and stucco noted principally in the neighborhood for having once been a whorehouse
set up by the Japanese for the convenience of their troops. The
French had assigned this place to the Americans as one of their
many "in" jokes. I never did find out the genesis of my own
particular shed.

My move to a daily stint in this shed at MAAG came after
I volunteered for the Franco-American organization that had
been agreed upon in December as the instrument for training
the Vietnamese Army. While details of just how the French
and the Americans were to work together were being thrashed
out, General O'Daniel gathered together the Americans selected
to staff the new organization and put us in the only available
space at his headquarters, the sheds in the yard, to do some
advance planning for the work ahead. There were four staff
divisions: army, navy, air force, and pacification. I headed
pacification, which was to guide the Vietnamese Army in its
moves to reoccupy former Vietminh zones as well as to oversee
any security operations in areas where guerrillas were still
terrorizing the population.

The next couple of weeks saw most of our basic planning
done, including suggested directives for the Vietnamese whenever they were ready to start the program. Although my own
planning drew heavily upon the lessons I had learned in the
Philippines and from my travels around the Vietnamese countryside, it also was tailored and shaped by the Vietnamese. I
discussed each step with the prime minister, the minister of
national defense, and the leaders of the Vietnamese Army,
whom I was continuing to see almost daily. This Vietnamese
input was the most important element in the planning. We
Americans and French would be guiding the Vietnamese into
taking control of their own affairs. If they were to succeed, the
proposed operations would have to be wholly understood and
accepted by the Vietnamese.

The first change they made was in the name of our program.

They objected to the word *pacification,* saying that it denoted a French colonial practice devised by General Lyautey in North Africa and applied in Vietnam by GAMOs (Mobile Administrative Groups) which had set up local governments and home guards in areas cleared by French Union forces. (I had seen the work of the GAMOs and thought that much of it was excellent.) The Vietnamese leaders did agree with the concept of using the Vietnamese Army to help and to protect the people, so I insisted that if they didn't like *pacification,* they pick a name themselves. After much head-scratching, the leaders chose a Vietnamese term for the work, which translated into English as *national security action.* We adopted this name promptly. Amusingly enough, the Vietnamese themselves (along with the French and Americans) continued to speak of the work as *pacification.* Years later, despite other official changes of name, it still is spoken of as *pacification.* Habit dies hard.

Toward the end of January, the new Franco-American training organization, TRIM, became a reality. The French command made the Cité Lorgeril, a walled compound in Cholon, consisting of a collection of pleasant villas around a courtyard, available as headquarters. Its organization was balanced, with scientific precision, between the Americans and the French. General O'Daniel was the chief of TRIM but acted under the authority of the top French commander, General Ely. TRIM's chief of staff (and my immediate boss) was that French briefing officer, Colonel Jean Carbonel, who had told the witless tale of my taking a suitcase full of money to Ba Cut. His deputy was an American, Lieutenant Colonel Bill Rosson. Under them were the chiefs of the four staff divisions (army, navy, air, and national security), two of whom were French and two American, each with a deputy of the other nationality. I was chief of the national security division. My deputy was a French paratrooper, Lieutenant Colonel Jacques Romain-Defosses. Our staff division had equal numbers of French and American officers.

There was too little amity in TRIM for me. The French

chief of staff who was my immediate boss seemed perpetually piqued at me and showed his feelings by refusing to speak to me directly. Instead, he would position his adjutant, a French officer, next to him and, while looking at me, would ask the adjutant to relay such and such a message to me. When the adjutant had finished, I would reply directly to the chief of staff, who promptly would ask the adjutant, "What did he say?" My reply would be repeated. It was lugubrious, since we all were being stiffly correct in military fashion and were speaking English face-to-face. He carried this practice into our official social life. At receptions he would stamp his feet and turn his back when I approached. I hardly endeared myself to him by my own behavior. I would put an arm across his shoulders familiarly and announce to those standing nearby in a grating American manner, "This guy is my buddy. You treat him right, you hear?" This made him explode, angrily shaking my arm off his shoulders. I found out that he continued to believe the convoluted fictions about my bribing Vietnamese with huge sums of money.

Most of the French officers in my staff division let me know openly that they were from various intelligence services. Once in a while, they would have the grace to blush when I came upon them as they were busy writing reports of my daily activities, presumably for a parent service. On the other hand, all of them had served in Vietnam for periods of six years or more and were exceptionally well-informed about Vietnamese life and geography. Thus my problem was to divert them from an unduly psychotic suspicion of everything I did and toward genuine help in the Vietnamese preparation for the serious and complex national security operations then underway. I was only partially successful.

For example, one of the French officers was from a clandestine service. He sat at a desk facing me, busied himself with paper work for a time, and then just sat there, staring. I noticed that his stare became more and more fixed on a telephone near me which was designated for English-language use. Even the telephones at TRIM were evenly divided between the two nationalities, although the execrable service was impartial. Both the French- and English-speaking phones were subject to sound effects apparently from outer space, additional voices picked up in midsentence or in shouts of "Allo, allo!" and dead silences. Nearly every incoming call would begin with blasphemous complaints about the long delays and frustrations involved in getting the call through to us. Then the caller would hurriedly shout his message before he was cut off. Knowing the performance record of the telephone, I assumed that the French officer staring at it was simply giving it a silent hate treatment.

But one morning, this English-language telephone rang. The French officer, who had been scribbling on a piece of paper and referring frequently to his French-English dictionary, jumped to his feet, snatched up the piece of paper, and rushed over to the ringing telephone before an American could reach it. Holding up the paper and reading from it, he spoke carefully into the mouthpiece, "I do not speak English, goodbye." Then he hung up. He looked at me to see if I had noticed his zany prank. I laughed aloud. He looked a bit surprised at my reaction and then grinned himself.

I went back to his desk with him. The French officer at the next desk was fluent in English and I asked if he would mind interpreting for the two of us. It was time that we all became better acquainted. We embarked upon a session of mutual talk. The prankster admitted that he had only three months longer to stay in Vietnam and frankly was sitting out the time until departure. I confessed that I didn't have all the answers on how to help the Vietnamese at the present moment. Since he had served many years among them, surely there must be at least one thing that he had long wanted to do for the Vietnamese that the war had prevented him from doing? If he named it, and if it could be fitted into our work, he could spend all of his remaining time at such a self-chosen task and have all the support I could muster.

He replied thoughtfully that he had long wanted to assist Vietnamese children and would like to draft an explicit proposal for a youth program to fit in with the national security concept. This sounded good, I said, worthy of backing, and his eyes lighted up. With such work to do, he told me that he would put in for further service in Vietnam, although he did want some brief home leave first because he had been away from his family for years. We parted on this agreeable note. The next day, at TRIM, he stood at attention before my desk, saluted, and informed me in formal tones that he had been ordered rotated back to France. His departure was set for the next day. Did he ask for an extension of duty in Vietnam, as we had discussed? He answered brusquely, "Yes, sir," his eyes showing a silent inner hurt. He told me that he would have to go. We said farewell.

Other French officers in my division also had deep feelings about ways in which they would really like to help the Vietnamese. I dug patiently for their ideas and put them to work on self-projects whenever I could. Abrupt departures continued. The staff division gradually settled into an atmosphere of surface civility, marred occasionally by outbursts pinned up on the bulletin board anonymously by both nationalities. We tackled a heavy workload of operational and logistical planning with the Vietnamese. Two large-scale national security campaigns and scores of other activities were enough to keep us all busy for a time. I will describe this work in the next chapter. It became part of the history of Vietnam.

The preoccupation of the French establishment in Vietnam with my presence led to a confrontation in this period. Apparently the various stories about my doings had been collected by the French clandestine service, whose officers made complaints about me to the CIA, their normal liaison. They claimed they had a long list of charges against my conduct. I learned of this from the ambassador, who said that the French wanted to confront me, make the charges one by one, and record my answers. Although he warned me that he objected to such a confrontation, because of the star-chamber aspect of the proceeding, I was eager to accept. I had had my fill of attempts at character assassination by so many of the French, and it was time to meet them head-on.

When this was being discussed in the ambassador's office, the CIA chief, a smug smile on his face, offered to host the meeting with the French at a luncheon at his home, saying that this would be acceptable to the French. He seemed to be relishing the meeting, apparently expecting me to get a severe verbal mauling or worse from his French associates. The French, he added, would let him sit in as an observer of the interrogation, and he promised to give the ambassador a complete report for forwarding to Washington. I said quickly that I would submit a report also, which could be forwarded concurrently. I felt like Daniel about to enter the lion's den.

So, one noon soon afterward, I met with the French at the home of the CIA chief in Saigon. The local director of the French clandestine service, a colonel with whom I had had a most friendly association in my work with the O'Daniel mission to Indochina in 1953, sat at a card table, papers spread out before him, face stern, back rigidly erect, and started the meeting by formally requesting that I respond as I wished to any of the charges which were listed in the papers before him. Since the list was very long, it was doubtful that all the items could be taken up before luncheon. We could break the meeting long enough to dine and then return to the inquisition. There were several of his officers present who were thoroughly knowledgeable about the incidents on his list, and did I mind their presence, since they would be advising him on the correctness of any answers I gave? I assured him that I was pleased to have them present.

The first item charged me with supplying arms to Ba Cut, the Hoa Hao rebel, by an airdrop on a specific date. I could hardly believe my ears. I broke out laughing. The French officers glared. My laughter offended them. When I caught my breath again, I explained to them that on the specific date they had named, an airdrop indeed had been made to Ba Cut (who had been made a colonel in the Vietnamese Army by General Hinh just before his departure for Paris, although Ba Cut remained antagonistic toward the Saigon government). However, the operation demonstrably wasn't mine.

The Vietnamese Army, I informed them, had observed this airdrop and had investigated it. The Vietnamese Army had recovered three of the parachutes and traced them by their markings to a French military unit. French officers had been present with Ba Cut when he received the airdrop. The tail markings of the delivery aircraft had been noted, and a check with flight operations records and personnel at Tan Son Nhut airport had revealed the names of the French pilots and crew who had been aboard the aircraft at the time the delivery was made to Ba Cut. The Diem government had lodged a formal complaint to the French command about this incident, thoroughly documented. Whatever made them feel that, by some magic, I had had a hand in this purely French operation?

My inquisitors were shaken. The colonel turned aside and whispered urgently to the panel of "informed experts" who were sitting in. Then he gamely read off the second item. I was charged with supplying arms to Trinh minh Thé, thus assisting him in his fight against the French who, after all, were allies of the Americans. I answered this assertion in as quiet a tone as I could. Trinh minh Thé and his Lien-Minh troops were on their way to Saigon to be integrated into the regular Vietnamese Army and were certainly not about to fight the French unless the French tried to stop this move and thus interfere with the best interests of the Vietnamese Army— which they had asserted formally that they would aid. The

fighting had ended *after* I had visited Trinh minh Thé in Tay
Ninh, and I trusted that the significance of this fact, along with
the safe return of three French prisoners whom the Lien-Minh
had held, wasn't lost on them.

However, I continued, speaking of weapons, I had noticed
several U.S. machine guns which the Lien-Minh had captured
from French forces sent against them, and I had copied down
the serial numbers of these guns to have them checked against
U.S. lists in Saigon. They had been supplied originally by the
U.S. to the French in Hanoi in 1951, to support French actions
against the Communists. I had some sharp questions in my mind
about how these weapons had been switched from use against
the Communists to use by French forces against a Vietnamese
officer who was known to be fighting the Communists, since
he had captured the weapons in question from the French.

At this point in the proceedings, luncheon was announced.
The French officers told our host that they couldn't stay for
lunch. As a matter of fact, they couldn't continue the meeting
any longer because they had urgent business to attend to elsewhere. They rose, gathered up their papers, and prepared to
depart. Their faces were flushed with embarrassment. The first
two items had blown up against them like exploding cigars, and
they didn't want to sit there and be exposed to further humilia-
tion. I insisted that they stay and finish the inquisition, whether
they ate lunch or not, since the whole business was their idea,
not mine. Reluctantly, they sat down again and we worked our
way through the whole list. It was clear that the French officers
thoroughly regretted having to go through with the farce they
had begun.

All but one of the charges were patently inventions, easily
destroyed fictions. The exception was the charge that my team
in Haiphong was planning "to blow up the harbor of Haiphong."
I admitted that they had talked about this subject and then
explained the background. The French admiral commanding in
Haiphong was an older man who lived next door to the house

where my team and other Americans lived. The Americans had noticed that the French admiral's water closet was only a few feet from their house and that he spent an unusually long time seated on the toilet every morning; and whimsy had seized them. How could they give the old gentleman a thrill while he sat there of a morning? Should they throw firecrackers through the window? No, his heart might not stand the strain. They had hit instead upon the idea of talking loudly about blowing up the whole harbor, water and all, before it had to be turned over to the Vietminh. The admiral, overhearing this, bolted out of the bathroom to send an urgent message to General Ely. I had been informed of the incident promptly and had told these American officers to stop scaring French admirals. They had promised to behave. However, if the French Navy officers were still frightened, I would take further measures. The French officers told me curtly that that wouldn't be necessary.

The meeting ended. Presumably, the French command received a report of these proceedings. I gave my own summary report to our ambassador, to forward to Washington with whatever information the local CIA chief was reporting. The whole business should have ended there. Of course it didn't, the perversity of human nature being what it is. French attempts at character assassination continued, reaching their peak some weeks later in the spring of 1955. The fictions invented by French circles in Saigon found their way into the French press and eventually into the lurid journalism of weekend supplements in newspapers of other European countries. Well-meaning people would clip these stories and send them to me. They added a Mad Hatter touch to the events I was living through.

The whistle could have been blown on me for other activities in early 1955, though. For example, I passed along some psywar ideas to a group of Vietnamese nationalists who were getting ready to leave North Vietnam for the South. They described the

long barrage of Communist propaganda which they had suffered for years. They were burning to strike a final blow in
return before they departed from their northern homes. Did
I have any suggestions? Indeed I did. I gave them two, which
they promptly adopted.

The first idea was used just before the French quit the city
of Hanoi and turned over control to the Vietminh. At the time,
the Communist apparatus inside the city was busy with secret
plans to ready the population to welcome the entry of Vietminh
troops. I suggested that my nationalist friends issue a fake Communist manifesto, ordering everyone in the city except essential
hospital employees to be out on the streets not just for a few
hours of welcome but for a week-long celebration. In actuality
this would mean a seven-day work stoppage. Transportation,
electric power, and communication services would be suspended. This simple enlargement of plans already afoot should
give the Communists an unexpectedly vexing problem as they
started their rule.

An authentic-looking manifesto was printed and distributed
during the hours of darkness on the second night before the
scheduled entry of the Vietminh. The nationalists had assured
me that they could distribute it safely because the chief of
police in Hanoi was a close friend of theirs and would rescue
any of them who might be caught and arrested. The next day
the inhabitants of Hanoi read the fake manifesto and arranged
to be away from homes and jobs for a one-week spree in the
streets. The manifesto looked so authentic that the Communist
cadre within the city bossily made sure, block by block, that
the turnout would be 100 percent. A last-minute radio message
from the Communists outside the city, ordering the Communists
inside to disregard this manifesto, was taken to be a French
attempt at counterpropaganda and was patriotically ignored.
When the Vietminh forces finally arrived in Hanoi, their leaders
began the touchy business of ordering people back to work. It
took them three days to restore public services. A three-day

work stoppage was a substantial achievement for a piece of paper.

When the nationalists saw me later in Saigon, however, they were woebegone. One arrest had been made when the manifesto was distributed. Their friend, the chief of police, became so imbued with the spirit of the affair that he had taken a stack of the manifestoes out in his car to help directly in the distribution. The French caught him in the act and, with the evidence of the copies of the manifesto in his possession, were convinced that he was a Communist agent. They had arrested him and put him in his own prison. He begged to be taken south as a prisoner. The French had done so and had turned him over to the Vietnamese government in Saigon. Nobody believed his story that the manifesto was a fake. He was being held in jail. Would I help? I explained what had happened to Prime Minister Diem. It took me until January to overcome his skepticism and obtain the release.

The second idea utilized Vietnamese superstitions in an American form. I had noted that there were many soothsayers in Vietnam doing a thriving business, but I had never seen any of their predictions published. Why not print an almanac for 1955 containing the predictions of the most famous astrologers and other arcane notables, especially those who foresaw a dark future for the Communists? Modestly priced—gratis copies would smack too much of propaganda—it could be sold in the North before the last areas there were evacuated. If it were well done, copies would probably pass from hand to hand and be spread all over the Communist-controlled regions.

The result was a hastily printed almanac filled with predictions about forthcoming events in 1955, including troubled times for the people in Communist areas and fights among the Communist leadership. To my own amazement, it foretold some things that actually happened (such as the bloody suppression of farmers who opposed the poorly-executed land reforms and the splits in the Politburo). The almanac became a best seller in Haiphong, the major refugee port. Even a large reprint order was sold out as soon as it hit the stands. My nationalist friends told me that it was the first such almanac seen in Vietnam in modern times. They were embarrassed to discover that a handsome profit had been made from what they had intended as a patriotic contribution to the nationalist cause. Unobtrusively, they donated this money to the funds helping the refugees from the North.

N O T E S

FREEDOM COMPANY. Freedom Company of the Philippines expanded its services into Laos as well as Vietnam, becoming particularly noted for its skillful training of mechanics and artisans. After the death of President Magsaysay, the leaders of Freedom Company formed a new profit-making corporation called Eastern Construction Company, Inc. (ECCOI), which took over Freedom Company contracts in Vietnam and Laos, retaining much of the spirit of the original group.

PLANNERS. The staff of Americans who worked with me in the shed at MAAG in January 1955, developing pacification plans, were Army Lieutenant Colonels Chuck Hash, Sam Karrick, and Ed Quereau, Navy Lieutenant Joe Redick, and Army Lieutenant Rufe Phillips.

★ ★

CHAPTER THIRTEEN

1955 PACIFICATION CAMPAIGNS

THE EARLY WEEKS of 1955 were filled with work on pacification, or what Diem insisted on calling national security action. There were long planning sessions between my TRIM staff division and the Vietnamese, almost continuous briefings of officials to make sure that they understood the program, inspections of troop training and logistical effectiveness, and then guidance and support for the operations themselves when they got under way. It was the kind of constructive effort that made it fun to get out of bed in the morning and go to work.

As 1955 began, there still were two large regroupment zones in South Vietnam for the Vietminh, as provided in the Geneva accords. When the Vietminh moved out of the zones to go north of the demarcation zone at the 17th Parallel, the Vietnamese government was to move in and assume control. It was this moving in and assuming control that was the main effort of the pacification program; it had to be handled correctly so that the inhabitants of these areas would welcome the arrival of the Saigon government. The agreement was that the first regroupment zone, the Camau Peninsula at the southern tip of Vietnam, would be available for takeover on February 8. The second zone, the provinces of Quang Ngai and Binh Dinh along the coast in the central region of Vietnam, would be taken over in phased steps, a section a day, starting on April 22. Apart from the need of these two regroupment zones for government authority, there were other areas already supposedly under Saigon control but in actuality ruled only sketchily and in disorderly fashion, with much banditry and terrorism. These other areas required attention also.

Vietnamese capable of doing this work were in short supply. There were few college graduates in Vietnam; and most of them were professional people outside of government. By and large, affairs in Vietnam were being run by high school graduates who had made up the civil service and the officer corps of the military under the French. The civilians had been restricted to relatively minor posts during French rule; the senior military officers had risen only to command of a battalion, with few allowed the experience of commanding even a temporary grouping of two or three battalions in a mobile force. Now, in the pacification program, we were asking these Vietnamese to run much larger and more complex operations than anything they had ever handled previously. Nearly all high school graduates were city-bred, since few farm families could afford to send their children to school in the cities, where the high schools were. This was also a problem, for pacification would take place in the countryside, and familiarity with what to expect there could be a key to its success.

In my talks with Diem, I had underscored the paucity of talent in the civil service for duty in the provinces, although training such as Cung's Civic Action program eventually would produce more. The military forces were richer in executive talent, both numerically and in knowledge of the countryside. Most of the troops were country-bred lads who had been inducted into military life by army recruiters moving around with the troop units, and most of the fighting and the troop movements had been away from the cities and in the provinces.

Furthermore, the Vietnamese Army was the only organization with a nationwide communication system, since the civil radio and telegraph system still suffered from wartime damages. The army could send orders to any unit in the country and get disciplined action as desired. The civilian ministries couldn't. All of this argued for the interim use of the army in quickly extending Saigon's administrative control throughout South Vietnam.

Diem had agreed with the thrust of these remarks. He also shared my views that soldiers trained to fight would need further training if their main task were diverted to giving help and protection to the people. It was important, however, that the Saigon government should strive for the ideal of that civil rule instead of military rule. The use of military forces should be kept to a minimum and even then should be clearly acknowledged as a temporary expedient. Readying civil servants to replace the military must be given high priority, with an orderly and established plan of replacement.

After much thought and talk, the pacification program was initiated with a directive issued by Diem as prime minister, and implementing directives quickly followed from the defense minister and the chief of staff of the Vietnamese armed forces (composed now not only of the army, but also of the new navy, air force, and marines). A suggestion of mine was incorporated. The situation in each province would be judged to determine which of three categories applied most closely to it: national security, transition, or civil. A national security province was one deemed to be too lawless for civil authorities to be effective; troops would be deployed there to halt terrorism and to start the rule of law, and the military commander would serve as province chief for civil matters as well as his military duties. A transition province was one making good progress toward a peaceful condition; the military commander would have a civilian deputy for civil matters—and their roles would be reversed as progress continued. A civil province was one peaceful enough for civilian rule to be effective; a civilian would be province chief.

Arbitrarily, we decided that the provinces in the Vietminh regroupment zones should be graded "national security" in those initial days when the Saigon government moved in to occupy them after the Vietminh left. We simply didn't know enough about conditions there to warrant taking a chance on anything else. It made sense to use troops in these provinces. What about the other provinces in Vietnam? There were more than thirty that would have to be considered and assigned an appropriate category. Diem was about to designate these provincial categories by fiat, when I hit upon an idea. Why not give officials who knew these provinces a voice in judging the proper category? All the top civilian and military officials throughout South Vietnam had been invited to a meeting in Saigon, February 3–5, to be told about the new pacification program. Why not let them present their views openly in this meeting and have a board of ministers present to make the final determination right on the spot?

I had put forward this suggestion with the thought that a healthy, open debate would bring out all the pertinent facts about current conditions in each province. I was unprepared for the emotional storm that broke upon the February meeting when this was tried. The hall in Saigon was packed with Vietnamese and French civilian officials and military officers, hundreds of them. Each, it seemed, had an opinion about each province. Those currently holding local power in a province tended to make it sound like paradise. Those hoping for these jobs or simply envious of the jobholders tended to make a province sound like hell on earth. Others simply sounded off about how disgusted their provincial friends were with the war, with the Saigon government, with the price of rice, or with a thousand other things. The French participants made speeches about each province, the burden of which was that only they could bring back the halcyon days a province had known, halcyon days which were then described. Tempers flared, of course. Shouted rebuttals were much in evidence throughout three feverish days of meeting. Finally, though, it was over. Each province had been assigned a category. Nobody could say that it hadn't been discussed exhaustively first.

The training of troops for pacification operations centered largely on improving the behavior of soldiers toward the civilian population. Some of this training took, some didn't. For example, one of the earliest efforts was to correct the bad habits of military drivers. A soldier put behind the wheel of a jeep or a big truck became a Walter Mitty who envisioned himself the underdog entry in a Grand Prix road race, coming from behind the pack to roar in first at the finish line. Cooperation sagged whenever military vehicles careered wildly through village roads, scattering inhabitants, chickens, and pigs in their path.

The troops assigned to move into Camau were lectured on the courtesy of the road. Then a good driver contest was held, with prizes and medals for the most courteous driver in each unit. The awards ceremony was held in a public square in the town of Soc Trang. It was a big event, attended by most of the town's population. An army band gave a concert. Medals and prizes were bestowed upon the most courteous drivers. After the ceremony was over and the large crowd was breaking up, the honored drivers jumped into their trucks, gunned their engines *varoom-varoom*, and went roaring off for home right through the crowd. People jumped for their lives, clearing lanes for these juggernauts, cursing the bemedaled drivers.

The psywar officers and men of G-5 in the Vietnamese Army were assigned the task of troop indoctrination. A series of playlets were written and performed by G-5 teams before troop audiences, with compulsory attendance. Each playlet gave a dramatized example of good and bad troop behavior among civilians, emphasizing the consequences. The cast consisted of a Good Soldier, a Bad Soldier, and the Villagers. In one playlet the Good Soldier would pay the villagers for a chicken, while the Bad Soldier would steal one over the Villagers' protests; afterward the Villagers would talk about the soldiers, with friendly words for the Good Soldier's unit but with Villagers going to help the local guerrillas attack the other unit, the Bad Soldier's unit. In another playlet the Villagers mouthed the current Vietminh propaganda against the Saigon government, and the Good Soldier answered this reasonably with accurate facts, while the Bad Soldier surlily told the people to shut up. There were a dozen of these playlets, performed from the back of trucks.

This behavioral training and indoctrination fell far short of efforts common to Asian Communist forces, where the early rules for behavior in the Chinese Communist 8th Route Army are still the basis for constant lectures by political officers and are enforced by iron discipline. (Offenders are often shot.) The Communist rules are known as the "three great disciplinary measures" and the "eight noteworthy points." The measures are "Act in accordance with orders; do not take anything from the people; do not allow self-interest to injure public interest." The points are "Put back the door (after being used as a bed); tie up straws (after use as a mattress); talk pleasantly; buy and sell fairly; return everything borrowed; indemnify everything damaged; do not bathe in view of women; and do not rob personal belongings of captives." The rules are the very essence of people's warfare. When the troops unite with the people, the war starts being won. Asian Communists understand this. Too few on our side do. People still get trampled under as our soldiers strive for the tactical goals given them. As long as this happens, we cannot win.

The xenophobia of the Vietnamese became marked on the eve of the occupation of Camau, or "Operation Liberty," as this occupation campaign was called officially. All the Vietnamese concerned with the operation, from Diem on down, made it plain to me that they wanted no foreigners present when they marched in. Communist propaganda had pictured the Saigon government people as the "running dogs" of French colonialists. Saigon leaders wanted the population to see only Vietnamese in the occupying force, to permit a fair chance to rebut the Communist propaganda and to start convincing the people that Vietnam was independent and was able to govern itself. I admit that I was sympathetic to this expressed need. But there were some practical things that needed doing, and there were no Vietnamese to do them. Reports of health conditions in Camau were alarming. To help the people, medical teams should enter Camau with the troops. The single Vietnamese doctor with the troops would have his hands full taking care of soldiers. If the population were to be given medical assistance, foreigners would have to be used.

The French military, the French Red Cross, and the Filipinos of Operation Brotherhood all offered to send in medical teams to help the people of Camau. I pleaded their case with Diem and other officials. The Vietnamese were adamant. No foreigners! I had some wry moments as the French blamed me for this turndown and, on their part, the Vietnamese accused me of pushing the "French cause."

Since the Vietnamese were gentler in their refusal of Filipino help, I decided to change tactics. The refusers were male, and there were some mighty pretty girls among the the Filipina nurses. I suggested that Operation Brotherhood take several of the prettiest nurses on a visit to Soc Trang, where I was meeting with Vietnamese Army leaders for a last-minute check of the Camau march-in. When our Soc Trang military meeting broke up for a bountiful luncheon, I managed to have the Operation Brotherhood group invited to join us. The senior Vietnamese officers vied with one another to have pretty Filipinas seated beside them at the luncheon. Lunch had hardly started before the Vietnamese had decided that Philippine medical teams simply must accompany them into Camau. Arrangements were made on the spot. There is an ancient Asian custom of using a pretty girl as a negotiator. I kicked myself for not thinking of it sooner. (Operation Brotherhood went into Camau by Vietnamese Army truck and set up a field hospital in an abandoned schoolhouse, with mobile teams visiting the villages. The inhabitants loved them. The parents of the first baby born in this hospital named the child "O.B.," in gratitude.)

The Francophobia of the Vietnamese complicated my work in other ways. For one thing, they didn't want the French to know the detailed plan for the occupation of Camau, such as the timetable for the arrival of each unit; they suspected that the French would find some way to louse up the operation and make the Vietnamese Army look bad. Yet I had both French and U.S. officers of my TRIM division helping to prepare the Vietnamese forces for the operation. They needed to know enough to be effective in their help. I finally got the Vietnamese to disclose details so that we could do practical things about logistics, but not before one excruciating episode took place. The scene was a briefing session given by the commander of the Camau operation, Lieutenant Colonel Duong van Duc, with General O'Daniel and assorted French and U.S. officers present. Lieutenant Colonel Duc described his operational plan without using notes. General O'Daniel found a lot of faults in Duc's oral presentation and started pressing him with questions. I whispered in O'Daniel's ear that Duc had invented a fake plan on the spur of the moment, just because O'Daniel had brought French officers to the briefing—which I had warned him against. Later, I showed O'Daniel the real plan. Still later, I got Duc to go over his real plan with my TRIM staff.

The Vietnamese prohibition against foreigners accompanying the troops into the operational area was extended to include the officers in my TRIM division, whom I'd wanted to go along as advisers. Lieutenant Colonel Duc finally gave in to the pleas of his own officers and let me place in the operation zone two of my U.S. officers who were popular among the Vietnamese.

Lieutenant Colonel Sam Karrick would advise on logistics at the operation's base. Second Lieutenant Rufe Phillips would accompany an irregular force which would enter the zone via rivers and canals and join with the road-bound main Vietnamese Army force at Camau town. Phillips, who had played football at Yale, was a towheaded six-footer, a giant among the smaller Vietnamese. He stood out like a sore thumb. Some French officers resented his inclusion bitterly and, one day, pointed out Phillips to Vietnamese officials and asked point-blank, "When you say no foreigners can go along with you, why do you take *that* foreigner with you?" The Vietnamese looked at Phillips and explained, "He's no foreigner. He's our *friend!*"

Word of Phillips' presence evidently went up the French chain of command to General Ely and from him to General Collins, the American ambassador. In the next U.S. Country Team meeting, Collins took General O'Daniel to task for there being only one TRIM adviser with the Vietnamese troops in the Camau operation, and a second lieutenant at that; with all those battalions going in, there should be dozens of advisers, hopefully including some lieutenant colonels at least. "He's one of Ed's people," O'Daniel answered, turning to me. "Oh, that's different," said Collins. I hastily explained what was happening in the operation at that point, how it was succeeding without a bossy mob of French and American advisers tagging along. Diem was flying down to Camau for a visit. After the prime minister had his day in Camau, there would be ample time for all foreigners who so wished to visit and see whatever they wanted.

The Camau operation went down in Vietnamese history as a success. The people responded to the friendliness and humanitarian attitude of the Saigon government forces whenever and wherever exhibited. The Communist cadre had urged the people to display only sullen acquiescence, and at first the people dutifully attempted this. But it was impossible for the people to remain aloof in the face of so much willingness to help, so much evidence that someone really cared about them. Many thousands of brightly colored pictures of the nationalist Vietnamese flag and of Ngo dinh Diem were handed out to villagers who tore down the faded old pictures of Ho chi Minh in their households and replaced them with the new Saigon pictures. More significantly, the people voluntarily started to reveal the location of secret caches of weapons and ammunition, to give names of those in Vietminh stay-behind organizations, and to pitch in to work alongside the soldiers in rebuilding and repairing destroyed or neglected public structures.

Diem, busy with affairs in Saigon, delayed his visit to Camau for a week. I nagged him in daily talks until he went, as much to shut me up as for any other reason. Just about every man, woman, and child in Camau town turned out to greet him. It wasn't too orderly. People waved excitedly and called out to him. Some broke out of the crowds to talk with him. It was an infectious scene. Troops drawn up as an honor guard, rigidly at present arms to salute the visitor, forgot their discipline and broke out in cheers. The scene was repeated over and over as he rambled through the town and neighboring areas. When Diem returned to Saigon, he seeemd revitalized, bubbling over with new energy. He had received a heady dose of genuinely demonstrated popularity.

In the euphoric aftermath of the Camau operation, Duc was promoted to colonel and then became Vietnam's first ambassador to Korea. Rufe Phillips was promoted to first lieutenant.

There was one serious error made in the Camau operation, for which I blame myself. It concerned the U Minh forest on the east coast of the Camau Peninsula. The forest was a vast tangle of mangrove swamp. The scouting force (mostly ex-Vietminh who had rallied to the government) told me that perhaps a hundred Vietminh soldiers were hiding in the U Minh. Local folks and public health officials said that this mangrove area was notorious for its high incidence of cerebral malaria and other deadly diseases. Thus, when it came to the question of using troops either for a thorough search of the U Minh or for other pressing duties, I suggested the latter course. With the U Minh borders guarded, I figured that the Vietminh in the forest would waste away or come out and surrender. The fact is that, despite a high death rate, the Vietminh stayed, survived, and built up a considerable base complex in the U Minh. Later, it became an area for supplies, training, and rest for Vietcong guerrilla forces. Eventually, captured Americans were among the prisoners held there. It remains today a hygienically and politically pestilential sore threatening the life of South Vietnam.

Once the Camau operation was well under way, plans were drawn for the occupation of the last remaining large area being vacated by the Vietminh. This area was what the Geneva accords called the "Central Vietnam provisional assembly area—last installment." It ran along the coastline for about a hundred and fifty miles and inland for some fifty to sixty miles, totaling about eight thousand square miles, and included the provinces of Quang Ngai and Binh Dinh far to the north of Saigon. There was a coastal plain running back several miles from the China Sea, then foothills and valleys, and finally a heavy mass of mountains, mostly covered by dense jungle. A paved highway and a railroad followed along its length, near the coast. Another paved highway ran into the interior near the southern end of the area, and there were a few other sketchy roads and trails. The Saigon government was scheduled to start moving into this area on April 22, entering at the northern end and proceeding south one section at a time, adhering to a rigid timetable. The Vietminh would embark at the port of Qui Nhon at its southern end, from where they would go by sea transport to Haiphong in North Vietnam.

This was more than double the area of the Camau operation. Obviously, more troops would be needed. The Vietnamese

Army was undergoing a touch of Americanization in its organization, including the creation of regiments and divisions from its former hodgepodge of separate battalions. The newly formed 31st and 32nd Divisions of the Vietnamese Army were designated as the force to be used. Diem and the army's General Staff picked a name for the campaign: Operation Giai-Phong, meaning liberating from a dungeon or breaking from chains. Colonel Le van Kim was appointed commander. He was secretary of the General Staff at the time, was believed to be an officer capable of handling so large a body of troops, had his ancestral home in the operational area, and had worked closely with my TRIM staff in preparing a study of "Lessons Learned in Camau." The "lessons" were published in Vietnamese, English, and French and were widely distributed within the Vietnamese government as a guide to the proper way to extend Saigon's administration over the country.

Colonel Kim was that rare creature, a Vietnamese graduate of the French War College. It made our planning sessions with him go quickly and well, but it also aroused the suspicion of Diem and his brothers, who thought that perhaps Kim had been so favored by the French that he had become more French than Vietnamese. When the Vietnamese General Staff and the defense minister proposed to Diem that Kim be appointed commander, Diem had hesitated, worried mostly because Kim was so proud of being a French citizen. This led to a private session between the two men, in which Diem asked Kim to choose between French and Vietnamese citizenship. Kim chose Vietnam. Even this didn't satisfy Diem's brothers Nhu (who lived with Diem) and Can (who lived with Diem's mother in Hué). Each brother put his own agents into the group of civil administrators who were to accompany the troops in Operation Giai-Phong. During the campaign itself, the agents sent in a flood of reports about Kim's activities. Some of the reports were so venomous that I finally urged Diem to pick somebody himself whom he personally trusted and have this man check closely on the truth of the reports. Diem did so. The poison-pen reports stopped.

As in Camau, the Vietnamese insisted that only one foreign adviser, Lieutenant Phillips, accompany their troops in Operation Giai-Phong. Again, the French and American officers of my TRIM staff provided backup support for the operation from the outside. We were in constant voice communication by radio with Phillips, who lived and worked with Kim, the operation's commander. By now people had become used to the arrangement. No longer were there complaints about only one American junior officer advising the Vietnamese, even though Giai-Phong deployed what essentially was a full corps of troops. Our method worked.

As in Camau, Filipino doctors and nurses of Operation Brotherhood followed the troops into the zone, where they set up a temporary hospital and undertook public health services. A typhoon struck the coast, broaching their supply ship and flooding their work areas. Dario Arellano, who had been photographing the Philippine medical work, managed to get back to Saigon in the storm to give me details for our efforts to relieve their situation. Among other things, he mentioned that the Filipinos had found an old building on a hill above the flood, empty, ancient, but with a roof still sound, and had moved into it. It was a fine shelter, but the first night the Filipinos had discovered that it was full of ghosts, spectral figures in the habits of priests and monks! Would I please tell the Filipinos what in the world they had found? Nobody there seemed to know. The next day I asked Diem. He was a walking encyclopedia of facts about his country. Sure enough, he told me about a Catholic monastery built on the site long ago. Some fifty years before, it had become a nunnery, but the nuns had moved out nearly ten years ago. The building had remained deserted until the Filipinos moved in for shelter from the typhoon. I then told him about the ghosts seen by the Filipinos. Patiently, in matter-of-fact tones, he explained to me that the ghosts probably were monks and priests who had died there a hundred years ago. When I passed this along, the Filipinos surprised me by staying there. They said the ghosts were friendly!

Operation Giai-Phong also went down in the history books as a success, despite efforts at spoilage by the Communists. When the Vietnamese Army entered the zone from the north, the Vietminh troops were withdrawing to their port of embarkation in the south, leaving behind destroyed bridges, a main highway scarred by deep ditches cut every few feet, torn up railroad tracks, confiscated telegraph and telephone lines, and scare stories among the population—the "they eat babies for breakfast" sort—about the ruthlessly inhumane behavior they could expect from the Vietnamese Army soldiers. The discipline and friendliness of the Vietnamese Army troops, along with their evident willingness to help the people by rebuilding destroyed markets, the roofs of homes, roads, and bridges soon overcame the fears the departing Communists had instilled among the people.

The hate campaign of the Communists boomeranged, largely because of the exemplary behavior of the nationalist troops. By the third day, news of their brotherly attitude had spread ahead of their march. Villagers lined up along the road, cheering them and passing out food and drink. By the fourth day, villagers were showing the nationalist troops where the Communists had hidden caches of weapons, ammunition, and other supplies. Meanwhile, at the southern end of the zone in the vicinity of Qui Nhon, the port of embarkation, the people were turning hostile toward the Vietminh soldiers. Communist political officers with these troops had been dragooning teen-agers, to take them north for schooling, promising their eventual return. Families began hiding their children in the hills. When the dragooning finally reached down to twelve-year-olds, popular feeling erupted. As the last units of the Vietminh troops marched through the streets of Qui Nhon town to board their transports, the aroused population threw rocks at them, screaming invective. It was hardly a noble exit. All this happened while the Vietnamese Army was still miles away on its march toward the town.

When reports came in from intelligence agents about what was happening there, I urged Diem to break away from his work in Saigon and fly to Qui Nhon, timing his arrival for the entry of the Vietnamese Army into the town. The mood of the people there justified his appearance as the nation's leader. When Diem ordered an aircraft for the flight, I suggested that now also was the time to take some foreigners with him, including French officials who had been so skeptical of his status among the people. I felt it was worth waiving the injunction against the presence of foreigners, since the town's reaction to having a nationalist leader share in its liberation should prove to be an eye-opener for even the most cynical observer. Thus it was that a French general and several French journalists journeyed to Qui Nhon with Diem.

Diem arrived at Qui Nhon just as the Vietnamese Army was entering town. His aircraft circled overhead and then landed at the airport. The nationalist troops went racing out to the airport, joined by the town's inhabitants as word spread of Diem's arrival. Only a handful of people were present when he stepped out of his aircraft. Moments later, troops and people came swarming in, forming a dense crowd around him. The diminutive Diem seemed to disappear among them. Then the excited people did something hitherto unknown among the Vietnamese. They boosted him up on their shoulders, so that all the crowd could see. A great cheer went up. The startled look on Diem's face, at the unexpected manhandling, turned into a wide grin. He let go of a head he had been clutching to steady himself and waved. Another great cheer went up. Diem pleaded to be put down. They set him down on the ground and he made his way through the crowd on foot, happily exchanging greetings. It was a vivid and turbulently happy scene. The French onlookers found it incredible. One told me that he wouldn't have believed it unless he had seen it, adding, "I didn't know the people loved him. It's much more than Ho chi Minh ever got." I hoped that it was a moment that all would remember—Diem, the foreigners, the troops, and the people.

NOTES

PACIFICATION. "National Security Action" was established by Diem in his directive 278/PTT/OP/M. In the February 1955 implementing orders from the Ministry of National Defense, there were explicit descriptions of the work to be done by troops and administrative teams in the former Vietminh zones. The tag line of these descriptions was: "To sum up, the inhabitants, treated as loyal subjects of a liberating regime, will be led to choose for themselves the regime which they will defend against any current sabotage or any future threat."

OCCULTISM. The Vietnamese had small need of Filipino ghost stories. Vietnam was so filled with the arcane that I used to advise Americans to read Kipling's "Kim" and pay heed to the description of young Kimball O'Hara's counterintelligence training in awareness of illusions. Nearly every Vietnamese leader I knew had, at some time, consulted a soothsayer from among the hosts of practitioners in spiritualism, numerology, astrology, palmistry, phrenology, necromancy, geomancy, and animistic wizardry. According to believers, even the streets of Saigon were haunted by those killed in traffic accidents, causing the vision of live drivers to blur momentarily as they passed scenes of past fatalities. However, it was by the good or ill omens of numbers that the Vietnamese were most affected, particularly dates. There was almost universal Vietnamese belief in the bad luck of 5, such as the 5th, 14th, and 23rd days of the Chinese lunar month used in Vietnamese calendars (with 1 plus 4 and 2 plus 3 each adding up to 5). Commercial airline travel fell off sharply on those days, and officials or generals who started operations on such days were regarded as ill-fated or foolish. I would caution Americans about Vietnamese superstitious dates but would also remind them of our own ethic by quoting Psalms 118:24, "This is the day which the Lord hath made; we will rejoice and be glad in it."

★ ★

CHAPTER
FOURTEEN

UNITED SECTS FRONT

T HERE IS THE WAY the rest of the world does things. And then
there is the Vietnamese way. The Vietnamese seem to insist
upon being different and unpredictable, and sometimes a touch
of this perversity rubs off on the foreigner in their midst, causing
him to add twists of his own to what is already going awry.
Ordinarily, such cantankerous behavior is absorbed in the daily
tumult of life in Vietnam and earns only momentary notice.
This wasn't the case in 1955, however. In the first months after
the spring 1955 Tet celebration ushering in the Lunar Year of
the Goat, there was a sudden madness that nearly tore Vietnam apart at the seams.

The signs of the times offered every expectation of a peaceful
spring full of national progress. Diem was mastering his duties
as prime minister, daily showing more executive skill. Hundreds
of thousands of northern refugees were building new lives and
new homes in the South. The Vietnamese Army had left the
troubled days of General Hinh far behind and was absorbing
the new ways taught by French and American advisers in
TRIM. The pacification campaign in Camau had gone well, and
the upcoming one in Central Vietnam (Operation Giai-Phong)

promised to go better. New hope had been born in the country-side as farmers worked land that had lain fallow during the war years. The sect warlord problem was being solved, with the integration of several sect forces into the national army: the Lien-Minh guerrillas of Trinh minh Thé, 10,000 Cao Dai troops under General Nguyen thanh Phuong, the remaining Hoa Hao regiment under General Nguyen giac Ngo (whose other regiment had been integrated previously), and four Hoa Hao battalions under Lieutenant Colonel Nguyen van Hue. The way had been opened for integrating other sect forces. General Ely, the top French commander, was becoming amenable to giving up French control of the Vietnamese armed forces and had even started thinking about the removal of the French Expeditionary Corps from Vietnam.

On March 5 the upbeat pattern faltered. That day the leaders of the Vietnamese sects met together in Cholon and decided to take the government away from Diem and divide it up among themselves. Their meeting was called by Bay Vien, the vice lord of the metropolis, who had bought authority over the police from Bao Dai and who had his own Binh Xuyen sect army. He was smarting under decrees issued in January by Diem, which were aimed at keeping underage youngsters away from houses of prostitution and at curbing the narcotics trade. Bay Vien told the gathering of Cao Dai and Hoa Hao leaders (his Binh Xuyen henchmen were mixed in among them) that the people of South Vietnam needed a better government than "that fool" Diem was providing. If the sects could unite long enough for a political act, they could demand and get the government posts controlling the fiscal and manpower resources of the country. Diem would be kicked upstairs to be an honorary prime minister while they actually ran things. If they pooled their military forces into a single mighty army, Diem would be frightened into accepting their demands. It should be easy.

Bay Vien's words fell on some ready ears, men who could anticipate the taste of money and power that he was promising each of them. They set about organizing themselves for the coup. A formal United Sects National Front was agreed upon. Pham cong Tac, Pope of the Cao Dai, was to be its Supreme Commander, contingent upon his contributing all Cao Dai forces to the front's cause rather than integrating them into the national army. Although the various sect armies were to remain independent under their present commanders (whom the meeting promised to upgrade in rank), they would become a single field army in case of need. The Hoa Hao guerrilla leader Ba Cut (with the missing finger joint) was named the field commander. Bay Vien sweetened his nomination of Ba Cut by promptly placing his Binh Xuyen army under Ba Cut's command for any emergency. The meeting ended with pledges of support to the new front and its program.

I heard about the meeting of sect leaders when Generals Trinh minh Thé and Nguyen thanh Phuong stopped by my house en route home from it. They were laughing. They thought this front a huge joke and seemed surprised when I not only took the news seriously, but pointed out that both of them had been suckered in an obvious confidence game. If the two had signed up as members of the front, it meant that they had placed their armed forces, which were their only source of power, under the control of Ba Cut for a political game devised by the boss gangster Bay Vien. Once they started playing his game, they would find themselves hooked, unable to get out. In the case of Trinh minh Thé, his recent oath to the government put him in a position where undertaking actions for Ba Cut and Bay Vien would make him vulnerable to charges of treason and rebellion. Nguyen thanh Phuong, whose Cao Dai army was in the final stage of being integrated into the national army, was in practically the same boat. It would be understandable if they shared the beliefs of Bay Vien, but they had professed much higher ideals. Seriously now, had they really signed up as members of the front?

The much sobered generals admitted that they had indeed signed up. They could not see how treason and rebellion could be claimed against anyone in the front, since Chief of State Bao Dai appeared to be involved. Some of the men who worked closely with Nguyen De (Bao Dai's "man in Saigon") had been present at the meeting and had encouraged the formation of the front and its aims. If it ever came to armed action against the Diem government, Bao Dai presumably would give the action legitimacy.

I commented that the two generals were in very strange company. Nguyen De had a forbidding reputation among the Vietnamese as a schemer whose plots somehow always seemed to use a cat's-paw who would end up on the short end of a deal while Nguyen De grew richer and more powerful. There were fervent *colons* among the French who were influencing Bay Vien and Ba Cut, *colons* whose self-interest ran counter to the interests of those Vietnamese who desired full independence for their country. Had Thé and Phuong changed their goal of an independent Vietnam, a goal they had proclaimed so stoutly in previous meetings with me?

Generals Thé and Phuong assured me that their ideal of an independent country was as strong as ever. The politics of what they were involved in was different than I thought it to be. Perhaps I didn't know the game. I commented that perhaps they didn't know the game either and had been trapped in it. I suggested bluntly that they resign from the front. They replied no, they wouldn't resign just now. Perhaps the objectives of the front were different from their own. They couldn't tell yet. They would retain their membership in the front for the time being and do their best to discover what was really afoot. The time might come when they could scotch a scheme harmful to the country by resigning. But not yet. We parted on this equivocal note.

After the generals left, I drove over to the embassy residence and informed Ambassador Collins of the sect development. He didn't think it was necessarily a bad thing, since it could lead to Diem's being forced to "broaden the base" of his government, an action that he had heard me favor in the past. "Yes," I replied, "broaden, but not devalue." The aims of the front smelled of a naked power grab, with the sect armies to be used as black-mail, a threat to coerce Diem into turning over the government to a handful of warlords. Such a coup would be a shabby and false foundation upon which to build a decent future for Viet-nam. This new move would give power to individuals noted for their extralegal actions. A government in which they actually did the ruling would be a government based upon the lack of respect for law and order and thus would reign under the motto "crime pays." I couldn't see the United States continuing any support for a Vietnamese government if it became so strangely perverted.

Collins suggested that I curb my emotions a bit but told me to keep after Thé and Phuong about resigning from the front. Maybe I could get others to resign as well. Meanwhile, he continued, he had been talking with General Ely about the problem of the sects, and they both felt that a group of Americans and French should make a thorough study of the problem. Given sound recommendations, he and Ely would present them to Prime Minister Diem and urge their adoption, promising French and U.S. support within reason. With this in mind, would I accompany Collins to meet with Ely for a discussion? Of course I would.

When we saw Ely the following morning, the French commander said that he and Collins were in agreement about a Franco-American study of the sect problem and that both of them wanted me to take charge of it. General Gambiez would be responsible for the French half of the effort since he commanded French Union forces in South Vietnam where the sects were located, and he was under instructions to give me full assistance. The study was an urgent bit of business for the Franco-American allies, of such top priority, in fact, that I couldn't be given much time to complete it. Hopefully, it could be done in a week or ten days. It must propose some specific solutions.

I agreed promptly. For the study, I would need the full-time help of military officers who were intimate with the affairs of the sect armed forces, economists who knew the agrarian situation in areas where the sects were located, political officers who could assay the sensitive social factors involved, information specialists who could plan ways to convince the sects of the benefits awaiting them from recommended actions and, finally, officials designated by both Ely and Collins who could assure the feasibility of any recommendations the Franco-American study group came up with, particularly if large sums of money were embodied in the proposed solutions. However, something else came first. I was concerned about the makeup and direction of the Franco-American study group. Gambiez was a brigadier general and obviously outranked me, as a colonel. It would be most awkward to have someone senior to me acting in the number two position.

General Ely told me flatly that Gambiez would help me. Both Collins and Ely assured me that the study group could draw all of the expert Franco-American manpower required and use it full-time. They reminded me again of the urgency of the work.

With Joe Redick accompanying me as an interpreter, I promptly called on General Gambiez at his headquarters in the Camp Chanson area. He waved us affably to seats at a small table in the middle of his spacious office. A large Alsatian dog lay on the floor next to it and eyed me warily. General Gambiez sat with us and told me cheerily that he was a guard dog who could attack and kill me at one word from him. I commented just as cheerily that the reason my hands were in my pockets as we sat down was that I had a tiny .25-cal. automatic in my pocket and I hoped the dog didn't make my trigger finger itchy, since the gun was aimed at my host's stomach or perhaps a little lower down. Gambiez laughed and took the dog over to the other side of the room. I politely put my hands on top of the table.

After these amenities we quickly got down to business.

Gambiez named some assistants who were expert on sect affairs to sit in for him full-time on the study project. I assured him that he needn't participate directly unless he desired to do so. Arrangements were made for a first meeting of the Franco-American group that same day.

This first meeting, attended by five French officers and an equal number of Americans, was held at my bungalow. I explained the work plan. First, we would compile the plain, hard, unvarnished facts about the sects. Once we had sufficient information, we would attempt to draw conclusions and to make recommendations. We would start by pooling the information each of us already had, see what might be missing, and then seek out specified missing pieces of information. I asked a French colonel to take notes as we pooled what we knew already and to have the preliminary fact sheet written up by the next day, with copies for all of us.

But tension grew when we started contributing facts known to us. Some of the French officers couldn't resist telling the kind of romantic fiction that passed for "facts everybody knows" in the French camp, and I insisted upon the need for precise evidence and truthfulness even if it hurt to tell. For example, we talked about a small unit of Hoa Hao under a colonel in Can Tho. Exactly how many men and weapons were in this unit? To whom were they loyal? Some of the French officers commented, with snickers, that I should answer the question since I had given the Hoa Hao colonel a Cadillac on the previous Monday. I explained patiently that we were after facts, not fiction, and noted that the car in question wasn't a Cadillac but reportedly was a Buick. Vietnamese authorities had the name of a French major who was said to have made this particular gift in Can Tho. Since the major was in the sect liaison section of General Gambiez's staff, I felt that the officers of that section who were present with us might answer my questions without reciting some wild fairy tale. And so went the sharing of information in the meeting.

The French colonel didn't have his account of our pooled information the next day, so I wrote up the first findings of the Franco-American group myself. Aside from unrevealed hanky-panky that might be going on currently, the sect armies had had their regular military pay as *supplétifs* stopped by the French in January, but the Diem government had continued the pay until the United Sect Front was formed, when this also was stopped. However, the sect armies took a share of the southern rice harvest in January through March and normally were afflu-ent until June, when lack of regular pay would pose a real prob-lem. The sect armies had a total of about 40,000 armed men in positions capable of threatening the security of Saigon-Cholon. There were supposedly 9,000 Binh Xuyen in the city and its immediate suburbs, plus a small band of Catholic militia under Colonel Leroy, the same man who had introduced me to the Hoa Hao months before and who had now allied himself with Bay Vien. Of the 40,000 total, about half had been recently integrated (or were in the process of being integrated) into the national army, mostly still within their original unit formations.

In the following ten days, the Franco-American group was kept hard at work on the study. I gave up my normal sleep in order to gather information and then try to make some sense out of it. In our final meetings, we concluded that Vietnam couldn't afford to have the private armies of the sects, although there was need to supply livelihoods for the men in them, security in the areas where these armies operated, and political positions for the sect leaders. We recommended a program for dissolving the sect armies and letting their soldiers be absorbed into the national armed forces or the Civil Guard (rural police), or into public work programs for postwar reconstruction. Politi-cal needs were met by a proposal to set up a national elective body with legislative powers, to be chosen by the people three months hence; the sect leaders or their designated henchmen could run for office. The economic needs were met largely by proposed agricultural projects to open up new farmlands and to increase profitable yields on lands currently owned by sect farmers. There were other detailed proposals, including the initiation of a large public school program, including high schools, in the sect regions.

The study, with its hard-won facts and its down-to-earth ideas for making a peaceful life more worthwhile for the sects than militancy, was given to Collins and Ely within the ten-day time limit they had set. I had gone without much sleep in order to finish it on time and was somewhat groggy from over-work. So the reaction of Collins came as a dull thud instead of a shock to me. After reading through the study, Collins told me that the study was "inadequate" to serve his needs. He would have his own personal staff of experts prepare another one. He didn't explain why it was "inadequate," although I surmised that he had wanted me to recommend some formula that would place Bay Vien, Ba Cut, and the others in the government while putting Diem on the shelf as a ceremonial figurehead. I commented that the political situation was about to explode over the sect issue, that my recommendations would defuse it if they were used promptly, and that if he didn't mind I was going to my house and catch up on sleep. With that, I drove to my house and went to bed. The next thing I knew, it was twenty hours later.

Much refreshed, I met with Generals Thé and Phuong, two of the sect military leaders, once again. They told me that the United Sects Front was about to issue an ultimatum to Diem, demanding that he give them the choice spots in the government and the major say in how the government was run. Diem could continue to preside as a straw man. The ultimatum must be complied with in five days. If Diem refused, the sect armed forces would make a show of strength, and force him to give in. I told Thé and Phuong that, if they were ever to withdraw honorably from the front, the time for doing so was at hand. Their withdrawal might give pause to the others who were rushing into actions that would wreck the progress being made in Vietnam. The two generals said that the greatest bar to withdrawal was what the Cao Dai Pope could do about Phuong's position as chief of the Cao Dai military forces. Maybe I was right, though, about its being time to act. How about our meeting again that night? I agreed.

I saw Ambassador Collins and told him what was afoot, noting that time for studying the problem had run out. The threat of a show of force by private sect armies against the government was a challenge that Diem would rise to meet. He was a scrapper. Moreover, the Vietnamese Army would support him. Its officers had little use for the sect armies. Despite rumors to the contrary, I was sure that the Vietnamese Army would fight in a showdown. The United Sects Front was on a collision course leading to a civil war, unless its leaders could be persuaded to act rationally. A firm stand by Generals Thé and Phuong might initiate a pause in which cooler heads could prevail. It was time for fast, positive action.

Collins told me to see what I could do with Thé and Phuong that night, and to keep him advised. I stayed up most of the night talking with the two generals at Phuong's Saigon residence, through Joe Redick as interpreter. They had decided firmly to quit the front, so our talk was on how best to do this and still keep their positions of strength and use them for constructive ends. I had telephoned Collins about their decision. He asked me to bring them by his house in the morning. I remarked that they would be rather tired in the morning, but a private meeting in which he congratulated them for their resolve might be useful in bucking them up.

In the morning Thé, Phuong, Redick, and I drove to the residence of Collins, bushed from the long night of talk and in need of showers, clean clothes, and breakfast. I assured them that it would be just a brief and friendly call, and then we could all be on our way again. I was surprised, when we entered, to find that Collins had his own special staff of political, economic, and information experts with him. As we sat down with the two sect generals, I sharing a couch with Collins and Redick seated on a footstool next to the generals to act as interpreter, the bevy of American experts pulled up chairs in a semicircle around us, put large notepads in their laps, took out pens and pencils, and sat poised, apparently ready to record every precious word for posterity.

Collins started the proceedings by telling his visitors how shocked he was as a military man over the disloyal behavior of the two generals toward their government. I stopped Redick as he dutifully started to translate this and pleaded with Collins to congratulate the generals for their decision to remain *loyal* to the government. This led to a fervent argument between Collins and me, while the two sect generals sat there puzzled, watching the scene and unable to understand the English we were speaking. I pointed out that, as Collins had suggested, I had invited Generals Thé and Phuong for a private meeting with him. Instead, there was a group sitting with pads and pencils who might be taken for journalists by his guests. The least that might be done was to explain who the notetakers were. Beyond that, I urged that he simply offer his congratulations on their commitment to be loyal; they shouldn't be scolded. Collins merely repeated his original remarks in a louder voice, adding that he was trying to prevent bloodshed.

Obviously the meeting was getting nowhere, and I was afraid that Thé and Phuong might catch the import of his words, become angry, and let their ire overrule their decision to pull out of the front. A clash between the sects and the government would then become a certainty. It was hardly the way to avoid bloodshed. So I forced a smile, stood up, and motioned the two generals to come along with me. I explained to Collins that I would give them breakfast and tell them that he had lauded their decision. We left.

After breakfast Thé and Phuong went to the meeting of the front where the ultimatum to Diem was to be decided upon. The two generals voiced their objections to the ultimatum and then resigned from the front, making it plain that they also were speaking for the armed forces under their command. They left the front meeting in an uproar. When I heard this news, I saw Collins and told him what had happened. By that time he and his staff were at the luncheon table. We had a bit of uproar among ourselves, too, about the way the early-morning meeting at the residence had gone. I know that I didn't endear myself to the others by my contribution to the conversation about the morning confrontation. I was grateful, however, that the headlong rush of the sects toward violence had received a check. I urged that whatever action the Americans and French were to take with Diem to resolve the sect problem be done promptly. The respite given by the courageous stand of Thé and Phuong might prove to be fleeting.

The respite was indeed all too brief. Those remaining in the front decided to go ahead with their scheme without the backing of Thé and Phuong and their forces. The front sent the ultimatum to Diem on March 22, telling him that he had until March 27 to agree to it, "or else." Diem mastered his temper and coolly offered to negotiate with the front leaders, saying that he had some proposals of his own wherein all good patriots could participate with him in constructing something more solid and lasting for the benefit of the country. The offer to negotiate was refused. The Binh Xuyen positioned mortars for a bombardment of the palace if Diem refused to accept the ultimatum.

The crisis quickly became public knowledge and wound up the nerves of the residents of the capital city more and more tightly as each hour passed. Rumors flourished like weeds, covering up the simple facts of the confrontation. Perhaps the most effective false rumor in the foreign community was that the Vietnamese Army was close to mutiny, its officers and men pictured as vehemently opposed to Diem. The canard was believed so strongly in high places that my personal firsthand check of battalions in the Saigon area and my findings of high morale and loyalty among the troops were dismissed as romantic fiction. Misleading reports that the Vietnamese Army wouldn't fight were sent to Washington and Paris, coloring judgments there. My contrary view went to Washington as a minority post-script. Many Vietnamese officials subscribed to the false rumor, too, and cabinet ministers started resigning, among them Minister of National Defense Ho thong Minh. When Ambassador Collins and I saw Minh to urge him to stay at his post, he admitted that he hadn't checked personally on any of the Vietnamese Army units. But he still believed that the troops wouldn't fight; he resigned and left town.

On March 29, the morning after the resignation of the defense minister, Redick and I drove to the palace to see Diem. It was clear that the guard battalion at the palace was taking seriously the reports that a Binh Xuyen attack on the palace was imminent. Unlike the comic-opera days of General Hinh's threats, the troops were busy putting finishing touches on fortified positions in the spacious grounds of the palace and were in combat gear, weapons at the ready. In the palace itself, there was a bustle of activity, telephones ringing, officials hurrying along hallways and up and down stairways, their faces intent and serious. There was no sense of panic in the air, just a quickened pace, the feel of getting everything shipshape before an expected emergency actually happened.

We were purposely early for our appointment with Diem, since I wanted to check on the installation of radio equipment I had arranged with the Signal Corps for the palace. It would keep the prime minister in touch with the military radio nets and other parts of the country, in case the palace was cut off from normal communications in an emergency. Redick and I stopped by the small office of Vo van Hai, who served as confidential executive secretary to Diem, and asked him about the new military radio equipment. Hai was his usual cheerful self, greeting us with a big welcoming smile. He showed us the new equipment, installed in good working order in an alcove adjacent to Diem's office. While we were looking at it, Diem joined us. He grinned as he thanked us for the equipment, saying it might come in handy. I told him that the radio had led to express orders to me from the U.S. Mission to stay away from the palace in case of an attack. The U.S. didn't want an American present at one of the command headquarters in the event of conflict between nationalists. I had been strictly forbidden to use the radio. Diem said dryly that he understood.

In his own office, Diem spread out a large-scale map of the metropolitan area and pointed out the locations where Binh Xuyen mortars had been reported. As far as he could tell, they were all 60-mm. mortars, although there were reports that the Binh Xuyen were trying to get some of the heavier 81-mm. mortars. If so, that might be bad. The 60-mm. mortars would do little damage to the thick palace walls if everyone remained behind them. Diem told us this in the detached tones of a briefing officer, professionally descriptive and seemingly indifferent to the fact that he would be the main target of the attack whose preparations he was enumerating. I was struck by his calm. This was a man in control of himself. His personal behavior must have stiffened the backbones of all those around him.

Then I asked Diem about the status of Ho thong Minh, the defense minister. Diem laughed bitterly. He had heard that Minh had gone to Dalat, where a number of Bao Dai's people had gathered when the Binh Xuyen had started making preparations to attack the palace. Presumably Minh was with them. It didn't really matter, Diem said, for he had taken the Defense Ministry portfolio for himself and would hold it personally for the time being. He remarked, with a fleeting smile lighting his face, that the army commanders had seemed to like this. They were disgusted with the rumors of their fear of the Binh Xuyen and their supposedly low morale. In Diem, they knew they had someone who would hold firm and who would give them clear orders if it came to a fight. He had had talks with unit commanders that confirmed their readiness and loyalty. Realistically, he didn't intend to take on all the detailed, daily paperwork of the Defense Ministry himself. He had asked Tran trung Dung, secretary of state at the presidency, to move over to the Defense Ministry and administer its routine affairs.

We changed the subject and talked about the possible alternatives to an open clash between the government and the Binh Xuyen. Both the French and U.S. governments had resources that perhaps could be contributed to help out once Diem found a feasible and acceptable way to resolve the problem.

Diem said he had offered to negotiate with the front leaders, but Bay Vien had made it very plain that he wanted Diem to step down or get out of his way while Vien and his cohorts took over the government. A basic moral issue was at stake. Bay Vien had fattened on the weaknesses of the people through his control of gambling, prostitution, and the opium traffic. He had shored up his position by making the deal with Bao Dai whereby he had named his own man as chief of police. Now, by use of force, this vice overlord was going to attempt to seize the reins of government. It would end the hopes of millions of decent Vietnamese nationalists. As a patriot, Diem couldn't let this happen.

Diem told me he had raised the issue of control of the police with Bao Dai, noting that the chief of state had promised him "full powers" as his prime minister. Surely, such powers encompassed control of the police. He had asked Bao Dai to rescind the agreement with Bay Vien, freeing Diem to appoint a new chief of police. Bao Dai had replied with a flowery message of trust in Diem but had avoided answering the request. Meanwhile, messages had passed information about Diem's request from Bao Dai's court circles to Bay Vien, and to Bao Dai's people in Saigon, alerting them. Subsequently, the front had been formed and the ultimatum issued. It was evident that Bao Dai was encouraging Bay Vien to act.

I told Diem that I respected his stand on the moral issue. If venality became the basis of government, the free part of

Vietnam would crumble, and venality seemed to be the name of the game that Bay Vien was playing. The Vietnamese nationalists would need all the moral strength they could muster for the days ahead. Involving the government in vice, in illicit deals to benefit individual officials, and in the other payoffs that Bay Vien seemed to have in mind would debase it to a point where it would have no honor left among the people. Then the people would have no fair or worthy choice in the 1956 plebiscite. Diem need not feel lonely at this moment of decision. Other men of goodwill throughout history had had to face similar moments and were his companions in spirit. A time like this came to test every good leader. I was sure that Diem would pass the test.

Diem thanked me and came with us to the stairway, waving farewell as we walked down to the car. We waved back and left. The doughty figure in the white suit, alone at the head of the stairs, stayed in my mind as we drove back to my house, an antidote to the decay one sensed in the air. Along the streets, I noticed that the flowering junipers and the tulip trees were losing their petals. The profusion of beauty at Tet, the traditional *bong-mai* blossoms, the chrysanthemums called *bong-cuc,* the *van-tho* Buddha flowers, *mong-ca* rooster combs, *mandariniers,* and dahlias had withered and gone.

N O T E S

Politics. The talk about Diem "broadening the base" of his government in March 1955, by giving key posts to sect leaders, ignored the steps already taken in this direction. On September 24, 1954, Diem had reformed his government, appointing eight members of the Cao Dai and Hoa Hao sects to cabinet positions (out of a total of fourteen positions in the cabinet). He picked these men for their executive competence as much as for their sect connections. The rub came when the men refused to be puppets for the sect leaders and, instead, tried to serve the best interests of the nation. The sect leaders, like General Hinh before them, yearned nakedly for greater personal power. So the fact that some respected sect people were already in the government simply didn't satisfy the appetites of the leaders.

★ ★

CHAPTER FIFTEEN

CONFRONTATION IN SAIGON

GREAT EXPLOSIONS brought me out of bed at midnight, March 29–30. They sounded as though they were four or five blocks away, in the direction of Doc Lap Palace. Between explosions, I could hear the stutter of machine guns and the popping of rifles, although these sounds seemed to be at a greater distance. Infantry troops evidently were fighting, some place, but not at the palace. Listening intently to interpret the sounds, I also heard a ringing which puzzled me for a moment until I realized that it was the telephone.

As I picked up the telephone receiver, I saw that my dog Pierre, a big blue-black clown of a French poodle, had squeezed into the narrow space under a bed, evidently his idea of a safe haven from the loud and angry night. All I could see of him were two big eyes appealing to me. He tried to wriggle out of his hiding place to come to me but was stuck. I lifted the edge of the bed to let him get out and was laughing at the ludicrous fix he had gotten himself into when I remembered that I still was holding the telephone. I said hello into the mouthpiece.

The call was from officers of my team who lived in a house on Rue Taberd, two blocks the other side of the palace from me. I was told rather sharply that it was no laughing matter.

Shells were falling all around the house. Hadn't they better get out of there and escape to a safe part of the city? I told them to stay put and keep away from windows and doors. The walls were thick and strong enough to withstand mortar shelling. It wouldn't be safe outdoors. I asked them about the infantry weapons fire that I'd heard in the distance. Yes, they'd heard the firing, too, but it was blocks away. And, oh yes, they'd had one casualty. One of the officers had tripped over some tubs of water set out in the hallway against the possibility of fire. No, no bones were broken. He was just shaken up and would be all right. I told them to let me know of any change in the situation and then hung up.

Joe Redick arrived at the house as I hung up. His wife and two small children had come to Saigon shortly before and were living in an apartment in the center of town. I told him to go back to the family, since a fire fight in the city in the middle of the night was hardly a reassuring event for new arrivals. He replied that the fighting was blocks away from them, and, as a matter of fact, they were sort of enjoying the excitement. What did I want him to do? I asked him to cope with the telephone system and attempt to talk with someone at the palace. Was Diem all right? Was the palace secure?

Redick finally completed a call to Vo van Hai at the palace after the usual arguments with switchboard operators and the usual frustrating disconnections in midsentence. Hai said that Diem had just come in. He had been outside in the palace grounds, dressed in pajamas and slippers, checking on the troops, seeing that the wounded were cared for, and making certain that they were alert in case of a ground attack. No, there hadn't been any infantry attack at the palace by the Binh Xuyen, only mortar shelling, which was still going on. Other than some chipped walls, the palace was intact. The ground fighting was in the Cholon area where the Binh Xuyen had attempted assaults on national army installations, such as the General Staff compound, and were being driven back.

Diem broke in to tell me that army troops in trucks had been ambushed by the Binh Xuyen around Rue Gallieni. The heaviest firing had come from a drugstore, of all places, and there had been army casualties. Army reinforcements were having difficulty moving by truck through the city because French tanks blocked some of the streets and main intersections. Diem said that a few Army troops had occupied the police station house in the 4th Arrondissement and he was concerned about their situation if more troops couldn't get through to help them. The police station was under heavy fire from the Binh Xuyen. Diem was going to try again to get General Ely on the telephone and request that French tanks not block the route being used for army reinforcements. I told him to take care of himself and to stop running around outdoors in his pajamas. We said goodbye.

I then telephoned Collins and told him of the news from the palace. He asked me to come over to his residence, if I could, in about an hour, when he was going to have a conference with Ely. I decided to drive to his residence a dozen blocks away by a roundabout route, in hopes of picking up some firsthand information. The shelling around the palace seemed to be tapering off, but I could still hear the distant racket of ground fighting.

I set out in my car. At the first corner, I noticed some national army troops moving cautiously toward my street, lugging a machine gun. They were in combat formation, with riflemen leading as point men. I looked back down my street, suddenly remembering that one of the Binh Xuyen politicians had a house a block away from me. Sure enough, the street light a block back revealed khaki-clad figures behind a wall, each wearing the green beret of the Binh Xuyen. I couldn't spot a machine gun, but several submachine guns were in evidence. It looked as though a fight was in the making right on my own block. I called a soft "good luck" to the national army men as I passed them and headed for the street past the palace and toward Cholon.

There was little visible activity at the palace. National army troops were scattered through the surrounding blocks, each tree trunk, shrub, alley, and fence sheltering armed men on the alert for trouble, their weapons and eyes following my car as I drove along. Toward Cholon, light French tanks were on the move in the streets. Finally, at a circle intersection of boulevards, I came upon a formation of tanks blocking the street.

A column of trucks filled with Vietnamese Army troops had been halted by French tanks, the column stretching back into the darkness, its commanding officers in angry argument with French officers standing on the street beside their tanks. The sound of infantry fighting close by made a deafening racket. The French officers were shouting that the Vietnamese couldn't pass; the troop convoy would have to turn around and go back to camp. The Vietnamese officers were shouting just as angrily that they had to get through and help their comrades on Rue Gallieni. I hopped out and joined the argument. The Vietnamese Army reinforcements must get through! The French officers said no. I took out a notebook and asked for their names. They refused to tell me and shouted that I'd better clear out before the tanks cleared me out along with my car.

More French tanks came rumbling up. The Vietnamese truck convoy started turning around on the street and heading back in the direction from which it had come. I drove to the residence of Ambassador Collins, the sound of infantry conflict still making a din from the fighting nearby.

I told Collins about the French tanks blocking the movement of Vietnamese Army reinforcements. Apparently the French Army was deliberately aiding the gangster Binh Xuyen forces which had ambushed the Vietnamese Army troops on Rue Gallieni and had attacked the army installations in Cholon. If these small, beleaguered national army units weren't helped immediately, they might well be wiped out. I could only conclude that the French military wanted the Binh Xuyen to win, inflicting defeat not only on the national army but on Diem

and his government. It was as shameful a case as it would have
been if the U.S. Army had ever been used, back in the 1920s,
to help Al Capone and his gang take over the city of Chicago.

As I expressed these views to him, there was a strange, somewhat puzzled look on Collins' face, a bit of patrician patience
with someone none too bright, even a bit fatherly. It was
enough to stop my talking and start my listening. Collins told
me softly that he had just agreed with General Ely that there
should be a stop to the bloodshed in Saigon-Cholon. Ely had
expressed concern about the safety of the thousands of French
civilians living in the metropolitan area. Further, there were
perhaps a million Vietnamese civilians in the city, many of
whom might become casualties if the fighting between the
Binh Xuyen and the Vietnamese Army continued, since the
battleground was within the city itself. Therefore, the U.S.
and French leaders had agreed to impose a cease-fire on the
two contending sides. With the agreement of General Collins,
Ely was getting in touch with both Diem and Bay Vien immediately and telling each to issue orders to his troops to stop
fighting and to remain quietly in place until further orders. The
French Union forces had been brought into town to make
certain that the truce was obeyed and kept, as well as to protect
the neighborhoods where most of the French lived.

The sound of infantry fire from the fighting in Cholon was
plainly audible as Collins stopped talking. We both listened to
it. It might take a little time for all the troops to get the word
about the cease-fire, Collins added, but the fighting must be
stopped by early morning. He went on speaking, almost as
though talking to himself, saying that the shedding of blood
must be stopped.

I told him I thought this humanitarian impulse of the French
military was coming at a strangely late time and I couldn't
understand why the U.S. had to be a part of it. French military
men were in close liaison with the Binh Xuyen, under the orders
of General Ely, and easily could have stopped the Binh Xuyen

from initiating the attack on Diem and the Vietnamese Army. It was patently implausible that the Binh Xuyen would have started this fight without tacit French approval. I must conclude that these French military men believed their own fiction that the Vietnamese Army was a pushover for the Binh Xuyen. When that army, caught in ambush and attacked in isolated positions by large forces, showed it was no pushover and started fighting back vigorously, I imagined that the heart started to go out of the Binh Xuyen soldiery and that this had shocked the French. A few more Vietnamese troops in town would have chased the Binh Xuyen right out of the city, but the French had prevented this reinforcement. A cease-fire now merely put off the day of reckoning for which each side would prepare more thoroughly. When that day came, there was going to be much more blood-letting than was likely this night.

Collins listened to this and said we could do only one thing at a time. Right now, we must prevent further shedding of blood. It was something we *could* do and we were *going* to do. Period. I drove back to my bungalow, saddened by the rhetoric which seemingly placed those of us who were trying to help the Vietnamese establish high principles in government into the opposite category of callous, bloodthirsty types.

When I turned the corner into my own street, I noticed that Vietnamese Army soldiers were still present on my block, obviously ready for combat. It was about three o'clock in the morning and the street lights were on; but beyond their patches of brightness was the dark of night, the black shadows of trees and shrubs and walls screening the presence of the troops. In the distance was the sound of continuing infantry battle. On my block the soldiers were in position to start a fight of their own, evidently having used the time since I had seen them last to creep silently inch by inch to their present positions, careful not to draw the fire of the Binh Xuyen in the next block. I looked down the street to the house beyond the next corner, where the Binh Xuyen troops had been manning a garden wall.

Nobody was in sight. The house itself was dark. I could only guess, but it seemed probable, that the Binh Xuyen were also in combat position, silently awaiting the next move of the army soldiers.

I drove quickly into my yard. From there, I called softly out to the army soldiers, asking them to check with their commander about a cease-fire. I heard a grunt of acknowledgment and then a hushed voice calling the commander on a radio. I started into my house and was almost bowled over by my dog Pierre who welcomed me with frantic leaps at my chest—and then took off like greased lightning for the street. I went to the gate and called him. No response from the dog. My searching eyes finally picked him out, standing, head lowered, sniffing interestedly at two soldiers stretched out prone behind a machine gun. I called him again, with more authority. Pierre, usually well-behaved, reacted by starting to run around sniffing at other soldiers in combat positions; then he cavorted out into the middle of the street, crouching playfully and barking at the soldiers. If they were ready for some sort of game, why so was he. It was a dead giveaway, of course, of the positions they had crawled into so carefully and surreptitiously during the night. I was afraid one of the army soldiers might open fire in exasperation, or that one of the Binh Xuyen troopers might start shooting at one of the army people, now that his location had been pinpointed.

I called loudly into the night for everyone to hold his fire and remain calm. It was one of my better shouts and carried for blocks. With that, I stepped out into the street, the potential battleground, and tried to catch my dog. He cocked his head, crouched, and then went prancing out of my reach when I got to him. It was great fun, and he played the game over and over again.

In the darkness around us, I heard subdued laughter from the soldiers. Then some of the Binh Xuyen troopers in the next block started whistling at Pierre, bringing laughs from *their* comrades. The army soldiers took up the whistling. The summonses from all directions baffled him. He came up to me, looking from side to side in annoyance at all the whistling, and stood there. I hauled him up into the house, knowing that the amused soldiery of both sides were no longer in a mood to assume their combat attitudes. I thought philosophically that at least Pierre had prevented *some* bloodshed that night.

In the morning the French-imposed, U.S.-supported truce was in effect. At my office I learned that the cease-fire had been imposed three hours and fifteen minutes after the Binh Xuyen had opened up on the palace with mortars at midnight.

The next two weeks were filled with the unease of the truce in Saigon-Cholon. The soldiers of both the Binh Xuyen and the Vietnamese Army were still held in the positions they took when the fighting ceased, in some places situated on opposite sidewalks of boulevards and streets, easily within talk and insult range. The positions were strengthened with sandbags, so little forts and strong points dotted the town, and the intervening no-man's-land was a street filled with its normal flow of daily traffic. Since the soldiers were alert, standing by their weapons, each side waiting for the other to start up the fighting again, driving along the streets between the opposing forts added a little extra zip to the already zesty business of maneuvering through the town's wild traffic pattern.

The French forces had also moved into town, building their own sandbagged forts along the streets and boulevards, laying miles of tangled webs of barbed wire, parking tanks on sidewalks and in traffic circles where they would have fields of fire down the streets, and manning this whole martial complex with thousands of troops. The French military zoned the districts and neighborhoods of the metropolitan area, declaring many of them to be under French protection. These territories, screened off by the military might of France, were promptly dubbed "French zones." Many of the fortified positions of the

Binh Xuyen forces were in the French zones, and the Binh Xuyen were able to move around freely and openly behind the protection of the French military. The location of some of these protected positions made them ominous. For example, one French zone was close by Doc Lap Palace where Diem lived and worked. Behind the French forces, only eight hundred yards from Diem's office and bedroom, the Binh Xuyen had fortified the National Security Police headquarters on Rue Catinat.

Diem estimated angrily that the French zones occupied half of the urban area of Saigon-Cholon, quite apart from substantial French deployments in the suburbs. French forces within the city itself totaled some 30,000 men, with about four hundred tanks of all sizes. (He was not amused by my comment that, at long last, a use had been found for French armor which had played an inglorious role in the gluey mud of rice paddies and at unfordable rivers during the Franco-Vietminh war.) When Diem mentioned the size of the French forces, he couldn't restrain himself from recrimination against the French authorities. "One of the French generals, Jacquot," said Diem, "went to our General Staff and notified them that half a brigade of French troops would be brought into town. But General Ely refused my bringing in three battalions. If I had had three more battalions in town, the Binh Xuyen would have hesitated to make these follies!"

The Vietnamese Army in town numbered little more than a battalion. One company had been ambushed on Rue Gallieni, and another had occupied the police station at the 4th Arrondissement, where there had been a fight. Other troops were scattered about in small detachments. Opposing them were sixteen battalions of Binh Xuyen, averaging about 400 men in each battalion, plus the police under Binh Xuyen control. The generous proportion of automatic weapons among the Binh Xuyen was worrisome, although one of my main fears was that French officers would furnish the Binh Xuyen with artillery heavier than the 60-mm. mortars they had used in the shelling of Doc Lap Palace. The French had already given the Binh Xuyen three *vedettes*, or gunboats, and these gunboats were significant in a waterfront city such as Saigon-Cholon. (The minuscule Vietnamese Navy was under strict French command and control at the time, unable to lift a finger against either the Binh Xuyen "navy" or its waterside forts that controlled the Saigon River.)

During this queasy lull, I quietly checked on how well the Vietnamese Army was doing in collecting tactical intelligence about the Binh Xuyen. French officers were running the Deuxième Bureau of the Vietnamese General Staff, just as French officers were guiding the Binh Xuyen. With French officers on both sides collaborating among themselves, any information they gave the Vietnamese Army would be highly suspect. Yet the Vietnamese Army needed honest facts upon which to base their plans and decisions.

The top Vietnamese Army leaders, Le van Ty and Tran van Don, had no funds for the collection of intelligence since they were supposed to rely on the Deuxième Bureau. Those Vietnamese Army leaders commanding troops facing the Binh Xuyen were a different proposition. Both were named Minh. One was short and slender, the other tall and husky, so they were quickly given distinguishing nicknames. Colonel Tran van "Little" Minh commanded the First Military Region, covering the capital and territory south and west of the city. Little Minh had a fund of a hundred thousand piasters for intelligence and a million piasters for the purchase of arms (from dissidents), yet he didn't seem well informed about the forces opposing him. Or, to put it differently, he seemed to have more curiosity about the location of Binh Xuyen wealth than about military aspects. He wasn't alone in this.

Many other Vietnamese were extremely curious about the ill-gotten gains of the Binh Xuyen vice lord, Bay Vien, and where he kept his treasure. The opium traffic (mostly from

Laos and South China, then via the Binh Xuyen to Europe and other markets) reputedly amounted to two hundred million piasters per month, or nearly two and a half billion piasters per year. (The legal exchange rate then was 35 piasters for $1 U.S.) The Binh Xuyen take from their control of gambling and prostitution added millions more in income. Bao Dai reportedly was paid a million U.S. dollars by the Binh Xuyen to cede them control of the police, along with a percentage of the opium profits; his income was said to amount to 3.4 million U.S. dollars a year.

Lieutenant Colonel Duong van "Big" Minh commanded the Vietnamese Army forces in the Saigon-Cholon sector. He had no official funds for the collection of intelligence, yet he seemed to be informed in great detail about the Binh Xuyen forces he was facing. I discovered that he had been collecting information from every source he could think of, including volunteer and paid informants. Money for the latter had come from Big Minh's sale of his own car and furniture, as well as a mortgage on his house. When I learned this, I was most favorably impressed. Here was a man who put duty before self. I discussed his money problems with Diem, and arrangements were made to transfer Defense Ministry contingency funds for his use.

Diem had intelligence sources of his own, mainly from his brother Nhu but also direct sources independent of his brother. These included Mai huu Xuan of the MSS and Nguyen ngoc Tho, who had served in provincial administrative posts among the sects for some years. Xuan had a wealth of knowledge about the Binh Xuyen from his days in the Sûreté, when he had held a top post in criminal investigation. And there were other individuals seeing Diem privately, of course. His principal contact with Chinese affairs in Cholon was through Ly giai Han (known as Ly Kay). On April 8 this venerable Chinese banker was kidnapped from a Cholon restaurant by three armed men. Diem asked General Gambiez to intervene with the Binh Xuyen in this case, without luck. (Kidnappers racked up a high score in this period. Among the victims were some thirty Vietnamese Army men living in Saigon-Cholon.)

Ngo dinh Nhu was working around the clock to provide information for his brother Diem. He had established intelligence networks of his own and was collecting massive piles of reports full of fact and fancy. In addition, he had been active in labor union politics for some years and received much voluntary information from workers living in Binh Xuyen areas. Further, he had become Diem's liaison with the loyal sect forces, such as General Ngo of the Hoa Hao and General Phuong of the Cao Dai. General Phuong and 8,000 Cao Dai *supplétifs* had been integrated into the Vietnamese Army on March 31, the day after the Binh Xuyen attack, and were keeping an eye on the suburbs and approaches to Saigon-Cholon on the west. Nhu also had urged Trinh minh Thé to engage in clandestine activities against the Binh Xuyen command post at the "Y" bridge over the Arroyo Chinois in Cholon, but Thé was feeling misused by the government at the time and refused. Indeed, Trinh minh Thé and his troops had been left in a sort of bureaucratic limbo, which he described to me as "muddy," saying that he and his men "had no orders, no nothing."

Trinh minh Thé admitted that he was rather well informed about the Binh Xuyen. He had introduced technicians surreptitiously to the Binh Xuyen, and they were busy at a score of Binh Xuyen projects, including running Bay Vien's radio transmitter at the Y bridge, which was making daily broadcasts to inflame the public. Did I want it blown up? (Afterward, I asked Ambassador Collins if we should have this transmitter blown up. He said no.)

During the confrontation with the Binh Xuyen, I also was flooded with voluntary information. Vietnamese from neighborhoods I had visited the previous summer, when "social action" committees were elected, started to call at the house to make sure that I knew what "really" was going on. The Ocampo family, long-time Filipino residents who had flown an American flag from their house when British troops took over Saigon from the Japanese in 1945, asked their friends among the *cyclo* and taxicab drivers to help and surprised me with daily gifts of detailed information. Colonel Jose Banzon, the Philippines observer, was equally generous with information from the Filipino community, whose musicians and singers were intimate parts of the metropolitan night life run by the Binh Xuyen. Along with all this, my friends among the American and Vietnamese journalists in the city, who were as indignant as I over the mockery of the political game being played in Saigon, went out of their way daily to share what they knew. I was deeply touched that so many wanted to help.

A strange sidelight was given to the scene of armed-but-waiting forces within Saigon when commercial flights brought the latest news publications to town from the U.S. The April 4 issue of *Time* magazine had a portrait of Diem on the cover. Displayed on newsstands around town, it made a striking background to the soldiers' sandbagged forts on the sidewalks.

Toward the middle of April, I was told that Collins and Ely finally had come to some conclusions about the sects. I was asked to help arrange a Franco-American meeting with sect leaders. Using the French and American officers of my previous study group as messengers, I extended invitations for this meeting to all the main leaders of the sects, staggering their arrivals so that loyal leaders and those in the front wouldn't have to be together in the same room lest they shoot each other. The uneasy armed truce of the city was much in evidence as the invited conferees drove to the meeting place in Cholon. Each had to make his way past French tanks which were parked in many streets, their crews idling atop them in the sun or camped nearby.

The meetings were conducted in French and French officers presided. Each sect leader was given "his day in court," to report upon his situation, his total troop strength and his needs, while French and American officers who composed the audience took notes. Each sect leader also was sounded out about his feelings toward a "more broadly based government" and "preventing the shedding of blood." Yes, yes, they responded, the government needs to be broader; some almost drooled as they envisioned the power coming their way. And yes, they would like to prevent bloodshed; some were plainly worried about keeping their own hides intact. Several of the French officers in the conference audience couldn't keep straight faces during the question-and-answer periods and were laughing among themselves over the farce of the proceedings. For once I agreed with them, although the sinking feeling at the pit of my stomach kept me from laughing with them. I smelled a "political solution" coming up that would turn control of the government over to Bay Vien and his French friends.

One of the Binh Xuyen conferees at this Franco-American meeting was yet another Colonel Minh in this drama—Colonel Thai hoang Minh, the chief of staff of the Binh Xuyen forces. Tall, husky, with a soldierly bearing and a lack of bombast in his talk, he struck me as a most impressive man. What was he doing amongst these gangsters? Hurriedly, I searched my memory for what I had learned about him. He had had an impressive combat record while leading the Binh Xuyen *supplétifs* against the Vietminh when the road to Cap St. Jacques was opened in February 1953. He had been put out of action when he stepped on a land mine.

When Colonel Minh left the platform after his stint, Redick and I introduced ourselves. French officers closed in on us fast like worried mother hens. I congratulated Minh on his ability to walk without a limp after so serious an injury. His exploits were known even to an American such as myself. Would he mind showing me the way his wounds had healed? Minh, laughing, said that he had heard of me too and rolled up his pant legs to show me how the extensive damage to his legs had healed. I squatted down to examine them. The French officers moved off, disgusted by my maudlin curiosity. As soon as they were out of earshot, I told Minh softly that we only had a few moments to be alone. I wanted to talk to him most seriously about something else. "What in hell are you doing on the wrong side?" I asked him. "You belong where the other patriots are, not with gangsters."

Minh's true feelings tumbled out in fierce whispers. He said that he hadn't participated in the decision to make the midnight March 29–30 attack or in the fighting. He thought it to be stupid and wrong. There were four battalions loyal to him personally, all located south of the city, across the arroyo. He wanted to bring them over to Diem himself, not to the government or to the Vietnamese Army. Would I tell Diem this? If Diem agreed, Minh would make the necessary arrangements. I promised to inform Diem. We had no further chance to talk because the clucking French officers came back to us, suddenly worried about having left us alone for a few moments. They accompanied Colonel Minh to the door. As he left, he gave me a friendly smile. It was the last I ever saw of him. A few days later, he was dead.

After the Franco-American sect meeting, Trinh minh Thé surprised me with some news about himself. He was going to Indonesia as one of the official Vietnamese delegates to the twenty-nine-nation Asian-African Conference that would meet in Bandung from April 18 to 23. I urged him to wear his black pajama uniform at the Bandung meetings. Some of the Communist delegates were sure to show up in pseudopeasant dress. He came by his rice-paddy uniform more honestly than they and should wear it proudly.

I saw Diem the next afternoon and told him about Colonel Minh of the Binh Xuyen. Diem was intensely interested in Minh's proposal to bring over his four battalions and promptly asked his brother Nhu to start making arrangements with Minh. We all agreed that great caution should be used in doing this, to protect Minh.

Diem had other matters on his mind as well. He was very worried about the trend of events. For one thing, he had sent his brother Luyen to France to talk to Bao Dai. The two had once been close to each other. Now, however, Bao Dai seemed to be avoiding Luyen, who was anxiously seeking an audience. Meanwhile, Bao Dai's confidants in Saigon appeared to be busy with some new scheme. The word was that Bao Dai would be coming back to Vietnam. If true, there was bound to be a sharp popular reaction against him. Already people were linking Bao Dai to the Binh Xuyen, and signs were starting to appear saying *"da-dao Bao Dai"* ("down with Bao Dai") in the streets.

Diem realized that Binh Xuyen behavior was purposely generating further unrest and insecurity among the populace, perhaps to provide an excuse for imposing stricter police restraints on the people by Bay Vien's police chief, Lai van Sang, or by the French military. Jeeploads of men raced through the streets of Cholon at dusk, firing submachine guns. Civilian casualties were mounting. That very noon, armed men in a jeep had fired at the main entrance to the General Staff building in Cholon.

Diem looked musingly out of the window for a time, his face grim as he reflected on his troubling thoughts. He turned to me finally and said he now knew what Ely and Collins had in mind as a solution to the sect problem. He had been talking with each of them. In fact, he had talked with Collins that morning.

Their proposed solution, as outlined to him, had five main points. (1) The Vietnamese government would become provisional only and would be composed of a coalition cabinet that included a number of persons in opposition to Diem. (2) A new chief of police would be named by Diem, subject to the approval of both the new coalition cabinet and the Binh Xuyen, "to prevent bloodshed." (3) Delegates would be appointed to form a Provisional Assembly, which would meet on May 15; among these appointees, sixty would be from the sects, sixteen would be northerners, and ten would be named by Diem. The

Provisional Assembly would recommend to Bao Dai whom he should name as the new prime minister. (4) An honorary High Council would be appointed as a consultative body, with sect leaders included as members. (Diem paused at this, adding, "as though sect leaders would be satisfied with honorary jobs when they want piasters.") (5) Diem's brothers Luyen and Nhu would be exiled from Vietnam, pro tem.

Diem had sent his own solution to the sect problem in a letter to General Ely that morning. In essence, the letter said, "The French Expeditionary Corps armed the sects and should be the ones to disarm them now."

I met with General Collins shortly after I'd left Doc Lap Palace. I told him of Diem's remarks and gave him my best opinion of Diem's reaction to the new Franco-American proposed solution: Diem wouldn't knuckle under. Furthermore, most of the Vietnamese people would be on his side. When word of the proposed solution became public, it was going to generate great popular unrest. It would be taken as a provocation rather than a solution. Unless there was a realistic way of absorbing some 40,000 armed sect soldiers into other pursuits, serious trouble in Vietnam lay ahead.

Collins was sure, imperfect though it might be, that the solution could be made to work. The main objective still was to defuse an explosive situation in order to prevent bloodshed. He himself was making a quick trip to Washington. He outlined some of the urgent matters he wanted to take up there. There was the sect problem. Also, there was the problem of reduction and reorganization of the Garde Civile (rural police) and similar problems with the Vietnamese Army. Further, there was a pressing need for more funds for the resettlement of refugees.

I reminded Collins that I was seeing Diem almost every day. It seemed clear to me that Vietnam was heading straight and fast into real turmoil. When trouble hit, Diem was sure to ask me if the U.S. would support him as head of the government. Diem would deserve an honest answer. What should I tell him?

Collins replied flatly that I should tell Diem that the U.S. would support him. Diem was the head of the legal government recognized by the U.S. But then Collins added a strange remark. He told me that I might hear all sorts of rumors of other things, even stories that the U.S. wouldn't support Diem. I was to disregard such tales. I could be assured that the U.S. would continue to support Diem and should so inform him.

As General Collins left Saigon for Washington, Ngo dinh Diem was making a radio broadcast to the Vietnamese people. He renewed his invitation to the leaders of the Binh Xuyen and the Hoa Hao to come to see him. He admitted that the government was no longer paying the *supplétif* forces but said that he would try to work something out to help them if they were willing to work with him. Further, a new move was being taken to let the people participate more in the government. General elections were to be held in three months' time, to elect representatives to a General Assembly. The electorate would be canvassed, meanwhile, for opinions on exactly what the business of the General Assembly should be. Diem called for unity, saying that it was essential if Vietnam was to realize independence after being divided for eighty years under a colonialist regime. He also noted that the national army had all the means necessary to oppose any attempt at violence.

I heard of this broadcast at my office in TRIM, where we were busy with final preparations for Operation Giai-Phong, which was scheduled to start in three days in Quang Ngai. It wasn't until evening that I could get away and call upon Diem. I asked him if there had been any response to his broadcast from the Binh Xuyen or the Hoa Hao. There had not. I then asked about the proposed General Assembly and the canvass of voters' opinions. Diem replied that the Assembly not only would have elected representatives, but also would have appointed representatives of armed groups and political parties as a means of easing present tensions in the country.

His proposed canvass of the electorate would be done through a simple questionnaire distributed to voters in all villages. They would mail their replies to the government, using stamped, self-addressed envelopes. Voters would be asked to answer three main questions. Do you want a General Assembly elected? Do you want a single national army? Do you want a reform program? The reform question would have a number of subquestions concerning land reform, a national university, public works, and the revival of the national economy. A copy of the results from the canvass would be sent to Bao Dai for his guidance, to show him what people were thinking.

The questionnaire was now being drafted and should be ready for distribution in a week. A week after that, the replies should start coming in. I cautioned him against overoptimism in expecting response from the electorate in time for it to be tabulated correctly, the results announced, and preparations made for holding a general election throughout South Vietnam. He was talking about millions of opinions and votes, which would have to be handled by an administrative organization that was now somewhat crippled and had never done such work before. Diem was certain that the Vietnamese could do it.

I asked him then about the Franco-American proposal to resolve the current situation. Was he refusing to consider it? Diem said that he was considering it, but how could he give traitors positions of power in the government and still retain enough respect from the people to be able to govern? Clearly, Chief of Police Sang would have to go right away. Kidnappings and shootings were continuing. Although Diem had been doing his best to show restraint, lack of decisive action, such as changing the chief of police, would bring dire results. His government was on the point of quitting. The army was growing disgusted by the apparent indecisiveness. Many of the police who had come over to the government after the Binh Xuyen attack were losing heart. The people themselves were starting to feel betrayed and were becoming really restless.

Diem had received a telegram from Bao Dai, stating that the truce in Saigon should be extended at least until the end of April. Bao Dai, he said, also asked for thirty million piasters, but Diem didn't have the funds to give him.

I made my own preparations for the violent days so obviously coming. Since I had to drive through the city daily to and from work, I did my best to learn the back streets and alternate ways by changing my route each time I drove around town. My self-education was stimulated by getting shot at a few times over my usual route and, once, barely frustrating an attempt to ram me with a truck. I had moved to a larger house on Duy Tan, and there was growing talk that it was to be the target of a terrorist attack soon. Several officers of my team had moved in with me, and we stashed loaded weapons and hand grenades near windows and doors to have them handy in an emergency. My Filipino friends of Freedom Company were concerned about my safety and finally prevailed upon me to let one of them, Proc Mojica, move in and keep an eye on things at night. Proc was learning to play the guitar, so I fell asleep each night to the soft strains of Philippine guerrilla songs drifting through the house. These lullabies seemed fitting for the mood in Saigon then.

Trinh minh Thé came back from the Bandung Conference full of stories. He had enjoyed one moment of his own making, in which he had presented a personal declaration against imperialism to the assembly. Dressed in his black pajama uniform, he had read his declaration aloud from the floor in front of the Chinese Communist delegation, which was headed by Chou En-lai. The declaration began with bitter words about ways in which the French colonialists had repressed the freedom of the Vietnamese. Delighted by what they were hearing, the Communists turned up the volume on the public address system to make sure that all delegates heard the words of this slim and youthful Vietnamese revolutionary in black pajamas. They boomed out into the hall. Yes, the French colonialists were bad. But, as bad as they were and as much as the Vietnamese hated them, there was an even greater evil today, an evil that the speaker would resist as long as there was breath left in his body—*the imperialism of the Communists!* They were the worst enemies of all to the people! With that, Thé had looked hard at the stunned Chinese Communists, then walked back to his seat.

On April 25 Diem told me that the situation was becoming "inextricable." The next day he dismissed Lai van Sang, the Binh Xuyen's director of national police, and appointed Nguyen ngoc Le to replace him. Le had been organizing the veterans with the help of Filipinos in Freedom Company. On April 27 Diem told me that Bao Dai had reacted by sending him a telegram from France, ordering him to change the commander of the Vietnamese armed forces for a man of Bao Dai's choosing, General Nguyen van Vy, now in Dalat with Bao Dai's Imperial Guard battalions. I had met with Vy a number of times, knew him to be one of the most competent Vietnamese combat commanders, and was quite taken with his evident integrity and thoughtful manner. Diem conjectured that Vy would not only assume command of the Vietnamese armed forces but also declare himself the interim head of the government in the name of His Majesty Bao Dai, pack Diem off to France, and prepare the way for Bao Dai's return to Vietnam. I doubted this; Vy was too honorable a person to undertake an action that would so tear Vietnam apart. One consequence would be that the Binh Xuyen would become much more powerful in such an interim government. If this were pointed out to Vy, I was sure that he would follow the tradition taught him by the French and refuse to accept such orders. Diem felt, however, that Vy was too honorable an officer to refuse to obey the orders of his chief of state.

When I left Diem, he had started to draft a reply to Bao Dai's telegram. He was going to try to make Bao Dai realize the truth of the situation in Vietnam and awaken him from his deluding dreams.

NOTES

TERROR. Colonel Tran van Don (later a general and a senator) confirmed Diem's story about the machine-gunning of the General Staff building. The firing came from a jeepload of men (one of them apparently a Caucasian) wearing the green berets of the Binh Xuyen. The firing was timed for the moment the Vietnamese Army leaders were going out of the main doorway for lunch. They took cover instantly and none were hit.

★ ★

CHAPTER SIXTEEN

BATTLE FOR SAIGON

I SPENT THE MORNING of April 28 at my office in TRIM, busy
with the demands of the "national security action" program
which by now had operations in progress throughout the country. I was working on the problem of replacing destroyed
bridges in Central Vietnam. Operation Giai-Phong was being
hampered in crossing rivers; makeshift ferrying by small boats
slowed the timetable for the march of the main body of troops
and the truckloads of relief supplies for the population. The
French Expeditionary Corps had bridge-building material, but
it was earmarked for shipment to France and North Africa.
Colonel Kim and Lieutenant Phillips wanted to fly to Saigon
from Operation Giai-Phong the next morning to take up the
problem. I told them to come ahead and arranged to have them
meet with General O'Daniel at his MAAG office in western
Cholon when they arrived. Perhaps O'Daniel could help us
find material for bridges.

At noon a telephone call from Doc Lap Palace asked if I
would please come and see Diem right away. Joe Redick and
I set out for the palace by the shortest route. Approaching Place
Khai-Dinh, a traffic circle where five boulevards and streets

meet, I noticed something amiss. Bicyclists were bumping into each other and falling in the street. Cars were stopping, their doors popping open and spewing passengers onto the pavement where they lay huddled. At first glance it looked like a massive slapstick scene. I slowed down, amazed. Then I heard the machine gun fire, a sound that had been muffled by the houses along the street. It was so unexpected an event in the heavy traffic that it seemed to take me forever to link the dropping of people onto the ground with the firing of machine guns. When I caught on, I stopped the car. Redick and I dropped flat on the pavement with the others.

The firing died away after several minutes. We got back into the car and drove past the scramble of stilled traffic at the circle. Seeing us on the move, people started getting to their feet again, apparently shaken but unhurt. The firing must have been over our heads. In the spacious public park behind the palace, I noticed that something new had been added: batteries of artillery with Vietnamese Army crews camped around the guns. They looked incongruous among the tennis courts, playgrounds, bridle paths, and beds of brilliant flowers beneath the tall tropical trees.

Diem was pacing up and down the long second-story porch of the palace's eastern portico when we arrived. Instead of going inside to his office, as was customary, we stood on the porch and talked. Diem had received word from Washington just before telephoning me. It had been reported to him that Ambassador Collins had obtained President Eisenhower's approval for a change of U.S. policy toward Vietnam. Diem was to be "dumped" in favor of a coalition government. Was this report true? Diem looked at me intently as he asked this. I said firmly that I didn't believe the report. Collins had assured me before his departure that the U.S. would support Diem, despite any rumors to the contrary. Diem refused to tell me the source of his information. I said that I would initiate a check with Washington by radio to make doubly sure of what

I'd just told him. Since it was midnight in Washington on the other side of the world, it would be hours before a reply could be expected from top U.S. officials.

Diem relaxed a little at my reassurances. He said there had been reports of shooting in the streets all over town, and I described what had happened on our way to see him. Diem thought the Binh Xuyen probably were working themselves up toward an action to break the truce. He grinned impishly and added that he had some new tactical intelligence about the Binh Xuyen. Their mortars had been freshly sighted in on the palace. The very spot on the porch where we were standing was the exact target for an 81-mm. mortar acquired by the Binh Xuyen during the truce. We might get blown up even as we stood there talking to each other.

I asked Diem about the Binh Xuyen chief of staff, who was to come over to the nationalist side, Colonel Thai hoang Minh. Diem said arrangements had been made to pass Colonel Minh and his four battalions (which were then near Go Cong south of Saigon) through the lines, where they would be integrated into the national army. Minh had said that his own troops and six Binh Xuyen battalions of "Sûreté assault troops" were practically at swords' points. One platoon loyal to Minh was in the Rue Catinat area, in the French security zone close to Doc Lap Palace.

We left after I had suggested to Diem that he get off the porch if it was indeed to be the target of 81-mm. mortar shells "at any moment." I drove to my house on Duy Tan, about eight blocks from the palace. There was scarcely any traffic on the streets. It was a little past one o'clock in the afternoon, and all sensible people in Saigon were at home for lunch and siesta. Just as I was turning into the driveway at my house, there came a series of loud explosions from the direction of the palace. Obviously, the attack on the palace had started. When I entered my house, the telephone was ringing.

It was Ngo dinh Diem calling me. His voice sounded calm,

unperturbed. I asked if he was all right. Yes, he told me; he was calling General Ely and had arranged with the switchboard for me to hear the conversation, as a witness. Before I could ask further questions, Ely came on the line. I did my best to follow the conversation, which was in French (later verifying it with Redick and Diem). Diem told Ely that Doc Lap Palace was under fire from the Binh Xuyen and he wanted Ely to know that this hostile action broke the truce. Ely said that he couldn't hear any sounds of an attack on the palace at his house. (He lived about half the distance from the palace as my house, where the explosions were a loud din in the midday air. I wondered if Ely could be inside a closed room, perhaps with an air-conditioner drowning out the sound of close-by artillery explosions. Was this possible?)

Diem seemed surprised that Ely couldn't hear the shelling. Just then, there came a great *wha-a-am* over the telephone. A long pause. Diem came back on the line, his voice a bit shaky. He asked if Ely had heard *that!* A shell had exploded against the wall of the bedroom from where Diem was speaking. He wanted Ely to understand that Diem hadn't broken the truce. The Binh Xuyen had. Diem was giving orders immediately to the Vietnamese Army to fight back. Ely started to say something, but Diem broke in to state that he had informed Ely of the facts and was taking action. He hung up.

I sat down to a belated lunch, writing notes about what was happening with one hand while I ate with the other. Before I was through, the telephone rang again. By this time there was a great noisy fuss going on over toward the palace, where the artillery in the park was returning the Binh Xuyen fire. I had to cup the telephone with both hands in order to hear.

The caller was my friend John Mecklin, correspondent for *Time* and *Life* magazines. He sounded excited. He was telephoning from the 4th Arrondissement police station. He and photographer Howard Sochurek were there. Mecklin was talking to me from the floor of the police station, lying under a desk for protection, and Sochurek was behind the building's cement wall next to the door. A company of Vietnamese Army soldiers was in the police station with them. A battalion, maybe more, of Binh Xuyen troops was attacking the police station from across the boulevard. The attackers were pouring heavy submachine gun fire into the police station and closing in fast. They would be inside the station any moment. If I had any bright ideas on what Sochurek and Mecklin should do next, now was the time to tell him.

I started asking Mecklin about the back exits to the police station, when he yelped, "My God! Oh my God!" "What is it?" I yelled back. Mecklin said the company of army soldiers had dashed madly out of the building, just as the Binh Xuyen troops had reached it. It was a counterattack. Sochurek was crouched there, photographing the scene. "God, look at 'em fight, Howard," were Mecklin's next words. Then there was an "oh, oh!" followed by a gasp of relief. Mecklin told me that he would have to hang up. He and Sochurek were leaving the police station because they both were looking at an incredible sight. The army company was chasing a battalion or so of Binh Xuyen down the boulevard, as if in a footrace, past the green berets littering the street as the Binh Xuyen snatched off and threw away their identifying headgear. "Who said these army guys wouldn't fight!" shouted Mecklin as he hung up.

I went back to finish my lunch but was destined not to do so. I remembered suddenly that Major Lou Conein was in a situation of possible danger. He had come to Saigon from Haiphong and had spent last night at my staff house on Rue Taberd. During dinner two heavily armed men had walked in and said that they were emissaries from Bay Vien. They wanted Conein to accompany them to see their boss, who had a message for me. Conein had telephoned me, and I had advised him not to go with them to the Binh Xuyen headquarters. We had no guarantee of safe-conduct from the gangsters. Instead,

Conein could arrange to see them again, in some safe place of his own choosing, to receive Bay Vien's message. The two emissaries and Conein finally had agreed to meet this noon on a broad, open street in the French security zone. By now, an hour and a half had passed since the meeting time and I hadn't heard from Conein or from the other officers who were going along to keep a protective watch on him and on the meeting place.

I called the Rue Taberd house. No, there had been no word from Conein. A lot of shells were exploding all around the house, cars burning out in the street, so maybe he hadn't been able to get back. Everyone in the house was safe. It had been hit but the damage was minor. I told them to stay there and keep under cover. I'd see if I could find our elusive comrades.

I went out to my car in the driveway. Just then, Conein and the others drove up, followed by a jeep. To my surprise, Major "Bo" Bohannan, and an army lieutenant colonel and a marine corps lieutenant unknown to me, climbed out of the following jeep. They all had arrived in Saigon at one o'clock on the day's Pan-American flight. Bo said that he figured he might be missing some fun and games, so he had impulsively put in for leave and luckily had found a seat on the commercial flight from Manila that morning. I was very glad to see him! The two strangers were reporting in for duty on my team. They all had met while hunting a ride to my house from the airport.

Conein was pale, apparently in shock. I asked about his rendezvous with the Binh Xuyen. "Five of them killed, right in front of me. Children, too!" he told me. The others explained that the Binh Xuyen hadn't shown up but that a mortar shell had hit a tiny Renault taxicab right in front of Conein while he awaited them. The direct hit had blown to bits the taxicab, its driver, and its passengers, a family group with three little children. I made Conein go in the house and poured him half a tumbler of whiskey.

I telephoned his Rue Taberd house with the news of his arrival. When I was informed that there hadn't been any recent shelling around the house, I said that I was sending Major Bohannan over with Conein and the others; Bo would be in charge. I packed them off to Rue Taberd, where there were beds and food for all. I would stop by when I could. First, I had to get over to the embassy to tell the officials there what I knew of the situation and to make sure that correct information was going to Washington. (I was worried by what Diem had told me about a change in U.S. policy. Maybe it *was* being discussed. If so, facts about the fast-changing situation in Saigon must get to Washington promptly.)

I drove toward downtown and the embassy. French tanks and barbed wire barred some of the streets completely. I detoured. At a schoolhouse, Vietnamese Army troops were scrambling out of a convoy of trucks. I paused, and several of the officers and men noticed me and called to the others. They waved their weapons and yelled, dancing around. They were all keyed up ready for a fight. At the next corner, Vietnamese Army MPs stopped me and insisted I take another detour. There was fighting going on just ahead. I turned into a main boulevard leading to Cholon and heard the sound of heavy infantry fighting. A Vietnamese Army battalion jogged along the side of the boulevard, heading toward the fighting. General O'Daniel drove by in his staff car just then and gave me a wave. As he drove past the running troops, he leaned out of the car and impulsively shouted, "Give 'em hell, boys, give 'em hell!" They yelled back, a lusty responsive cheer.

Arriving at the embassy after all the zig-zagging, I found a squadron of light French tanks drawn up before it in defensive positions. In the chargé's office, the senior embassy officials were seated around a desk composing a radio message for Washington. To my astonishment, they were debating which adjectives to use to describe the low morale of the Vietnamese Army troops who now had to stand up to the high-spirited Binh Xuyen! I could hardly believe my ears. Apparently they had stayed in the embassy building and relied on telephone reports from French friends about what was happening. It was all a fantasy. One of the attachés even said that he had been informed that I had personally led a Vietnamese Army attack against the Binh Xuyen headquarters and had been killed. French officers claimed to have seen this.

I told the gathering what I knew of the situation. My words were greeted skeptically. I urged them to delay the drafting of the message for another fifteen minutes while they went out into the streets for a firsthand look at what actually was going on or telephoned General O'Daniel to ask him, since he had been driving around town. The army attaché, an infantryman, came in just then and confirmed my observations. The debate broke out again. I told the chargé that I wanted to send a separate message bearing my name as the source, so Washington could sort out conflicting views in radiograms from Saigon. He said okay. With that, I sat down and wrote a detailed radiogram describing events as I knew them so far that day. After showing it to the chargé, I saw it on its way. The group debate over the official message was still going on.

It was late afternoon by the time I left the embassy. Dense clouds of smoke darkened the sky above Cholon, where a large section of the city was burning, and each side claimed the other had set it. The fire raged virtually unchecked, since firemen couldn't get through the combat lines. Thousands of people ran through the streets from their burning homes, seeking safety but trying to avoid the strong points where infantry fighting raged. The Vietnamese Army and government workers were opening temporary shelters for these refugees in schoolhouses in an attempt to organize care for them, although many spent the night in the streets. I learned later that a hundred people had died in the fire, another five hundred known casualties went to hospitals, and many thousands were left homeless. More than a square mile of the most densely populated section of the city had been burned out.

I stopped by the big house on Rue Taberd where most of

my team lived. Burned-out and shell-shattered vehicles gave the street outside a junkyard look, and a crumpled sedan lay across the front steps, blocking the door. I climbed over a wall to get in. Everyone and everything inside was intact. I asked Major Fred Allen of the team, who knew General Nguyen van Vy quite well, to try to see Vy or to find out what he was doing. Vy reportedly was carrying out Bao Dai's orders. Our embassy officials had told me that Vy had come to Saigon from Dalat with one battalion of Imperial Guards and had taken over the command of the Vietnamese Army, presumably to stop the counterattack against the Binh Xuyen. Allen made fruitless attempts, but Vy, though in town, wouldn't or couldn't see him. Later, Vietnamese Army officers told me that Vy was issuing orders as a commnader, but that nobody was obeying them. They added that Vy had unsuccessfully attempted to relieve Big Minh of command over the troops fighting against the Binh Xuyen in the city, in order to replace him with one of Vy's officers.

After dark, in savage nighttime battles, the army stormed Binh Xuyen strongholds at the Grand Monde gambling casino and at the Petrus Ky High School, both in Cholon. General Phuong of the Cao Dai stopped by to tell me about the Petrus Ky attack, saying that some Frenchmen had been captured there along with the Binh Xuyen. (The next day, Diem confirmed this report about Frenchmen at Petrus Ky, giving me the names of those then being held by the Vietnamese Army. Later, he reported that a total of thirty-seven Frenchmen eventually had been found at Petrus Ky, some of whom admitted they were members of a *colon* militia organization.)

Late that night I heard from Washington. There were blunt words for me: my radio message had contained statements at variance with other information being received; if it was true that Diem was alive, was still the head of the government, and actually was being supported by the national army as I claimed, then I should get my statements confirmed by the senior U.S. officials on the scene. Tiredly, I wondered how I was going to get some of these Americans to see what was under their noses. I fell asleep thinking about it.

Early the next morning, April 29, I was awakened by a hubbub on the street in front of my house. I looked out. The block was filled with people along the sidewalks and curbs on both sides of the street, where pedicabs, taxis, and even an old truck were jammed into parking areas. There were several small fires laid against garden walls, where people were cooking breakfast. My first guess was that the people were refugees from the conflict and great fire in Cholon, which I judged from the smudges in the sky must still be burning. The fighting was continuing, too, its sounds plain in the morning air. Yet the people didn't look like refugees. I could see no children, no bundles of possessions.

My houseboy came in and told me that the people had started arriving before dawn. No, they were not refugees. They had come to where I lived to *protect me* because of the "papers" and the radio broadcasts. He showed me several of the "papers." They were leaflets in various sizes, some from a printing press, others from mimeograph machines, my name displayed prominently in each. It seems that different groups had come up with the same idea at the same time of offering a large sum for my head. The leaflets had been distributed last night and earlier this morning. As for the radio broadcasts, they were a new hourly appeal on the Binh Xuyen radio station, offering a large sum to anyone bringing me in *alive* to the Binh Xuyen. The broadcasts hastened to explain why I should be lugged in alive, in case a listener got the wrong notion that the gangster Binh Xuyen forces were turning effete. The radio audience was assured that I would be suitably tortured, until, finally, my stomach would be torn open, my guts stuffed with mud, and my body floated down the Canal de Derivation for all to see. Leaflets and broadcasts blamed me for all the current troubles in Saigon-Cholon.

I went out on the street to meet the crowd before my house.

They were some of the elected neighborhood officials from the days of the social action committee who had come from all over the city, along with taxicab and *cyclo* drivers who were friends of the Ocampo family, and even a group of well-dressed bureaucrats who explained to me that they were residents of a nearby apartment house. From their many remarks, I gathered that I represented something "good" to them and that it had become evident "the bad ones" were out to destroy me. They didn't want it to happen and were at my house to prevent it.

It was a stunning way to start the day. I must have stood there amongst them for several minutes, unable to speak. It was one of the grandest moments of my life.

When my emotions were under control again, I thanked them for coming to me in an hour of need and asked if all had had breakfast. There was a chorus of assent. I reassured them that there was no need to guard the house. I was leaving it for duties elsewhere in the city, and I was sure that they had affairs of their own and of their families to look after that day. I climbed into my car, backed out, and headed down the street waving and smiling. As I drove away, the crowd was dispersing.

I made the rounds of the homes of the senior U.S. officials, to catch them at breakfast or before they left the house for the day's work. By now, there was general agreement with what I had reported to Washington. (The Vietnamese Army storming of the Binh Xuyen stronghold at the Grand Monde gambling casino seemed to have been especially convincing about the fighting quality of the army.) The only official I missed seeing was General O'Daniel, who had left a few minutes before. His wife Ruth told me, "You know Mike whenever there are troops fighting. He was eager to get out of the house this morning." She showed me where shrapnel from mortar bursts had rained down around the house, on the porches, in the yard. She looked out of the door wistfully at the beautiful, sunny morning, saying that she guessed she should stay inside as her husband had asked. There still were mortar bursts, the crash of artillery firing, and the popping and rattling of infantry weapons not too far away.

I drove to my office at TRIM to meet Colonel Kim and Rufe Phillips, so that I could take them out to MAAG at the far end of Cholon for the meeting with General O'Daniel about getting material for the Bong Song and other bridges in Operation Giai-Phong. Fighting was going on around the area, so there were no traffic cops. It was a fast drive to the TRIM compound, ending in a scene just the reverse of the one at my house. A crowd of French officers had gathered in the street in front of my office. One of them held a little Vietnamese girl in his arms, her leg bleeding from a shrapnel wound, and was making an impassioned speech to the others. "Look what Lansdale has done," he said. "He makes war on children!" As the crowd glowered at me, I took the girl away from him and handed her to Lieutenant Colonel George Melvin, who had come up, so that he could take her to our dispensary a few yards away for treatment. The loss of his human prop didn't deter the speaker, who continued describing my villainy. It seems that I had been directing the fighting against the Binh Xuyen, at the same time had been hiding under the bed with a quaking Diem, had my hands dripping with the blood of innocent people, and was to blame for "everything." Kim and Phillips were standing nearby, amazed at the tirade. I told them, "Let's get out of here. We have a meeting with General O'Daniel."

We climbed into two cars, Phillips with me and Kim in a Vietnamese staff car. Kim jumped out of his staff car suddenly and ran over to us. Having just come from the operations in Central Vietnam, he had forgotten momentarily about the situation in the city. We would have to drive past the Binh Xuyen lines to get to MAAG, and his Vietnamese Army car was sure to get shot up in the process. As Kim got in with us, we all grinned sheepishly. We had come close to being fatally stupid.

West of the TRIM compound, my recently acquired knowledge of city streets came in handy. Several blocks would be empty of people, their houses shuttered. Then there would be a block with troops in combat. Brakes on. Back up. Detour. Often soldiers would look up from weapons they were firing and wave us away. The trip became a series of detours. I recalled a back way to MAAG, through alleys and lanes almost too narrow for a car, that would bring us in from the northwest. The route was peaceful until I turned the last corner just before arriving at MAAG—and drove us right into the middle of a sandbagged barricade swarming with Binh Xuyen troops! As they swung their weapons toward us, I smiled my number one smile, waved my hand, said a cheery "hello boys," and drove slowly around the sandbagged position. They stood and watched us. I kept going. In a moment we were at the MAAG headquarters. Binh Xuyen soldiers, prone behind a machine gun on the sidewalk, didn't even look up as we drove in the entrance.

Moments after we had sat down with General O'Daniel to discuss material for bridges, the neighborhood around MAAG turned into a battleground. We had to shout to be heard over the din of machine gun fire and exploding grenades. I excused myself from the conference and went to the men's room at the rear of the building. I discovered that the windows above the urinal had a fine view of a nearby Binh Xuyen strong point, where defenders in green berets were busily firing down the street. I went back to the conference and urged O'Daniel to go to the men's room for a unique way to watch a battle. He did, after a quizzical look at me. Peering out the window, he told me, hell, there was nothing to see. I looked again. The Binh Xuyen had deserted the outpost in the few moments I had been away. The erstwhile defenders evidently had snatched off their berets as they scampered off. The sandbagged positions were littered with green headgear.

The firing in the neighborhood died down as our conference ended. I spent a minute or so privately with O'Daniel, telling him about the radio message to me from Washington. It seemed to surprise him. He had very positive views about the loyalty and capability of the Vietnamese Army, which coincided with mine.

When we left MAAG, children were out on the sidewalks and streets, excitedly picking up the brass casings from expended ammunition. The flagpole in the courtyard had been hit, but the American flag was still flying. A squad of Vietnamese Army soldiers was moving westward along the street, toward the sounds of combat now a couple of blocks away. I drove Kim and Phillips back to TRIM, where they could confer with my staff about other operational needs in Central Vietnam. It was much easier driving through the streets. Only a few Binh Xuyen strongholds remained in the main sections of the city.

When I returned to my own house on Duy Tan, there was none of the early morning crowd in front of it. The street once again was its quiet, backwaterish self. The temporary security man, Proc Mojica, was sound asleep after his long, watchful duty the night before. I put a cup of coffee and a pad of paper on the dining room table and had barely sat down to write some notes about the changing situation in town when Colonel Jean Leroy walked through the door. I glanced out the door past this guerrilla leader who had introduced me to the Hoa Hao and who now reportedly had joined forces with the Binh Xuyen. A squad of his troops, heavily armed, had taken up guard positions along the front of my house.

Leroy told me to come with him to the Binh Xuyen. Since the Binh Xuyen radio was still broadcasting gory threats of disemboweling me, I told Leroy, "No, thanks. I'm not coming." I added that I was worried about his own safety and told him of the success the army was having in defeating the Binh Xuyen. Leroy and his men were risking death every minute they stayed in this area. He'd better get to a safe zone pronto. Leroy grinned and repeated his request to come along with him. Again I refused saying we were too good friends for me to resist since if I did both of us were bound to get hurt. By then, we were standing face to face in the living room. My hand was only inches away from some hand grenades I had hidden on a ledge behind a window drape. At this point, Bohannan and several of my staff officers walked in on the scene. Bohannan said I really didn't need all those armed guards in front of the house, because the Binh Xuyen were on the run. I told him that the "guards" were just leaving. I put my arm around Leroy's shoulders and walked him to the door, where we said farewell. He and his troops went roaring away in their jeeps.

I didn't see Leroy again for ten years, when we met in Washington for a drink to "the old days." (Leroy had to flee Vietnam in 1955, and he made his way to France. He and his men became building contractors in France, quickly picking up skills, and made a success of their lives far from home.)

That afternoon Conein and Allen of my team had a talk with General Nguyen van Vy, who supposedly was trying to take command of the Vietnamese Army for Bao Dai and stop the fighting against the Binh Xuyen. They told me that Vy had obtained some armored howitzers from the French military, who were eager to fulfill any of his requests, and, to the dismay of the French, had turned these howitzers over to the Vietnamese Army. The army promptly started using the howitzers against the remaining Binh Xuyen strongholds in the city. Apparently Vy, when the chips were down, found that his heart was with his comrades in the Vietnamese Army. Instead of playing the whole tangled political game that Bao Dai, the Binh Xuyen, and the French expected of him, Vy had acted to make sure that the army would at least win the battle in the city. But Vy was still bent on taking command in Bao Dai's name, and the army's combat commanders were still refusing to obey him. When I heard this, I concluded that Vy was trying to act honorably under orders that were practically impossible to follow with honor.

In the late afternoon, Diem asked me to come to the palace. It looked like a battleground. There were shell holes and martial litter in the gardens, walks, and driveways and great gouges cut in the palace walls. Windows were shuttered, sand-bagged defense positions could be seen throughout the palace grounds, and heavily armed troops were very much in evidence. A platoon was dug in at the front gate, evidently not expecting friendly visitors. I managed to squeeze my car past them and entered the grounds.

Diem met me in an alcove off his bedroom, where there was a small desk, its top burdened with great stacks of papers. He was doing most of his daily work in this sheltered spot, which was relatively safe from shot and shell. I looked at him closely to see how he was standing up under the strain. He had gone without sleep the night before and his tired eyes showed it. Instead of pacing the floor and gesturing energetically, as he so often did, he sat in a chair, his figure a bit slumped. His face and voice showed the results of the emotional battering he had been taking. There were strain lines around the eyes and mouth. His speech was much slower than usual.

The tiny alcove forced an intimacy on us. There was barely room for his chair and desk, let alone other furniture. Two narrow chairs were brought in for Redick and myself. We squeezed into them and sat knees to knees with Diem.

Diem said that the Vietnamese Army had advanced as far as the Arroyo Chinois in Cholon, but the troops were exhausted and needed a rest before attempting the crossing. The Binh Xuyen still held the Y bridge and the southern part of the city beyond the canals and the arroyo. The army would try to cross early in the morning. Some of Colonel Thai hoang Minh's Binh Xuyen troops had managed to get across the canal to the Vietnamese Army side, as he had arranged. More were coming in but were having to fight their way through other Binh Xuyen troops to reach the Vietnamese Army's lines.

Diem had bad news about this Binh Xuyen officer, Minh.

Apparently Minh had gone home to get his wife before crossing over into the army lines. Some of Bay Vien's bodyguards
had been waiting there. An eyewitness reported that Minh
and his wife had been seized, wrapped up in bicycle chains,
given a murderous beating while lying helpless on the ground,
and then shoved into a car which had driven off. Presumbly,
Minh and his wife were dead, or shortly would be.

Diem's voice was heavy with emotion as he told me this. I
suggested that the smartest thing he could do right then would
be to take a nap for at least an hour. He replied that he would
like to do so, but he really had asked me to see him concerning another matter. Would I please wait while he told me about
it? Tears had come to his eyes as he spoke. I nodded yes. We sat
there silently for some moments.

Diem finally reached over to his cluttered desk and picked
up a lengthy telegram. In a choked voice, he said it was a
telegram from Bao Dai. He read it aloud. It was evident that
the author had composed it in a savage fury. It stated that
Diem had been selected as the head of the government in
order to unite and help the welfare of the Vietnamese people.
Instead of that benign action, what had he done? He had been
disobedient toward the desires of Bao Dai, had alienated the
friendship of France, and had acted as a monster, plunging the
peaceful Vietnamese into the horrors of fratricidal conflict. His
willful hands were dripping with the blood of his innocent
fellow country men. Thousands more were left homeless when
their houses were burned in the fires he had caused. Their agony
was on his head. Instead of being a good leader, he had
brought disaster. Therefore, he must leave Saigon upon receipt
of this telegram and take the very first flight to France, where
he was to report immediately to Bao Dai. Diem was to turn
over the government to the proper person, whom Bao Dai already had designated. This was General Vy.

When he finished reading the telegram, Diem looked at
me imploringly. I remarked softly that his real time of decision

had come. If he was wondering what to do—as I presumed from the look on his face—I had a suggestion to aid his thinking. He could review his acts that led up to this moment, judging each upon its ethical merits or demerits and upon how it affected the majority of the people. In doing this, he would arrive at the sum of the strength or weakness of his present position and, from this sum, could make his decision. As national leaders, he and Bao Dai must think of the larger good. If it would help, I would sit with him as a friend while he thought this through.

Diem touched my knee with his hand, gesturing me to stay. Slowly, painfully, he recounted to me his past actions that bore on the present crisis. It was a long process.

Gradually, there emerged the principles he had followed and which, fundamentally, made up the issue at stake. Governmental power should be used for the benefit of those governed. If the government turned its responsibility for public safety over to those who preyed on the public, such a government would have ceased to act for the benefit of those governed and thus no longer would be true to the people's trust. It had been unprincipled to give the police powers to the Binh Xuyen, but it had been principled to take them away from the Binh Xuyen and make them a government responsibility. If Diem left Vietnam, the police powers undoubtedly and wrongly would go back to the Binh Xuyen. In the eyes of the people, there would be no moral basis upon which the government could govern. The Vietnamese government must not be based upon ideas despised by the people. Given a solid basis of ethics in government, the people would want to participate in it more fully and should do so. Otherwise, freedom would founder.

Diem's brother Nhu came to the doorway at this point. He, too, appeared to have taken an emotional battering. He leaned tiredly against the doorjamb, no longer looking the part of a boyish leading man playing the young surgeon or freshman congressman in a Hollywood movie, as he usually did. This was another man running out the string to exhaustion. When Nhu had Diem's attention, he told him that the Binh Xuyen radio station was broadcasting the contents of the Bao Dai telegram. Evidently Bao Dai's people who were associated with Bay Vien had received a copy. Diem gritted his teeth at the news. His chief had made this coded message available to those trying to destroy him. It must have been the decisive straw. Diem said firmly that he was staying in Saigon and would continue to run the government. I asked him if he was sure of his decision. He was. "I know I'm doing the right thing!"

I left the palace and got busy at the task of informing the U.S. leadership about the state of affairs in Saigon. After giving the news of Diem's decision to Randy Kidder, the deputy chief of mission who was acting head in the absence of Collins, I sent a message of my own to Washington, summing up what I had heard from Diem and what I had seen of a loyal army driving the Binh Xuyen out of the city.

It must have been this particular message that Secretary of State John Foster Dulles mentioned to me months later. His staff had brought him my message while he was at a dinner party. After reading it, he had excused himself and gone over to the White House to see the president and inform him. President Eisenhower had then made the decision to support Diem, as far as the U.S. could. Before that, the president had given his representative, General Collins, a free hand in this political matter. Dulles told me that Collins had discussed with him the formation of a coalition government in Saigon. The president's final decision had come after Collins had left Washington and was en route back to Saigon. None of these high-level deliberations in Washington were known to me in Saigon at the time. I hadn't believed Diem's reports from Washington that the U.S. was about to "dump" him and had thought I was being honest when I had expressed my disbelief. From the little I ever learned, I concluded eventually that my unwitting role had been that of an expendable pawn in a political game.

That night Trinh minh Thé stopped by my house briefly. He wanted me to know that he had brought two of his Lien-Minh battalions, 1,300 men, into town from the suburbs. Diem had asked him to get around to the rear of the Binh Xuyen forces and prevent them from moving out of the city into their old river-pirate hideouts between Saigon and the China Sea. French tanks had stopped the movement of the Lien-Minh battalions along provincial roads to the river-pirate hangouts (such as the Rung Sat swamps), so Thé had slipped into the city after dark with his troops. He was hopeful of finding some way of flanking the Binh Xuyen forces and getting down river behind them. I wished him luck. Shortly after he left, I started getting telephone calls. Rumors were flying wildly around the American and French communities that savage guerrillas in black pajamas were in town for a "night of the long knives" in which all our throats would be cut. I did my best to reassure callers that the black pajama troops were part of the army forces protecting the city. Finally, I simply stopped answering the telephone and went to bed.

The Binh Xuyen radio broadcasts of Bao Dai's vituperative message to Diem, along with the presence of French forces in Vietnam's capital city and the savagery of the street fighting between the Vietnamese Army and the Binh Xuyen, made an emotionally explosive mixture. The explosion itself came on the last day of April and continued until May 4, in the form of a series of frenzied political actions by Vietnamese nationalists. By May 4 the political facts of life in Vietnam were unlike anything anyone had envisaged. Even by May 2, when Ambassador Collins returned from Washington, it was to a vastly different Vietnam from the one he'd left. Events had outdistanced the pundits and "big picture" officials.

There were two polarizing forces with similar names busy in Vietnam in this hectic period, each working with furious energy. One was the Revolutionary Committee, which included some of the more fiery political ideologists among the Hoa Hao and the Cao Dai who had supported Diem against the Binh Xuyen. Perhaps the most thoughtful of these was Nguyen bao Toan, the organizer of a rice-roots political party among the Hoa Hao followers of General Nguyen ngoc Ngo. Generals Thé and Phuong participated in this new Revolutionary Committee. It wanted some fast action. Bao Dai was declared to be deposed. Diem was to be considered as having resigned on April 29. A new regime was to assume power, although there was wild debate over the composition of this new regime. Diem might be made president by the Revolutionary Committee. Or the committee itself might rule, with the legislative support of an enlarged revolutionary body having three representatives each from every province in Vietnam. (Although known as the Revolutionary Committee, its more formal name was "The General Assembly of Democratic Revolutionary Forces," with its main body composed of three hundred young patriots who said they represented eighteen nationalist political parties.)

The other polarizing force was the National Revolutionary Movement, sparked by Ngo dinh Nhu and Tran quoc Buu, the leader of the Vietnamese Federation of Labor, among others. It formed revolutionary groups in several provincial capitals and in the labor unions of Saigon-Cholon and planned to hold a Revolutionary Congress in Saigon on May 1, with many thousands of participants. Its aims initially were to rally support for Ngo dinh Diem and then to plan national elections for a republican form of government. Bao Dai would have to take his chances along with other candidates, although many of the revolutionaries in this movement were deeply angry over Bao Dai's recent activities. "Stupid" was one of the milder labels they gave him. Delegations arrived in Saigon for the May 1 congress, but combat conditions in the capital city were too prominent to make a large gathering feasible. (Who would enjoy meeting with his peers on an artillery target?) The Revolutionary Congress finally convened on May 4, with about six hundred delegates from the provinces and trade unions in attendance. The major resolution was in support of Diem. In the days immediately afterward, massive popular demonstrations took place in nearly every city and provincial capital of South Vietnam, in alliance with the National Revolutionary Movement.

On May 2 Doc Lap Palace was the stage setting for an incredible melodrama. The Revolutionary Committee went there to demand that Diem "bow to its will, for the sake of the people." The committee discovered the presence of another caller, General Nguyen van Vy, who had received further prodding from Bao Dai. Vy told Diem that he would have to leave Vietnam. Vy was to take over the government with "supreme powers." He had 1,500 troops of the Imperial Guard deployed nearby in the French security zone, where the Vietnamese Army was prohibited. The civilians on the committee, brandishing revolvers, promptly declared that Vy was under arrest. Vy, in turn, promptly declared that the committee was illegal and that he didn't recognize its powers. At this point members of the Vietnamese General Staff telephoned the palace to ask Vy to join them for dinner, to celebrate the howitzers delivered to the army through his efforts. He told them that he doubted he would be able to dine with them, since he was being held under arrest by something called the Revolutionary Committee. The General Staff officers said that they would send army troops to the palace and rescue him.

Two Americans, my journalist friends John Mecklin and Howard Sochurek, were at the palace while this was going on. Sochurek was busy with his camera, recording the scene (one photo was published later as the center spread in an issue of *Life*). Mecklin found a telephone and called me at my Duy Tan house to describe the scene. I asked him to let me speak with Trinh minh Thé and his interpreter Hoai. General Thé came to the telephone and, through Hoai, told me that the revolutionaries with him were stumped about what to do next, since the Army was coming to the palace and they might end up as casualties or prisoners themselves. I told him that it sounded like a damn fool predicament for him to be caught in and suggested that he get the committee out of the palace immediately. If he wished, he could bring them to my house for dinner. They would be right over, said General Thé, but please hold on, Diem wanted to talk to me. Diem came on the telephone. He said that he was all right and, now that the committee was leaving for my house, he would straighten out the situation quickly. He had asked Vy to have dinner with him or leave promptly along with the committee. In either event, Diem wasn't taking orders from Vy or anyone else at the moment.

The members of the Revolutionary Committee arrived shortly afterward. My cook had improvised a hasty dinner by borrowing food from the neighbors, which we ate buffet style while we sat around and talked. After listening to the excited revolutionaries, I urged them to do more thoughtful planning in the future and suggested that they would be wise to unite with the National Revolutionary Movement. Somehow, all the Vietnamese nationalist revolutionaries would have to work as a team. After dinner the committee left, saying that they were going to hold a secret meeting. I learned later that they composed a brief manifesto and, around midnight, started printing it in leaflet form. But because of the events on May 3, only a handful of the leaflets were ever distributed.

On the morning of May 3, General Collins met with his "Country Team," made up of the principal officers in the U.S. Mission. He had been away from Saigon for two weeks and opened the meeting with the remark that he found all of us quite changed in our attitudes since he had last seen us. Apparently, *somebody* had fomented a revolution among us Americans also. He politely refused to explain his remarks when I asked him what he was talking about. Then he told us the current U.S. policy directions in Vietnam, which had been conveyed to him in a radio message upon his arrival. We were to support Ngo dinh Diem in the present crisis. We were to help unwind anti-French emotions among the Vietnamese. (By this time, there was considerable overt popular expression against the French in Saigon. On their part, the French seemed to have overlooked the connection between their own behavior and this Vietnamese reaction and were convinced that, by some magic or other, I was to blame personally for their sorry political position. Some claimed I was trying to start World War III.)

The afternoon of May 3 Trinh minh Thé arrived unexpectedly at my house. He had a serious problem to solve. With that statement, he spread a map open on the dining room table. As he smoothed out the map, a flesh wound on his hand caused blood to drip from his fingers. I bandaged his hand for him while he talked.

He said that he was still under orders to get around to the rear of the Binh Xuyen and block their retreat to down-river redoubts. That morning, however, the Vietnamese Army had told him to take the left flank, with the two battalions he had in town, as the army crossed the canals to drive the Binh Xuyen from positions in the districts and suburbs just south of the city. They were to cross over two canals and then rush down Route 15 to Nha Be, far to the Binh Xuyen rear.

He and his troops had moved through the waterfront district of Saigon that morning, past French positions in the city, and came to the Tan-Thuan-Dong bridge over the Canal de Deriva-tion, close to where the canal met the Saigon River. The Binh Xuyen had a fort just beyond the bridge. Trinh minh Thé had moved about half of a battalion across the bridge, for an as-sault on the fort, when three Binh Xuyen gunboats showed up. The gunboats had the bridge under fire. There were many casualties. The crossing of the canal was stopped. How in hell could he fight those gunboats? His men were out there dying right now.

I told him that he needed artillery both to take care of the gunboats and to assist in the assault on the fort. He said he had been at the Vietnamese Army headquarters begging them for artillery but was told there wasn't a single gun available for his use at this time. He would have to make do without artillery. Later, when it could, the army would try to move over some artillery to support him.

I asked him what his largest weapons were. He had two armored scout cars with .50-cal. machine guns. They were his heaviest weapons. He would have to make the best use of these, I said, as a temporary measure until he got artillery help. The .50-cal. machine guns would have to concentrate their fire on the armor protecting the gun crews aboard the gunboats. If possible, he should try to get some bazookas from the army and add their fire to that of the heavy machine guns. Under this covering fire, he should try to get his men out of their fatal trap on the bridge. Once he got his command together again, he must insist on artillery support before attempting that long, exposed assault approach a second time.

Trinh minh Thé nodded agreement. We gave each other a hug of encouragement. He ran out to the street, jumped into a jeep, and drove off. I ran out to my own car and sped over to Doc Lap Palace.

At the palace I walked in on a conference between Diem and a group of Vietnamese Army officers. General Ty and Colonel Don were among them, as were both of the top commanders in the battle against the Binh Xuyen, Little Minh and Big Minh. They were jubilant. The army had crossed the Arroyo Chinois in Cholon and the Binh Xuyen were on the run. Wasn't I going to congratulate them? I told them hell no, not yet. While they were all standing around praising each other, their attack across the canal at the river was getting clobbered because they wouldn't give it artillery support.

I reminded them, as they knew, that I was under strict orders not to give them any commands. However, my orders didn't forbid me telling them a story. Now hear this! Once upon a time some Vietnamese Army commanders were drinking tea together with their boss and telling him how wonderful they were when they should have been moving one of the artillery batteries from Doc Lap Palace, or from in front of the chief of staff's home, or from the General Staff headquarters courtyard, and used that artillery to support Trinh minh Thé at Tan-Thuan-Dong bridge. His unit was the only one on the entire front coming up against big guns protected by armor plating. It also was the only unit without artillery support. The military commanders were about to be condemned by the people, who would become savage when they heard this. Right now, I was damned mad and was waiting for my listeners to finish the story for me.

There was a stunned silence when I stopped. Diem broke it by telling Little Minh to get artillery over to Trinh minh Thé right away. Little Minh hurried off and the others started leaving. I congratulated them on the crossing of the Arroyo Chinois. They looked at me a bit dubiously. I had been very angry when I had interrupted their meeting. I assured them again that I was happy over their success so far. The battle was still far from won, however, and it was no time to start relaxing.

Diem asked me to stay on and talk with him. We went to a small sitting room furnished with a couch and some heavy chairs positioned too far from each other for easy conversation, so I suggested that we sit together on the couch. Diem opened the conversation by saying that he had never seen me as angry as I had been just now. After all, Trinh minh Thé was a military man and would have to take his chances along with others in battle. I shouldn't become so concerned about his affairs. Even though Trinh minh Thé was a friend, he was just one of the many Vietnamese patriots who were my friends and was perhaps not as well educated or as experienced as some of the others. I told Diem to stop this line of talk. It was leading to a point where he might say something that would make me angry all over again. Trinh minh Thé had given Diem his support when men with more education and experience had hung back. Right now, he was out risking his neck for Diem. His sort of friendship was worth more than all the fair-weather friends put together. Furthermore, somebody had been criminally stupid in putting Thé's guerrilla troops, who were neither well enough trained nor well enough equipped, into a formal assault with no fire support. It was a lousy use of guerrilla capabilities.

Diem changed the subject. He told me, in detail and at great length, about all the revolutionary activities then afoot among Vietnamese nationalists. He gave me thumbnail biographies of a number of the leaders. These had been active in the 4th International agitation. Those had been with the Vietminh as political cadre. Still others had been discredited in this, that, or another activity which had failed. Diem, seeing my interest, delivered a monologue about revolutionary Vietnamese personalities for over two hours. As he talked, evening came to Saigon. The lights went on inside the palace. I reminded Diem that he had things to do, and so did I. I was starting to say goodbye when his brother Nhu came into the room.

Nhu walked right up to where we were sitting on the couch and stood silently for a few moments, just looking at us. Finally, he said softly, "Trinh minh Thé has been killed. At the bridge. I've just heard and thought you should know." The news hit me hard. I was scarcely listening as Nhu explained that he had checked carefully for details before coming in to inform us. He was sorry to say it, but the news seemed to be true. Trinh minh Thé had been struck behind the ear, apparently by a rifle bullet. From the angle at which he was hit, the rifleman had been behind and above Thé. The troops there were saying that it must have been a sniper. There was talk about a French sniper from the nearby French defense positions.

Nhu left the room. Diem and I sat wordless on the couch. I

rose to leave, to be alone with my grief. I turned to Diem and told him, "We have lost a true friend." I couldn't trust myself to say more. Diem looked at my face and started crying. Great sobs racked his body. I sat down again and held him in my arms. He asked me brokenly to forgive him for the way he had talked about Trinh minh Thé a little earlier. I told him there really was nothing to forgive, but he must always remember. True comrades were rare. He must never turn away from the unselfish ones who served freedom. We sat there quietly after that until he regained control. Then I left for my house. The tears made it hard for me to see as I drove.

On May 4, there was a great public funeral ceremony for Trinh minh Thé in Saigon, followed by another public ceremony in Tay Ninh. Thousands upon thousands of people participated. He had been very close to the hearts of the Vietnamese people, and many took his loss personally. With Thé's friend, Le khac Hoai, I made arrangements for the Vietnamese government to provide for his widow and children. The oldest, Nhut, was only six, and there were a younger sister Thu, a little brother Chau, and a fourth child due to be born any day now. Trinh minh Thé was practically penniless when he was killed.

I was with the family when we buried him on his beloved mountain, Nui ba Den, alongside the men who had fallen with him at the bridge. His remaining troops kneeled on the slopes of the mountain below the grave, almost hidden in the trees and by a mist that had crept up the heights, and chanted words that I couldn't make out. Hoai told me that they were pledging comradeship with me, whom their fallen leader had taken as his brother. I stood there with his family and asked his men to be true to the beliefs of Trinh minh Thé and serve their country well.

In Saigon on the morning of May 4, amid the great upsurge of feeling over Trinh minh Thé's death, Diem firmed up his hold on the governmental leadership. He convened a cabinet meeting which approved his decrees revoking the powers of General Nguyen van Vy, removing Le van "Bay" Vien as a general in the Vietnamese Army, and confiscating the properties of the Binh Xuyen leaders. The proceeds from the sale of these properties were to go to housing for fire victims and similar relief projects. (The properties included many hotels, nightclubs, and trucks; and in the accounting, a large number of stolen automobiles were discovered in Binh Xuyen hideouts.) Another May 4 decree permitted Diem to place any army officer "on extended leave" when deemed necessary; the weeding out of those who had been active against the government began.

Diem, in a radio broadcast, said that the Binh Xuyen forces were finally being driven out of the city. Now that the people and the army were joined in a common effort, the city could no longer be threatened. Vy had attempted a stab in the back against the army when it was fighting to protect the people, so Vy had to leave. Demonstrations against the French must be curbed. "When one is winning, one must not be proud. Do not show hatred toward foreigners who understand us, have good intentions toward us and help us." He ended the broadcast by talking about the need for a legislative assembly, noting that he had been alone in 1933 when he had fought for having a popular assembly "but today all the people are fighting alongside me."

By May 9 all the Binh Xuyen were out of the Saigon metropolitan area, and a thousand of their remaining forces had retreated down the river to the old pirate hangout in the Rung Sat swamp. The last of the Binh Xuyen forces in Saigon had been guarding the PTT national communications center near the palace, the National Police headquarters, and the National Bank building, all of which were in the French security zones. When word of the French easing of the truce restrictions arrived at Doc Lap Palace, I was talking with Diem at the palace entrance. We both were amazed when Major Huynh van Cao, one of the palace guard battalion officers who had received special training with the Presidential Guard Battalion at Malacanang in Manila, ran past us, jumped into a jeep, stopped at the gate to pick up three soldiers from the guard detail, and drove off with them. Twenty minutes later Cao returned. Diem asked him why he had gone off in such a hurry. Cao said that when he had received a report of the French ending their security restrictions, he suddenly remembered the Binh Xuyen troops who were still occupying fortified positions in vital government buildings. He and his handful of soldiers had driven to the buildings and asked the Binh Xuyen there to surrender. They did. It was a bit of quick thinking and initiative. Diem promoted Cao.

After several days of fighting through the mangrove swamps, with soldiers tying themselves to mangrove trees at night to keep their heads and shoulders above water while they slept, and with the fledgling Vietnamese Air Force attempting to support the infantry by jury-rigged bombing from light training aircraft, the last remnants of the Binh Xuyen in the Rung Sat swamp surrendered. Bay Vien and several other leaders escaped by boat and eventually made their way to France.

NOTES

BRIDGE. My executive officer at TRIM, Lieutenant Colonel George Melvin, devoted himself to procuring material for bridging the Lai Giang River at Bong Song, a crossing that vexed the steady progress of Operation Giai-Phong. In later years when Melvin and I would meet, it became our habit to toast "the Bong Song Bridge" and recall those hectic times in Vietnam.

HERO. My houseboy, Pham van Ty, followed a Vietnamese custom and had two wives, both of whom lived with him and helped keep house for me. I was fascinated and awed by the conjugal duty chart the wives had posted on the door to their quarters. It had ruled spaces for the hours he was supposed to be at leisure, spaces which were filled in by the name of whichever wife was to be his companion for bed, for meals, and so on. He had been complexly divided between the two

wives on a very heavy schedule. Despite the demands on his time and
energy, he retained his blithely happy ways around the house, earning
my continuing admiration. What a man!

DIXIE. The Binh Xuyen radio broadcasts during the fighting in Saigon-
Cholon became particularly obnoxious at one point. Binh Xuyen gun-
ners shot down a light, unarmed sport plane flown by a French civilian
and carrying Dixie Reese, a photographer with the U.S. economic mission. Reese had asked the pilot to fly low so he could photograph
scenes of what was happening to the city. Both men were killed in the
crash. The Binh Xuyen radio promptly claimed that Reese was a secret
agent working for me and had therefore deserved to be killed. Reese,
a happy-go-lucky sort, was one of the most peaceful men I have ever
known. The claim that he was working for me would have astonished
him as much as it did me. It simply wasn't true.

ALONE. When Diem mentioned in his May 4, 1955, radio broadcast that
he had been alone in 1933, his Vietnamese listeners understood what
he meant. Diem had been minister of the interior for Emperor Bao Dai
(ruling the empire of Annam) in 1933 and had pushed for more Vietnamese autonomy, including a national assembly. French colonial
authorities refused, and Diem resigned in protest. Bao Dai stayed on as
emperor under the French until 1945, when he abdicated the throne
and ended the vassal empire.

★ ★

CHAPTER SEVENTEEN

MIDYEAR 1955

SAIGON PRESENTED a battered and frowzy look to passengers arriving aboard airliners on May 10. Coming in, the planes flew above the remnants of the Binh Xuyen fleeing down river, the battle wreckage of buildings, the clutter of French tanks and troops along the streets, and vast patches of charred and blackened ruins in Cholon districts where the great fire had raged. Among the arrivals that day was George Frederick Reinhardt, the new American ambassador. A career foreign service officer, he replaced the president's special envoy, J. Lawton Collins. Clearly, the United States was giving up its attempt at a quick and simplistic fix of Vietnam's complex problems, through a powerful lieutenant of the U.S. chief executive, in favor of a more conventional approach through professional diplomacy.

At the time, Diem could give only the barest acknowledgment to the change of American leaders in Saigon. He was preoccupied with his military problems at home, problems which had taught him some hard lessons in the days just past. Although the Binh Xuyen forces obviously were close to being finished, their allies, the Hoa Hao "armies" of Soai and Ba Cut, had blockaded the Mekong and Bassac rivers, had put cities in the far south under siege and had tried unsuccessfully to open an escape route for the defeated Binh Xuyen. It was a grim Diem who went about the business of dealing with the last sect armies still opposing him. When I reminded him of his recent radio speech about the need to be a graceful winner, he said shortly that he hadn't won yet.

Diem became very much the commander in chief of the national military forces. He moved battalions, changed commanders, kept track of the exact amount of units of fire in every battalion that might be faced with combat, and knew precise and current details of the behavior of officers and men in all combat units. He argued pointedly with French military commanders over ceding their control of road and waterway lines of communication for his troop movements, over the command and equipping of river forces, over the presence of French military men among the dissident forces, and over the quality of ammunition supplied to the national army. He suspected the French of supplying better ammunition to his enemies than to the Vietnamese Army. Once he queried a French general about Ba Cut's receiving such dubious help. "Impossible!" the French general told him angrily. "We have cartridges marked 1949 and 1950," Diem snapped back. "A few marked 1951. Ba Cut shoots at us with cartridges dated 1954. That's what is impossible!"

(Months later, when U Nu of Burma came to Vietnam, I asked Diem his opinion of his visitor. Diem thought U Nu didn't seem to have the quality required for rule in Southeast Asia at that time. What quality is that? "He doesn't know anything about his army," Diem told me. "He couldn't even tell me how many men were in it, how many battalions he had, or what weapons the Burmese have!")

On May 13 General Soai proffered a peace feeler to Diem. His Hoa Hao forces would pledge loyalty to the government if Diem would give him seventeen million piasters to take care of arrears in troop pay and then subsidize the force at the rate of four and a half million piasters monthly. Diem replied bluntly that Soai's blockade of the river was harming the national economy, and he would not pay. Soai set his troops to digging trenches at his citadel of Cai Von, across the Bassac River from the city of Cantho. Ba Cut brought his own guerrilla forces into this citadel. The dissident Hoa Hao commenced bombarding with mortars the city across the river. It was evident from their public statements that the Hoa Hao leaders were still confident that they could defeat the Vietnamese Army and Diem.

Diem acted. He sent the 1,500 men of the Imperial Guard Regiment south to take up positions against the dissidents at Cai Von. It was a shrewd psychological blow. Soai and Ba Cut claimed that, as supporters of Bao Dai, they opposed Diem, but here was Diem sending Bao Dai's personal regiment against them. (It had been brought to Saigon from Dalat by General Vy in his abortive attempt to oust Diem for Bao Dai. When the attempt failed, Diem had changed the regiment's officers and had won it over to his side.) Diem's action made it plain to nearly everyone in South Vietnam that he was firmly in command.

Soai and Ba Cut sent word to Pham cong Tac, pope of the Cao Dai, who was still the titular head of the United Sects Front, that a Cao Dai army was needed to help in the fight against Diem. (The old Cao Dai army under General Phuong had remained loyal to the government and had been integrated into the Vietnamese Army.) So Pope Tac named Le van Tat as his new general and charged him with raising another Cao Dai army.

From the stories I heard, the French were encouraging the regeneration of Cao Dai forces to oppose Diem. Diem told me that a French general had visited Pope Tac in Tay Ninh. When I suggested that the French general might have been trying to dissuade Pope Tac, Diem said he knew I was not that naive. Two French officers had followed up the general's visit by delivering a large sum of money to Pope Tac. After I heard this story from Diem, I checked privately with General

Phuong, who confirmed the visit of the two French officers and gave me their names. He had been offered a million piasters, which had been displayed temptingly, if he would add his forces to the new Cao Dai army. Phuong had turned this down flatly. The memory of Trinh minh Thé was too fresh and strong for him to go against the course they both had decided was best for the country.

While the confrontation grew in the countryside, emotions were seething in the city. There were many frustrated Europeans in Saigon, people who had deluded themselves that Diem was sure to be overthrown by his sect opponents. When the opposite happened, they gave vent to their anger. Diem was the main butt, of course, but blows also were aimed at Americans in general and at me in particular. It was an instance of human misbehavior that remains indelible in my memory.

Part of the anger took the form of journalism. French and British correspondents had filed wildly exaggerated stories of recent events in Saigon. Now they tried to cover their mistakes with impassioned editorials, the mildest of which still advocated that Bao Dai should form a coalition government, including the Binh Xuyen, as the only means of saving Vietnam. Diem was pictured as a hapless little man whose hands dripped with the blood of innocents. I was the mastermind American behind him, at once impossibly naive and impossibly clever. These stories appeared in notable French and British journals and flooded back into Saigon via the news services— stirring up emotions all over again. It was a self-perpetuating tumult.

The journalistic attack was bearable, even diverting in a sick way. What happened next wasn't. A group of soreheads among the French in Saigon undertook a spiteful terror campaign against American residents. Grenades were tossed at night into the yards of houses where Americans lived. American-owned automobiles were blown up or booby-trapped. French security officials blandly informed nervous American officials that the terrorist activity was the work of the Vietminh and other Vietnamese, in retaliation for American meddling in Vietnamese affairs. Didn't we realize that it was the Americans, not the French, whom the Vietnamese resented?

The women at the American embassy asked me for advice and help. What does a woman, living alone in a foreign city, do when a grenade explodes against her door at midnight? How does one make sure a car isn't booby-trapped before turning the ignition key? In response to these requests, members of my team ran an informal school at our Rue Taberd staff house, where we demonstrated to the American girls how one takes precautions against booby-trapping and grenading. One of the pupils was Anita Lauve, a political officer at our embassy. Our lessons weren't enough to help her. Early the next morning, her car, parked on the street in front of her apartment, was blown up. She forgot caution and chased the perpetrators down the street in her nightgown, furious when she couldn't catch them.

Apparently I was on the list to be shot. A drive along the streets was enlivened by the whir of a bullet past my head or a suddenly shattered car window. The hazard was underscored one morning. A Frenchman with a mustache like mine had parked a car almost identical with mine in front of my house while he spent the night in a house across the street. In the morning, as he drove away from his parking place, a car came out of hiding from the next corner, passed him, and fired submachine gun bursts at him point-blank, killing him and riddling the car. Police investigators said the victim had been mistaken for me.

By then I had bits and pieces of information about the identity of the French soreheads behind this reign of terror. Some were associates of the French colonel who was the chief of staff of TRIM, the one who had refused to address me directly. When I arrived at TRIM headquarters that morning, therefore, I went to see him. As usual, we spoke through his adjutant. I told him about the death of the Frenchman who had been mistaken for me and said that I was aware of the identity of the instigators. The cruel farce was going too far, and I added impulsively, "I hereby inform you that I am withdrawing my protection from the French Expeditionary Corps. Don't forget that you are ten thousand miles from Metropolitan France. Whatever happens to you from now on is on your own heads."

That night my words took on sober meaning as concussion grenades exploded outside the quarters of the ringleaders of the French soreheads. Also, three junior officers of the French Army were caught red-handed by the Vietnamese police, with a supply of explosives in their jeep and a target list of Americans in their possession. They went to jail. I suggested to Diem that they be held until General Ely personally requested their return. I was certain that the French commander wasn't aware of the aberrations of the sorehead clique in his forces; this was a sure way of educating him. Diem ordered the three junior officers held until further notice from him.

The following morning found me on the carpet at the American embassy. Formal word had come that I had threatened to remove my protection from the French Expeditionary Corps. My action was contrary to the U.S. policy of friendship toward our French allies. I kept a straight face and replied that as long as the French continued attempts to terrorize Americans, my staff of ten U.S. officers and I definitely refused to "protect" the French Expeditionary Corps of 80,000 men. I was willing, however, to negotiate an arrangement with the French. I then told our ambassador about the three French junior officers caught red-handed the night before and the circumstances under which they were being held.

General Ely was informed about his officers in jail. He talked to Diem about their case, and they were released. In exchange the sorehead clique was disciplined. The reign of terror stopped.

In the last week of May, France agreed to move some 80,000 men of the French Expeditionary Corps from camps and posts in and around Saigon and to station them in embarkation zones on the coast. As French tanks and troops started pulling out of the city, many tensions departed with them. For the first time in ninety years, except for an interlude in 1945, the Vietnamese took control of Saigon.

As Saigon settled down to normalcy again, a group of French journalists arrived for a visit. Publishers and editors in France finally had come around to sending reporters from their immediate staffs to Vietnam to find out exactly what was happening. Their sober accounts doused the last inflammatory fictions. At their request, I met with them. Most of their questions centered on why the Vietnamese had become so anti-French in past weeks. I told them that it was because a number of the local French were false to the precepts of France. "What precepts?" they asked. "*Liberté, egalité, fraternité,*" I said. "When the French start treating the Vietnamese as free and equal brothers, the wounds will heal."

During the dangerous period in Saigon, Diem introduced me to a house guest of his, Bernard Yoh. Yoh had led guerrillas in Shanghai during World War II, including operations for Admiral Milton Miles, and later had fought against the Chinese Communists. I quickly discovered that Yoh had a rare understanding of the tactics and rationale of unconventional warfare, so we soon were deep in shoptalk. Noticing the smile of satisfaction on Diem's face, I asked if he minded my taking Yoh with me for lunch and more talk at my house. He was pleased, saying he hoped we would become friends.

Afterward, while bringing Yoh back to his host, Yoh scolded me for driving around the streets unarmed. Surely I must know that I was on several death lists? With that, he took off a snub-nosed .38-cal revolver and a waistband holster he had been wearing and insisted that I put them on immediately. I said I didn't need his revolver. He persisted, I protested, and finally, as he got out of the car, Yoh tossed the revolver and holster in my lap. "You must go armed," he said.

Years later, after we had become good friends, I confessed to Yoh why I hadn't put his revolver in my waistband that day in Saigon. My waistband already was toting a revolver and a pistol of my own, covered by my sport shirt. Within reach, under the seat, were other weapons. I simply hadn't wanted anyone to know that I drove around town accompanied by an arsenal. In Asia a man can get shot more readily for a pistol than for a wallet or wristwatch. I hardly needed to encourage any more thugs to use me for target practice.

The campaign against the Hoa Hao dissidents under Soai and Ba Cut took final shape near the end of May. It was patterned on the "national security operations" we had evolved for the takeover of former Vietminh territory, with heavy emphasis on political, psychological, social, and economic measures as well as military force. Lieutenant Colonel Duong van "Big" Minh, who had led the army troops against the Binh Xuyen in Cholon, was promoted and named commander of the new campaign. A civilian, Nguyen ngoc Tho, was appointed his political advisor and deputy. (In 1963, these same two men, Big Minh and Tho, took over the government after the death of Diem.)

The two commanders were southerners, sympathetic to the aspirations and feelings of the people in the rice paddies where their forces would be operating. They worked hard to educate the troops about the religious and cultural sensitivities of the people in the region and the imperative need for good behavior by the troops. The campaign followed the spirit of Magsaysay's axiom about offering the enemy the choice of "all-out force or all-out friendship." As a result, the dissident forces surrendered in large numbers after the first forceful actions by the Vietnamese Army, leaving only a handful of dissidents in small bands who went into hiding. Peace came to the countryside within a very short period, and Big Minh and Tho became figures of national repute and popularity.

The campaign started with a public rally in the Hoa Hao center of Long Xuyen, led by Hoa Hao General Ngo who had remained loyal. Some fifty to sixty thousand people participated in the pro-government demonstration and waved partisan banners and placards reading "Long Live Diem" and "Down with Bao Dai." Then the dissident bastion at Cai Von was subjected to an intense artillery attack and a follow-up infantry investment of what was left of the fortified positions. Ba Cut and his guerrilla followers had fled the Cai Von trenches and bunkers before the devastating attack, reminding me a bit of how Bedford Forrest had left Vicksburg before *that* citadel had capitulated in our Civil War. General Soai also got away with a handful of his men. News of this major defeat of the front's military forces sped to Tay Ninh. Pope Tac of the Cao Dai, with members of his family and a few close associates, fled to the safety of exile in Phnom Penh, Cambodia.

Soai and Ba Cut remained elusive for many months, their followers dwindling away. Soai finally rallied to the government in March 1956, receiving a pension and a house in Saigon from Diem. Ba Cut met a more tragic fate.

With the national army hunting for him, Ba Cut sent a message to Nguyen ngoc Tho, the political director of the operations against him. He was ready to negotiate and designated a lonely spot to meet alone with Tho. Despite the possibility of ambush, Tho met him, only to discover that Ba Cut had set exaggerated demands as the condition for his "rallying" to the government. Tho turned down the proposal but agreed to meet Ba Cut again to discuss more modest terms. A second meeting was set, again in a lonely spot at midnight. When Diem heard of this, he ordered Tho by radio not to take such risks. Tho asked the radio officer not to deliver the message formally to him until later and slipped away to the meeting anyhow, only to find Ba Cut's demands unchanged. I was with Diem in Saigon that night and commented on the courage shown by Tho in going alone to meet Ba Cut. Diem frowned at this. "Tho is a fatalist," Diem said, "and that's different from the courage you meant."

Since Tho had turned him down twice, Ba Cut then sent me a message, requesting a meeting. I named a site of my own choosing which would be safe for us both, but noted that my language handicap meant that I would have to bring along an interpreter. When this was accepted, Joe Redick and I held two meetings with the Ba Cut dissidents. Ba Cut had large ideas about the honors, status, and funds that Diem should grant him and his men for ceasing their dissidence, and he would not reduce his demands. After our second meeting I had no more dealings with him.

Ba Cut was captured by a government patrol on April 13, 1956, while I was back in Washington discussing other Vietnamese matters. A patrol had stumbled onto him accidentally. He had a notebook in his pocket when captured, filled with jottings about his affairs and including one sentence in English he credited to me. Diem asked me later if I really had told Ba Cut, "Don't be so damn greedy"? I admitted that I had. Despite my pleading for clemency, Ba Cut was sentenced to death by a military court and was guillotined at Cantho on July 13.

About the time of the beginning of the end for the front dissident forces at Cai Von, a much happier beginning took place in Saigon. The Vietnamese Veterans Legion held its first national congress on May 29, 1955, in Saigon's City Hall. Ponce Enriquez and other Philippine Veterans Legion members of the Freedom Company of the Philippines were active advisers for this founding event. A monument to the Unknown Soldier was dedicated in the plaza before City Hall, and General O'Daniel laid a wreath for the United States.

NOTES

PHILIA-PHOBIA. If I believed in reincarnation, I could have startled the European correspondents with a true story to add to their already lurid Sunday supplement pieces about my supposed anti-French attitude. When I was a young man, I once had a vivid dream about being a French artillery lieutenant, my cannons on a sandy shore under bombardment from British men-of-war which dared sail in close, their gunports belching flame and smoke, because my guns were out of ammunition. In my dream I could see the cannonballs hurtling at us, some falling short in shallow water near the beach. I waded out to pick one up and see if it wouldn't fit my guns, to fire back at the British. When I grasped a cannonball under the water, I was startled to find it burning hot. The shock of the burn awoke me from my dream. The dream seemed so realistic that I had noted it in my journal. Years later, reading a history of Napoleon's campaign in Egypt, I came upon a description of this exact incident. Wouldn't it be ironic if I had been a French officer generations ago and the dream a whisper from the past?

CHAPTER EIGHTEEN

BEGINNINGS OF THE REPUBLIC

NOTHING ABOUT THE FUTURE was predictable in the summer months of 1955 in South Vietnam. The country's leadership was included in this limbo. Diem had been repudiated by Chief of State Bao Dai yet doggedly continued in office as prime minister, insisting that he was acting in the best interests of the majority of the people who, on their part, clearly were willing to follow him for now. But where were he and they going? This question was underscored by the revolutionary ferment evident in the land. Rival nationalist movements sprang up, and their various leaders impatiently urged Diem to act in a number of contradictory ways. The social unease was stirred further by the resettling of nearly a million northern refugees into new homes in the South, their alien accents jarring on southern ears, their raw new communities needing huge public programs, among them the digging of hundreds of miles of canals in the southern lowlands, if they were to become a viable part of the local economy.

Military affairs were in transition, too. The French Expeditionary Corps not only was moving into coastal camps, as agreed, but also was packing up vast dumps of military supplies in South Vietnam and shipping them out of the country. Diem and the Vietnamese military leaders were worried about the availability of supplies for South Vietnam's needs. The Vietnamese Army had plans for reducing its forces, for reorganizing, and for retraining, but most of its battalions were still too busy in operations against the Hoa Hao dissidents and in national security actions in former Vietminh zones to do more than barely start such programs. The U.S. insisted on Vietnamese force reductions for budgetary economy; and as the French prepared to depart, disquieting reports from North Vietnam told of new Communist divisions being formed, trained, and equipped with massive amounts of Soviet and Chinese artillery, armor, and vehicles. Since the French were leaving and the Vietnamese Army was widely known to be preparing to cut back, the South Vietnamese were worried that the increased military strength and mobility of the Communist North was intended to invade the South. Hanoi wouldn't attack China and didn't need such a huge force to invade Laos. This left the remaining neighbor, South Vietnam, logically assuming that it was to be the victim of the military buildup in the North.

At this moment of uncertainty in Vietnam, the British and others (including Americans) reminded Diem that he was due to participate in talks with the Hanoi leaders about plans for holding a plebiscite in 1956. The 1954 Geneva conferees had directed North and South to get together about this one year before the plebiscite. That meant talks had to be initiated in July 1955. Diem, harassed, said that talking with the Communists about an election made no sense to him. I started to describe the improving factors that could mean a victory for the free Vietnamese nationalists in the plebiscite, but Diem admonished me for underrating the dirty-trick capability of the Communists. He cited a long list of Communist violations of the Geneva accords. No election with them! Diem informed the British diplomatically of his stand. On July 16 he made a radio broadcast to the Vietnamese people. "We did not sign the Geneva agreements," he told them in part. "We are not bound in any way by these agreements entered into against the will of the Vietnamese people. . . . We do not reject the principle of elections as a peaceful and democratic means to achieve unity. But elections can be one of the foundations of true democracy only on condition that they are absolutely free. And we shall be skeptical about the possibility of achieving the conditions of free elections in the North under the regime of oppression carried on by the Vietminh."

The restless summer brought changes for me also. I was transferred from TRIM, where my French confreres and I had rubbed each other raw and where the Franco-American part of Vietnamese national security action was practically finished. I was assigned to MAAG and asked to form a new staff section there to deal with what we called "unconventional" matters. The work included training the Vietnamese Army in intelligence operations, psychological warfare, and troop information. We helped organize and train the first Vietnamese Army Rangers. I continued seeing Diem almost daily.

Shortly after I had transferred to MAAG, the French commander, General Ely, and the U.S. MAAG chief, General O'Daniel, met to discuss what the buildup of Communist military forces in the North might portend. One result of the meeting was to start the Vietnamese Army on planning the defense of South Vietnam in case of invasion. They also gave me the task of organizing the Vietnamese for guerrilla resistance in case of an invasion by the Communists. I did the practical thing and took the problem to Diem, pointing out to him that the most effective guerrilla resistance could be formed by political partisans among the nationalists. Since he was the political leader of the Vietnamese nationalists, it was up to him to appoint a political executive group for me to advise. In turn, a staff section should be formed in the Vietnamese

Army to work alongside the political partisans and ensure coordination between conventional military forces and the guerrillas. Diem quickly appointed a resistance directorate as part of his own staff.

In the following weeks, potential guerrilla bases and operational areas were located along probable invasion routes, political cadre were enlisted and taught the basics of guerrilla warfare, and communication nets were established. The concept of arming people in hamlets and villages for self-defense was adopted, soon developing into a nationwide program known as the "Village Self-Defense Corps" (which later became the Popular Forces). Diem approved this arming of the citizenry because it was a realistic way of assuring democratic rule in South Vietnam. The status of the mountain tribes, who lived a migratory life astride the interior trails used by Communist forces and who had been organized by the French as maquis against the Vietminh, needed sharp revision upward. The Vietnamese treated the mountain people as subhuman, and their antipathy was reciprocated. Diem agreed to reforms in administration and official attitudes in tribal areas, and a new start was made. Along with improved social programs, tribal people organized anew for resistance against the Communists once again. Officers on my staff started sporting bracelets that denoted their adoption into tribes, although I kept the visits of the Americans brief, not wanting us to get between the tribes and the Vietnamese as the French had done—and as U.S. military men were to do a decade later.

As the summer wore on, I was an almost daily visitor at the palace. Diem was wrestling with his thoughts about the political future and apparently had found me a useful sounding board, someone familiar and companionable with whom he could afford to relax and be himself. External pressures had eased, particularly from the French government which had made friendly overtures toward him after a meeting of Dulles and Faure in Paris. But the internal problems of South Vietnam were far from being settled. As the national leader pro tem, the initiative toward a more viable basis for Vietnam's political welfare would have to come from Diem.

Our talks that summer were long. Diem would usher interpreter Redick and me into his office, where three heavy chairs had been placed for a tête-à-tête. Since the chairs were always in the same position, I would tease him about hidden microphones by saying, "Testing . . . one . . . two . . . three," as I sat down. We then would settle into talk over innumerable cups of tea and packs of cigarettes; Diem's chain-smoking surpassed even the heavy smoking of Redick and me. (With all that smoke, we should have called the place the Blue Room.) Thanks to all the tea, we would have to break from time to time for trips to the bathroom. I recall one time when Diem responded to a provocative question from me about the effect of Christian teaching on the Vietnamese by lecturing me for five hours straight. Such sessions would exhaust our interpreter, Redick, although gradually my understanding of French improved enough to relieve his burden somewhat.

I did my best to encourage Diem to think through to some conclusions about the nature of a political structure that would give South Vietnam, with a free citizenry, a chance for survival in the modern world. Diem would discourse on the political philosophies dominant in Europe early in the century, a subject upon which he was exceptionally well-read. I would demur on some of the points he made, reminding him of the human misery that certain political ideas had brought when ambitious men had adopted them to corrupt ends, such as Mussolini's use of syndicalism. Then I would turn his attention to subjects even closer to his heart: the history of Vietnam and the social evolution of its people. His knowledge of his country and his countrymen was immense, a fascinating mixture of erudition, gossip, and affection that could have given him a career as Vietnam's foremost historian if he had so chosen. After this,

I would lead into discussions of the adaptability of foreign ideas to Vietnamese culture, given the Leninist impositions of the Communists under Ho, the Western innovations of the French, and the long influence of Chinese and Confucian thought upon the Vietnamese.

Since Diem had been exposed most of his life to people in Asia and Europe who held narrow political views of the United States, people who saw it mostly as a materialistic industrial giant using brute strength and money to get its way as the world's leader, I took the time to teach Diem a little about *my* country and countrymen. I stressed the humble beginnings of the United States, the years of hard work it took the American farmers, artisans, and shopkeepers to win freedom from a colonial power, and their further years of work to create a means for self-government. Diem had known that the American Declaration of Independence had come in 1776, but he seemed surprised when I told him that the U.S. Constitution was written eleven years later and didn't come into effect until March 1789. I described some of the problems that had to be overcome in a rural society, and both the dreams and the quarrels of the Founding Fathers.

Diem asked me sharp questions about the "checks and balances" among the three branches of the U.S. government and asked me to describe in detail how the chief executive exercised power. Once, I had to draw him a diagram to illustrate the "chain of command" from the U.S. president down. Noting Diem's deep interest in the U.S. presidency, I also told him how George Washington had seen the position, setting its customs and acting as a political arbiter above partisan factions. I pointed out that few men in history had the opportunity Washington had to become "the father of his country." Perhaps Diem could be one of those few men. As the national leader when Vietnam had become independent, Diem would, I hoped, use his strength of leadership as wisely as Washington had, so that future generations would hold him in esteem.

Later, when the political pot boiled anew in Vietnam, I would remind Diem from time to time that he had to keep future generations in mind in his actions. I would ask him, "Do you think that's the right thing for 'the father of his country' to do?" Usually he would pause and reflect before he acted. One time, though, during an argument over the freedom of the press (in which I had pleaded against closing a small nationalist journal), Diem had rebutted me sharply, ending up by saying, "and stop calling me *papa!*"

Meanwhile, others had been pressing Diem for political action. Foremost among them were his brothers Nhu and Can, each of whom led revolutionary factions, sometimes in rivalry. Nhu, who worked with Diem daily at the palace as his political and intelligence assistant, clearly had the edge in this rivalry; his influence on Diem increased from mid-1955 on. However, Diem also saw Can, the youngest in the family, from time to time, either on Diem's visits to his mother in Hué (where Can ran the family household) or on Can's brief visits to Saigon. I wanted to meet Can, about whom I had heard both flattering and unfavorable stories. Diem kept assuring me that he would arrange a meeting, but somehow it continued to be postponed, and finally he said that Can was simply a stay-at-home and that I shouldn't take the time to visit his "kid brother." Respecting Diem's wishes about his family, I never met Can.

The Movement for National Revolution (MNR), which had flamed into such hot political life in May, now had chapters throughout the country. Although its governing executive was made up of energetic nationalist leaders, each with a considerable following of his own, the dominant MNR executive was Diem's brother Nhu. As summer turned into fall, MNR became increasingly clamorous and militant about dethroning Bao Dai and in its support of Diem. Nhu and his MNR confreres proposed many other political innovations, some enlightened and some merely sly throwbacks to unhappy instruments of the past. One such instance, which I opposed so strongly that Diem shelved it, was a plan to create an ostensible "community self-help" program. Built into the proposed program were the same devices for making the inhabitants of a community inform on one another as the Japanese Kempeitai had used when they had created "neighborhood associations" to control populations in invaded areas during World War II. I warned Diem not to use totalitarian defenses against the totalitarian threat of the Communists. They would frustrate the true yearnings of the people for freedom and lead to a resentment which could be aggravated and exploited by subversive political agents. Why should Diem help Ho instead of the nationalist cause?

As fall days passed, unrest among the revolutionary groups and nationalist political parties increased. They wanted action. I reminded Diem of his long-held dream of a popular assembly for Vietnam, believing that electing and forming such an assembly would turn all these political energies into a more productive form. Diem told me flatly that Bao Dai remained opposed to such an assembly. I pointed out that the true sovereignty of a nation could come only from the people. As a leader, Diem must act to help the people find the means to express their sovereignty in some practical form. If South Vietnam were to remain free and to govern itself, then it was high time that the Vietnamese found the way to handle their own affairs.

Diem agreed that South Vietnam's political structure must be changed dynamically if Vietnamese nationalists were to survive. He quoted to me numerous expressions of this thought from MNR and other politicians, adding that the body politic was nearing an explosion point; if he didn't act soon, the revolution would overrun him. I guessed the conclusion that these remarks were leading toward and interrupted him. If he was thinking of the overthrow of Bao Dai and of his own elevation to replace Bao Dai as chief of state, *through the fiat of MNR actions and MNR-led mass demonstrations*, I said, he should forget it. His family was too closely associated with the MNR. Neither the Vietnamese people nor the free people of the world would believe in the validity of such sponsorship. The look on Diem's face confirmed my guess of what he had been about to say.

I explained to Diem that the only acceptable, viable way to bring about the drastic change that he and the MNR had in mind would be through suffrage, a free expression of the people's will through the ballot box. If Diem was so sure that the people were about to explode unless there was a change, he should let them say so by a vote. The results would be recognized throughout the world, since there was wide acceptance of the principle of the people's ultimate sovereignty.

Further, a plebiscite designed only to let the people choose a new chief of state at this point wasn't enough. Since Bao Dai had stepped down from emperor to chief of state, Vietnam had been governing itself itself through a mishmash of laws and decrees that stemmed largely from its days of colonial rule. Some of them were clearly outmoded in a nation that now was independent. If the people were to be given the say in electing their leadership, the people would want the process to continue and to grow. That meant a whole new set of rules, embodied in a constitution. Even North Vietnam had such a constitution. In an electoral contest between the old customs under Bao Dai and something new under Diem, Diem would have to spell out what that something new was. At the very least, he would have to link his candidacy with a mandate for the creation of a constitution written by representatives chosen by the people. He would have to set a definite date for an election of representatives to a Constitutional Assembly, meanwhile—if the people chose him over Bao Dai—holding office as a public trust until the Constitution came into being, at which time he would have to abide by it.

This conversation took place late in September. It left Diem in a very thoughtful mood. Several days later, Diem showed in his conversation with me that he had accepted the idea of a popular election. He was already planning how it could be held throughout the country in a single day.

On October 6, 1955, Diem announced a referendum to be held on October 23 to let the people decide who should be chief of state, Bao Dai or Ngo dinh Diem with his pledge of initiating constitutional government. The voters would be given two ballots, one bearing the name and picture of Bao Dai, the other the name and picture of Ngo dinh Diem. The voter would cast the ballot of his preference and discard the other. I urged Diem to use a good photograph of Bao Dai on these ballots, since I was sure that Diem would use a good one of himself. Also, I cautioned him against a possible stuffing of the ballot box by the MNR, since he and the electorate would have to believe fully in the validity of the vote results in case he won and set about constructing a new political system. Cheating would be building the future on a false foundation and this would mean that whatever he did next would be short-lived. He must look ahead to 'the needs of still unborn generations if he was running for the position of "father of his country," which would be the import of the referendum.

Diem was dubious about helping Bao Dai too much in the referendum. After all, Bao Dai had been a political power for many years, and Bao Dai's people in Vietnam would be pulling every trick they knew to win. They already were widely publicizing an October 18 cable message from Bao Dai, dismissing Diem. I reminded him that Diem had many more supporters active on his side than did Bao Dai. The most that Diem might do, if he felt that custom and superstition might work against him, would be to add some subliminal insurance by the use of color in the ballots, printing his own in red, the Asian color of happiness. Bao Dai's ballots could be printed in black or blue or green.

Diem's face lighted up at this suggestion. In the October

23 election, the ballots for Diem were printed in the cheerful red of Asian weddings and other cheerful events. Bao Dai's ballots were in an uninspired shade of green, although the picture on them showed a handsomer man than the portrait on Diem's ballots.

The final tabulation of the vote, as street sweepers brushed away a great litter of discarded green ballots was 5,721,735 votes for Diem and 63,017 votes for Bao Dai. On October 26 Ngo dinh Diem proclaimed the Republic of Vietnam, naming himself as its president.

NOTES

POTABLES. "Adoption" by a mountain tribe in Vietnam included a drinking spree which would make a gypsy out of anyone. Hosts and guests drank out of a communal bowl, the brew a fermented mash which the tribal women had first masticated and then had spit into the bowl. Guests needed an iron constitution. After participating in remarkably similar ceremonies with tribes in Asia and South America, I finally was given some sound advice by my Chinese guerrilla friend Bernie Yoh. He told me to carry a flask of my favorite brandy to these gatherings, single out the chief, and share the flask with him as a special honor. Done courteously, it flattered the tribe and certainly made for better drinking.

★ ★

CHAPTER NINETEEN

LAST DAYS IN VIETNAM

O NE OF THE UNRECOGNIZED BENEFITS of military life is that
the man in uniform gets a healthy dose of humility from time
to time. I got a memorable one in late 1955. It came from the
new chief of MAAG. General O'Daniel's tour of duty and
years of service had ended, and he had returned to the United
States for retirement. His replacement, Lieutenant General
Samuel Tankersley Williams, arrived in Saigon on November
15. He was a noted combat commander, known far and wide
in U.S. military circles as "Hanging Sam."

A reason for his having so awesome a nickname soon became
apparent. General Williams set about "shaping up" the MAAG
to his liking, with fierce tongue-lashings of senior officers who
were responsible for whatever struck him as sloppy or out of
place. His roars could be heard all over the MAAG headquarters buildings, as one luckless soul after another stood before
him while the wrath poured ·down over his head. The new
chief's most frequent charge was that the officer was running
his work "like the Texas militia and this had damn well better
change." Strong men were driven to tears.

My turn came all too soon. On his second day at MAAG,

Hanging Sam called me to his office. As I neared the office, I could hear his powerful voice telling off someone for the higgledy-piggledy appearance of the motor pool. I hurriedly checked my own appearance. Yes, my uniform buttons were buttoned and zippers zipped. A brigadier general came out of the office, his face bloodless and stunned. He asked me if I was going to see Hanging Sam. Yes, I told him. He gave a fervent "God help you" as I went in. I walked past the desk of the aides, who kept their heads bent over papers in a show of great industry; they looked storm-bent to me. At General Williams' desk, I stopped at attention with a click of my heels, gave him my best salute, and reported in.

Williams looked at me for a moment, then told me in conversational tones that he had visited my staff section in my absence. He concluded with, "You run them like a band of gypsies. What have you got to say for yourself?" I looked back at him, a vision quickly coming to mind of some of my staff just back from visits to mountain tribes, undoubtedly sporting new tribal bracelets on their wrists. They'd be a gypsy-looking crew indeed. So I grinned and admitted the truth of General Williams' charge, adding, "I like gypsies, sir."

There was a long silence. Then came the deluge. I got a blistering lecture about maintaining discipline that seemed to go on forever and that undoubtedly was meant not only for my own ears but for every living creature in the entire metropolitan area and maybe even the ships at sea. While it was going on, the aides tiptoed out of the office, heading for shelter from the verbal storm. Finally, the lecture ended and General Williams told me that I was dismissed. I said that I had another matter to take up with him. "What's that?" he asked. "How about having dinner with me tonight at my place?" I asked.

After some further talk, in which he insisted that I hadn't paid sufficient attention to his lecture and in which I insisted just as stoutly that I had heard every word, he accepted my invitation. I didn't tell him this, but his tongue-lashing had reminded me strongly of some I had received from my indomitable grandfather, so much so that affectionate memories of him were very much in my thoughts during that long lecture. Hanging Sam not only came to dinner that night, but the two of us gradually gained an understanding of each other, and a rare friendship developed which had a very deep meaning to me. Some weeks later, while I was visiting Washington, I talked to a group of officers in the Joint Chiefs of Staff in the Pentagon. One of them interrupted the talk in amazement. "You mean to say you *like* Hanging Sam?" I assured him that I did. I meant it, then and now.

I spent the holidays outside Vietnam. General Williams didn't. He told me that he had been with the Vietnamese Army at the Demilitarized Zone between North and South over Christmas and New Year's Day and had never felt lonelier in his life. He had received reports of North Vietnamese troop movements toward this border, along with reports of their being equipped with new Soviet tanks and artillery. The reports were many days old, so he kept wondering what might be happening *now* as he looked to the North. The meager intelligence reports he got only added to his apprehension. He kept visualizing a surprise invasion by the Communist forces and had small confidence in my own prediction that the North Vietnamese would come south secretively, not in an overt invasion. He was a veteran of Korea, where Communist forces *did* make open invasions across borders. He remembered the lesson they taught him. My own crystal-ball predictions were based on what I knew of the characters of Ho, Giap, and other North Vietnamese leaders. Despite the fluke of the vast open battle at Dien Bien Phu, I believed that they still thought in terms of guerrilla and clandestine operations. An open invasion would be looked upon by them as too unconventional and hazardous, when they had more proven means to use.

General Williams' foreboding of an invasion from the North

resulted in his doing his best to help the Vietnamese armed forces ready themselves to meet such an attack. This meant organizing and training the South Vietnamese in units large enough and with enough firepower to resist an onslaught by many North Vietnamese divisions. As the South Vietnamese prepared for the expected large-scale warfare, their armed forces gradually took on the image of U.S. forces, not only with regiments and divisions (as initiated by General O'Daniel), but also with corps. The day of isolated and independent battalions scattered over the landscape was past. Men and firepower now could be massed for defense.

Years later, armchair critics with the dubious valor of hindsight claimed that it was stupid to make the Vietnamese Army into so conventional a force. These critics, of course, didn't have to look across a border where heavily armed Communist divisions were forming for an action that looked suspiciously like an invasion. When General Williams questioned my own prediction about a secret infiltration, I had to admit honestly that I might be wrong. The Vietnamese are not that predictable and, further, I didn't know how hard Giap and other Communist military leaders were listening to the advice of Soviet officers who then were busily instructing the North Vietnamese in methods of sweeping attacks with massed artillery and armor. A formal invasion could not be ruled out as a possibility by those who would be responsible for meeting it.

General Williams spent much of his time visiting Vietnamese troops. Watching him do this, I grew impressed by the relationship he soon established with men from the rank and file who came up to him, privately seeking his counsel in personal problems or telling him of births and deaths among their relatives. Officers would confide in him about command problems in a way they seldom did with their own Vietnamese superiors. Americans who looked at Williams and saw only the hardbitten combat commander missed this wise and understanding side of the man, which somehow, using a sort of "personal

339 / Last Days in Vietnam

radar," the Vietnamese military men had discovered. Few of the many thousands of Americans who served afterward in Vietnam ever had bonds with the Vietnamese as close as those General Williams enjoyed.

Williams tried to open the way for Americans in his command to follow his example. I commend his method to anyone responsible for the training and advising of foreign troops in their own homeland. Once a month, American military advisers stationed throughout Vietnam were brought together in Saigon. At the meeting there not only was an exchange between Americans about the problems at hand, but a period in which Williams turned the floor over to the Vietnamese. In this period General Tran van Don, the chief of the Vietnamese General Staff, would tell the gathering of American advisers exactly and candidly how the Vietnamese military men thought these Americans were succeeding or failing. No names were mentioned, to avoid embarrassing individual Americans or Vietnamese; but behavioral problems, cultural differences, and the many frictions that could cause serious trouble between military men of two nationalities were all laid open for discussion. It was a revealing exercise, blowing away false notions and giving each American in the audience a chance to start understanding what hitherto had seemed alien to him.

Other Americans were working closely with Vietnamese, of course. Some of the relationships led to a development which I believed could bring only eventual disaster to South Vietnam. When I discovered what was happening, I strove to have the turn of events modified and even journeyed to Washington to appeal personally to the secretary of state. My efforts failed.

This development was political. My first inkling came when several families appeared at my house one morning to tell me about the arrest at midnight of their menfolk, all of whom were political figures. The arrests had a strange aspect to them, having come when the city was asleep and being made by heavily armed men who were identified as "special police." The families who had come to me for help or assurance were almost incoherent in trying to answer my questions about why their men had been arrested. They didn't know for sure but conjectured that their menfolk, who were not criminals or law-breakers, were victims of political reprisal by the Can Lao party. They said that every official in the government was be-ing pressured to join and that their men had refused. Their men loved Vietnam and worked hard in the government but hated the notion of joining a secret society in order to keep their jobs. Part of their repugnance came from what they had heard of the initiation ceremony, in which new members had to kiss a picture of Ngo dinh Diem and swear undying fealty to him. Secret cells of the Can Lao were being organized rapidly throughout the civil service and the military forces.

I knew a little about the Can Lao, and what these distraught people told me simply didn't fit into that picture. The genesis of the Can Lao came in 1953 when six political thinkers formed a new political party which they called the Revolutionary Party of Workers and Peasants. The six were Ngo dinh Nhu, Dr. Nguyen tang Nguyen, Tran quoc Buu, Tran van Do, Tran trung Dung, and Tran chanh Thanh, a mixture of labor leaders and intellectuals from the three main regions of Viet-nam. Their hope was to organize urban laborers and rural farmers in a joint nationalist effort with the intelligentsia throughout the country, forming neighborhood, village, and hamlet chapters. Nguyen tang Nguyen served as the party's first chairman. About three months after its founding, the new party changed its name to Le Parti Travailliste (Labor party) and adopted a humanist program more closely in keeping with European parties of the same name. After the advent of Diem as prime minister and his confrontation with the French, the party translated its name into Vietnamese, *Can Lao,* and Diem's brother Nhu became its secretary general. He gradually maneuvered his five fellow founders out of leadership positions in the party. The last I had heard, it still was a relatively small party, although it had some vigorous and able members directed with considerable skill by Nhu.

I had a scheduled meeting with Diem later that morning. I used the opportunity to tell him about the dead-of-night arrests and gave him the names of those I had heard were arrested. He recognized them and was visibly surprised by the arrests. He excused himself and left the room for about twenty minutes, informing me when he returned that it had all been a mistake and that the men were being released. He was a bit flustered and embarrassed as he said this. I guessed that he had taken the matter up with his brother Nhu, who had an office in the rear of the palace, and really hadn't known about the event before I told him.

Deciding that the time was right, I also told him what I had heard of the secret recruitment of Can Lao members throughout the civil service and the military forces and of the initiation ceremony in which new members kneeled and kissed his portrait. Diem laughed at this description and said that it was nonsense; he was certain that no such thing was being done. As for the Can Lao, it was true that many new members were joining the party, supporting him only because they shared his ideas on how best to have Vietnam develop and grow. All that his brother Nhu really was doing was building a political party behind the newly elected president of the Republic of Vietnam, no different actually than in the United States where each president had a political party supporting him.

I said emphatically that he was more nearly in the position of George Washington, who didn't have his own political party, than of later U.S. presidents. In Vietnam members of long-time nationalist parties had voted for him in the belief that he was going to give everyone a fair chance to participate in the national political life. If the Can Lao now was being organized by his brother as a clandestine political organization throughout the government, with use of secret police also controlled by his brother to put down any opposition, the Can Lao was going to force the other nationalist parties to go underground in order to survive. It would leave the body politic in South Vietnam deeply divided, in a covert and deadly game of nationalists struggling against nationalists, at the very time that thoughtful patriots needed to come out into the open to write a constitution and found a new political system to rival the Communist system in the North. What was being started now could lead only to a ghastly repetition of past tragedies among such nationalist partisans as the Dai Viéts, the VNQDD, the Hoa Hao, and the Cao Dai. To repeat the turbulent history of betrayals, murders, and ill-fated uprisings such as the historic one in Yen Do would only benefit the waiting Communists ultimately.

Diem said little after my outburst. I left him, in what I hoped was a thoughtful mood, and drove to the American embassy. There I told Ambassador Reinhardt about the events of the morning and concluded by saying that it was a moment when the Americans under his direction who were in regular liaison with Nhu, and who were advising the special branch of the police, would have to work harder at influencing the Vietnamese toward a more open and free political concept. As I talked, a strange look came over the ambassador's face. After a pause, he informed me softly that a U.S. policy decision had been made. We Americans were to give what assistance we could to the building of a strong nationalist political party that would support Diem. Since Diem now was the elected president, he needed to have his own party.

The news that such a U.S. policy decision had been made, and that it had been made without my knowledge or chance to say anything while it was being considered, shocked me. I said as much to Reinhardt, pointing out that he and the U.S. policy-makers in Washington were well aware that I had almost daily discussions with Diem, mostly on political subjects. No other American was doing this so frequently, although Diem was meeting with other Americans from time to time, such as Wesley Fishel, who was preparing the Michigan State training program for Vietnamese administrators, and Wolf Ladejinsky, who was advising on land reform measures. Although I often saw Fishel and Ladejinsky, neither had mentioned U.S. encouragement of a secretive presidential political party, and I doubted that they knew of it either.

Reinhardt told me firmly that the U.S. policy decision had been made and that I should guide my actions by it. At my request he brought in his political staff to meet with me. We had a long discussion, and there were some angry moments. The staff members were adamant that their reasoning as political scientists was sound; there should be a strong nationalist party supporting the incumbent leader. I admitted that this would be ideal *except at this moment in Vietnam*, when the creation of such a party by Vietnamese who would organize it along clandestine lines, secret cell by secret cell, meant that all the other nationalist parties would have to conceal their own activities. The new party, the Can Lao, would be in control of the police, the military, and the economic sanction functions of the government. The midnight arrests of political oppositionists showed how these powers could be used. The Can Lao party might grow to a fair size, but the body politic of South Vietnam would be badly wounded. The timing couldn't be worse, coming just before the writing of a constitution and creation of a new political system for the country. A viable, open system of democracy—a goal that U.S. officials felt was desirable—simply couldn't grow from such a beginning.

My arguments were rejected. So, having been stopped in Saigon, I turned to Washington and requested a chance to come home for consultation. It was granted. Arriving in Washington, I set out on the customary round of "debriefing" meetings with policy-makers, operations executives, support administrators, and their staffs. I argued my case without success. The meetings included one private session with John

Foster Dulles and Allen Dulles, since the brothers had decisive voices in determining the U.S. relationship with Vietnam. I was as unsuccessful with them as with the others, despite the friendliness of the meeting. I gathered that they felt the pragmatic course to be the one their political experts in Saigon had recommended, though they looked sympathetically at my views even while judging them to be too visionary and idealistic. My statement that this was one of the times when principled idealism was the most pragmatic and realistic course only drew from them the advice that I should disengage myself from any guidance to political parties in Vietnam. It was a moment of bleak frustration for me.

Upon returning to Vietnam, I took the only course left open to me. I spent every moment I could, when meeting with Diem, in talking about the necessity of having a loyal political opposition and about how to encourage it to participate in public affairs. In this I was none too successful. For one thing, the Vietnamese have a strong touch of Potemkin in them and are as ready to put up false fronts as he was to build fake villages for Catherine the Great to view. Thus it wasn't too surprising to find new Vietnamese political parties coming into being, founded by associates of Nhu and dutifully calling themselves the "loyal opposition," while the long-established opposition nationalist parties underwent increasing oppression.

As an observer, first in Vietnam and later from the distance of Washington, I watched the Can Lao party grow. It attracted many fine people to its ranks, among them warm friends of mine, and soon was the dominant elite of the country. It flourished for nearly a decade, with an ideology of its own called "personalism" (supposedly upholding the integrity of the individual) and with firm party discipline. Increasingly, it acted against dissent. As the prisons filled up with political opponents, as the older nationalist parties went underground, with the body politic fractured, Communist political cadre became active throughout South Vietnam, recruiting followers for actions against a government held together mainly by the Can Lao elite rather than by popular support. The reaped whirlwind finally arrived in November 1963, when the nationalist opposition erupted violently, imprisoning many of the Can Lao and killing Diem, Nhu, and others. It was heartbreaking to be an onlooker to this tragic bit of history.

In my meeting with the Dulles brothers early in 1956, I asked the secretary of state to use his influence with the U.S. military to get me transferred from Vietnam, just as he evidently had used it to have me sent there in 1954. I told him that my days for constructive work there seemed to be ending anyhow, thanks to U.S. policy restrictions. My request appeared to surprise him. He told me flatly that there was much more work with which I could help in Vietnam. He brought up the subject of the 1956 plebiscite as proposed at the 1954 Geneva Conference. I surely wanted to stay in Vietnam and see my friends there through whatever problems and perils the plebiscite would bring, didn't I? I should stay in Vietnam at least through 1956.

I wondered if I had heard correctly. The 1956 plebiscite? I said I doubted there would be any plebiscite; too much had happened since the conference at Geneva. He said that of course there would be a plebiscite and asked me to explain my doubts. I reminded him of Diem's refusal, in 1955, to meet with Hanoi's Communist leaders on the subject and noted that there had been no change in his attitude since. Moreover, if the U.S. did some official arm-twisting and forced Diem into meeting the Hanoi officials to arrange a plebiscite, another obstacle probably would arise. The Communist officials who had waged a successful war against the French were terrible bunglers at running a government. Their stock with the public in North Vietnam was so abysmally low that they wouldn't dare put it to a vote, let alone chance a contest against Diem, whose popularity was at a peak. (Diem's landslide victory over Bao Dai at the polls wasn't lost on Hanoi's leaders.) I felt certain that the Communist leaders, while declaiming loudly about holding a plebiscite, would do everything they could to postpone it.

When pressed for the reasons behind these conclusions about the probable attitude of Hanoi officials, I told the Dulles brothers what I had heard from refugees and travelers from North Vietnam. The Communist land reform program had been carried out in too radical a fashion, too abruptly, with even small family farms taken away from the owners and handed over not to the poor, but to village ne'er-do-wells, beggars, and the indolent. Apparently the thought was that when they failed at farming, the farms then could be impounded by the state as idle land and be made into collectivized state farms. Rural sections of North Vietnam were in revolt, especially in Ho chi Minh's home province of Nghe An where troops had been called in to reestablish governmental control. On Soviet advice, the Politburo had suspended the land reform program and had publicly censured the officials in charge of the program, but the agrarian population was still seething against the government.

Another Communist agrarian measure had disillusioned the North Vietnamese population further, particularly in the Red River region where the majority lived. Wanting to make up the deficit in rice production, the Hanoi government had followed Chinese advice and denuded the hills of trees in order to plant upland rice. With the natural cover gone, the water rushed off the hills when the rains came, bringing unprecedented floods and misery to the lowlands. On top of earning all this resentment in the rural areas, the Hanoi regime had also managed to be maladroit with its most prized asset, the youth. Revolt was stirring at the University of Hanoi, where students were demanding relief from the heavy input of political indoctrination in all their lectures. Students complained that their instructors skimped even highly technical subjects in favor of long dissertations on dialectical materialism. Much the same thing was happening in the high schools of North Vietnam. Its most promising youth were finding fault with the regime.

For these reasons I felt that the Communist leaders in Hanoi would discreetly inform the Soviets (co-sponsors of the 1954 Geneva accords) to go slow on pressing for a plebiscite in any meeting with the British (the other Geneva co-sponsor). None of this ruled out the possibility of a Communist adventure into South Vietnam, overt or covert; traditionally, making trouble in a neighbor's land can divert attention from trouble at home. In Vietnam there would be powerful motivations for the rice-deficit North to gain control of the rice-surplus South. All I was saying was that I was sure the Communist leaders knew that they couldn't win this goal via the ballot box.

My argument about whether or not the plebiscite would be held had no discernible effect on the length of my tour of duty in Vietnam. I returned to Saigon "for the rest of the year." Thus I was in Vietnam when the next action about the plebiscite took place in London in April 1956. On April 11 representatives of the nations sponsoring the 1954 Geneva Conference, Lord Reading for the United Kingdom and Gromyko for the Soviet Union, agreed that the proposed plebiscite was unfeasible under prevailing conditions in Vietnam and therefore wouldn't be held. The news was quickly overshadowed by a more sensational mystery story, the April 19 disappearance of British frogman Commander Lawrence Crabb near the Soviet cruiser *Ordzhoni-kidze* which had brought Khrushchev and Bulganin to England the day before. (At the time, the frogman mystery fascinated me more than the agreement not to hold the plebiscite.) The Geneva-proposed election date in July passed quietly.

In 1956 "Democracy" was the number one topic in the *quan pho* and *xe pho* of South Vietnam. These soup stands in the markets and on the sidewalks are the equivalent of the American corner drugstore or neighborhood bar. In Vietnam people exchange news, gossip, and opinion over bowls of soup. *Pho* is a northern soup of beef (or chicken) and half-dried rice noodles; it is a favorite in Saigon, along with a Chinese soup

of pork and undried rice noodles called *hu tieu*. In Central Vietnam, the most popular soup is *bun bo* with chopped peanuts,
mint, and leafy vegetables. In the southern regions of the
Mekong and Bassac rivers, it is *mi*, a soup with Chinese sheet
noodles or wonton. Thus, anyone who wants to see the Vietnamese at their gregarious best and to find out what the public
is saying about current events needs to go on a gastronomical
excursion among the soup stands. It's a delicious way to take
a political survey.

Mostly, the people spoke of Democracy with a big *D*, as if it
were some magical word describing the ideal solution for all
political wrongs, a panacea that would turn Vietnam into a bit
of heaven on earth. Yet the last national elections the Vietna-
mesé held in 1946 to found a democratic republic had ended
disastrously for Vietnamese nationalists, since the minority Communists had used the election to gain control of the government
and to institute a police state. The Communist government in
Hanoi, calling itself the Democratic Republic of Vietnam, based
its mandate on the 1946 election and apparently hadn't dared
to hold an election since, despite its borrowing from Jefferson
and Paine for parts of its Constitution. Perhaps the fact that
the Communists had made an ugly travesty of political ideals
caused groups of politicians in South Vietnam to quarrel against
every step toward democracy taken in 1956 that they believed
to be less than perfect; they had been burned in that flame a
decade before. The dreams and hopes of the people of South
Vietnam were still for the creation of a peaceful and idyllic
state.

Diem had one eye on the lack of democracy in Hanoi when
he added some words of warning to his countrymen in his
speech proclaiming the Republic of Vietnam, three days after
his victory over Bao Dai at the polls the previous October. He
said: "Democracy is not a group of texts and laws, to be read
and applied. It is essentially a state of mind, a way of living
with the utmost respect toward every human being, ourselves

as well as our neighbors. . . . Democracy demands from each of us, then, infinitely more effort, understanding, and goodwill than any other form of government."

Also in his proclamation that October, Diem had promised a commission "to set up a project for the Constitution," a project which "shall be submitted to the National Assembly elected before the end of the year." On November 28 he named an eleven-man commission, chaired by Vu van Mau and with members drawn from the legal profession, six of them cabinet officials. I pointed out to Diem that the commission members were city boys and, even though he felt that they were brilliant intellectuals, I couldn't help wondering if they understood the Vietnamese of the countryside well enough to speak for them in the Constitution. Diem explained that the Assembly, when elected, would have a full chance to represent all the people in the final wording of the Constitution. I crossed my fingers as the commission started work.

My anxiety was eased somewhat when Diem announced in January 1956 that elections would be held on March 4 to elect 123 delegates for a Constituent Assembly, each to represent the electorate of a particular district. Politicians in the old-line nationalist parties objected vociferously to this, claiming that the government intended to rig the election and pack the Assembly with its own people; instead, they wanted a group to be selected by established political parties—in effect a self-appointed elite —for the writing of the Constitution. These politicians threatened to boycott the election. I had some noisy sessions with a number of them, in which emotions ran high and in which I failed to convince them that the March 4 election would be an opportunity for them to get their organizations working for an effective modern political life in Vietnam. The emotionalism in these meetings stemmed in part from my taunts that they were afraid to test their self-esteem at the ballot box.

My anxiety was eased further when a group of rural politicians, mostly Hoa Hao and Cao Dai, asked the Freedom Company of the Philippines to sponsor Juan C. Orendain for a visit to Vietnam, as a friendly counsel to those drafting the new Constitution. Orendain (whom I mentioned previously as one of the courageous editors of the *Free Philippines* in 1953) was willing to help out. Diem heard of the invitation and asked me about him. I told him that Orendain had devoted years of his life to championing man's liberty, both as a journalist and as a noted constitutional lawyer in the Philippines; he was one of the Filipinos for whom I had the deepest respect and affection. Diem showed considerable interest and, when Orendain arrived in Saigon, had several long talks with him. Orendain spent months in Vietnam, helping all who sought his counsel.

The election campaign for the Constituent Assembly ran from February 20 to March 2. Some four hundred candidates vied for the 123 seats. About half the delegates stated that they opposed (in varying degrees) the Diem regime, although few of the old-line politicians entered the race. The electorate the candidates appealed to was younger than in the U.S. at that time, since the voting age had been lowered to eighteen. The campaign itself saw a remarkable innovation in the democratic process: the government footed the cost of the campaign, providing posters, leaflets, radio time, and transportation to candidates on an equal basis, with a council of representatives of the candidates deciding in each district where posters would be put up and the timing of political meetings. To weed out frivolous candidates, those who polled less than 5 percent of the vote in their district would have to pay for their share of the cost of printing leaflets and posters out of their own pockets.

When the March 4 vote was tabulated, 80 percent of those registered had voted. Candidates in open support of Diem had won 84 of the 123 seats in the new Assembly, among them Mr. and Mrs. Ngo dinh Nhu, the president's brother and sister-in-law. It was a much cleaner election than others I have seen in Asia, and I have little doubt that some of the nationalist leaders in the opposition would have had a good chance of winning if they had entered the race instead of sitting it out on the sidelines. The elected delegates believed that they had won fair and square. One of the first actions of the new Assembly, when it started meeting, was to declare that it wouldn't approve the draft written by the Diem-appointed commission. It was going to write every word of the new Constitution itself. Diem said fine, do it yourself then. He gave the Assembly some general guidelines and asked it to finish its writing in forty-five days. It set to work, selecting fifteen of the delegates to do the actual drafting. They hadn't finished at the end of forty-five days, so Diem extended the time. Finally, the Assembly's work was done and, on October 26, 1956, the new Constitution was promulgated.

The Constitution was a mixture of tradition, advanced social ideas, and potentially dangerous restrictions. It established two independent branches of government, the executive and legislative, with the executive branch giving the president strong powers as in the American system. It detailed the obligations of citizens as well as their rights. It recognized the family as the foundation of society and charged the government with specific responsibilities toward Vietnamese families. The government also was charged with helping, insofar as it could, the unemployed, the aged, and the victims of illness and natural disaster. Fair wages, the right to organize trade unions and to strike were included among the rights and duties of citizens. Business monopoly was outlawed.

The restrictive measures, giving the president unusual powers over the public safety in times of emergency, crept into the Constitution while the Assembly was drafting it. I felt, then and now, that this was caused primarily by the launching of a new campaign of terror in the countryside by Communist guerrillas. Although it was a relatively light campaign compared to previous and subsequent terrorist moves by the Communists, it was vicious enough to remind all the elected delegates in the Assembly that the new nation had deadly enemies who still intended to impose their will by force.

The Constitution had no sooner been completed and approved than it was amended. Unlike the similar event in the United States, when the Bill of Rights came into being as the first amendments of our Constitution, the Vietnamese amendments were more mundane. One of them perpetuated the office-holding of the delegates of the Constituent Assembly, making them automatically members of the new National Assembly until the next elections were held. Another amendment empowered President Diem to appoint a vice-president, an office that was to be elective in the future. On December 29, 1956, Diem named Nguyen ngoc Tho as his vice-president. Tho, as you will recall, had served as political adviser to Big Minh in the campaign against the dissident sect guerrillas. He also was secretary of state for national economy.

The campaign of terror by the Communist guerrillas mentioned above was the old nightmare of savagery with murders and kidnappings. It was prompted this time by the burgeoning success that Diem and his government were having in establishing an effective rule throughout South Vietnam. The Communist leaders in Hanoi couldn't afford to let this continue. Communist stay-behind cadre in the villages dug up their cached weapons and undertook secretive raids. Cadre who had gone north in 1954-55 started returning in small groups to their home areas in the South, fortified with refresher training in political methods and small-unit tactics. By the end of 1956, there were hundreds of Communist guerrillas in scattered bands throughout South Vietnam trying to impose a hold on the villagers.

The government relied mainly on the Civil Guard, its national police constabulary, to maintain law and order in the provinces. The Civil Guard was badly outmatched in trying to cope with the guerrillas. I had remembered the lessons taught by the Huk campaign in the Philippines and had urged Diem to designate the Civil Guard as a military reserve organization, with training and equipment for at least company-sized military operations as well as their normal police work. However, the

U.S. Mission in Vietnam decided on a firm policy of keeping police and military forces separate and persuaded Diem that the only way he could get American help for his police was to keep them as a strictly civilian organization, with American civilian police "experts" as advisers and trainers.

The result was a police force sketchily trained and armed along the lines needed for keeping order in an American city and pathetically unready for the realities of the Vietnamese countryside. A squad of Civil Guard policemen, armed with whistles, nightsticks, and .38-cal. revolvers, could hardly be expected to arrest a squad of guerrillas armed with submachine guns, rifles, grenades, and mortars; the Civil Guard squad would be dead or dispersed by the guerrillas long before they got close enough to be effective. Even so, the Civil Guard tried to do what their American advisers insisted upon. Fortunately, before the Civil Guard experienced too many casualties, General Williams quietly convinced the Vietnamese Defense Ministry to make a back-door delivery of military weapons and ammunition to the Civil Guard, giving it a fighting chance for survival. By that time Diem was begging the U,S. Mission to change its policy of assisting the Vietnamese police, but to no avail. American bureaucrats are a stubborn breed.

The Civil Guard had posts housing a squad, platoon, or company in strategic places throughout the country. These outposts were homey affairs, in which the Civil Guard police lived with their families. As I drove along the provincial roads past these outposts, I saw how well they seemed to fit into the bucolic scenery, the family wash drying in the sun and scads of children playing around the yard. Apparently the Communist guerrillas noticed this homey touch, also, and devised a tactic incorporating it. One group of guerrillas would fake a noisy attack on a village, to lure the Civil Guard police out of their outpost. When the police rushed to help the village, another group of guerrillas would move in on the outpost, murdering the women and children left there. It was a brutal Pavlovian lesson, conditioning the Civil Guard not to go to the aid of villagers but to stay and

guard their families in the outposts. With no Civil Guard protectors, the villagers became easy prey for the guerrillas.

One answer to the growing terrorism in the countryside was
to arm the villagers for self-protection. When I discussed this
with Diem, he readily agreed, adding that by arming the electorate, perhaps Vietnam could be sure to have a real democracy,
since no leader could become a dictator in the face of a public
bearing weapons. Village self-defense units were started
throughout the country, manned by local volunteers and armed
mainly with outmoded weapons, such as Lebel rifles, retired to
warehouses by French colonial officials years before. (Later,
the village self-defense militia became today's Popular Forces,
a home guard that has suffered more Communist guerrilla attacks than have any of the regular military forces fighting in
Vietnam.)

Paradoxically, the Communist campaign of terrorism started
just as life in the countryside was beginning to show great
promise for the people on the land. It wasn't only that the
armies had departed from the former battlegrounds in the rice
paddies, letting farmlands be tilled in peace; there were, as
well, a multitude of new efforts being made to improve the
whole agrarian economy of Vietnam. Each time that I visited
President Diem in his office, I would find him deep in the study
of some new program, often of vast dimensions—such as the
draining of the great swamps of the Plaine des Joncs along the
Cambodian border or the creation of a major cattle industry in
the highlands that would provide new opportunities for both
mountain tribesmen and for émigrés from the impoverished
farms of the central coast lowlands. Some of these plans remained as dreams, but many of them came into being.

One of the actualities was the development of the trans-
Bassac region, the land between the Bassac branch of the
Mekong River and the Gulf of Thailand. The first phase called
for settling over a hundred thousand people in new model farm

communities in the Cai San area and draining the low-lying land by constructing 125 miles of navigable canals. Model villages and canals were constructed mostly by hand labor. Whenever I saw the thousands of local inhabitants with shovels and buckets toiling away at the new canals that would be their lifeline linking them to the rest of Vietnam in an area of few roads and many waterways, it brought to mind a vivid picture of the building of the pyramids in ancient Egypt. American officials who administered U.S. aid for this project seemed to be as awed as I was by the sight of these thousands of toilers. The settlements were planned to sandwich a community of refugees from the North between similar communities of farmers from the South, alternating northerners and southerners throughout the region in a cultural melting pot that hopefully would give each equal opportunity.

Diem also was full of enthusiasm for new crops. Under his guidance, floating rice was grown in huge experimental plots along the Vaico River where seasonal flooding turned the lowlands into vast bogs, and communities of northern refugees located in foothills of the Vietnam cordillera were urged to grow kenaf, whose fiber could be woven into bags for sugar. Once, when I replied to some of Diem's boasting about the superlative fruit grown in Vietnam by praising the superior mangoes of Cebu in the Philippines, Diem sent agriculturists to Cebu—and soon after, plantings were made in Vietnam. (I had tempered my comment about the mangoes by praising the Vietnamese mangosteens, noting that they were Magsaysay's favorite fruit as well as my own. Diem gave me a basketful of mangosteens to ship to Magsaysay, which I sampled generously before sending along: the temptation of this wonderful fruit was too much for me.)

Wolf Ladejinsky, the American land reform expert, had left his position with the U.S. government at the time, and Diem immediately employed him. The two men became close friends in 1956, and Ladejinsky was given a house next to the presidential palace and joined Diem at breakfast nearly every morning. Thus Diem's daily routine began with these breakfast sessions, discussing the implementation of the land reform measures drafted by Ladejinsky and issued as decrees by Diem, as well as the myriad problems of the whole range of agricultural projects afoot. Both men shared the dream of making an Eden of Vietnam, with bounty for all its inhabitants and with ample foods for other nations in the Pacific basin.

Unnoticed by me at the time, Diem took a seriously wrong step in the development of the countryside, a step that was to have disastrous political consequences later. In a decree he changed the old custom of village self-government and replaced it with a system of appointed leaders, the new village leaders being named by district and province chiefs, who themselves had been appointed by Diem. Apparently, his intention was to federalize local government as one means of unifying the nation. The disbelievers of this world may find it incredible, but I learned of this decree only long after I had left Vietnam. How I missed knowing about it at the time remains a mystery to me, since it was on a subject close to my heart. The memory hurts.

In my own talks with Diem, I often had stressed the importance of having officials elected at local as well as at national levels, starting in the villages; Diem had seemed sympathetic, only warning that it would take time to introduce. But his decree about village officials went in the opposite direction. It took away much of the local initiative upon which modern democracies are founded, transgressed the ancient Vietnamese edict that "the Emperor's rule ends at the village wall," and gave Communist agitprop cadre a highly effective argument to turn villagers against the Diem regime; everything that went wrong in a village could be blamed upon the Diem-appointed officials, whether they were responsible for it or not.

The last weeks of 1956 found me drawn into a confrontation between Diem and the Chinese community. I attempted to be a peacemaker.

There were perhaps a million Chinese living in Vietnam in 1956, although there was no precise census and responsible Vietnamese and Chinese could give me only vague guesses when I asked them. Whatever the true number, the Chinese were a significant minority group in Vietnam, "foreigners with privileged status" under the 1935 Treaty of Nanking, culturally separate from the Vietnamese and lords of the economy of South Vietnam. The principal Chinese city was Cholon, the twin urban area extending westward from Saigon and now part of a single metropolis. In return for high taxes, French administrators had permitted a degree of economic autonomy to the Chinese, excepting only mineral extraction. The Chinese dominated the commerce in rice, owning nearly all of the rice mills, as well as the country's retail and wholesale trade, most of its light industry, and food processing. Chinese autonomy was marked further by a form of self-rule, with the heads of Chinese *congregations* (families) collecting taxes and acting as arbiters in the affairs of the community for the government of Vietnam.

As in other countries of Southeast Asia, there was considerable envy of the Chinese for their prosperity, although antipathies didn't run toward the eruptions of flaming hatred that happened elsewhere from time to time. In Vietnam the success and special status of the Chinese were more a dull ache than a deep wound in the body politic. Offsetting this was the rich borrowing of Chinese culture by the Vietnamese in their daily lives, a greater infusion than in any of the other nations of Southeast Asia. The Vietnamese have high respect for Chinese civilization. (I have yet to meet a Vietnamese who didn't know the stories of "The Three Kingdoms" or who wasn't aware of Confucian precepts.) But the Vietnamese do have a historic fear of Chinese political domination, and the most revered Vietnamese heroes were those who had defeated Chinese armies in the past. In turn, many of the Chinese residents felt morally and culturally superior to the Vietnamese; a popular saying among these Chinese characterized Vietnamese women as licentious (*chien*) and Vietnamese men as playboys (*niao*). Despite these differences, there was free intermingling among the Vietnamese and Chinese, and there was no stigma attached to intermarriages.

In August 1956 Diem issued two decrees that affected the Chinese residents of Vietnam. The first removed the special status of the Chinese, required them to register as aliens, and prohibited aliens from engaging in eleven types of merchandising. The second decree, issued a few days later, conferred Vietnamese citizenship upon all Chinese born in Vietnam. The new citizens were required to obtain new identity cards, for which they would adopt Vietnamese names. The second decree eased some of the prohibitions in the first decree, by permitting Chinese with legal Vietnamese wives to continue in some of the proscribed businesses as well as permitting Chinese investments in Vietnamese enterprises. In essence, the two decrees were aimed at eliminating a vital minority group by absorbing it into the citizenry.

The decrees came as a shock to the Chinese. Some of the families fled to Cambodia, where their old special status still prevailed. Although thousands of the younger Chinese started registering as Vietnamese citizens, the older generations recoiled in hurt and angry bewilderment, holding long, acrimonious meetings among themselves. I recall my own feeling of surprise at the time, caused mostly by the abruptness with which Diem had acted, and the officious zeal with which his Vietnamese officials were attempting to carry out his edicts. I did my best to convince Diem that issuing decrees that brought sharp social and economic changes needed thoughtful and politic presentation to the people if they were to succeed. Diem told me determinedly that the Chinese understood well enough and that he was going to make the decrees succeed. Several days after this exchange between us, we had an argument over the punitive deadline set for changing all commercial signs into the Vietnamese language, among them hundreds of elaborate neon and electric bulb signboards that made the nights in Cholon vivid with light and color. Diem finally agreed to ease the deadline and give the Chinese community a more reasonable period in which to make the changes.

Some days after the issuance of the two decrees affecting the Chinese community, several of the leaders of congregations in Cholon visited me. They had heard that I'd once helped the Chinese in Manila with the Philippine government and asked if I would do something similar for the Chinese in Vietnam now. I promised to listen to them and then determine whether or not I could help. This led to meetings in Cholon with groups of Chinese leaders, mostly in French; Ogden Williams acted as interpreter for me, having taken the place of Joe Redick, who had returned to the U.S. I was impressed by how very divided the Chinese leaders were in their opinions. Some felt that they owed a great deal to Vietnam and only wished to make the transition to Vietnamese ways more amicable; they particullarly wanted Vietnamese officials to carry out the decrees with less apparent vindictiveness and greater understanding. Other leaders felt that they had done enough for Vietnam by paying taxes and threatened to either resist the decrees or leave the country.

My advice to them was that the Chinese needed to come to some agreed-upon views among themselves as a community. When they had done so, they should then make these views known to President Diem and his government. If they wished, I would attempt to set up a meeting for them with Diem; if, however, they were just going to argue with one another in front of Diem, I doubted that such a meeting would be very useful. I reminded them that they were living in a country with hazardous security problems, yet few of their sons had offered their services to the military. Most had stayed in a cushy, draft-exempt status and earned some resentment from families whose sons were risking their lives in the nation's service. I suggested that the Chinese community might give more visible indication that it cared about what was happening to their Vietnamese neighbors if the Chinese wanted the Vietnamese to care about what happened to them. Some of the younger Chinese had helped in Operation Brotherhood. They did so as individuals; thus their acts were seen as personal rather than as a Chinese contribution. Perhaps the Chinese could subscribe to a Red Cross unit of their own with the Vietnamese Army or set up similar service units to help Vietnamese refugees or orphans, of whom there were so many in need. Such tangible evidence of care could help make the political climate more favorable for them.

Gradually, the leaders of the main Chinese congregations settled their differences. I was able to persuade Diem to meet with them, alone and informally, so that the talk could be candid and constructive. Several such meetings were held. As a result, the integration of the Chinese into the Vietnamese citizenry continued, but at a slower pace and with waivers of many of the harsher penalties in the decrees. Several of the more officious Vietnamese dealing with the Chinese were re-placed by persons of greater understanding. The Chinese community itself started contributing to the Vietnamese welfare more openly, while the sons of Chinese families entered their terms of Vietnamese military service. Although cultural differences kept the Chinese from becoming absorbed altogether into the Vietnamese body politic, the separation line for this minority group did grow shadowy.

Orders had arrived ending my duty tour in Vietnam at the close of 1956 and returning me to Washington for another assignment. Before departure, there was a last act of friendship for Ngo dinh Diem which I hoped to perform. I wanted to find a restful vacation spot for him where he could relax naturally and recoup the energies and calm thinking he would need for being an effective chief executive of his country.

I was mindful of the fact that each man has his own best

way of vacationing. I recalled the mistake made by Hitler, when he had brilliant psychological and physiological tests devised to tell him when one of his German leaders needed a rest—and then spoiled it all by ordering the tired-out leaders to vacation near him at Berchtesgaden, often leaving them further exhausted by their dislike of the mountains or the tensions of being so close to the boss. In the Philippines, Magsaysay had had a government vacation house in the mountains at Baguio where he could take brief rests, although he still was too accessible to visitors and the problems they brought; the moments of vacation he loved best were at the family farm in San Marcelino or at a fish-fry with boyhood friends alongside the river near the farm. Magsaysay's parents, as well as his older brother Jesus, saw to it that these boyhood haunts were ready for him at a moment's notice when he wanted to duck away from presidential chores.

Ngo dinh Diem wasn't as well favored as Magsaysay when it came to vacations. It was true that he had a government vacation home in the mountains at Dalat, whose pine forests, strawberry beds, truck gardens, and G-stringed mountain people bore a remarkable similarity to the scene at Baguio just across the China Sea. But when Diem returned to Saigon after brief stays at Dalat, he was often haggard and would confess to me that he had been unable to sleep. The nights in Dalat were so quiet that he would stay awake waiting for some noise. The only moments he cared for at Dalat were those when he could be alone with a book in front of a log fire; yet he felt that even these intervals were only a pale imitation of the pleasure he felt shut away at night in his own study in Saigon, surrounded by reading matter of his own choosing.

Aside from Dalat, his other vacation place was at the family home in Hué, where his mother and youngest brother lived; but he returned to Saigon from visits in Hué in much the same fatigued state as from Dalat. I gathered that family affairs and local politics consumed the moments when he should have been resting. I once urged the bachelor Diem to call upon the still unmarried sweetheart of his youth in Hué and follow the local custom of taking her for a boat ride on the Perfume River while he serenaded her with his mandolin—which he admitted to me that he hadn't played since boyhood. A blushing Diem confessed to me upon his return from Hué that he had lost his nerve at the last moment, certain that he would have made a poor Lothario.

When I asked him about a seaside vacation, Diem was noncommittal. I had a place in mind, a government cottage among a stand of pines on a bluff above a private cove, just north of Long Hai and within an easy drive of Saigon. With a trade wind making a lullaby through the pines and with the constant wash of the surf in the cove below, it was ideal for relaxing. Although Diem had been enigmatic in his response, his family was enthusiastic. His brother Nhu, Mme. Nhu, their children, and I had a picnic at the beach cottage, after which they embarked upon a campaign to talk Diem into taking a weekend rest there. My contribution to the campaign was a couple of oil crayon sketches I made of the cottage and its cove; Mme. Nhu had these sketches pinned up in Diem's bedroom at the palace, as propaganda posters. Finally, Diem agreed to a weekend at the cottage and invited me to come along.

We had two lazy days at the beach, family style. I had brought some swim trunks for Diem, but he insisted upon jumping into the surf in his underwear; I was amazed to discover that he wore old fashioned long johns. On the road to the beach, I had stopped at a town market and bought sacks of rambutan, "the poor man's lichi," for the local crop of this delicious fruit had ripened for harvest. The grownups in the family disdained my lowly offering, so the children and I gorged ourselves in between swims. Thuc, the elder brother, practiced his English by telling me about combat leaders of militia near Mytho, men of great natural ability but of too little education to obtain commissions in the Vietnamese Army; we agreed that such men should be selected for special training and a chance at advancement. Although his wife warned me not to play him, I accepted a challenge from Nhu to play scrabble in French, losing to him steadily until I insisted that we play the game both in French and English; when I won the double language game, Nhu promptly told me that he was tired and quit the play. "He doesn't like to lose," said his wife.

Diem and I conversed mostly about Confucian principles, concepts which practically all Vietnamese start learning from infancy on and which I believe form the true Vietnamese ethos upon which their government should be based. When we discussed this subject in Saigon, the scholar in Diem would come out and he would discourse in a most animated manner. At the beach cottage, though, with the steady sound of the surf and the wind through the pines, his eyelids would droop and I would stop talking and steal away, while he closed his eyes and napped. He dozed off time and again over the weekend, as well as sleeping deeply at night. When we set out upon our return to Saigon afterward, he said that he had never before felt so refreshed from a vacation.

In later years, when I heard in Washington of the troubles Diem was having in his leadership, I noted that he had returned to his habit of flying to Dalat for brief, sequestered vacations at the mountain resort. I wondered if he had ever learned to relax there, or if he was returning to his burdens in Saigon afterward still tense and tired. Once, when I suggested in a letter that he try the beach cottage again, he wrote that Communist guerrillas had infested the locality and that he didn't want to risk soldiers' lives just to safeguard a vacation place. Perhaps it made a difference in the course of Vietnam's history.

NOTES

JOHNNY. Johnny Orendain, to whom the Vietnamese turned for constitutional advice, was the first Filipino to invite me to his home in 1945. At the first dinner with his family, I listened to stories of their escape from the Japanese occupation forces of World War II. One memorable story concerned the time the family was stopped by Japanese soldiers and their five-year-old son sang to the soldiers the only song he knew, "God Bless America." The non-English-speaking soldiers patted him on the head for the pretty song and fortunately didn't ask him his name, which was MacArthur Orendain. Dinners with the Orendains had another memorable feature. Johnny made the best apple pies I ever tasted, having learned the art while working his way through Stetson Law School.

BEACH. My favorite beach near Long Hai, which I introduced to Ngo dinh Diem as a rest spot in 1956, had caught my eye in 1953 when it was part of the realistic training ground used by the French clandestine service for preparing Vietnamese and Montagnard irregulars for maquis duty. Vietminh guerrillas infested the area, and the French sent their trainees into operations there as a graduation exercise. A pine forest and sand dunes ringed the beaches, providing ample cover for guerrillas. Its unspoiled beauty, loneliness, and potential danger caused me to be highly selective in those I brought there for picnics and swims in the early days. One visitor was Joe Alsop, just after he had proved in 1954 that he was more than a city room journalist by making a nervy solo trip into a Vietminh zone to interview Communist leaders. Before Diem's 1956 weekend at the beach, troops made a thorough security check of the area. It was safe at that time.

★ ★

Chapter Twenty

A COURSE FOR AMERICA

M AGSAYSAY HAD ASKED me to stop off for a visit in Manila
en route from Saigon to Washington late in December 1956.
So I spent a day and a night in the Philippines, all too brief
a time to be with old friends. Instead of the expected quiet
evening with Magsaysay and cronies, I found myself his honor
guest at a formal dinner at Malacanang Palace—a dressy diplomatic affair arranged by his new socialite advisers and very far
from the khaki shirt and trousers I was traveling in. Borrowed
black pants, tucked in with safety pins, and *barong tagalog*
(Filipino dress shirt) from Magsaysay's wardrobe, managed
to get me through the long dinner with its toasts and speeches.
I suspect that both Magsaysay and I would have been happier
with one of the meals we had shared during the Huk campaign,
the bully beef, the rice and fish eaten with fingers, among companions with whom we could relax.

Although there were some old friends at the dinner, several
of the guests were strangers to me, among them American officials who had come to the Philippines after my time of service
there. Two of these men eyed me strangely throughout the
meal. Later, when I was saying good night to them, their fare-

wells were hedged with some verbal knifings. My borrowed attire evidently had offended them, along with my presence in the Philippines. It seems that relations between the United States and the Philippines were being put on a "normal" basis, something I could apparently spoil. After some remarks in this vein, one of them spluttered, "Thank God you are leaving this part of the world," and, with that, both departed.

The next day, flying eastward across the Pacific toward home, I thought about that petty valedictory. I wondered what a "normal" relationship between Americans and Asians would be in their terms.

During these past years in Asia, the patterns of behavior I had observed in U.S. officials were about as broad as all humanity. There were some officials who affected a studied aloofness, saying that Americans couldn't represent the United States properly if they became too involved with local people. There were others who strove for comradeship with the Asians around them: some who went too far by going native and some who struck a good balance by remaining themselves while making friends. There were Americans of the "take charge" type, bossing everyone within sight, often in order to get some worthwhile job done but stifling the initiative and stomping on the dignity of the very Asians they were trying to help. There were technicians blind to everything outside their immediate programs, at times gullibly and unwittingly aiding Asian political sharpies and money grubbers eager for the "pork barrel" opportunities in some U.S. program. There were Americans who behaved nobly and those who behaved atrociously. There were bored Americans putting in career time and Americans who made every moment count. What was "normal"?

The United States was undertaking vast aid programs in Asia to give the free nations a chance at life in the world that emerged from World War II. In these programs, it long had been my conviction that the manner in which our help was given was far more important than the substance of what we gave. Human affairs are full of examples of assistance doled out badly enough to earn the envy, jealousy, resentment, or contempt of the recipient or to sap his moral fiber. Human affairs also are full of examples of true friendship wherein help was given the right way, ennobling both the giver and the taker. I recalled two stories told me by Filipinos after my arrival in their country in 1945, stories told so often that they became memorable for me. At the time, the Filipinos had had more chance to get to know us Americans than had other Asians, thanks to two generations of intimate association. The stories taught me much of Asian feelings about American attitudes.

One of the stories was a favorite of Filipino politicians and intellectuals whom I came to know. It concerned the ceremony held at the completion of a bridge built by American engineers over the Pasig River in Manila before World War II. A ranking U.S. official spoke to the assembled throng at the ceremony, praising the American builders and noting how the U.S. was bringing civilization to the Philippines. The next speaker was Manuel Quezon, president of the Commonwealth and an ardent nationalist. Quezon scorned what he took to be the condescension of the U.S. official and declaimed passionately that he would rather live "in a Philippines run like Hell by Filipinos than in a Philippines run like Heaven by Americans!" It was a classic dig at insensitive American paternalism. Yet most of the Filipinos who told me this story had gone to public schools started by American teachers, and these teachers had earned their deep affection. The contrast between the way they looked upon the American at the bridge ceremony and at their American teachers made its point. The teachers had accorded them their dignity as individuals while the official had been blind to it.

The second memorable story was told to me by Filipino leaders of the guerrilla resistance against the Japanese occupation in World War II. It concerned the darkest hours of the Philippines in early 1942. Philippine government leaders had fled to the safety of our military stronghold on Corregidor Island off the tip of the Bataan peninsula. The story goes that Quezon sent a radio message to President Roosevelt. In it he noted that the Philippines had declared war against Japan under its agreements with the United States. Now, however, the Japanese military swarmed over the Philippines. The Filipino people were suffering. There had been great destruction. Only small remnants of the country's military forces were still holding out. With heavy heart, the conclusion had been reached that it was time to give up. Would the United States please release the Philippines from the agreement to fight alongside the Americans?

Back came the reply from the White House. Yes, the Philippine government was released from any obligation that would bring suffering to the Philippine people. Quezon was free to act as he thought best. However, the United States had pledged itself to defend the Philippines. Thus, even though it also was being grievously hurt in doing so, it would remain true to its pledge and continue trying to defend the Philippines as long as there was one American left alive to do so.

This exchange of messages, in the midst of the tragedy unfolding for both Filipinos and Americans, touched a usually hidden Asian psyche. The Filipinos who told me the story would end it by asking, "What else could we do but keep on the fight through the people, whatever the government did? You Americans trusted us and showed it by dying to defend us. We *had* to stay by your side and remain men ourselves." The years of war that followed this incident are filled with events marking unusually close bonds between Filipinos and Americans, bonds that astonished the world by holding despite adversity. To me, this story—which the Filipinos believed and which I did because they did—depicted the ideal relationship which should exist between peoples who share the same principled beliefs. It is a brotherhood wherein we love, trust, and help one another.

Now I was leaving Asia at the close of 1956, a tumultuous decade after the end of World War II. I was convinced, more than ever, that the most pragmatic course for Americans serving in Asia was to heed the idealism of our country's political tenets and make them the basis for our acts. We had become involved in an immense struggle in Asia with opponents, the Communists of Mao's persuasion, who fanatically believed that they must convert all others to their viewpoint even if at the muzzle of a gun barrel. They waged a theocratic-like political warfare, with ideas as their heaviest weaponry. We fought against their ideas with strength of our own, sharing this strength with allies. But I was dismayed by what many of my fellow Americans looked upon as strength. We said "in God we trust" and then put our main trust in material things—money, machines, goods, and battalions—to win this struggle. I had no quarrel with the use of weapons, dollars, and materiel to aid our fight, as long as these remained the secondary support to what should be our main reliance, our principles as Americans. We couldn't afford just to be *against* the Communists. We had to be *for* something ourselves.

I had personal views about the Asian Communists from my brushes with them. I was saddened by what had happened to some of them who had joined the Communist ranks initially for idealistic reasons, such as the righting of social injustices, and who then had found themselves bound to a system they gradually lost faith in, kept there by vindictive security measures or feelings of guilt for acts they had been induced to participate in. These captives of the system included a number of the Communist notables, men whose private agonies must have been Promethean.

But I also had seen the ruthless savagery of our Communist opponents. My heart really went out to their victims and my anger had hardened against those responsible. By 1956 countless thousands had been proscribed by name and murdered by the Communists for such innocent reasons as having been born into families or circumstances disliked by the Communist elite. Since the end of World War II, some 700 million human beings had been conquered by the Communists through political-military force, in a blatantly imperialist chapter of history that mocked all men of good will by bearing its Communist label of "liberation." The "liberated" millions had been fixed to their neighborhoods and their places of labor, permitted no meaningful voice in their future, and subjected to frightening penalties for infractions of the system's regulatory ordinances. Kept from the rest of the world by Iron and Bamboo Curtains, they lived in vast prisons.

There was the prospect that the Communists would continue their role of conquest in the world, imprison yet more populations. Communist theoreticians had an *idée fixe* about expanding their revolution into other territories, including the United States, as a necessity for the successful birth of the utopian society they hoped would be established eventually. The fact that these theoreticians were like little children believing a fairy tale, with simple faith in there being a happy ending after all the horror, was no consolation to those of us facing them.

The Communist methods of conquest I had seen were the Asian tactics of waging "people's war." Instead of using a regular army to invade and subjugate a country, they employed a cheaper way, one that poor men could afford. The start could be made with a handful of militant believers in the political idea of communism, from a base where they would be initially safe from the police or other governmental forces. Trained as proselytizers and guerrillas, the band would feed upon local grievances and fix the blame on established authorities, recruiting those it convinced or cowed, arming them, and then, as their numbers increased, attacking government forces at places and times where victory seemed certain. Growth would continue until the Communist forces dominated the countryside, ringing the cities, choking them off from the countryside and finally forcing them to succumb. This, in other words, was political struggle waged by armed adherents taken from the popular masses—people's warfare.

People's warfare succeeded under Mao in China and under Ho in North Vietnam and had been suppressed only after great difficulty in the Philippines, Malaya, and Burma. There was evidence that it was being initiated in Indonesia, where Communist preparations in the villages of Central Java had earned the nickname of "the Yenan Line" for the area, and in Thailand where a heavy infiltration of Vietnamese settlers in the northeast region offered many villages as safe havens for trained cadre from Hanoi. During my stay in Vietnam, Ho chi Minh, Vo nguyen Giap, and other Vietnamese Communists had done much public crowing over their success with this homespun method of waging war in their defeat of the French. It was a testimonial which I clearly felt would appeal to power-hungry have-nots in other countries around the world, including countries whose governments would turn to the United States for help when their turn came as targets. How would the Americans respond? Would they see each new problem as another Korea?

The war in Korea was an anomaly, fought conventionally in a time and a part of the world where unconventional and revolutionary warfare had become the new rule. In Korea, the Communists neither practiced what they had preached nor what they had found to be so successful in other Asian lands. It struck me, from their use of guerrillas only as auxiliaries to regular forces and their use of masses of ground troops, that the Communists in Korea had attempted to fight in Soviet style, instead of using the method by which Mao had won China. In return, the Americans and their allies had fought back in their own conventional way, much as they had in a mixture of World Wars I and II but with updated weaponry. It was a brutal experience, but it taught no lessons about people's warfare. I felt that the Asian Communists, who had been severely hurt in Korea, would revert to their old familiar ways the next time they started a war. I just hoped that Korea hadn't left too many Americans too singularly and tragically misinformed about Asian Communist warfare. The next confrontation would demand much wisdom from us, if we helped and were to give our help pertinently.

My hard-knocks schooling in the Philippines and Vietnam had stressed the demotic strategy practiced by Asian Communists and the need for demotic defense against it. Fundamentally, the people of a country are the main feature on a battleground of Communist choosing, since the ensuing struggle becomes one between the Communists and the government over which side will have the allegiance of the people. Whichever side wins that allegiance will win the country, defeating the other side. Thus the Communists strive to split the people away from the government and to gain control over decisive numbers of the population. The sure defense against this strategy is to have the citizenry and the government so closely bound together that they are unsplittable. In other words, a country's strength lies in having what Lincoln described at Gettysburg: a government "of the people, by the people, for the people." Given such a government and an informed and vigilant citizenry, the Communist's vaunted methods of waging people's war simply cannot get off to a meaningful start.

Based on this understanding of prime defense in a country being helped by the United States, the role of Americans in our assistance programs becomes plain. The mere fact that we are giving aid already means that we are influencing the internal affairs of the country. So we need to use that influence consistently toward guiding the country to attain its true strength, a strength that becomes part of the friendship between its people and ours. Our long-range self-interest demands that every action by our officials in such a country serve to encourage the building or maintaining of government responsive to and participated in by the people. It may be a slow process, small step by small step, but we should not deviate from the goal with excuses of expediency or to save the false pride of officialdom.

This means that U.S. officials in an aided foreign country should spend every moment possible in gaining understanding of its people and then act within earned friendship. Our political counselors should stress the need for a government that upholds the spirit of the country's laws and processes, giving social justice to the people and urging that justice be adhered to, buttressed, or enlarged as necessary. Our military assistance should make sure that the troops it arms are dedicated to the protection of the people as their constant and highest objective in becoming proficient in the martial arts. Our economic aid should be given only in ways that increase the self-reliance of the people and not in ways that increase local bossism or other entrenched corruptions. Social injustice, bullying by military or police, and corruption must be seen as grave weaknesses in the defense of a country, errors that can lead to its downfall and eventually, as our friends are eliminated, to the downfall of the United States.

If every country allied with us worked conscientiously on its prime defense among its own people, and if the United States became the champion of its expressed principles by channeling all our foreign aid singularly into such defense, Communist expansion through the use of politicized guerrilla terrorism could be brought to a stop. As a practical American, however, I had and have few illusions that Washington would adopt this attainable ideal. The back rooms of Washington policy-makers are too full of articulate and persuasive practitioners of the expedient solution to daily problems, of the hoary art of power politics, and of the brute usages of our physical and material means. They can scarcely comprehend the pragmatism of sticking to the ideal of having a government "of the people, by the people, for the people" as the strongest defense any country could have against the Communists, and they seek other ways of defeating the Communists, ways that they can see or touch or inventory on paper. Thus, I could only conclude that U.S. aid would fall short of helping to build true defenses, that vulnerabilities would continue to exist around the world, and that sharp-eyed Communists would recognize and exploit them. This means that we can expect more people's wars, Maoist-style, in our time.

In the next people's wars in countries we were aiding, I hoped that we wouldn't forget the political basis of such conflicts and mistakenly place our main reliance on military, police, and economic actions without recognizing that they are merely implements of political will. If we erred in this way, the Communists could continue their pose of speaking for the people, exacerbate every transgression by a government they sought to destroy, recruit those wronged by the government along with their relatives and friends, and keep right on growing ever stronger. In such a downhill situation, the only salvation is to switch defense priorities back to what they should have been all along—the building and strengthening of a national political structure that was at one with the people—and insist that all other actions contribute to this goal. Even as a wartime priority, such sensitive work takes time.

If we are to succeed, impatient Americans will have to remember our own heritage. The revolutionaries who founded our country understood the imperative need to wage their struggle upon a political foundation. Yet it took five wartime years after the Declaration of Independence before the first Articles of Confederation were ratified, and an additional seven years before the U.S. Constitution was established. The twelve years we needed to build a viable political structure in the eighteenth century might even be insufficient, given the destructive skill of the Communists. People's wars are not for fighters with short attention spans.

Our Founding Fathers left another legacy of revolutionary strategy that their inheritors should heed in people's wars. They selected the head of their opponents—George III—as the main target in the psychological warfare they waged consistently throughout the struggle, a type of warfare they counted on more heavily than the guns of the Continental Army. The success of this psychological campaign was such that even generations later, in the twentieth century, a mayor of Chicago was elected mostly on a platform of opposition to the long-dead George. We might laugh at the naivete of latter-day citizenry, but we cannot discount the emotional effectiveness of the original attack. The strategy of directing psychological blows at an enemy's leadership in a political war is hardly new. It is a fundamental necessity of such warfare, of which today's people's wars are merely the latest examples.

The authoritarian leadership of Communist forces in a people's war looms definitely as a target. The process which selects a Communist to speak for "the masses" in such a war is as patently questionable as was "the divine right of kings." The falseness of a Communist leader's position with the people and the guilt of the premeditated savagery he commits in their name beg for strong and constant exposure to the truth. A government that has the morality of a base in the popular will can make an effective psychological attack upon such leadership, bringing about the isolation of these leaders from the people, their increasing impotence, and their eventual downfall. The strategy is as potent today in people's wars as it was for Americans in 1776. Tyranny remains tyranny, whatever its current name.

In sum, I concluded that Americans who go out to help others in people's wars must understand that these struggles are composed of the means that shape the ideological end. Essentially, they are conflicts between viewpoints on the worth of individual man. The Communists see man materialistically as little more than a zero, a cipher of the state to which he is subservient. We Americans, to be true to ourselves, must see man as an individual endowed by his Creator "with certain unalienable

Rights" and that "to secure these Rights, Governments are instituted among Men." In people's wars, this is an American's battle cry of freedom.

NOTES

BEHAVIOR. Of course, one of the precepts I wanted American officials to follow was the Golden Rule, "Do unto others as you would have others do unto you." It was as meritorious in Asia as elsewhere in the world. I recall that the Filipino banker Albino SyCip had cards printed stating this rule in the many forms in which it was known in Asia. His card cited quotations from Jesus, Buddha, Confucius, Mahomet, Brahmanism, Hinduism, Judaism, Parsee, Taoism, and Zoroastrianism.

FILIPINISM. Although the more bumptious among us should remember the fierce national pride portrayed by Quezon in his "Hell and Heaven" remark at the Manila bridge dedication, all of us can treasure another remark by another Filipino. The martyred Philippine hero Jose Rizal once said, "A man retains his freedom so long as he preserves his independence of thought." In these days of Pavlovian behavioral controls subtly created by skilled propagandists, as in Rizal's day of colonial repression, we need to hold fast to such truth.

LESSONS. In a list of what I learned from my experiences in the Philippines and Vietnam, I would include the following:

—There are no secrets in Asia, only the need to determine which story is true.

—The harder a Communist political attack on a weak point in the social fabric, the more honest we must become in strengthening it.

—An insurgency depends upon its leadership, about which there is always more to learn.

—The poorest view of an insurgency is from an office desk.

—A good smile is a great passport. Use it!

—In guerrilla territory, the children are a barometer.

—If alone in a road ambush, keep moving if possible.

—In military civic action, remember that friendship is earned, not bought.

—A pistol on the hip invites death or robbery; conceal it unless prepared to use it instantly.

—Always keep vehicles ready for long trips, fueled, lubricated, and with every reachable nut and bolt tightened.

—In a campfire, dry bamboo gives light; dry coconut shells (not husks) give cooking heat but little light.

POSTSCRIPT

TRAGIC ENDS (which came when I was far away in Washington) awaited both Magsaysay and Diem. (I was stationed at the Pentagon from 1957 to 1963.) Distance did not cushion the shock of their deaths.

Magsaysay was killed during his presidency when his aircraft crashed into a mountain on the island of Cebu on March 17, 1957. When the plane was overdue in Manila and his whereabouts were still unknown, his wife Luz telephoned me in Washington and I did my best to reassure her. His senior aide, Colonel "Borro" Borromeo, telephoned soon afterward to give me the news of the death, his voice so choked with tears that I barely understood his words. It was in the small hours of the morning in Washington. I gave the news to Carlos Romulo, the Philippine ambassador, and we sat together for hours trying to console each other.

Diem was overthrown in a coup on November 1, 1963, and was brutally murdered, along with his brother Nhu. In Washington the flash news of the coup came in over the press wires close to midnight of October 31 (noon of the next day in Saigon). My long-time friend Spencer Davis, Washington bureau chief for the Associated Press, called with the news and asked if the government was sending me out to Vietnam again. He was surprised when I informed him that I had been retired from the air force that very day and doubted that I would see Vietnam again. I had been shunted from Washington work on Vietnamese problems in 1961 and had been busy with other duties. The coup and murders in Saigon seemed incredible.

I served in Vietnam again from August 1965 to June 1968 in a civilian capacity, as an assistant to the U.S. ambassador and with the rank of minister. The presence of American youngsters fighting and dying in a war there and the shaky Vietnamese political structure at the time were cause enough for my volunteering to help as I could. But that's another story, quite different from the experiences described in this book.

INDEX

Acheson, Dean, 91
Adevoso, Terry, 95
Advisory practices, author's, with
  Diem, 157–159, 177, 258 f.,
  298 f., 307 f., 327 ff.; with groups,
  46–47, 76–77, 89, 103, 304,
  327 ff.; with Magsaysay, 37, 42,
  66–67
Agitprop, Communist, 70, 92–93
Aglao barrio attack, 66–67
Airborne troops, 78–80
Air-Sea Rescue, US 31st Sqdn., 128
Alba, G. R., 124
Allen, Fred, 290, 296
Allen, James, 113 n.
Almanac, Vietnamese, 226 f.
Alsop, Joseph, 364
Ammunition, contaminated, 75
Aquino, Benigno, 151
Aragon, M., 124
Arellano, Dario, 240
Arellano, Oscar, 169, 170, 182 n.
Arellano brothers' movies, 138
Asian-African Conference 1955, see
  Bandung Conference
"Asuang" psywar, 72–73
ATOM (Allied Training and Operations Mission), 181

Ba Cut, 152 f., 173 f., 320 ff.; airdrop,
  222; and Thé, 198 f.; sect front,
  246, 313, 315
Bagong Buhay, 114
"Bamboo telegraph" (Philippines),
  42
Bandung Conference 1955, 274, 279 f.
Bank of Indochina, 181
Banzon, Jose, 48, 178, 214, 272
Banzon, Luz, see Magsaysay, Luz
Bao Dai, 129, 143, 145, 147 f., 302;
  and Diem, 154 ff., 258, 279, 280,
  298 ff., 301, 312, 324, 331–334;
  and sects, 247, 280
Barbero, Carmelo, 83 n.
Barre, Jean, 183
Bataan, 26, 34, 50, 97
Battalion Combat Team (BCT), 20,
  32, 49, 70
Bay d'Along agreement, 129
"Bay" Vien, 147, 153, 177, 269 f., 310,
  311; sect front, 245 ff., 286 f.
BCT, see Battalion Combat Team
"Big" Minh, see Duong van Minh
Binh Xuyen, 146 ff., 153, 176 f.; city
  combat, 261 f., 268 f., 281, 284 ff.,
  291, 292, 297, 310 f., 312; rackets,
  269 f.; sect front, 245 ff.

Bohannan, Charles T. R., 30 n., 32, 41, 62, 287, 296
Borromeo, Emilio "Borro," 377
Broger, John, 81
Browder, Earl, 113 n.
BUDC (Barrio United Defense Corps), 7
Bulganin, N. A., 347
Bullitt, William, 179
Bumgardner, E. F., vii
Bunker, Ellsworth, vii
Buu Loc, 135, 145
Byrne, Pat, 151

Canfield, Cass, vii
Can Lao party, 340–345
Cannon, Robert M., 121
CAO, see Civil Affairs Office
Cao Dai sect, 146 f., 152, 153, 315 f., 342; integration, 245, 271
Cappadocia, Guillermo, 82, 86
Carbonel, Jean, 217
Castaneda, Mariano, 19, 20 f., 37, 41, 43, 44 f., 68
Castelo, Oscar, 106
Casualties: Franco-Vietminh War, 163; Huks, 50–51; inflicted by Huks, 8
Catholic Action, 117
Chanson, General, 187, 188
"Charlie" company, 7th BCT, 88
Chinese Communist 8th Route Army, 7, 84, 233
Chinese community; Philippines, 76–78; Vietnam, 357–360
Chou En-lai, 279
CIA, 220, 221, 224
Citizens party, Philippines, 103
Civic action: Philippines, 70–71, 84; Vietnam civilian, 210 ff.; Vietnam military, 210, 232 f., 241
Civil Affairs Office (CAO), Philippines, 70 ff., 83 n., 91, 137
Civil Guard, VN, 251, 353–354
Clandestine services, French, 220 f.
Clausewitz, Carl von, 105
"Coffee klatsch" sessions, 46–48, 89; see also Advisory practices
Cogny, René, 80
Collier's, 99

Collins, J. Lawton, 175 f., 202 ff., 256, 283, 300, 301, 313; and sects, 247 ff., 252 ff., 263 ff., 275 ff.; country team, 203 f., 304 f.
Committee for Good Government, 117
Communist Party: Philippines, 6, 7, 8, 16, 23, 64, 113 n.; Vietnam, 16, 146; see also Politburo
Conein, Lucien, 162 f., 286 ff., 296
Constitutions: Philippines, 24; U.S., 329, 374; Vietnam, 332, 333, 348–352
Copuano, Donald, 65
Country team, U.S., 114, 203
Cowen, Myron M., 18, 25, 26, 77, 90, 91
Crabb, Cmdr. Lawrence "Buster," 347
Crisol, Jose, 83 n.
Czech medical teams, 170

Dai Viet party, 145 f., 342
Dap Chu'on, Khmer leader, 183
Davis, Spencer, 377
de los Reyes, Isabelo, 113 n.
Democratic Party, Philippines, 109
Democratization Ministry, VN, 145
Diem, see Ngo dinh Diem
Dien Bien Phu, 129 f., 151
Do van Bong, 179
Draper, William H., Jr., 59
Drivers, military, 232
Droge, Dolf, vii
Dulles, Allen, 182 n., 344
Dulles, John Foster, 106, 126, 182 n., 300, 343 f., 345–347
Duong van "Big" Minh, 270, 290, 306, 320
Duong van Duc, 183, 235, 237

Eastern Construction Company, 227 n.
East German medical team, 170
EDCOR (Economic Development Corps), 48, 50–58
Eisenhower, Dwight D., 127, 175, 300
Elections: Philippines 1949, 25, 28, 29; Philippines 1951, 88–94; Philippines 1953, 102–109, 115–122; Vietnam national, 144–145, 278, 332–334, 348, 350 f.; Vietnam proposed plebiscite, 164 f., 204,

Elections (contd.)
  325 f., 345–347; Vietnam social
  action, 141–142
Ellis, A. C., 31
Ely, Paul, 175 f., 217, 224, 318, 326;
  and sects, 248 f., 252, 264, 275 f.,
  285
Enriquez, Ponce, 322
Evangelista, Crisanto, 113 n.
"Eye of God" psywar, 73–75

Far Eastern Broadcasting Co., 81
Faure, Edgar, 328
Ferrer, Jaime, 328
Fishel, Wesley R., 343
Fookien Times, 76
Force strengths: Franco-Vietminh
  War, 112, 114; Huk campaign,
  20, 22, 23, 50–51; Huks in WWII,
  6–7; pacification, VN, 239; Saigon
  front, 251, 268 f.
Foreign Legion, French, 112, 146
Foronda, C., 124
Forrest, Nathan Bedford, 321
Franklin, Ben, ix
Freedom Company, 95, 213 ff., 227 n.,
  279, 280, 322, 349 f.
Free Philippines, 119–120, 124, 350
French agreements, VN independence,
  129, 147, 181
French forces, 110 ff., 114, 147, 324 f.;
  in Saigon, 262 f., 267 f., 288, 318,
  319
Fuentes, Elias, 113 n.

G-5, Vietnamese Army, 137 ff.
Gambiez, General, 248 ff., 270
GAMO (Mobile Administrative
  Groups), 217
Garcia, Carlos P., 116
Garde Civile, 276
Geneva accords, 130, 154, 163 ff.,
  325 f., 345–347; timetables, 209,
  228 f., 238
George, Harrison, 113 n.
Giap, see Vo nguyen Giap
Golden rule, 376
Gomez, Dominador, 113 n.
Go Puan-seng, 76–77, 97
Greek guerrilla war, 14

Grenades, hand, 75, 148–149, 296
Gromyko, A. A., 347
Guerrilla warfare, Communist con-
  cepts, 370 ff.; Philippines, 7, 12,
  13, 23, 64, 65 f., 69 f., 75, 94;
  Vietnam, 352 ff.

Habeas corpus writ, Philippines, 65
Hall, Charles, 34, 59 n.
Hannibal, 1
Hardie, Mr. and Mrs. John, 65–66
Harris, Ann, vii
Hash, Chuck, 227 n.
Heath, Donald, 127, 154, 157 f., 186;
  country team, 203; on refugees,
  166 f.
Hellyer, George, 158 f.
Hinh, General, see Nguyen van Hinh
Hitler, Adolf, 361
HMB, see Huks
Ho chi Minh, 110, 152, 153, 156, 337,
  371; as examiner, 161; popularity,
  155, 243; purger, 188
Ho quan Phuoc, 182 n.
Ho thong Minh, 195 f., 210, 256, 257
Hoa Hao sect, 146 f., 152 f., 313,
  314 f., 320 f., 342
Hobbs, Leland S., 18, 25, 26, 36, 43,
  46, 77
"Huklandia," 9, 11, 56, 64, 86, 91, 93 f.
Huks (HMB), 13, 19, 21–24, 25, 65 f.,
  80, 86–87, 88, 123, 128; Aglao,
  66–67; as HMB, 12; early history,
  6–9; Makabulos, 26, 27; MIS in-
  filtration, 82–83; 1951 election,
  85 f., 92–94; politburo, 60–64;
  political action, 10, 11, 23, 69–70;
  psywar against, 72, 73–75, 92;
  Sierra Madre, 96–98
Hunters ROTC guerrillas, 95
Huynh phu So, 152
Huynh van Cao, 311

Iglesia ni Kristo, 80, 81
Ileto, Rafael, 49
Imperial Guard, VN, 280, 290
Intelligence collection, 24 ff., 71,
  269 ff.
Intelligence, military, 5 f., 63, 74, 81–
  83, 110, 137, 326

Jacquot, General, 268
Janequette, William, 113 n.
Jaycees (Junior Chambers of Commerce), 117, 164
Jefferson, Thomas, x
Johnston, Myriam L., vii
Joint Chiefs of Staff, U.S., 43, 105, 337
Jones, Helen, 31
JUSMAG (Joint U.S. Military Advisory Group), Philippines, 2, 17, 18, 25, 26, 36, 43, 45–46, 78, 79, 107 f., 121

Kapatagan, Lanao, 52–56
Karrick, Samuel N., vii, 227 n., 236
Kelly, Patrocinio M. Y., vii
Kempeitai, Japanese, 152, 153, 331
Khrushchev, N. S., 347
Kidder, Randolph A., 204, 300
Kieu cong Cung, 207 ff.
Korean War, 1, 15, 78, 99 f., 371 f.
Kublai Khan, 143
Kuomintang, Vietnamese, 145 f.

Lacy, William S. B., 104 f., 114
Ladejinsky, Wolf, 343, 355 f.
Lai van Sang, 275, 278, 280
Lam thanh Nguyen, 195
Land courts, Philippines, 48
Lansdale, Carolyn, vii
Lansdale, Helen, vii
Lapus, Ismael, 82, 83
Laurel, Jose, 103
Lauve, Anita, 151, 317
Lava brothers, 23
League of Women Voters, 117
Le Duan, 188
Le khac Hoai, 190 f., 309
Le ngoc Chan, 171, 173, 183
Lenin, Nikolai, 105
Le quang Vinh, see Ba Cut
Leroy, Jean, 147, 251, 295 f.
Le thanh Nghe, 182 f.
Le van Kim, 239 f., 282, 293 f.
Le van Tat, 315
Le van Ty, 269, 306
Le van Vien, see Bay Vien
Liberal Party, Philippines, 29, 102–103, 106, 107, 109
"Liberty wells," 77–78

Lieberman, Henry, 56
Lien-Minh, 153, 309; integration, 199 ff.; star-chamber charges, 222–223; strength, 187, 199, 301
Life magazine, 285, 303
Lincoln, Abraham, 372
Lions Clubs, 99, 117
"Little" Minh, see Tran van Minh
Liwanag, Silvestre, 26
Lopez, Fernando, 51, 109
Luyen, Mme., 160
Lyautey, General, 217
Ly giai Han (Ly Kay), 270

MAAG (Military Assistance Advisory Group), Vietnam, 127, 134, 294 f.; author at, 215 ff., 326, 335 ff.; with refugees, 166, 182 n.
Magsaysay, Jesus, 67
Magsaysay, Luz, 34, 35, 68
Magsaysay, Milagros, 35
Magsaysay, Ramon, 18 f., 21, 25, 68, 81, 83, 90, 98 ff., 127, 128; Aglao, 66–67; airborne, 78, 79; assassination tries, 46, 82, 120; author meets, 13 f., 33–37; Chinese, 77; death, 377; EDCOR, 51–57; habeas corpus, 65; military reforms, 43–45; oatmeal, 59 n.; on promotions, 45; Politburo, 60–63; post-election, 121–124; presidential campaign, 102–104, 106, 109, 115–121; rural credit, 76; the people, 48 f., 100 ff.; vacations, 361; Vietnam, 136, 175, 178, 191, 198, 355; with troops, 37–43, 86 ff., 94
Magsaysay, Ramon, Jr., 35
Magsaysay, Teresita, 35
Mai huu Xuan, 149, 270
Malony, Harry, 89
Manahan, Manuel, 114, 119, 124, 125, 151
Manila Bulletin, 114
Manila Railroad, 65
Manila Times, 114, 151
Manolo, Bishop, 81
Mao Tse-tung, 13, 24, 85, 100, 105, 161
Marshall, George C., 78, 89

Maryknoll Fathers, N.J., 156
McClintock, Robert, 140
Mecklin, John, 285 f., 303
Melvin, George, 293, 311
Merchant, Livingston, 15
Merrill, Gyles, 34, 99
Michigan State University, 209, 343
Miles, Milton, 319
Military Intelligence Service: Philippines, 6, 32 f., 63, 81–83, 92, 108; U.S., 4, 5
Miller, Anne, vii
Miller, Henry L., vii
Mirasol, Ciriaco, 52, 53
MIS, see Military Intelligence Service
Movement for National Revolution (MNR), 302 f., 330, 331
Mojica, Proculo L., 279, 295
MSS (Military Security Service), Vietnam, 149, 270
Murphy, Camp, 19, 35, 36, 38, 68
Mussolini, Benito, 328

Nacionalista Party, 103, 109
Nanking, 1935 treaty of, 357
Nasser, Gamal, 137, 172
National Bank of Vietnam, 181
National Institute for Administration, Vietnam, 208 f.
National Movement for Free Elections (NAMFREL), 90, 95, 108, 115 ff.
National security action, see Pacification
Navarre, Henri, 110, 111, 113, 114
Nazareno, Rod, 107
Negritos, Philippines, 66
"New villages," Malaya, 57
New York Times, 56
Ngo dinh Can, 160, 239, 330
Ngo dinh Diem, 152, 154 ff., 180 f., 283 f., 302 ff., 327 ff.; author meets, 156–159; Bao Dai, 155, 258, 275, 279, 280, 298 ff., 324, 331–334; Chinese, 270, 357–360; death, 345, 377; as executive, 210 f., 313 f., 326 f., 354 ff.; French, 222, 276, 290, 310, 314; Hinh, 172, 174; lectures, 308, 328; 1956 plebiscite, 325 f., 345; pacification, 229 f., 239, 242 f.;

with people, 178 f., 237; Philippines, 178, 214, 349, 355; political beliefs, 277 f., 312, 328, 348 f., 356; refugees, 165 ff., 355; sect confrontation, 245 ff., 252, 255 ff., 259 n., 261 f., 274, 275 f., 277, 278, 280, 284 f., 297 f., 313 ff.; Thé, 185, 191, 193, 200 f., 307 f.; U Nu, 314; vacations, 360–363
Ngo dinh Khoi, 155
Ngo dinh Luyen, 160, 185, 299 f.
Ngo dinh Nhu, 160, 185, 299 f., 308, 345, 362 f., 377; and intelligence, 210, 239, 270, 271; political activities, 302 f., 330 f., 340 f., 350
Ngo dinh Thuc, 160
Nguyen bao Toan, 302 ff.
Nguyen Binh, 153, 188
Nguyen De, 143, 247
Nguyen giac Ngo, 152, 195, 196, 245, 302, 321
Nguyen ngoc Le, 280
Nguyen ngoc Tho, 320, 321 f., 352
Nguyen tang Nguyen, 340
Nguyen thanh Phuong, 245, 246 ff., 252 ff., 271, 302, 315
Nguyen van Hanh, 140 f., 151
Nguyen van Hinh, 136, 137, 138, 149; coup, 171 ff., 183
Nguyen van Hue, 245
Nguyen van Minh, 183
Nguyen van Tam, 145
Nguyen van Thieu, 152
Nguyen van Vy, 176, 280, 290, 296, 298, 303 f., 310
Nhu, see Ngo dinh Nhu
Nhu, Mme., 160, 362, 363
Nieto, Manuel, 122
Nixon, Richard M., 123, 183
Nui ba Den, 189, 201 n.

OB, see Operation Brotherhood
Ocampo family, 271 f., 292
O'Daniel, John W., 110, 127, 133 f., 136, 139, 158, 294 f., 322; air help, 175; with French, 176, 216, 217, 326; refugees, 166; Vietnamese military, 181, 186, 235, 288, 292
O'Daniel, Ruth, 292

Operation Brotherhood (OB), 168 ff., 182 f., 234 f., 240 f., 360
Operation Giai-phong, 238 ff.
Operation Liberty, 233 ff.
Opium crops, Laos, 112 f.
Ora, Antonio, 113 n.
Orendain, Juan C., 124, 350, 363 f.
Orendain, MacArthur, 364
Osmena, Sergio, 8
OSS (Office of Strategic Services), 4, 162
Ouerbach, Dr. Sol, 113 n.
Overseas Chinese 48th Det., Huks, 7

Pacification, 216 ff., 228 ff., 243 n.; Camau, 228, 233 ff.; Central VN, 229, 238 ff., 282; Chinese Communist, 113; Long My, 178 f.
Paine, Tom, ix
Panay, Huk activities, 82–83
Palaypay, Jerry, 35, 61
Pathet Lao, 112 f.
Paul of Tarsus, 105
PCAC (Presidential Complaints and Action Commission), 122 f., 124, 214
Peabody, George, vii
Peace Fund, Philippines, 51–52
People's Anti-Japanese Army, see Huks
People's Liberation Army, Philippines, see Huks
Pham cong Tac, 246, 253, 315
Pham van Ty, 311 f.
Pham xuan Giai, 137 ff., 138, 139
Phan huy Quat, 136, 137, 195
Philippine Armed Forces, 15 n., 19, 20 f., 32, 97 f.; airborne, 78 f.; in elections, 90, 91 f., 93 f., 108, 116, 121; Magsaysay's impact, 38–45, 86–88; morale, 13, 26 f., 102; psywar, 14, 70, 71–75; scout rangers, 48, 49 f.; 7th BCT, 73, 88; social conscience, 47–59, 70 f.
Philippine News Service (PNS), 90 f., 118, 119
Philippine Veterans Legion, 95, 108, 117, 215, 322
Phillips, Rufus C., 3rd, vii, 178, 227 n., 236, 237, 240, 282, 293 f.

Pierson, Albert, 107
Plebiscite proposal, VN, see Elections
Police, VN national, see Civil Guard
Police, "special," 339 f.
Politburo, Philippines, 8, 9, 12, 23, 61, 62, 70, 85, 93; capture, 63–65
Pomeroy, William, 98, 113 n.
Popular Forces, Vietnam, 327
Presidential Complaints & Action Commission, see PCAC
Psychological activities (and psywar), 14, 69–75, 92–93, 137–140, 225–227, 333

Quereau, Ed, 227 n.
Quezon, Manuel, 113 n., 367
Quirino, Antonio, 25, 108, 119
Quirino, Elpidio, 14, 18, 43, 44, 61, 65, 90, 102, 103, 106, 107, 109, 118, 121, 124
Quoc-Gia Lien-Minh, see Lien-Minh

Radford, Arthur, 105
Rangers, Vietnamese Army, 326
Ravenholt, Albert, vii
Reading, Lord, 347
Recto, Claro, 103
Redick, Joseph P., vii, 162, 190, 194, 227 n., 328; in sect troubles, 249, 253 f., 256, 261, 273, 282 f., 297, 322
Reese, Dixie, 312
Refugees, Vietnam, 164 ff., 182 n., 324, 355; exodus blocked, 182 n.
Reinhardt, George Frederick, 313, 342 f.
Revolutionary Committee, VN, 301 ff.
Revolutionary Congress 1955, 302
Revolutionary Development, VN, 213
Revolutionary Party of Workers and Peasants, 340
Richards, Peter C., 80
Rizal, Jose, 61, 376
Rizal, Taciano, 61–63
Romain-Defosses, Jacques, 217
Romulo, Carlos P., 106, 109, 377
Roosevelt, Franklin D., 368
Rosson, William, 182 n., 217
Rotary Clubs, 117
ROTC, Philippines, 90

Roxas, Manuel, 151
Rural credit, Philippines, 76

Sabin, Lorenzo S., Jr., 183
San Juan, Frisco Johnny, 95, 124, 125, 213 f.
Santiago, Tomas, 51
Scout Rangers, Philippines, 48, 49–50
Sects of Vietnam, *see individual names:* Binh Xuyen, Cao Dai, Hoa Hao
Security of documents, 25, 26
Self-criticism by Huks, 23
Sessums, John, 108
Seventh BCT, Philippines, 73, 88
Shaplen, Robert, vii, 99
Sharpe, Lawrence, 183
Sihanouk, Prince Norodom, 113, 183
Slogans of Huks, 69
Sochurek, Howard, 285 f., 303
Social Action committees, 140–142, 151
Socialist Party, Philippines, 6
Spellman, Cardinal, 182 n.
Spruance, Raymond A., 104 f., 107, 114, 121
"Stalin university," 7, 98, 113
"Stay-behind" Communists, VN, 212 f., 236 ff., 352 ff.
Strategic Intelligence School, USAF, 12
Strengths, *see* Force strengths
Subic Bay, 34, 44, 50, 59
Sun Tzu, 105
Superstitions: Philippines, 72, 240; Vietnam, 226 f., 243
Supplétifs, French Army, 112, 147
Sûreté, Vietnam, 149
SyCip, Albino, 77, 376

Tactics: airborne, 78–80; Armed Forces, Philippines, 20 f., 32 f., 47–59, 70 f., 81 ff., 88, 97 f.; Communist pacification, 113; Huks, 21, 23, 26 f., 64, 65–66, 75, 94 f.; Vietminh, 131 f., 151, 167 f., 182, 212 f., 236 f., 241, 352–354; Vietnam pacification, 213, 228, 232 f., 236 f., 241, 243 n.
Tanada, Lorenzo, 103

Tan Malaka, 113
Tarlac, Philippines, 26–29
Taruc, Luis, 6, 8, 9, 23, 123, 151
Telegrams ten-centavo, citizens to secretary of defense, 48–49, 122–123
Terrorism, Communist, 369 f.; Philippines, 13, 26 f., 64, 65 ff., 94, 96, 101; Vietnam, 352–354
Thai hoang Minh, 273 f., 284, 297 f.
Thé, *see* Trinh minh Thé
Thirteenth Air Force, U.S., 108, 125
Tibet pacification, 113
Time magazine, 114, 272, 285
Train robbery, 65
Training Relations Instruction Mission, *see* TRIM
Tran chanh Thanh, 340
Tran quoc Buu, 152, 302, 340
Tran trung Dung, 258, 340
Tran van Do, 340
Tran van Don, 269, 281, 306, 339
Tran van "Little" Minh, 269, 306, 307
Tran van Soai, 152, 313, 314 f., 320 f.
Travailliste, Le Parti, 340
Tribes, mountain, VN, 327, 334
TRIM (Training Relations Instruction Mission), 181, 217 ff., 293, 317 f.
Trinh minh Chau, 309
Trinh minh Nhut, 309
Trinh minh Thé, 147, 153, 184 ff., 302, 303 f.; author meets, 189 ff.; Bandung, 274, 279 f.; city combat, 271, 301, 305 ff.; clandestine charges, 222 f.; death, 308 f.; sect front, 246 ff., 252 ff.
Trinh minh thi Thu, 309
Troop indoctrination, VN, 232 f.
Truman, Harry S., 31
Try-Tran bus company, 34
Twining, Nathan, 15

UMDC (Unités Mobiles d eDéfense de Chrétientés), 147
U Minh forest, Camau, 237 f.
U Nu, 314
United Sects National Front, 245 ff., 315
U.S. Information Agency, 138, 172
U.S. Military Assistance Advisory Group, *see* MAAG

Vagnozzi, Emilio, 80
Valeriano, Napoleon D., vii, 73, 88, 178
Van thanh Cao, 198
Vargas, Jesus, 91, 92
Vietcong, 213
Vietminh, 110 ff., 129 f., 146, 151, 152, 153, 325 f., 337, 345–347; Hanoi, 225 f.; refugees, 167 f., 182 n.; terror, 212 f., 352–354; training, 161; withdrawal, 163 ff., 168, 237 f., 241 f.
Vietnamese Air Force, 311
Vietnamese Army, 111 f., 114, 137–139, 325, 326, 338; pacification, 166, 216 ff., 229 ff., 238 ff.; vs. sects, 255 f., 261 ff., 286, 288 ff., 292, 297, 320 f.
Vietnamese Federation of Labor, 152, 302
Vietnamese names, 151
Vietnamese Navy, 269
Vietnamese Veterans Legion, 215, 322
Vietnam history briefs, 110–111, 142–145
Villages, Vietnam, 356

Village Self-Defense Corps, 327
VNQDD (Viet-Nam Quoc Dan Dang [Vietnamese Kuomintang]), 145 f., 342
Vo nguyen Giap, 151, 337, 371
Vo van Hai, 256, 261, 303
Vu van Mau, 349

Wachi, *see* Overseas Chinese 48th Det., Huks
Wachtel, J. C., vii
Wang tsio-Yong, 182 n.
Ward, W. T. T., 125
Washington, George, 329, 341
Williams, Ogden, 359
Williams, Samuel T., 335–339, 353
Winnacker, R. A., vii

"Y" bridge, Cholon, 271, 297
"Yenan Line," Indonesia, 371
Yoh, Bernard, 319 f., 334 n.
Young, Genevieve, vii
Yulo, Jose, 109

Zambales, Philippines, 34, 66–67

ABOUT THE AUTHOR

Edward Geary Lansdale was born in Detroit in 1908 and was educated in Michigan, New York, and California. After earning his way through U.C.L.A. as a writer-artist for various publications, he went into advertising. In World War II he served with the OSS and at the war's end he became a career officer in the U.S. Air Force, rising to the rank of Major General before his retirement in 1963.

Between 1957 and 1963 Lansdale worked with the assistant secretary of defense in the field of special operations. After he retired to civilian status, he served as senior liaison officer for the American ambassador to Vietnam from 1965 to 1968, with the rank of minister. The United States and the Philippines both awarded numerous decorations to General Lansdale.

Edward Lansdale died in 1987 and was buried at Arlington National Cemetery. His second wife, Patrocinio ("Pat") Yapcinco Lansdale, who enthusiastically supported the idea of a new edition of Lansdale's work, lives in McLean, Virginia, which has been home to the Lansdale family for over 300 years.